Front Cover: Opening ceremonies, XIX Olympiad in Mexico City. Photo, Jerry Cooke, "Sports Illustrated" © Time Inc.

Back Cover: Top, Dick Fosbury of the United States, gold medalist in the high jump. Bottom, 10,000-meter race, won by Naftali Temu of Kenya. Both photos, ABC-TV.

1969

THE
BOOK
OF
KNOWLEDGE
ANNUAL

THE YOUNG PEOPLES
BOOK OF THE YEAR

Grolier
INCORPORATED
New York

Grolier
of Canada Limited
Montreal

Standard Book Number: 7172-0600-9
The Library of Congress Catalog Card Number: 40-3092

COPYRIGHT © 1969 BY  Grolier
INCORPORATED

Copyright © 1969 BY GROLIER OF CANADA LIMITED

PRINTED
IN
U. S. A.

No part of this book may be reproduced without
special permission in writing from the publishers

STAFF

William E. Shapiro
Editor in Chief

Russell J. Sully
Art Director

Deborah K. Kaplan
Associate Editor

Wallace S. Murray
Vice-President and Editorial Director, Grolier Incorporated

EDITORIAL

Style Editors:	J. M. A. Raikes, chief Eleanor C. Wood	**Production Editor:**	Helen Riehl Hitchcock
Researchers:	Fern L. Mamberg, chief Lydia Cohen	**Production Assistant:**	Arlington S. Higgenbothem
Indexers:	Kathleen Leerburger, chief Ruth Hines	**Staff Assistants:**	Dorothy Baldo Janet H. Ramlow Gloria James

ART

Art Assistants:	John Keaveny Jane Schoenfeld Marilyn Gong	**Picture Editor:**	Allen Reuben
		Staff Assistant:	Ruth E. Northlane

MANUFACTURING

Director:	Edward C. McKenna	**Assistant Director:**	Walter Schenone

CONTENTS

CONTRIBUTORS

Amory, Cleveland, A.B.
Radio and television commentator; Columnist, *Saturday Review, TV Guide;* Author, *The Proper Bostonians; Who Killed Society?*
Television page 171

Benedict, Burton, A.B., Ph.D.
Professor of Anthropology, University of California, Berkeley; Author, *People of the Seychelles; Mauritius: Problems of a Plural Society*
Mauritius page 84

Birch, Guy
News Editor, *Toronto Star*
Canada page 122

Bohle, Bruce, A.B.
Usage Editor, *American Heritage Dictionary;* Editor, *The Home Book of American Quotations*
Dictionary Supplement page 395

Brackman, Arnold C.
Consultant, Asian affairs; Author, *Southeast Asia's Second Front*
Asia page 102

Brooks, Hugh C., Ph.D.
Director, Center for African Studies, St. John's University, New York; Author, *New Africa; Guide to College Geography*
Africa page 76

Buder, Leonard
Education writer, *The New York Times*
Education page 160

Button, Dick
Olympic figure skating champion (1948; 1952)
Winter Olympics page 337

Carlson, Jerry A., B.S.
Farm Management Editor, *Farm Journal*
Agriculture and Food page 90

Craib, Roderick, A.B., A.M.
Assistant Transportation Editor, *Business Week;* Author, *A Picture History of U.S. Transportation*
Transportation page 342

Cronkite, Walter
CBS News Correspondent
Top of the News page 49

Edelson, Edward, B.S.
Author, *Parent's Guide to Science; Poisons in the Air*
Science and Technology page 282

Field, Carolyn W., B.S.
Coordinator, Work with Children, Free Library of Philadelphia
Children's Literature page 226

Foderaro, Sal J.
Managing Editor, *The Americana Annual*
United States page 358

Frederick, Pauline, A.B., A.M.
NBC News United Nations correspondent; Author, *Ten First Ladies of the World*
United Nations page 350

Furness, Betty
Special Assistant to President Johnson for consumer affairs; Chairman, President's Committee on Consumer Interests
Protecting the Consumer page 157

Gilruth, Robert R., B.S., M.S., D.Sc.
Director, NASA Manned Spacecraft Center, Houston, Texas
Man on the Moon page 312

Gonzalez, Henry B.
United States Congressman, 20th District, Texas; initiator and organizer of HemisFair '68
HemisFair '68 page 386

Goodsell, James Nelson, Ph.D.
Latin America Editor, *The Christian Science Monitor*
Latin America page 208

Gordon, Leonard I., M.D.
Internist; Medical Editor, *Medical Tribune*
Medicine and Health page 230

Griffith, Geoffrey
Associate Editor, *Daily Mirror,* Sydney, Australia
Australia and New Zealand page 110

Harris, Leonard, B.S.S.
CBS News arts editor and theater critic
Theater page 168

Hattersley, Ralph
Contributing Editor, *Popular Photography*
Photography page 266

Herst, Herman, Jr., B.A.
Columnist, *Hobbies Magazine;* Book Review Editor, *Mekeel's Weekly Stamp News;* Author, *Nassau Street; Fun and Profit in Stamp Collecting*
Stamps page 203

Hinch, Derryn
Foreign correspondent, *The Sydney Morning Herald,* Australia
John G. Gorton page 115

Hoyt, Robert G., A.B.
Editor, *National Catholic Reporter;* Author, *Issues That Divide the Church*
Roman Catholicism page 277

Joel, Lydia, B.A.
Editor in Chief, *Dance Magazine*
Dance page 177

Kandel, Myron, B.S., M.A.
Editor, *New York Law Journal*
Law page 216

Kline, Bert F.
Managing Editor, *Baltimore Jewish Times*
Jews and Judaism page 280

Kupferberg, Herbert, M.A., M.S.
Music Columnist, *The Atlantic*
Music page 174

Leerburger, Benedict A., Jr., A.B.
Project Director, Crowell-Collier Macmillan Information Sciences; Author, *Josiah Willard Gibbs*
Antarctic Discoveries page 294

Lillehei, C. Walton, M.D., Ph.D.
Professor of Surgery and Chairman, Department of Surgery, The New York Hospital-Cornell Medical Center; president, American College of Cardiology, 1966–67; recipient, Albert Lasker Award, 1955
Transplantation page 238

Lonn, George
President, Pitt Publishing Company Limited, Toronto; Author, *Canadian Profiles; Builders of Fortunes*
Pierre Elliott Trudeau page 131

Manoogian, Haig P., B.S., M.F.A.
Associate Director, Institute of Film and Television, New York University; Author, *The Filmmaker's Art*
Motion Pictures page 180

May, Charles Paul, B.A., M.A.
Free-lance author, photographer and book reviewer; Author, *Chile: Progress on Trial; High-Noon Rocket; A Book of American Birds; Great Cities of Canada*
Adult Literature page 224

Meehan, J. J., B.A.
Editor, United Press International, London, England
Western Europe page 186

Mishler, Clifford
Numismatic Editor, *Coins Magazine;* Fellow, American Numismatic Society; Co-author, *Coins, Questions and Answers*
Coins page 205

Newbauer, John
Editor in Chief, *Astronautics & Aeronautics*
Space page 302

Perrot, Paul N.
Director, Corning Museum of Glass; Author, *Three Great Centuries of Venetian Glass*
Glass as Art page 261

Psomiades, Harry J., Ph.D.
Chairman, Department of Political Science, Queens College, The City University of New York; Author, *The Eastern Question: The Last Phase*
Middle East page 240

Ronberg, Gary M., B.A.
Staff Writer, *Sports Illustrated*
Sports page 318
Summer Olympics page 332

Ross, Edward S., B.S., Ph.D.
Curator, Department of Entomology, California Academy of Sciences, San Francisco; Author, *Insects Close Up*
Ants and Bees page 140

Schechter, David Charles, M.S., M.D.
Assistant Professor of Surgery, The New York Hospital-Cornell Medical Center
Transplantation page 238

Schwartz, Harry, Ph.D.
Specialist in Soviet affairs, *The New York Times*
The Soviet Bloc: Winds of Change page 18
Soviet Union and Eastern Europe page 194

Sherlock, Philip M., B.A.
Vice-Chancellor, University of the West Indies, Kingston, Jamaica; Author, *Land and People of the West Indies; This Is Jamaica*
West Indies page 390

Silverstein, Harry, A.B.
Director, Creative Arts-Alienated Youth Project, New School for Social Research; Editor, *The Social Control of Mental Illness*
Youth Revolution page 34

Stevens, Richard P., Ph.D.
Chairman, Department of Political Science and Director, African Language and Area Center, Lincoln University, Pennsylvania; Author, *Basutoland, Bechuanaland and Swaziland;* contributor, *Journal of Modern African Studies*
Swaziland page 87

Taylor, Robert, A.B.
Art Editor, *Boston Globe*
Painting and Sculpture page 256

Thompson, Era Bell, B.A.
International Editor, *Ebony;* Author, *American Daughter; Africa, Land of My Father;* Co-editor, *White on Black*
Nauru page 118

Trussell, Tait, B.A.
Managing Editor, *Nation's Business;* Co-author, *Dear NASA Please Send Me a Rocket;* editor (with others), *Successful Management*
Economy page 150

Van Precht, William H., B.A., M.A., Ph.D.
Publisher and Editor, *Craft & Model Hobby Industry Magazine*
Craft and Model Hobbies page 206

Wagner, Walter F., Jr., S.B., S.M.
Editor, *Architectural Record*
Architecture page 96

Wilson, Kenneth L., A.B., Litt.D.
Editor, *Christian Herald Magazine;* Author, *Angel at Her Shoulder; The Man with Twenty Hands; Bible Boyographies*
Protestantism page 279

Zill, Jo Ahern, B.S.
Fashion Editor, *Look*
Modern Living page 250

Zinn, Donald J., Ph.D.
Professor of Zoology, University of Rhode Island, President, National Wildlife Federation
Conservation and Nature page 134

ARTISTS

George Buctel
Alan Colby

Dick Harvey
Ron McKee

Joe Stonehill
Blaise Zito

R E T R O S P E C T

1968

CRISIS IN FRANCE and the near downfall of President Charles de Gaulle were brought about by disenchanted, rioting students and striking workers who almost paralyzed the nation. But millions of Frenchmen rallied to the Government's aid, as shown here in a pro-De Gaulle march down the Champs-Elysées, and gave the General a vote of confidence in June elections.

SUMMER OLYMPICS in Mexico City brought together thousands of athletes from nations the world over to compete in a rare spirit of international harmony. Here, Bill Toomey of the United States wins the final event of the decathlon and a gold medal.

THE RACE FOR THE MOON made great strides in 1968 with the 11-day earth-orbiting flight of Apollo 7 and the round-the-moon trip of Apollo 8.

ASSASSINATIONS of two outstanding Americans cast a shadow of gloom over the land. The death of Senator Robert F. Kennedy abruptly ended an exciting political career and left his wife, Ethel, a widowed mother of ten children (an eleventh child was born posthumously in December). The death of Dr. Martin Luther King, Jr., leader of the Southern Christian Leadership Conference, and the black apostle of nonviolence, left a void in the civil-rights movement. While his role in SCLC was taken over by Dr. Ralph Abernathy, his widow, Coretta, took a more active role in the civil-rights movement in the hope of keeping alive the principles for which her husband had lived and died.

THE INVASION OF CZECHO-SLOVAKIA by half a million Soviet and Warsaw Pact troops brought a halt—but perhaps not an end—to a proud people's quest for freedom.

THE PRESIDENTIAL ELECTION AND VIETNAM WAR occupied the attention of the American people during the year. Richard Nixon won the Republican nomination and went on to win the election, defeating Democrat Hubert Humphrey. Earlier, at the Democratic convention, U.S. involvement in Vietnam had led to violent clashes between police and antiwar demonstrators. Meanwhile the war continued and more lives were lost, even though peace talks were being held in Paris.

SOVIET BLOC: WINDS OF CHANGE

By HARRY SCHWARTZ
THE NEW YORK TIMES

NOT since 1956 has the Soviet Bloc been wracked by so much dissent as in 1968. The patterns of the Kremlin's troubles in both years were uncannily similar. In 1956 and in 1968 the Soviet Army had to invade a friendly country: Hungary and Czechoslovakia respectively. It also came close to invading a second friendly satellite nation: Poland both times. In addition, in both 1956 and 1968, internal unrest within the Soviet Union itself was of significant concern to the Kremlin rulers.

But the winds of change blew much more fiercely in 1968 than in 1956. And they accomplished much more. There are three striking contrasts between these fateful years of dissent.

In 1956 the storms that then threatened the Soviet empire were largely the result of a miscalculation by the empire's ruler, Communist Party leader Nikita S. Khrushchev. In 1968 the corresponding political hur-

The political turmoil that brought Russian tanks to Prague, Czechoslovakia, reflected forces that had long been working under the superficially tranquil daily routine of Russia and Eastern Europe.

The 1956 Hungarian Revolution was set off by Khrushchev's attack on Stalin.

ricanes had no similar single common cause. Rather, they reflected powerful forces that had long been working, though little noticed, under the superficially tranquil daily routine in Russia and Eastern Europe.

The 1956 events were all set off by the famous Khrushchev secret speech at the Soviet Communist Party Congress in February of that year. This speech, an exposure of Stalin, revealed that the man who had been worshiped as a faultless god was really closer to a devil incarnate. The shock produced by this speech precipitated the peaceful revolution in Poland, the violent revolution in Hungary, and the flood of literary destalinization in the Soviet Union. No such single dramatic event was required in 1968. Rather, that year saw the coming to fruition of forces long since working steadily in the countries involved.

A second difference between these two historic years is the greater durability—and therefore greater influence—of the most important single center of revolt. The Hungarian Revolution of 1956 lasted barely two weeks, from the first storming of the Budapest radio station in late October to the full-scale invasion by Soviet troops on November 4. In Czechoslovakia, in 1968, on the other hand, Alexander Dubcek became first secretary of that country's Communist Party in January, and the Soviet invasion did not take place until August 20. What Dubcek called the "Czechoslovak Road to Socialism" therefore had more than two hundred days to spread its democratic message.

Finally, there was no 1956 sequel to the almost incredible political defeat administered to the Kremlin in 1968 by a Czechoslovakia fully occupied by Soviet and satellite troops. In Hungary, in 1956, the invading army quickly overthrew the legal Government of Imre Nagy. It installed the new pro-Soviet regime of Janos Kadar even before the fighting had fully ended. But in Czechoslovakia, in 1968, it proved impossible for the Soviet Government to impose a pro-Soviet regime on Prague. Rather, the Soviets were given an unprecedented political defeat. This was the result of the relatively peaceful but united resistance of the Czechoslovak people. Another factor was the enormous pressure of world public opinion, including the protests of many influential communist parties. Czechoslovak Communist Party chief Dubcek, Premier Oldrich Cernik and National Assembly Chairman Josef Smrkovsky had all been arrested by Soviet troops. They were beaten, handcuffed, taken to Russia and put in jail. In effect they were deposed and made ready for trial and execution as traitors. But because of the resistance of the Czechoslovak people and the pressure of world opinion, these three men had to be freed, recognized as still in office, and permitted to negotiate with the highest Kremlin leaders. Hungary's Imre Nagy, on the other hand, never left his prison and was finally executed.

The basic source whence the winds of change of 1968 drew their strength was the desire for freedom. Related to this was the demand for the final end of the greater and lesser remnants of Stalinist dictatorship that still plagued and plague the countries affected. It is this concern with freedom that united in 1968 the student demonstrators in Poland, Czechoslovakia's people and its leadership under Dubcek, and various intellectual dissidents in the Soviet Union. A very important second element gave added strength to the forces for change in Prague, Warsaw, and the minority areas of the Soviet Union, notably the Ukraine. This was the desire for freedom from rule by Moscow.

After the invasion of Czechoslovakia, the Soviet Union began spreading the so-called "Brezhnev Doctrine." This, as voiced in *Pravda,* maintains that socialist countries do not really enjoy full sovereignty, independence and territorial integrity. All these rights, *Pravda* argued, can be violated if other socialist countries—meaning primarily the Soviet Union—feel that socialism in one of these states is endangered and decide to intervene militarily. This was, of course, an attempt to frame a legal justification for the invasion of Czechoslovakia after that invasion took place.

Hungary's Imre Nagy, above, was executed and replaced with pro-Soviet Janos Kadar.

From the intellectual, ideological and political point of view, the most important document written in 1968 was a small pamphlet entitled *Thoughts Concerning Progress, Peaceful Coexistence and Intellectual Freedom*. Its author is Dr. Andrei D. Sakharov. He is one of the Soviet Union's most eminent scientists. Dr. Sakharov's pamphlet could not be and has not been printed in the Soviet Union. But it has been circulated there in typewritten and hand-copied manuscript. It was smuggled abroad and published in July 1968 in *The New York Times*.

The remarkable feature of Dr. Sakharov's work is that it represents a broad-ranging examination of the chief problems facing both the Soviet people and the people of the world. This examination clashes sharply with Soviet propaganda stereotypes. And in general it is in agreement with the conclusions of liberal opinion in many parts of the world.

Dr. Sakharov's longest single discussion is devoted to the threat to intellectual freedom. He sees this as coming from a variety of sources. Thus in the Soviet Union he notes the repressive force of censorship, which, he writes, "kills in the embryo the living soul of Soviet literature, and indeed the same applies to all other aspects of social thought, giving rise to stagnation, monotony, and a complete absence of any fresh or deep thoughts. Indeed, deep thoughts can appear only in discussion, with the presence of opposition, only with the potentiality of expression not only of true but also of doubtful ideas. This was already clear to the philosophers of ancient Greece, and almost no one doubts this now. But after fifty years of uncontested rule over the minds of a whole country, our leadership seemingly fears even a reference to such a discussion."

But even the need for intellectual freedom is only one aspect of Dr. Sakharov's preoccupation in this remarkable document. Perhaps the best way to summarize the totality of his peroccupation is to quote his first sentences:

Andrei Sinyavsky and Yuli Daniel at the funeral of writer Boris Pasternak. Dr. Sakharov denounced the trial and imprisonment of these two Soviet dissenters.

"The division of mankind poses the threat of destruction for all. Civilization is endangered by the possibility of universal thermonuclear war, catastrophic hunger for a majority of men, stupefaction from the drug of 'mass culture,' and bureaucratized dogmatism.

"In the face of these perils, any action intensifying the split in humanity, any doctrine asserting the incompatibility of world ideologies and nations is madness and criminal. Only universal cooperation based on intellectual freedom and the high moral ideas of socialism and labor, accompanied by the elimination of dogmatism and of the pressures of the hidden interests of the dominant classes, can safeguard civilization."

At the core of the author's proposals for saving mankind is a plea for Soviet-American cooperation. This

The Czechoslovak drama began when Alexander Dubcek, above, replaced Antonin Novotny.

plea is founded on the belief that the two societies are and will continue to grow more and more similar to each other. He bases this belief on the conclusion that the Soviet Union must and will become more democratic. He also argues that the United States is moving toward convergence with socialism through "social progress, peaceful coexistence, worldwide cooperation with socialism and changes in the structure of ownership." Thus Dr. Sakharov feels that one day the United States and the Soviet Union will have healed their differences. When this happens the industrialized nations of the world will have reduced their huge arms budgets substantially. He thus proposes that these nations allocate 20 per cent of their national income to help underdeveloped nations emerge from their hunger and backwardness.

It should be underlined here that the great bulk of Dr. Sakharov's ideas are completely at variance with the current Soviet line. Thus Soviet ideology now insists that capitalism and communism must always be opposed until one or the other triumphs. The notion of convergence of the two systems toward some more or less common center is treated as heresy and claimed to be the invention of bourgeois propaganda.

Thus the Soviet leaders in 1968 further narrowed substantially the permissible area of intellectual freedom. They tightened censorship and sent more dissidents to jail. Indeed they produced the most intellectually confining situation in the Soviet Union since Stalin's death in 1953.

It was in Czechoslovakia, however, that the winds of change and of attempted self-liberation blew most strongly during 1968.

Formally the drama in Prague began on January 5, 1968. On that day Alexander Dubcek was elected first secretary of the Czechoslovak Communist Party, replacing Antonin Novotny.

The political convulsion that removed Novotny from power at the beginning of 1968 had four main roots.

One was the bitterness of the Slovak one third of the population. The Slovaks felt that the Czech majority—and particularly Novotny himself—had never given the Slovak minority a fair deal.

Second were the country's economic difficulties. These resulted in a stagnation of living standards in a country that had once prided itself on being among the most advanced in Europe. The Communists had mismanaged the nation's economy. In addition, Czechoslovakia had been cut off from Western competition and technical influence. As a result, much of the country's production was high cost and poor quality.

Third was the discontent of the intellectuals, particularly the writers. They rebelled against the capricious and strict censorship, which was relatively lenient one day and severe the next. They were also bitter about Czechoslovakia's subservience to the Soviet Union in foreign policy. This servility was most apparent during the Arab-Israeli war of June 1967. Much Czechoslovak sympathy was with Israel. But the Government adopted a Moscow-dictated, pro-Arab line. The writers' discontent came to a head in their congress at the end of June 1967. The speeches there induced the Novotny regime to retaliate. Individual writers were expelled from the Communist Party. And the newspaper of the Writers Union, a major organ of liberal expression, was taken away.

Finally, there was the rebelliousness of Czechoslovak young people. This was expressed at one level by the strength of a sort of hippie movement in Prague. It was expressed at another level by the demonstration of university students on October 31, 1967. This demonstration began as a protest against poor student living conditions. But the police brutality used against the students turned the whole matter into a major political confrontation between the Government and the intellectual elite of the university students.

The essence of the changes that Communist Party leader Alexander Dubcek tried to introduce can be

Economic stagnation and student unrest helped bring about Novotny's downfall.

Leading Czechoslovak liberals:
Premier Oldrich Cernik, above,
and Josef Smrkovsky.

expressed in the phrase "socialist democracy." Dubcek and his closest associates, particularly Premier Oldrich Cernik and National Assembly Chairman Josef Smrkovsky, sought to combine a very considerable degree of freedom with the continuance of the economic features of socialism.

The main ideas of the Dubcek era were reflected in the Action Program that was adopted by the Czechoslovak Communist Party Central Committee in April 1968. In this program the Communist Party was seen not as the dictator and boss of the society, but rather as the conciliator of the different group interests of the society. In this view the Communist Party was to rule by persuasion, not by force and threat of punishment. The Action Program also called for extensive freedom of speech and press.

Similarly, the Action Program saw the role of the security police as that of guarding the country against threats from abroad, not as the protection of communist rule by stifling dissent and questioning. Also, the Action Program provided for citizens to have the right to go abroad freely. And they could remain abroad as long as they wanted to. It was, in these and other respects, the most liberal and democratic program ever issued by a Communist Party closely allied with the Soviet Union.

Even before the Action Program was adopted, the influence of these ideas had become evident. The Czechoslovak press, radio and television enjoyed a new freedom. These media became the advance guard of the Dubcek revolution. They exposed the secrets of the Novotny regime. They revealed, for example, the torture used to extort false confessions.

In late February, Czechoslovakia was aroused by the flight of Major General Jan Sejna. The Czechoslovak press charged that he had been involved in a plot to save Novotny by means of a military coup. And the newspapers, radio and television told the Czechoslovak people that General Sejna and the son of Antonin Novotny had engaged in swindles that had enriched them at the expense of the nation. The anger caused by these revelations helped topple Novotny from his remaining post, that of president of Czechoslovakia, which was given to retired General Ludvik Svoboda.

Very quickly, however, this trend toward democratic socialism came under attack from two main sources, one domestic, the other foreign.

Inside Czechoslovakia, Novotny still had many supporters in the higher and middle echelons of the Communist Party, the Government and the economic bureaucracies. These people feared that they would lose their jobs as a result of the revolution at the top. As a result, they wanted to restore Novotny to power.

The tactics of the domestic opponents were based on fear and slander. They sought to convince the workers that the changes Dubcek favored would mean mass unemployment and lower wages. They spread rumors that Czechoslovakia had been caught in a "counterrevolution of the intellectuals" who had taken power at the expense of the workers. And they used the weapon of anti-Semitism. They took advantage of the fact that a few people prominent in supporting Dubcek were of Jewish origin. Among these people were Eduard Goldstuecker, head of the Writers Union, and Frantisek Kriegel, a member of the Communist Party Presidium. But despite all efforts, popular support of Dubcek grew.

Foreign opposition to the democratization of Czechoslovakia came primarily from the Soviet Union, Poland and East Germany. In each of these countries the reins of Communist Party control were being drawn tighter. This had intensified the contrast between the situation in each of these countries and that of Czechoslovakia. In Moscow, Warsaw and East Berlin, therefore, fear grew that the liberal ideas spread in Prague might prove contagious and stimulate resistance to the regimes in these other countries.

But there was another reason for Soviet, Polish and East German opposition to the new trends in Czech-

Ludvik Svoboda, above, president of Czechoslovakia, and Eduard Goldstuecker, head of the Writers Union: advocates of liberalization and reform in Czechoslovakia.

oslovakia. These countries became increasingly alarmed that Czechoslovakia might abandon the Soviet Bloc's foreign-policy decisions and emulate Rumania in taking independent positions. They feared that Czechoslovakia might establish diplomatic relations with West Germany—as Rumania had done—in order to get badly needed West German economic aid. They feared also that Czechoslovakia might reestablish diplomatic relations with Israel and switch to a more neutral or even pro-Israeli position in the Middle East. And above all, the most fearful men in the Kremlin argued that if Czechoslovakia were permitted to continue on its course, it would inevitably come under the control of non-Communists and change sides in the cold war.

These fears from Czechoslovakia's neighbors reflected themselves in ever-increasing pressures exerted on Dubcek to change his policies. As early as March a special meeting was held at Dresden, East Germany, at which Dubcek and his colleagues were pressed to change their ways. In May, Dubcek flew to Moscow for more conferences. And later, Soviet Premier Aleksei N. Kosygin visited Czechoslovakia. But liberalization continued. Dubcek's only concession was to

On August 20–21, 1968, Czechoslovakia was invaded by Soviet, Polish, East German, Hungarian and Bulgarian troops.

permit Soviet, Polish, East German and Hungarian troops to enter Czechoslovakia for Warsaw Pact maneuvers in June.

The first crisis came in mid-July. It was preceded by increasing evidence that the Soviet troops that had come for "maneuvers" would not return home as scheduled. Then came a demand from Moscow that Czechoslovak leaders meet with Soviet, Polish, East German, Hungarian and Bulgarian leaders in Warsaw. Since this obviously would be an attempt to dictate to Czechoslovakia, Dubcek refused. The Warsaw meeting was held anyway, without Czechoslovak representatives. The outcome of this meeting was a letter that was in effect an ultimatum. This letter charged that Czechoslovak socialism was in danger. It demanded that Dubcek reinstitute censorship, purge the Communist Party of elements considered untrustworthy, and prevent non-Communists from organizing politically. Behind this letter was a thinly veiled threat of an invasion if the demands were not met.

The crisis seemed resolved in early August, after Czechoslovak and Soviet leaders had met at the small Slovak town of Cierna, near the Soviet border. Here

The invaders seized control of all major cities. They met little physical opposition, for the Czechoslovak leaders had warned against armed resistance.

The Czechoslovak people offered passive resistance, painting anti-Soviet slogans on windows and walls.

and at a later meeting in Bratislava, which was attended also by Moscow's allies, agreement seemed to have been reached. The agreement appeared to be that Czechoslovakia would follow the Soviet foreign-policy line but would have freedom in its internal affairs.

But all these conceptions were scrapped on the night of August 20, 1968. Czechoslovakia was invaded by hundreds of thousands of Soviet, Polish, East German, Hungarian and Bulgarian troops. The invaders quickly seized control of all major cities. They met no resistance since Dubcek and other Czechoslovak leaders warned against offering armed resistance. Dubcek, Premier Cernik, Smrkovsky and other Prague liberals were arrested by Soviet troops and imprisoned.

Now it became the turn of the Soviet Government to be surprised. Moscow had apparently anticipated that anti-Dubcek conservatives would be able to form a Czechoslovak Government that would be approved by President Svoboda, and that would be supported by most of the Czechoslovak people. But Svoboda refused to approve an alternative Government. And the people of Czechoslovakia soon showed that they were united in supporting Dubcek and opposing the invasion. Some Soviet tanks were set on fire. But in the main the Czechoslovak people employed passive resistance. They chalked swastikas on Soviet tanks. They painted anti-Soviet and pro-Dubcek slogans on walls. And they tried to persuade the invading soldiers that they had committed a crime. Meanwhile world public opinion condemned the invasion. The Russians were attacked by many Western European communist parties, by Yugoslavia and by China as well as by the free world.

In this tense situation President Svoboda was flown to Moscow to negotiate with the Soviet leaders. He demanded that the imprisoned Czechoslovak leaders be freed and be permitted to join the negotiations as the leaders of the country. The Russians gave in. Soon Dubcek and his comrades were out of their prison cells and in the negotiating chambers of the Kremlin. The

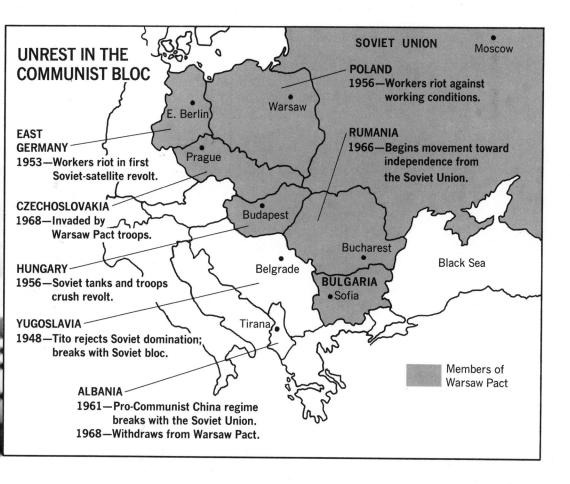

UNREST IN THE COMMUNIST BLOC

SOVIET UNION

Moscow

POLAND
1956—Workers riot against
working conditions.

Warsaw

E. Berlin

**EAST
GERMANY**
1953—Workers riot in first
Soviet-satellite revolt.

Prague

RUMANIA
1966—Begins movement toward
independence from
the Soviet Union.

CZECHOSLOVAKIA
1968—Invaded by
Warsaw Pact troops.

Budapest

Bucharest

Black Sea

HUNGARY
1956—Soviet tanks and troops
crush revolt.

Belgrade

BULGARIA
Sofia

YUGOSLAVIA
1948—Tito rejects Soviet domination;
breaks with Soviet bloc.

Tirana

Members of
Warsaw Pact

ALBANIA
1961—Pro-Communist China regime
breaks with the Soviet Union.
1968—Withdraws from Warsaw Pact.

The Soviet Bloc has experienced great unrest since 1948,
when President Tito of Yugoslavia rejected Soviet domination.

result was a published communiqué in which the Soviet
leaders promised to remove their troops once the situation in Prague had undergone "normalization." Because enemy troops occupied their country, the
Czechoslovak leaders were forced to agree to a secret
list of provisions: Soviet forces would remain indefinitely in Czechoslovakia. Censorship of the press would
be restored. And there would be no freedom for noncommunist or anti-communist political activity in
Czechoslovakia.

By the end of October, Czechoslovakia had formally
approved a public treaty agreeing to stationing of Soviet troops in the country. This was followed by the
beginning of a withdrawal of some of the invading

Soviet forces. Inside the country, censorship had been restored. And many of the democratic changes of earlier months had been entirely or partially canceled. Nevertheless, it was clear that the Czechoslovak people were still united around Dubcek and his democratic course. And they resented deeply the brutal invasion that had ended their freedom and sovereignty. Resistance continued, though it was moral and political rather than violent.

Poland, in March 1968, suffered the most serious internal disturbances that country had seen since the communist takeover was completed in the late 1940's. In virtually all major Polish cities pitched battles erupted in which thousands of young people, mainly students, battled the police. At the height of this mass rioting, there is good reason to believe, the Soviet Union contemplated the possibility that the fighting might develop into revolution that would require the intervention of Soviet troops.

The Polish rioting was precipitated by a Polish government crackdown on the freedom of writers, particularly the banning of a classic Polish play about the struggle of Poland against czarism in the nineteenth century. Audience reactions to anti-Russian remarks in the play turned each night's performance into practically an anti-Soviet demonstration. As a result the play was ordered off the boards. This resulted in massive student protests. These protests might have been kept at a low key, but another factor became involved: a struggle for power at the highest levels of Polish rule. Those anxious to displace Gomulka decided to use maximum force against the students as a means of discrediting Gomulka. The resultant police brutality outraged students all over Poland. This led to the spread of demonstrations and riots.

To combat this disaffection the Polish regime turned to anti-Semitism. It charged that the ringleaders of the student riots had been Jewish young people, many of them the sons and daughters of high officials. Thus

Polish Communist Party leader Wladyslaw Gomulka cracked down on antigovernment rioters in March 1968.

the riots were presented as a "Zionist plot" against Poland, even though the number of Jews in the country is under 25,000—many of them elderly people in homes for the aged. The result was that many Jewish officials, scientists, writers and the like lost their jobs. Many Jews began to flee the country.

It was these internal troubles that help explain the bitterness of the Gomulka regime in Warsaw against Dubcek's experiment in Prague. During the riots, Polish students shouted "Long Live Czechoslovakia!"

When Czechoslovakia was invaded, the five nations involved sought very carefully to present a picture of unanimous approval among their people for the occupation of this neighboring and allied state. Thousands of meetings were held at which resolutions of support for the invasion were adopted. But later it became clear that among students and intellectuals there had been bitter though ineffective opposition.

The most spectacular effort to show enmity to the invasion took place in Moscow's Red Square. At the height of the August crisis about a dozen people sought to stage a peaceful demonstration and unfurl banners supporting Czechoslovakia. The demonstration was promptly crushed by Soviet secret police.

In East Germany a series of trials began which revealed that young people and intellectuals had distributed leaflets against the August invasion, painted Dubcek's name on walls, and otherwise tried to make known their abhorrence for the violation of Czechoslovakia's independence and sovereignty.

At the end of 1968 it was evident that Soviet power, for the time being, had crushed the democratic forces in Czechoslovakia. But in the process of this repression it had alienated an entire nation, Czechoslovakia, and stimulated resistance in the Soviet Union and the other countries that had sent troops. The seeds had been planted, in short, for harvests of wrath in the future, when the winds of change in the Soviet Bloc may blow with a violence that may make the storms of 1968 seem like balmy breezes.

Pavel Litvinov, grandson of the late Soviet Foreign Minister Maxim Litvinov, and Mrs. Yuli Daniel, wife of the writer sentenced to prison, were arrested for supporting Czechoslovakia.

Walter Ulbricht of East Germany helped instigate the invasion of Czechoslovakia, but he faced internal opposition from many German students and intellectuals.

YOUTH IN REVOLT

By HARRY SILVERSTEIN
NEW SCHOOL FOR SOCIAL RESEARCH

THIS is the age of revolution. But it is not revolution in the ordinary sense of political upheaval against a particular government. By revolution is meant the most massive series of changes in almost every area of social and community life. It knows no narrow political or national boundaries. It is international in scope. And it is peculiar to modern civilization. The thrusts of this revolution go in every direction. They are political. They are technological and cultural. They are economic and ideological. They are social and individual.

Little that exists in the modern world is permanent or stable. The character of modern revolution is that of incredible speed and movement. Whatever at a given moment seems new and progressive soon becomes old and backward. Nothing stands still. Even revolution is followed by revolution.

This is also the time of the youth revolution. Those we call youth are not unlike the times that have spawned them. Many were born in those years of the "baby boom," the seven-year period following the second "War to End All Wars." They reflect—in mood, hope, disappointment and expression—the period of modern history in which they were reared.

Within five years, half the people in the world will be 25 years of age or younger.

The present youth generation is heir to our contemporary world. Consider some facts about this world:

1. The population has increased more than 50 per cent in their lifetime.

2. The speed of long-distance mass transportation has more than doubled in the last twenty years. It will triple within the next five years.

3. Computers can sort information and solve complex problems several thousand times faster than any human being.

4. In the last twenty years, several hundred governments around the world have toppled.

5. In the United States alone, 40,000,000 families change residence each year. This is 20 per cent of all families.

6. Nuclear weapons stockpiled by the United States, the Soviet Union and other nations can annihilate all life on earth.

7. Men have orbited the earth and will soon land on the moon.

8. Medical advances have greatly increased life-span in the past twenty years.

9. World literacy has increased twentyfold in the past twenty years.

10. Within the next five years, half of the people in the world will be 25 years of age or younger.

These extraordinary facts serve to dramatize modern social change. They form the backdrop against which young people and their problems must come to be understood. For no present-day social movement can be seen without some sense of a world in transition. The questions youth raise are important elements of this complex fabric called modern civilization. What they say and do are part of it. What they experience is part of it. These facts lend credence to the idea that today's youth are different from youth of past eras.

The theory that a unique youth revolution is taking place is supported by recent events around the world. What is of special importance is that youth not only are affected by the great changes that are taking place, but that they are also a major force in producing these changes. Moreover, these events seem to be independent of the type of society in which they take place. Whether a society is capitalist, socialist or communist, young people seem to be a vital, active force in that society. Whether a society is democratic or totalitarian, industrialized or underdeveloped, young people are a vital force there.

For example, in 1968, French youth were at the forefront of a national strike. This strike almost paralyzed France and ended the rule of President Charles de Gaulle. In the United States, young people forced universities to give them a greater role in policy-making decisions. They led civil-rights and anti-Vietnam-war movements. And they greatly influenced the 1968 presidential election. The Cultural Revolution in Communist China has been principally a youth movement. And the youth of Czechoslovakia were the first line of defenders against the Soviet occupation forces. These items illustrate eruptive situations. But the youth movement has also proceeded in less eruptive ways.

In modern art, new psychedelic forms are the expression of youth. In fashions and style, young people have set the creative patterns that are followed by adults. Music and dance each has its recent innovations from the young. Experimental "communal" groups are made up mostly of young people trying to develop new ways of social existence. Large communities of young migrants have emerged in the past two years. Best known of these are the East Village in New York City and Haight-Ashbury in San Francisco. It is indeed evident, then, that a youth revolution, sometimes disruptive, sometimes serene, is in process.

In a stable society, whenever a new generation is "promoted" to adulthood, it is expected to act more or less like the preceding generations. Indeed, successive generations ultimately take on the basic appearances of one another. In this way the society keeps its essential

In 1968, young people influenced the presidential election and led anti-Vietnam-war movements.

Bob Dylan, youth idol and musician, sings "the times they are a-changing."

form. The ideal society, then, changes only gradually. When this does not happen, the society is unstable.

At any given "moment" in the history of a society, various generations behave somewhat differently from one another. The behavior of young people is certainly different from the behavior of adults. Youthfulness of course can be regarded as a period of apprenticeship for future adult status. These differences are normal and expected. However, when societies are undergoing rapid change, unexpected differences can be seen. Such differences in youth behavior are in a sense "social mutations." If read correctly, modern society is in effect failing to reproduce itself with relative exactness. A large segment of today's youth generation is not acting more or less like preceding generations. There have emerged two generational worlds within a single period of social history. And these two worlds are often mutually antagonistic.

The more society rapidly changes, the more parents and children will have been reared in different "realities." Each generation then sees the other as out of touch with that part of the modern world each likes to believe is the "real world." As Bob Dylan cautions parents in song: "get out. . . , for the times, they are a-changing." This is a far cry from those days when "children were to be seen, not heard."

There is no simple explanation for the current youth movement. It is complex. And it has many determinants. This is a world, however, in which there are many voiceless minorities. And they have come to recognize their own potential for full participation in the events that shape their lives. One might speculate that young people also have come to recognize this potential. Thus, whatever the cause or shape of events in the past few years, it is clear that the voices of youth can hardly be overlooked.

There is another way of interpreting the youth revolution. We can examine three aspects of present-day society about which young people are very concerned.

There appears to be a general decline of authority, and young people are probing the limits of this authority, as they did at the 1968 Democratic convention and at the antiwar demonstration at the Pentagon in 1967.

For less-advantaged youth there are fewer alternatives: some become delinquents or take part in ghetto riots.

Young people are concerned about authority. They are concerned about the dehumanization of society—that is, the loss of warm, human qualities in everyday social life. And they are concerned about values—because they believe that adults have a self-contradictory system of values.

First, there appears to be a decline of authority.

Many young people believe that the authority of society's institutions is not absolute or permanent. As a result, young people constantly probe the limits of this authority. This probing, this testing, is condensed in the term "anti-Establishment." This concept is central to the idea of "alienation." By alienation we mean a complete rejection of the values and structures of a social system. Alienation results in many different forms of behavior. The form depends upon the individual's background and development.

For example, young people from well-to-do homes may withdraw from school or work. They may give up religion and family life and retreat to a hippie community. Or they may directly confront authority. This is what happened in 1968 on university campuses the world over. For less-advantaged youth there are fewer alternatives. Young people who grow up in poverty in ghettos may engage in delinquency or other illegal behavior. This is what happened in recent riots in ghetto areas of American cities. It is ironic that those who are "better off" often wish to withdraw from society. Yet those in less-fortunate situations often demand more complete participation.

Second, modern society seems to be moving toward a general condition of dehumanization.

The basic forms of our modern society are located within the urban-industrial complex. Within this complex there are large-scale bureaucratic structures. These structures can accomplish mass production, mass communication and mass education. But these bureaucracies tend to be impersonal and insensitive. They perform their functions—but they do so at the sacrifice of

Young people are concerned that society
is moving toward a general condition of dehumanization,
the results of which are insensitivity and conformity.

Revolutionary youth have many older heroes, including Che Guevara, Cuban revolutionary who was killed in Bolivia, and Albert Camus, the French existentialist writer. Others include pediatrician Dr. Benjamin Spock and philosopher Herbert Marcuse.

individual potentialities and needs. This produces a condition in which the aims and needs of the group far outweigh those of the individual.

This dehumanization is an important element in the alienation of young people from society. They feel that they cannot control and master their own fates. It is small wonder that many young people strongly identify with Monsieur Meursault, the principal character in Albert Camus' *The Stranger*. M. Meursault, caught in a web of circumstances, is unable to manage the course of his life. He commits a pointless murder, is tried and sentenced to death.

Many young people believe that their elders are essentially unfulfilled. They believe that many adults fail to explore their basic potentiality. The reason for this, they believe, is the adults' tendency to conform to the demands of large-scale social groups. To conform, adults have to submerge their personal and individual interests. Young people thus see a world populated by conforming, mechanical, insensitive men.

Several recent incidents underscore youth's concern about society's neglect of individual needs. For example, student demonstrations on college and university campuses almost always include demands for smaller classes. Students want to work more closely with faculty members. They want personal association. And they want individual assistance. In a sense, the movement toward decentralization of elementary and secondary schools contains the same basic element. Decentralization of education is antibureaucratic and anti-Establishment. Again, those who favor decentralization also favor more personalized education.

Most student demonstrations have included the demand for an end to large classes, a symbol of dehumanization and conformity.

The tumultuous activity at the Democratic convention was in part caused by the intervention of young people in the established political structure.

Similarly, political parties have been challenged by youth as bureaucratic—and too big. In 1968 the tumultuous activity at the Democratic national convention was in part caused by the intervention of young people in the established political structure. One primary aim of the young was the return of political control to smaller party units.

Even in the dramatic arts, a strong tendency has been in the direction of relatively small community theaters. These theater groups have sprung up throughout the United States. And they are basically the theaters of youth. The form of drama has also been shaped along antibureaucratic and prohumanistic models. These new forms are known as "guerrilla theater," "provo" and "street theater." Here, spontaneous events are staged in the streets or indoors. These events are designed to disrupt the mechanical patterns of daily life in contemporary society.

Unfortunately, young people do not always respond positively to a dehumanized society. Many young people, in fact, act in such a way that their human resourcefulness remains essentially untapped. Recent studies of hippie communities offer powerful evidence of this. In these communities, to which youth withdraw, there are visible signs of a basic social malaise. In their new environment, young people begin to engage in a new life-style. The central moral, or ideal, of many of these communities is that "you can do anything you want so long as you do not hurt anyone else." Many young people use this theme as a basic guideline for behavior—especially the part that states "you can do anything you want." This opens the floodgates of potentially destructive activities. Along these lines medical statistics are very compelling. In some hippie communities there are very high rates of upper-respiratory infection, hepatitis and venereal disease.

Further, drug use is quite marked in these communities. In general the use of drugs, particularly marijuana, has increased throughout the United States. In hippie communities it is almost universal. Perhaps the best indicator of the significant use of drugs among youth is the elaborate lexicon developed about it. Pot, acid, high and down are just a few of the terms.

There is, rightfully so, great concern about the dangers of drug use. But because of this concern the sociological significance of drug use is sometimes lost. To many, drug use appears to represent a countermeasure to dehumanization. Put simply, many young people believe that drugs enhance human potentiality. Drugs are used to expand experience beyond the limited, everyday feelings of mediocrity. In the most elementary formula, insensitivity and dehumanization plus drugs equals humanization. Also drugs are rarely used by young people when they are alone. Most often they are used in groups. Thus impersonality plus drugs equals intimate human interaction.

There is a third major characteristic of society that is of great concern to young people. This is society's self-contradictory system of values. Many young people

New-Left students have taken the lead in calling for changes in society. Above, Mark Rudd, head of Columbia University's Students for a Democratic Society. Below, Rudi Dutschke, West German student leader. Bottom, Daniel Cohn-Bendit, student leader in the forefront of France's May 1968 riots.

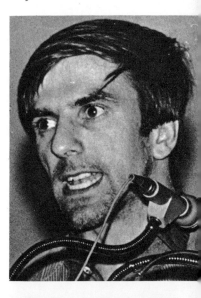

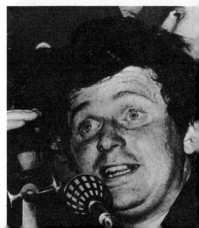

Society's system of values has led many young people to withdraw to hippie communities.

see society as being very hypocritical. They believe that ethical and moral codes are frequently violated. They also believe that those who espouse these codes are at the same time the most flagrant violators. In this sense, youth feel victimized by a lack of idealism among those of the older generation. The areas in which this most often is seen are religion, sexual behavior, politics and the business world.

For example, there is today deep concern for materialism. High value is placed on material things such as cars and television sets. This is in contradiction to espousal of humanism, where high value is placed on the human being. Young people feel that the quest for money and material things has assumed such proportions as to deny the quest for spiritual wealth. Moreover, some wealthy societies discover that their wealth has been obtained at a cost to those who still live in poverty.

Surely the major contradiction in the American value system is in the area of prejudice and discrimination. It is, as Gunnar Myrdal's well-known study indicates in its title, *An American Dilemma*. The credo of American society states that all are created equal. Yet minority peoples are treated as less equal than others. The most visible youth movement in the past decade has of course been the civil-rights movement. It should also be evident that this movement is international in scope.

Sexual morality and sexual behavior are also areas in which there are major value contradictions. Modern youth see this issue in three related ways. The sexual behavior of the older generation does not agree with the moral code. The sexual codes are too restrictive. The basis of sexual behavior should be love. What is interesting about these findings is that the attitudes of young people about sex are at the same time both traditional and revolutionary. In addition, studies indicate that youth appear to be more emancipated from restrictive moral customs of the past. Thus they are more tolerant of such behavior as premarital sex. Nevertheless, their sexual behavior has not substantially changed. The so-called sex revolution, then, is a revolution in values not behavior. Behavior, however, will eventually change in accordance with the new values. Indeed this has begun to happen.

The traditional component concerning sexual behavior of youth is romantic love. The idea of love is difficult to define. Yet it is very much a part of the act of sex. Again, young people are tolerant of others who engage in sexual behavior without love. But love is the most important part of their moral code. Hippie communities have gained a reputation for sexual freedom. Surprisingly, studies observe that in these communities the romantic, one-man one-woman tradition still predominates.

Such basic precepts as God and the afterlife and ethical concerns such as the notions of right and wrong are of deep concern to youth. Thus religious values are being closely studied by them. Many young people feel that established Judeo-Christian religious institutions are irrelevant to modern times.

In a sense, a religious revolution has begun to take place. Indeed, various churches are reexamining their basic principles. Religious institutions are also becoming more secular, closer to the people. At the same time, youth in particular have begun a widespread interest in Eastern and Oriental religions, notably Hinduism and Buddhism.

In many ways, the youth revolution can be thought of as the polarization of values and ethics between two generational groups. The views of youth and adults have become rather different and distinct. Adults have adapted to society's customs and traditions. For them to readjust to a new life-style and entirely new approaches is very difficult. Such adjustment requires great versatility. And few except the young have this versatility. Thus, as changes take place in society, those able to adjust with ease are likely to be youth.

It is no accident that the chronological demarcation of youth has been extended to include those of age 25.

Love is the most important part of youth's moral code.

The generation gap:
in many ways,
the youth revolution
can be thought of as the
polarization of values
between two
generational groups.

What society needs, it more or less receives. And what it needs is a human being prepared for future change and versatile enough to accept this change. What is revolutionary is that young people themselves are major influences in the process of change.

Those who speak of the generation gap speak about great differences between youth and adults. And these differences revolve about such issues as human priorities and those values which provide guidelines for them. The concept of the generation gap serves to emphasize these differences. The sense of history between the two generations is also distinct. For many of the young, sometimes called the "Now Generation," there is no past and little future. For adults the past and future are important. It is the present, and the younger generation's participation in it, which is most elusive.

The idea of a generation gap is useful. Yet it does not shed too much light on the complexities of the categories youth and adult. We are aware of the differences between young people and adults. But it is also necessary to take into account the many similarities. The generations after all are not absolutely distinct from one another. Consider the extent to which youth bear the characteristics of their elders. And at the same time, adults have taken on many of the attributes of youth. Adults also are quite attracted to youth. This is suggested by the large numbers of tourists who visit and spend time in youth communities each year.

It is also obvious that not all members of a single generation are alike.

Still, differences are experiences. And these experiences are sometimes quite profound. As one youth poetically summarized these differences between him and his parents, "Behind our home in suburbia there are woods. When I was a kid, I used to walk through the woods marveling at nature. I still do. So far as I know my parents never walked through those woods, and if they did, it would probably be to get to the other side."

TOP OF THE NEWS

WALTER CRONKITE

JANUARY

HUMAN HEART TRANSPLANTS. In December 1967 and January 1968, surgeons performed five heart-transplant operations, the first to be performed on human beings. Those of December 3 and January 2 were performed by Dr. Christiaan N. Barnard and his team, in Cape Town, South Africa. Dr. Adrian Kantrowitz and his group, in Brooklyn, New York, performed those of December 6 and January 10; and the team of Dr. Norman E. Shumway, in Palo Alto, California, performed that of January 7.

For each of the five patients, the drastic surgery involved in replacing his diseased heart with a healthy one (from a person who had just died) was the last hope. The critical part of the procedure was less the operation than the tendency of the body to reject foreign

A GI rushes to the aid of a buddy wounded during the Vietcong Tet offensive, which began on January 30.

tissue. This immunological reaction is a natural defense against disease. After a heart-transplant operation, various drugs are administered to suppress the reaction for the time being, at the risk of serious infection. By the end of January, only one patient, dentist Philip Blaiberg, in Cape Town, was still living.

NORTH KOREANS SEIZE THE PUEBLO. On January 23, North Korean patrol boats captured the U.S. Navy electronic intelligence ship *Pueblo* off the North Korean coast. The vessel and its crew of 83 were taken to the North Korean port of Wonsan. North Korea claimed that the ship had intruded into its territorial waters and was carrying out "hostile activities." The United States demanded the return of the ship and crew.

JANUARY 1968

	1	2	3	4	5	6
7	8	9	10	11	12	13
14	15	16	17	18	19	20
21	22	23	24	25	26	27
28	29	30	31			

1. Cecil Day Lewis was named poet laureate of Britain.

9. Sweden granted asylum to four U.S. Navy men who had deserted in Japan in October 1967 in opposition to the Vietnam war.

15. Earthquakes struck western Sicily, Italy, leaving 80,000 homeless and more than 200 dead.

16. In continuing terrorist shootings in Guatemala between communist and Rightist factions, two U.S. Embassy military attachés, Colonel John O. Webber, Jr., and Lieutenant Commander Ernest A. Munro, were shot to death.

19. President Johnson named Clark M. Clifford secretary of defense.

21. Four unarmed hydrogen bombs were fragmented and scattered when a U.S. Air Force B-52 crashed and burned near Thule, Greenland.

30. On the first day of Tet (lunar New Year), Vietcong raiders and North Vietnamese troops launched attacks on major cities throughout South Vietnam.

31. The South Pacific island of Nauru, a UN trusteeship, became an independent republic.

FEBRUARY

National Guardsmen patrol the streets of Detroit during Negro rioting in July 1967. Because of many such riots across the nation, President Johnson appointed the National Advisory Commission on Civil Disorders.

RIOT COMMISSION REPORT. On July 27, 1967, in the wake of destructive racial riots in Newark, Detroit and other American cities, President Johnson appointed an 11-member National Advisory Commission on Civil Disorders. The commission, headed by Illinois Governor Otto Kerner, was directed to find the basic causes of urban riots.

On February 29, 1968, the commission released its findings, with the disturbing warning that "Our nation is moving toward two societies, one black, one white—separate and unequal," and that the basic cause of this situation is "white racism."

To support this conclusion, the commission pointed out that white society condones the fact that most Negroes live in urban ghettos. In some ghettos the crime rate is 35 times higher than in white neighborhoods. Infant mortality is 58 per cent higher. Fully 40 per cent of all nonwhite Americans (mostly Negroes) live below the poverty level; 33 per cent of ghetto Negroes are unemployed or underemployed. As a daily routine, Negroes must cope with unsympathetic police forces, lack of jobs, and substandard housing. What is needed to correct these inequities, declared the commission, is a program "equal to the dimension of the problem." This program should include: 2,000,000 new jobs in the next three years; greater efforts to end school segregation; greater efforts to improve ghetto schools; establishment of uniform national welfare standards; income supplements; enactment of an enforceable Federal open-housing law; 6,000,000 units of housing for low- and moderate-income families in the next five years.

It was estimated that these programs would cost hundreds of billions of dollars. But, said the commission, "There can be no higher priority for national action and no higher claim on the nation's conscience" than to attack the causes of racial disorder. "To pursue our present course," the report continued, "will involve the continuing polarization of the American community and . . . the destruction of basic democratic values."

FEBRUARY 1968

				1	2	3
4	5	6	7	8	9	10
11	12	13	14	15	16	17
18	19	20	21	22	23	24
25	26	27	28	29		

7. Reverend Dr. Daniel A. Poling, a prominent Protestant Church leader, died at 83.

11. General Alfredo Stroessner was reelected president of Paraguay.

14. The United States announced that it would resume arms shipments to Jordan; such shipments were halted during the June 1967 Mideast war.

16. The Federal Government ended most deferments for graduate students. . . . North Vietnam released three captured American pilots: Major Norris M. Overly, Captain Jon D. Black and Ensign David P. Matheny—the first U.S. prisoners to be freed by Hanoi.

22. Cartoonist Peter Arno died at 64.

23. Author Fannie Hurst (*Back Street*) died at 78.

28. Stating that he had failed to win wide support among the voters, Michigan Governor George Romney announced his withdrawal from the Republican presidential race.

29. Continuing its feud with the Soviet Union, Rumania withdrew its delegates from the Soviet-sponsored meeting of 67 communist parties being held in Budapest, Hungary.

MARCH

PRESIDENT JOHNSON BARS RENOMINATION; CURTAILS NORTH VIETNAM BOMBING. On March 31, in a television speech, President Johnson told a surprised nation that "I shall not seek and I will not accept the nomination of my party as your president." The President's statement came at the end of a speech about Vietnam in which he announced that he had ordered a partial halt in the air and naval bombardment of North Vietnam. The demilitarized zone between North and South Vietnam as well as the southernmost part of North Vietnam were excluded from the bombing halt. Mr. Johnson also invited the North Vietnamese to join in a "series of mutual moves toward peace."

President Lyndon Johnson announces that he will not seek renomination.

GOLD CRISIS. On March 1, bankers and speculators throughout the world rushed to exchange dollars for gold. This wave of speculative buying caused the gravest international monetary crisis since 1931. The major factor behind the gold rush was a lack of faith in United States economic stability, caused by an increasing deficit in the U.S. balance of payments and the refusal of Congress to vote a tax increase in the face of rising government expenditures. It was estimated that, by March 14, speculators bought $2,000,000,000 worth of gold, betting on a raise in the U.S. official gold rate of $35 an ounce. The London gold market closed on March 15.

The United States and its allies in the London Gold Pool—the central banks of Great Britain, Switzerland, West Germany, Italy, Belgium and the Netherlands—took several steps to ease the situation. First, the United States repealed a law that required that 25 per cent of all U.S. currency be backed by gold. This freed the United States' $10,400,000,000 in gold reserves. Then, on March 16–17, international bankers met in Washington, D.C., with Pierre-Paul Schweitzer, managing director of the International Monetary Fund. The bankers agreed to stop buying and selling gold on the open market and to use their remaining gold only to settle debts between nations. The bankers also set up a two-price gold system: the official price of gold for intergovernmental transactions would be maintained at $35 an ounce; the free-market price for private buyers, such as speculators and industrial users, would be allowed to fluctuate according to the law of supply and demand.

One further, long-range step was taken to ease the world monetary crisis on March 30, when nine Western industrial nations, at the Stockholm Monetary Conference, voted to create new reserve assets known as Special Drawing Rights (S.D.R.'s), or paper gold. When this plan is ratified by the 107 member-nations of the International Monetary Fund, the S.D.R.'s will augment the gold reserves of the IMF member-states. This will facilitate the expansion of world trade.

MARCH 1968

					1	2
3	4	5	6	7	8	9
10	11	12	13	14	15	16
17	18	19	20	21	22	23
24	25	26	27	28	29	30
31						

6. Joseph W. Martin, Jr., former Speaker of the House of Representatives and a congressman from Massachusetts for 42 years, died at 83.

8. Terence J. Cooke, 47, auxiliary bishop and vicar-general of the Archdiocese of New York, was named by Pope Paul VI to succeed the late Francis Cardinal Spellman as archbishop of New York.

12. After 154 years of British rule, the Indian Ocean island of Mauritius was granted independence.

22. Wilbur J. Cohen was nominated to succeed John W. Gardner as U.S. secretary of health, education, and welfare. . . . President Johnson announced that General Westmoreland, head of U.S. forces in Vietnam, would be relieved of his post and appointed as Army chief of staff.

24. United Nations Security Council condemned Israel for its March 21 attack against Jordan, in which 15,000 Israeli troops, supported by tanks and planes, crossed the Jordan River and destroyed Arab guerrilla bases.

27. Soviet Colonel Yuri Gagarin, 34, who undertook the world's first orbital space flight, on April 12, 1961, was killed when his jet plane crashed.

APRIL

DR. MARTIN LUTHER KING, JR., ASSASSINATED. In the early evening hours of April 4, Martin Luther King stepped out onto the balcony of the Lorraine Motel in downtown Memphis, Tennessee. As he leaned over the balcony railing, a shot rang out, and the civil-rights leader fell mortally wounded by a bullet in the neck. Dr. King was rushed to St. Joseph's Hospital, but the 39-year-old Nobel Peace Prizewinner and advocate of nonviolence died less than an hour later.

The shot that felled Dr. King had come from the rear of a run-down rooming house, 200 feet away. Near the building police found a high-power rifle, binoculars and a suitcase. From fingerprints on the rifle, the Federal Bureau of Investigation identified the alleged assassin as James Earl Ray, alias Eric Starvo Galt. Ray, 40, had escaped from prison in 1967.

As news of Dr. King's assassination spread, so too did waves of rioting, arson and looting. In two hundred cities and towns across the United States, thousands of Negroes took to the streets to vent their anger. Hardest hit were Chicago and Washington, D.C. In the nation's capital, it took 12,500 troops three days to end the rioting, some of which took place three blocks from the White House. In all, more than 77,000 troops were deployed or alerted to cope with the crisis. Yet despite the widespread damage, there were fewer deaths than during the riots of 1967, primarily because police used their guns less and black leaders—militant and non-militant—walked the ghetto streets beseeching the people to keep calm.

Even as the rioting continued, Dr. King's body was flown from Memphis to Atlanta for burial. On April 9, after a service at the Ebenezer Baptist Church, 200,000 people marched to Morehouse College for a memorial ceremony. Dr. King's body was borne by a mule-drawn wagon, symbolizing his love of the poor of the nation. He was then buried in nearby South View Cemetery. His epitaph reads: "Free at last, free at last, thank God Almighty I'm free at last."

Martin Luther King, Jr.   1929–1968

APRIL 1968

	1	2	3	4	5	6
7	8	9	10	11	12	13
14	15	16	17	18	19	20
21	22	23	24	25	26	27
28	29	30				

2. In the Wisconsin Democratic primary election, Senator Eugene McCarthy won 57.6 per cent of the vote.

3. The United States and North Vietnam agreed to establish contacts leading to eventual peace talks and the end to the Vietnam war.

4. Terence Cooke was installed as Roman Catholic Archbishop of New York.

5. A 30,000-man relief column arrived at Khesanh, South Vietnam, to lift the 76-day siege of this embattled Marine base.

7. Auto-racing champion Jim Clark, 32, was killed when his Lotus-Ford auto crashed at Hockenheim, West Germany.

10. Forty-six persons were drowned when the ferry *Wahine* capsized in Wellington Harbor, New Zealand. . . . General Creighton W. Abrams was named to succeed General William Westmoreland as commander of U.S. forces in Vietnam.

16. Author Edna Ferber died at 82.

20. Pierre Elliott Trudeau was sworn in as prime minister of Canada. . . . A South African Boeing 707 crashed near Windhoek, South-West Africa, killing 122 persons.

M
A
Y

VIETNAM PEACE TALKS. On May 3 the United States and North Vietnam agreed to meet in Paris for preliminary Vietnam peace talks. During the talks, which began on May 10, the North Vietnamese negotiators, Minister of State Xuan Thuy and Colonel Ha Van Lau, demanded that the United States stop bombing North Vietnam and halt all other acts of war. The United States negotiators counterdemanded that Hanoi pledge military reciprocity in exchange for a bombing halt.

FRANCE IN TURMOIL. In early May, the Sorbonne and the University of Nanterre were closed because of what school officials termed "Leftist agitation." Immediately thousands of New Left students took to the streets of Paris. On May 11, after days of rioting and demonstrating, some 30,000 students charged police lines in Paris' Latin Quarter. In the melee, more than 350 people were injured and 450 arrested.

In support of the students, the General Confederation of Labor and the French Confederation of Labor called for a nationwide, one-day general strike for May 13. French workers then took matters into their

Amid clouds of tear gas, French policemen use riot shields as protection against a barrage of cobblestones thrown by French students.

own hands and by May 20, more than 10,000,000 people were on strike, demanding higher pay, a shorter workweek and a voice in management. Though in the midst of prosperity, the workers' wages had not kept pace with rising prices. The strike quickly brought the French economy to a standstill. There were no mail, rail, air or ship services. Schools were shut down and occupied by striking teachers. The banks were closed, and, as food became scarce, people began to hoard. Workers all over the nation occupied their workshops and factories, ousting management personnel. As a result of the turmoil, President Charles de Gaulle cut short a visit to Rumania.

The chaos resulting from the strikes and the student rioting and demonstrations threatened to topple the Fifth Republic. But the Goverment of Premier Georges Pompidou managed to survive a vote of censure on May 22. General de Gaulle then dissolved the National Assembly and called for national elections in June. On May 31, Premier Pompidou revised his Cabinet, and negotiations with unions got some of the strikers out of the plants they had occupied.

MAY 1968

			1	2	3	4
5	6	7	8	9	10	11
12	13	14	15	16	17	18
19	20	21	22	23	24	25
26	27	28	29	30	31	

3. A Braniff Airlines airplane crashed south of Dallas, Texas, killing 84 persons.

7. Alabama Governor Lurleen Wallace, 41, died of cancer. . . . In Indiana, Robert Kennedy won the Democratic primary with 42 per cent of the vote.

9. Actress Marion Lorne died at 82.

14. Robert Kennedy won the Nebraska Democratic primary with 53 per cent of the vote; Senator Eugene McCarthy received 31 per cent.

19. In the continuing Nigerian civil war, Federal troops captured Port Harcourt, the major port of Biafra (Nigeria's secessionist eastern region).

22. Black-power advocate H. Rap Brown was found guilty of violating Federal firearms laws and was sentenced to five years in prison.

28. Senator Eugene McCarthy won an upset victory over Robert Kennedy in the Oregon Democratic primary; he received 43 per cent of the vote to Kennedy's 37 per cent.

30. Panama's National Electoral Tally Board declared Dr. Arnulfo Arias the winner of Panama's presidential election, which had been held on May 12.

Robert F. Kennedy   1925–1968

ROBERT KENNEDY ASSASSINATED. During the first few minutes of June 5, after winning the California Democratic primary, New York Senator Robert Kennedy made a brief victory speech in a ballroom of Los Angeles' Ambassador Hotel, stepped from the podium and entered a rear corridor. There a gunman, later identified as Sirhan Bishara Sirhan, 24, a Jordanian immigrant, was waiting. Several shots rang out, and Senator Kennedy was hit by three bullets.

Fatally wounded, he was rushed to Good Samaritan Hospital, where surgery was performed to remove one of the bullets, which had lodged in his brain. But the damage was too severe. At 1:44 A.M., June 6, Robert Kennedy died. Later that day, the Senator's body was flown to New York City, where it lay in state at Saint Patrick's Cathedral. Throughout the day of June 7 and during the early morning hours of June 8, more than 150,000 people filed past the Senator's coffin to pay last respects to the man who was striving to be president of the United States, and who, to many, symbolized the promise of a better life, a better America. Later in the day, after a pontifical requiem mass was celebrated, the Senator's body was placed aboard a special train to Washington. At Arlington National Cemetery, Robert F. Kennedy, 42, was buried near his brother John, who, five years earlier, had also been assassinated.

TRUDEAU ELECTED PRIME MINISTER OF CANADA. On June 25, Canadian voters overwhelmingly endorsed Pierre Elliott Trudeau as prime minister. Trudeau's Liberal Party increased its number of seats in the 264-seat House of Commons from 127 to 155.

DE GAULLE TRIUMPHS. In May, France was almost totally paralyzed by striking workers and revolutionary students. President Charles de Gaulle's political days were numbered, said many observers. But once again, the General confounded the political pundits. In two days of voting (June 23 and 30), the Gaullists and their allies won 354 of the 487 National Assembly seats.

JUNE 1968

						1
2	3	4	5	6	7	8
9	10	11	12	13	14	15
16	17	18	19	20	21	22
23	24	25	26	27	28	29
30						

4. Film and theater actress Dorothy Gish died at 70.

5. The U.S. Navy announced that the nuclear sub *Scorpion*, which had been due at Norfolk, Virginia, on May 27, was "presumed lost," and that the 99 men aboard were "presumed dead."

6. Dr. Franklin Clark Fry, president of the Lutheran Church in America, died at 67.

8. James Earl Ray, accused of assassinating Dr. Martin Luther King, Jr., was captured in London.

14. Nobel Prize poet Salvatore Quasimodo died at 66.

19. Led by Dr. Ralph Abernathy of the Southern Christian Leadership Conference, more than 50,000 people marched in Washington, D.C., to support the demand of the poor people for a share of the nation's wealth.

26. President Johnson nominated Supreme Court Associate Justice Abe Fortas to succeed Chief Justice Earl Warren, who had announced his retirement; U.S. Court of Appeals Judge Homer Thornberry was nominated to take Fortas' place as associate justice. . . . Jazz trumpeter Harry (Ziggy) Elman died at 54.

JULY

Russians and Czechs meet at Cierna. On the left is the Soviet delegation (left to right): Presidium Chairman Nikolai Podgorny, Communist Party General Secretary Leonid Brezhnev, Premier Aleksei Kosygin, Central Committee Secretary Mikhail Suslov. The Czech delegation is on the right; Communist Party leader Alexander Dubcek can be seen full profile.

SOVIET BLOC SEEKS END TO LIBERAL CZECHO-SLOVAK REGIME. On July 29, leaders of Czechoslovakia and the 11-member Soviet Politburo met in Cierna, a small town in Czechoslovakia near the Soviet border, to discuss Czechoslovakia's liberalization policies. These policies had come under bitter attack by the Soviet Union and its allies.

The liberalization of Czechoslovakia had begun on January 5, 1968, when reformist Alexander Dubcek replaced Antonin Novotny as Czechoslovak Communist Party chief. In the following months, Dubcek ended censorship and promised the Czechoslovak people greater civil rights.

Threatened by the growing freedom in Czechoslovakia, the Soviet Union, Bulgaria, East Germany, Hungary and Poland called for a Warsaw Pact summit meeting and for an end to Dubcek's liberal policies. Czechoslovakia rejected these demands, but later agreed to meet with Soviet leaders at Cierna. While the Cierna conference was taking place, Soviet troops and tanks, which had been on Czechoslovak soil for War-

saw Pact maneuvers, lingered on, adding an ominous note to the proceedings.

POPE PAUL UPHOLDS CHURCH BAN ON BIRTH CONTROL. In a papal encyclical *Of Human Life,* dated July 25, Pope Paul VI upheld the Roman Catholic Church ban on artificial birth control. The encyclical generated considerable controversy. Many liberal Roman Catholic theologians stated that the encyclical was not binding. But the Roman Catholic bishops of the United States called for support of the papal stand.

UNITED STATES-SOVIET ATOM TALKS. The United States and the Soviet Union agreed on July 1 to open talks aimed at limiting and reducing offensive nuclear weapons and defensive antimissile systems. The agreement coincided with the signing by the United States, the Soviet Union, Great Britain and 59 nonnuclear nations of a treaty to prohibit the spread of nuclear weapons. France and Communist China, nuclear nations, refused to sign the agreement.

JULY 1968

	1	2	3	4	5	6
7	8	9	10	11	12	13
14	15	16	17	18	19	20
21	22	23	24	25	26	27
28	29	30	31			

2. The Soviet Union released an American airliner forced down on June 30 in the Kurile Islands north of Japan after entering Soviet airspace; the plane was en route to Vietnam with 214 U.S. servicemen.

10. President Charles de Gaulle appointed Couve de Murville to replace Georges Pompidou as premier of France. . . . In Boston, Dr. Benjamin Spock, Rev. William Sloan Coffin, Jr., Michael Ferber and Mitchell Goodman were sentenced to two years in Federal prison for conspiring to counsel evasion of the draft.

15. A Soviet Aeroflot Ilyushin 62 jet landed at Kennedy International Airport, New York, inaugurating direct air service between the United States and the Soviet Union.

17. In Iraq, President Abdul Rahman Arif was ousted by the military; former Brigadier General Ahmed Hassan al-Bakr was named president.

19. After abandoning his fight against extradition from Britain, James Earl Ray, accused assassin of Dr. Martin Luther King, Jr., was flown to the United States and jailed in Memphis, Tennessee.

28. German chemist Otto Hahn, discoverer of nuclear fission, died at 89.

AUGUST

REPUBLICAN NATIONAL CONVENTION. During the week of August 5, Republicans gathered in Miami Beach, Florida, to select a presidential nominee. Despite spirited bids for the nomination by New York Governor Nelson Rockefeller and California Governor Ronald Reagan, former Vice-President Richard Nixon, as predicted, swept to a first-ballot victory. He chose as his running mate Maryland Governor Spiro T. Agnew.

DEMOCRATIC NATIONAL CONVENTION. In sharp contrast to the orderly, businesslike Republican convention, the Democratic national convention, held during the week of August 26, was the scene of turmoil, bloodshed and party disunity caused primarily by differing views on the Vietnam war. While antiwar demonstrators and police and National Guardsmen battled in the streets of Chicago, Democratic delegates fought bitter verbal battles inside Chicago's huge convention hall. Though Vice-President Hubert Humphrey won easily on the first ballot, the bitterness engendered by the Vietnam issue seemed to leave the party in a shambles. Senator Eugene McCarthy, who fought unsuccessfully to deny the nomination to Humphrey and to force the

Citizens of Prague try to ignore the menacing presence of Soviet troops in an armored vehicle.

Democrats to include an antiwar plank in their platform, refused to support Humphrey and his running mate, Maine Senator Edmund S. Muskie.

SOVIETS INVADE CZECHOSLOVAKIA. The month of August began hopefully for the Czechoslovaks, who, under the leadership of Communist Party chief Alexander Dubcek, were groping their way toward a more democratic form of communism. During the first week of the month, Czech leaders met first with Soviet leaders in Cierna and then with the leaders of other Warsaw Pact nations in Bratislava, Czechoslovakia, where a unity document was signed. Soviet troops then pulled out of Czechoslovakia. For a time afterward it seemed that the Soviets had accepted Czechoslovakia's bid for greater internal and external freedom. Then, on August 20, Soviet, East German, Hungarian, Bulgarian and Polish troops raced across Czechoslovakia's borders, seized all major cities, including Prague, the capital, and took into custody several liberal Czech leaders, including Alexander Dubcek.

Ordered by their leaders not to fight the invading forces, the Czechoslovak people bravely resisted by carrying on a war of nerves, by taunting the Russians, demonstrating, marching, destroying road signs to confuse their enemies. A relatively few Czechoslovaks were killed and many Russian tanks were destroyed during several incidents.

On August 23, Czech President Ludvik Svoboda flew to Moscow for talks with the Soviets. He was joined there by Dubcek, who had been taken to Russia as a prisoner, and by Czech Premier Oldrich Cernik. During four days of meetings with Soviet and other Warsaw Pact leaders, the Czechoslovak officials, their country occupied by 600,000 foreign troops, were forced to make many concessions. They returned home at the end of August to tell their people that there would be less freedom and a reimposition of censorship, and that two divisions of Soviet troops would be stationed permanently on Czech soil.

AUGUST 1968

				1	2	3
4	5	6	7	8	9	10
11	12	13	14	15	16	17
18	19	20	21	22	23	24
25	26	27	28	29	30	31

4. In response to Arab terrorist attacks, Israeli jet fighters bombed and strafed a guerrilla training camp near Salt, Jordan, killing 23 civilians and five soldiers. . . . The Congo (Brazzaville) Army recalled President Alphonse Massamba-Debat, asking him to form a new Government; the Army had ousted him the previous day.

14. It was reported that more than 1,000 people had been killed by a week of floods in the Indian state of Gujarat.

22. Fourteen S. Vietnamese were killed when the Vietcong mounted a rocket attack against Saigon; this was the first such attack in two months. . . . Paul VI became the first Roman Catholic pope to visit Latin America when he traveled to Bogota, Colombia, to attend the three-day 39th Eucharistic Congress.

24. France joined the supernuclear-power club (U.S., U.S.S.R., Great Britain, Communist China) when it exploded its first hydrogen bomb.

28. John Gordon Mein, U.S. ambassador to Guatemala, was shot to death in Guatemala City by communist terrorists.

31. More than 15,000 people were killed by earthquakes in Iran.

SEPTEMBER

NEW YORK CITY SCHOOL CRISIS. On September 9, the first day of school in the fall term, members of the United Federation of Teachers went out on strike, closing the city's schools to more than one million pupils. The UFT members were protesting the ouster of ten union teachers from the Ocean Hill-Brownsville school district, being run by a locally elected governing board as part of an experiment in school decentralization. The predominantly Negro governing board and unit

Signs on an Ocean Hill-Brownsville school show support for community control—the main issue in the New York City school crisis.

administrator Rhody McCoy charged that the ten teachers, who were white, were poor teachers or were trying to sabotage the decentralization plan. The UFT, led by Albert Shanker, insisted that the local board did not have the right to oust the teachers. The strike continued for two days, during which time a settlement seemingly was reached. The teachers returned to their classrooms but struck again on September 13. The UFT charged that the governing board had gone back on its agreement to allow the ten teachers to teach in the district. This second strike lasted until September 29, when Mayor John Lindsay, the governing board, the UFT, the Board of Education and the New York State Education Commissioner reached yet another agreement to reopen the schools. This was accomplished on September 30. But the situation remained tense. Residents of the predominantly Negro area still insisted on the right to determine who would teach their children. And the union still insisted that the teachers have job security and that they be protected, by police if necessary, from threats and harassment by residents of Ocean Hill-Brownsville.

VIOLENCE IN MEXICO. On September 18, after several weeks of student disorders, Mexican Army troops seized control of the campus of the National University in Mexico City. The trouble had started in July, when Mexican riot police broke up fights between students. The students charged that the police had used excessive force. They then demonstrated against the police until President Gustavo Diaz Ordaz ordered the Federal troops into action. In the week following the Army take-over of the campus, clashes erupted between students and soldiers. At least 17 persons were killed, a hundred injured and perhaps two thousand arrested. Fearful that the students would disrupt the Olympics in October, the Government met some of the students' demands. Soldiers were withdrawn from the campus on September 30. And students were promised that riot-police squads in Mexico City would be disbanded.

SEPTEMBER 1968

1	2	3	4	5	6	7
8	9	10	11	12	13	14
15	16	17	18	19	20	21
22	23	24	25	26	27	28
29	30					

6. Swaziland, the last British territory in Africa, became an independent nation.

10. Charles E. Goodell was named by N.Y. Governor Nelson Rockefeller to fill the Senate seat vacant since the death of Robert Kennedy.

13. The Czechoslovak National Assembly reimposed censorship on newspapers, radio and television.

18. Actor Franchot Tone died at 63.

19. Country and Western singer Red Foley died at 58.

26. Portugal's critically ill Premier Salazar was succeeded by Marcelo Caetano. . . . Premier Daniel Johnson of Quebec died at 53.

29. A constitution drafted by the military junta ruling Greece since April 21, 1967, was approved by 91.87 per cent of Greek voters; the new charter took away most of the powers of exiled King Constantine.

30. The reactivated battleship USS *New Jersey* went into action for the first time since the Korean war; standing off the coast of North Vietnam, the battleship shelled targets deep in the demilitarized zone.

OCTOBER

VIETNAM BOMBING HALT. On October 31, President Johnson announced that he had "ordered that all air, naval and artillery bombardment of North Vietnam cease." The President went on to state that bombing would resume if North Vietnamese troops attacked South Vietnamese population centers or sent thousands of troops across the demilitarized zone between North and South Vietnam. In exchange for the bombing halt, North Vietnam agreed to expanded peace talks in Paris. This opened the way for participation of the South Vietnamese and the National Liberation Front.

APOLLO 7. On October 11 the Apollo 7 was launched into orbit by the massive Saturn 1B rocket. Aboard the spacecraft were astronauts Walter M. Schirra, Jr., Donn F. Eisele and R. Walter Cunningham—all tak-

The former Jacqueline Kennedy, widow of President John F. Kennedy, and Aristotle Onassis leave chapel on Skorpios after their wedding.

Associate Justice Abe Fortas had his nomination for chief justice of the Supreme Court withdrawn when it was blocked by a Senate filibuster.

ing part in the United States' first manned space mission in almost two years. During the 11-day, 163-orbit flight, the astronauts put Apollo 7 through tests designed to pave the way for a manned landing on the moon. A rendezvous test was made with the second stage of the Saturn 1B rocket. The rocket engine of the Service Module was test-fired eight times, which proved that it could be started in orbit. And various engineer and navigation checks were made. In addition, for the first time live TV transmissions were made from a manned U.S. spacecraft. Millions of viewers around the world saw the three astronauts, all of whom caught cold during the flight, as they orbited the earth at altitudes up to 282 miles. On October 22, after covering a distance of 4,500,000 miles, the Apollo 7 splashed down in the Atlantic.

OCTOBER 1968

		1	2	3	4	5
6	7	8	9	10	11	12
13	14	15	16	17	18	19
20	21	22	23	24	25	26
27	28	29	30	31		

1. Artist Marcel Duchamp (*Nude Descending a Staircase*) died at 81.

2. Associate Justice Abe Fortas withdrew as nominee for chief justice of the Supreme Court after the Senate refused to end a filibuster by those opposing the nomination.

9. French jurist René Cassin won the Nobel Peace Prize.

14. For the third time during the fall term, New York City schoolteachers went out on strike.

16. The Soviet Union and Czechoslovakia signed a treaty providing for the maintenance in Czechoslovakia of thousands of Soviet invasion troops.

17. Japanese writer Yasunari Kawabata won the 1968 Nobel Prize in Literature.

20. Jacqueline Kennedy and Aristotle S. Onassis were married on the Greek island of Skorpios.

31. The U.S. Navy announced that part of the hull of the nuclear submarine *Scorpion* had been found 10,000 feet below the surface of the Atlantic, 400 miles southwest of the Azores; the *Scorpion*, with 99 aboard, was last heard from on May 21.

NOVEMBER

THE ELECTIONS. On November 5, more than 73,000,000 Americans went to the polls and elected former Republican Vice-President Richard Nixon the 37th president of the United States. In one of the closest presidential races in American history, Nixon defeated Democratic Vice-President Hubert Humphrey by 449,704 votes. He received 31,770,237 votes (43.4 per cent of the total) to Humphrey's 31,270,533 (42.72 per cent). Nixon showed greater strength in the electoral-vote tally, winning 301 to Humphrey's 191. Nixon's running mate was Maryland Governor Spiro T. Agnew. Maine Senator Edmund S. Muskie was the Democratic vice-presidential nominee.

Former Alabama Governor George C. Wallace made a strong showing on the American Independent Party ticket. He received 9,906,141 votes, or 13.53 per cent of the total, and 46 electoral votes.

Taken together, the Nixon and Wallace totals indicated that there was a conservative trend in the

Richard Nixon raises his hands in victory after winning the election. With him are his wife, Pat, his daughters, Julie and Tricia, and Julie's fiancé, David Eisenhower, grandson of former President Dwight Eisenhower.

nation. Many observers believed that Nixon's strong stand on the issue of law and order won the election for him.

Although the Republicans won the White House, there was little change in the composition of the United States Congress. The Republicans gained five seats in the Senate and five in the House of Representatives. The Democrats would still control both houses when they convened in January.

In the senatorial elections, however, there were some surprising upsets. Liberal Democrat Joseph Clark of Pennsylvania was defeated by Republican Representative Richard Schweiker. Daniel Brewster of Maryland lost to Republican Representative Charles Mathias, Jr. In Oklahoma, A. S. (Mike) Monroney was defeated in a bid for a fourth term by former Republican Governor Henry Bellmon. And Wayne Morse of Oregon apparently went down to defeat, although he called for a recount of the votes. In other senatorial races, Barry Goldwater won handily in his bid to represent Arizona once again. And in California, Democrat Alan Cranston defeated Max Rafferty, who had jumped to political prominence by espousing an ultraconservative philosophy.

When the House of Representatives met in January, it would have three more Negroes among its membership, including the first Negro Congresswoman in United States history. She is Democrat Shirley Chisholm of Brooklyn, New York.

In the gubernatorial races, the Republicans picked up five statehouses for a total of 31. In 1960 they had controlled only 16 statehouses. Nevertheless, the Republicans lost two important races which can only be considered as major upsets. John Chafee, who had served as governor of Rhode Island for three terms, was defeated by a small margin by a political unknown: former Superior Court Judge Frank Licht. And Montana Governor Tim Babcock, who had served two successful terms, was defeated by Montana's Attorney General, Forrest H. Anderson.

NOVEMBER 1968

					1	2
3	4	5	6	7	8	9
10	11	12	13	14	15	16
17	18	19	20	21	22	23
24	25	26	27	28	29	30

14. Workers and students joined in a 24-hour, nationwide general strike in Italy to demand increased retirement payments and social-security benefits.

15. American bishops meeting at the National Conference of Catholic Bishops, in Washington, D.C., adopted a pastoral letter accepting the papal ban on birth control; but the bishops noted that Catholics who could not follow these teachings should not feel cut off from Holy Communion.

18. The United Federation of Teachers voted to end a five-week strike, the third teachers' strike in New York City in the fall of 1968, when the operation of the decentralized Ocean Hill-Brownsville school district was taken over by a trustee of the state of New York.

20. Explosions in a coal mine near Mannington, West Virginia, killed 78 men.

25. Author Upton Sinclair (*Oil!*, *The Jungle*, *King Coal*) died at 90.

27. President Nguyen Van Thieu appointed Vice-President Nguyen Cao Ky to head the South Vietnamese delegation to the expanded peace talks in Paris.

DECEMBER

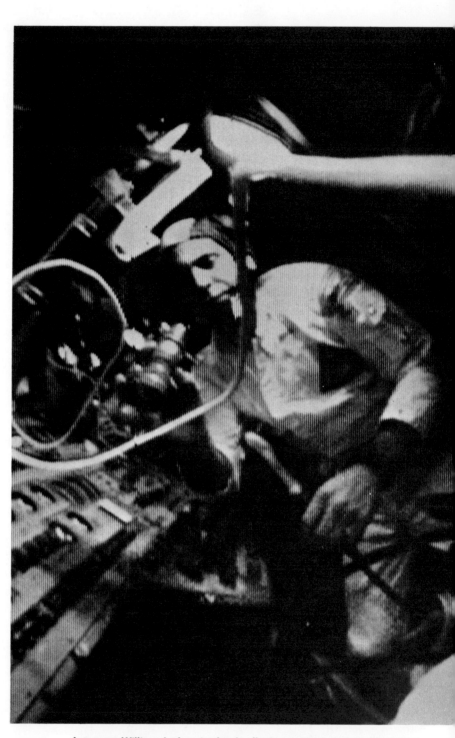

Astronaut William Anders in the Apollo 8 command module. The space-craft was 120,653 nautical miles from earth, traveling at a speed of 3,207 miles per hour when this television picture was transmitted from space.

APOLLO 8 GOES TO THE MOON. For six days, from December 21 to December 27, hundreds of millions of people around the world sat glued to their TV sets, watching a space spectacular that was almost beyond belief. Aboard Apollo 8, Captain Frank Borman, Captain James Lovell, Jr., and Major William Anders were boosted into earth orbit by the giant Saturn 5 rocket. Three hours later, the third stage of the rocket was fired, and Apollo 8 began its long journey to the moon. On the morning of December 24, Apollo 8 went into lunar orbit 69 miles from the moon's surface. After ten orbits, the spacecraft engine was fired, and the astronauts were back on course for a return to earth. At 10:51 A.M., after a perfect flight, Apollo 8 splashed down in the Pacific. The three astronauts had completed a flight of over half a million miles. The men and the spacecraft functioned so well that NASA officials went ahead with plans for a 1969 lunar landing.

RETURN OF THE PUEBLO CREW. On December 23, the 82 crew members of the U.S. Navy ship *Pueblo* walked to freedom across the Bridge of No Return which links North and South Korea. Released too was the body of Duane D. Hodges, the crew member who had been killed when the ship was seized on January 23. The release came after the United States signed a document apologizing to North Korea for the incident; the United States repudiated the document even before it was signed. Ship commander Lloyd M. Bucher and other crew members avowed that the ship had not violated North Korean territorial waters, and that they had been beaten by their captors.

ISRAELI COMMANDOS ATTACK LEBANON. In retaliation for an attack by two Arabs on an Israeli plane at the Athens, Greece, airport, Israeli commandos attacked the Beirut, Lebanon, airport on December 28, destroying planes worth $40,000,000. The UN Security Council unanimously condemned Israel.

DECEMBER 1968

1	2	3	4	5	6	7
8	9	10	11	12	13	14
15	16	17	18	19	20	21
22	23	24	25	26	27	28
29	30	31				

9. Protestant theologian Karl Barth, 82, died in Switzerland.

11. Senator E. L. Bartlett of Alaska died at 64.

12. Actress Tallulah Bankhead died at 65.

19. Cambodia released 11 U.S. soldiers held since July 17, 1968, when their riverboat strayed from South Vietnam across Cambodia's border on the Mekong River. . . . Norman Thomas, six-time Socialist Party candidate for president of the United States, died at 84.

20. Nobel Prizewinning author John Steinbeck (*The Grapes of Wrath, Of Mice and Men, Travels with Charley*) died at 66.

22. Julie Nixon was married to Dwight David Eisenhower 2d by the Rev. Dr. Norman Vincent Peale at Marble Collegiate Church in New York City.

27. Communist China resumed its nuclear-testing program with an explosion in the atmosphere of a three-megaton thermonuclear device in Sinkiang Province in northwestern China.

30. Norwegian diplomat Trygve Lie, the first secretary-general of the United Nations (1946–53), died at 72 in Norway.

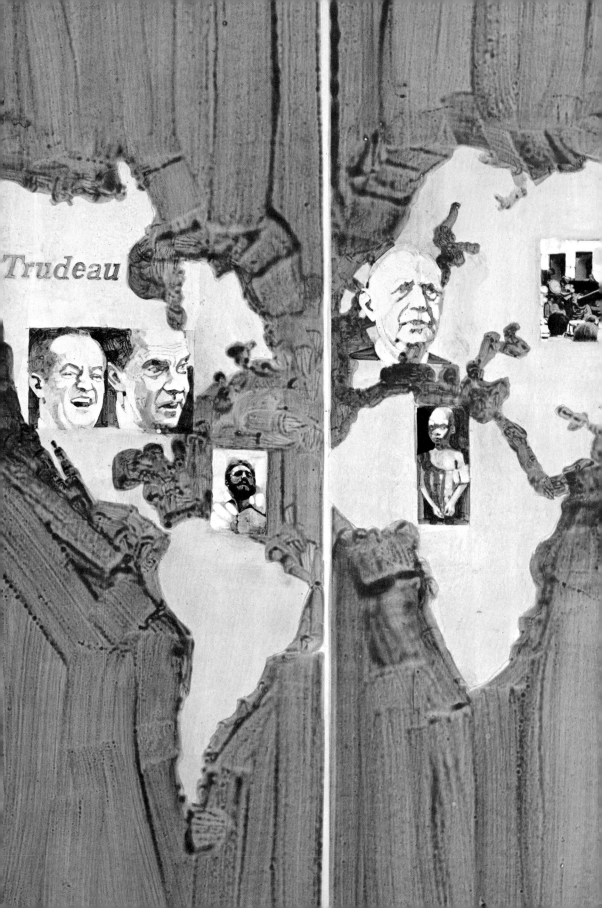

Red Guard

THE

YEAR

IN

REVIEW

1968

AFRICA

THE year 1968 saw the birth of three independent states on and near the continent of Africa. In March the island of Mauritius received independence from Britain in spite of racial rioting which resulted in Britain's sending troops to maintain order. Swaziland, in southern Africa, received independence in September. In October the island of Fernando Po, in the Bight of Biafra, and Rio Muni, on the mainland, merged and became independent. All three nations joined the United Nations.

South-West Africa, which is claimed by both the Republic of South Africa and the United Nations, had a slight political change during the year. The United Nations adopted a resolution changing the name to Namibia. The UN appointed a staff, including a governor, to rule Namibia. The Republic of South Africa, however, still controls the area. And it refused to allow United Nations personnel into the territory. Thus the change in name seems to be more of a diplomatic exercise than the birth of a new nation.

▶ CIVIL WAR IN NIGERIA

The Federation of Nigeria was wracked by a brutal civil war during 1968. Efforts by Britain and the Organization of African Unity and appeals by the UN and others failed to end the fighting.

Biafra, Nigeria's former eastern region, is inhabited mostly by people of the Ibo tribe. It had proclaimed independence on May 30, 1967. Fighting broke out in early July. Biafra was not recognized by any of the world powers. But in 1968 the African nations of Gabon and Tanzania established diplomatic ties with the nation. And France gave it informal backing. Britain continued to sell arms to the Federal Government. Belgium and Czechoslovakia, however, stopped their sales during the year. Biafra, on the other hand, was able to purchase supplies via Portugal. Because Nigerian troops conquered Biafra's coastline, supplies were sent in by air. Gabon and the offshore islands served as nearby air bases to bring arms and relief shipments.

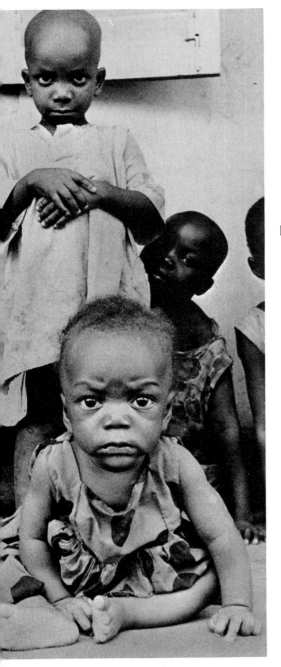

A Nigerian billboard stands in sad contrast to the reality of tens of thousands of Biafran children suffering from malnutrition or dying of starvation because of civil war.

During 1968, Biafra lost most of its 29,000 square miles of territory to the Federal troops, and lost all but one major town. All the Biafrans controlled at the end of the year was 6,000 square miles. This area was completely surrounded by Federal forces. Nevertheless, the Biafrans vowed to fight on. They claimed that all Biafrans would be killed if the Federal troops win the war. Whether this is true or not—and an international team that visited the area said it was not—the Ibos believe it is.

Fighting in 1968 not only deprived the Biafrans of most of their territory, it also disrupted their food supply. Starvation was a very serious problem, and in October large-scale relief shipments began to arrive in the country. If the present situation continues, as it seems likely to do, starvation may claim between 1,000,000 and 2,000,-000 people. This is in addition to the hundreds of thousands killed in the fighting.

▶WARFARE IN SUDAN AND CHAD

The less publicized but still brutal revolt in Sudan entered its seventh year. The Government in Khartoum is controlled mostly by the Arabic northerners. The black Africans in the three southern provinces want independence. In 1968 the Sudanese Government maintained control of the roads and the major cities in the south. But it was not able to maintain control over the countryside. By the end of 1968 the revolt had cost tens of thousands of lives, devastated large areas of the south and strained Sudan's relations with its southern neighbors. Unfortunately the revolt shows no signs of ending soon.

Open warfare also erupted in northern Chad at the end of August. At the urging of the Chad Government, the French sent in a military force to deal successfully with the situation.

▶MERCENARIES

The 123 white mercenaries who fled the Congo (Kinshasa) at the end of 1967 were flown out of Rwanda in April 1968 to various European countries, which promised not to allow their return to Africa. President Joseph Mobutu of the Congo also agreed to drop his demand that the mercenaries be returned to his country to face trial.

Mercenaries were reported to be fighting on both sides in the Nigerian civil war. Egyptian and British pilots flew for the Federal Government. Biafra has no air force, but it received supplies from abroad. These supplies were flown in by pilots of various countries. They were paid $500 per trip. An American who organized an arms airlift reportedly made $5,600,000 before the Government of Biafra dismissed him. In October, Biafra also dismissed some German mercenaries who had built up the best military unit in Biafra.

Nigerian troops won territory despite strong resistance by Biafran soldiers such as these.

POLITICAL INSTABILITY

The young nations of Africa continued their struggle to adapt political desires to economic capabilities.

In 1968, as in the previous year, Africa saw several coups, countercoups and attempted coups. Generally the Army replaced civilian governments or another group of officers. In Mali the Army overthrew the Government of Modibo Keita in November. The Republic of the Congo (Brazzaville) also saw its Government turned out of office by the Army. This coup took place in September, after fighting broke out between the regular Army and a young militant force, with Leftist leanings. The young officers had had the support of ousted President Alphonse Massamba-Debat. In April a coup in Sierra Leone ousted Andrew Juxon-Smith, the chief of state. He was replaced by Siaka Stevens.

AFRICA'S ECONOMIC PROBLEMS

During 1968, Africa was beset by many economic problems. Nevertheless, the year did witness several positive accomplishments. Foreign aid, while nowhere near the continent's needs, still was important. In landlocked Zambia, for example, Yugoslavia agreed to help build a dam on the Kafue River. This will ease Zambia's dependence on Kariba Dam. White-dominated Rhodesia controls the power-generating facilities of this dam, and relations between the two nations are strained. The United States aided in road construction, while the Chinese made plans to construct a railroad across Tanzania to Zambia. Italy finished an oil pipeline from the Indian Ocean to Zambia. Nevertheless, Zambia took control of 25 private companies in April. It did this in order to have greater control over its own economy. Yet this action might scare away some companies that might have invested in the country.

In 1968 the Congo (Kinshasa) settled most of its problems with Union Minière of Katanga over compensation for assets seized in January 1967. This opened the way for private investment in the country.

The most important economic news announced in 1968 was an increase in food supplies by nearly 4 per cent per person. The African coffee crop was up 10 per cent. The 1967 cacao yield was about the same as in 1966 (958,000 tons). But higher prices gave the producing nations a greater income. South Africa and Kenya exported significant amounts of grain.

ORGANIZATION OF AFRICAN UNITY

The tenth ordinary meeting of the OAU was held in Addis Ababa in February. Among the many resolutions adopted were several condemning trade with Rhodesia and South Africa. One of the most controversial resolutions was one demanding the immediate and unconditional withdrawal of Israeli troops from Arab territories they had occupied during the June 1967 war. The vote was by acclamation. But several delegates said they were not allowed to speak on the resolution. The Arab nations of North Africa belong to the OAU. Israel, however, has maintained very warm relations with several black African nations.

The OAU also condemned the International Olympic Committee, and called for a boycott of the games if South Africa was allowed to attend. The OAU prevailed and South Africa was excluded.

The OAU Liberation Committee met in Conakry, Guinea, early in 1968. President Sékou Touré of Guinea called on the committee to make greater efforts to free the rest of the continent from foreign control— including that of Israel. The committee in 1968 coordinated guerrilla fighting in white-controlled areas of Africa where the blacks are not politically free.

In September the fifth heads-of-state meeting of the OAU was held in Algeria. Among the resolutions passed was one condemning the secession of Biafra and asking for them to stop fighting.

INTERSTATE POLITICS AND BORDER WAR

Guinea and Ghana's relationship became friendly in 1968. About 35 of the 100 Ghanaians who were staying with former

Guinea President Sékou Touré, who called for greater efforts to end white control of Rhodesia.

An April military coup d'état made Siaka Stevens prime minister of Sierra Leone.

Ghanaian President Kwame Nkrumah in exile in Guinea returned home. The Ghanaian Government had claimed they were being held against their will.

Ethiopia and Kenya reached agreement with Somalia over their ill-defined borders. Open warfare was stopped and all sides seemed to be trying to reduce tension in the area. In April, Somalia claimed that its Russian-equipped Army was the best in East Africa. But it appeared unwilling to test this Army in the field against the smaller Kenyan or Ethiopian (American and British equipped and trained) Army, and the area remained calm.

▶ RHODESIA

The minority white Government of Ian Smith continued to govern in Rhodesia despite world pressure. In April the Rhodesians considered a new constitution which in reality showed that the whites planned to continue in power over the African majority. To vote, a person would have to have an income of £900 or more. (The African average was £138. The white, colored and Asian average was £1,361.) This in itself would effectively ban most Africans from voting.

Britain held several informal and two formal meetings with Rhodesia to try to get the rebellious Government to return to its control. The meetings produced no results. While drought and economic sanctions held economic growth down to 3 per cent, the Government felt politically strong enough to end press censorship. On May 9 the UN Security Council had adopted a resolution calling on UN members not to import goods from Rhodesia.

African nations and world opinion were aroused in March when five Africans were hanged despite pleas for clemency from Queen Elizabeth II and others.

African governments continued to demand that Britain use force to end the Unilateral Declaration of Independence (UDI) of Rhodesia. But it is very unlikely that the British Government will act. The British Army would be so split by such

HEADS OF GOVERNMENT

Botswana	SIR SERETSE KHAMA, president	Malawi	H. KAMUZU BANDA, president
Burundi	MICHEL MICOMBERO, president	Mali	YORO DIAKITE, chief of state
Cameroun	AHMADOU AHIDJO, president	Mauritania	MOKTAR OULD DADDAH, president
Central African Rep.	JEAN BEDEL BOKASSA, president	Mauritius	SIR SEEWOOSAGUR RAMGOOLAM, prime minister
Chad	FRANCOIS TOMBALBAYE, president	Niger	HAMANI DIORI, president
Congo (Brazzaville)	MARIEN NGOUABI, chief of state	Nigeria	YAKUBU GOWON, chief of state
Congo (Kinshasa)	JOSEPH D. MOBUTU, president	Rhodesia	IAN SMITH, prime minister
		Rwanda	GREGOIRE KAYIBANDA, president
Dahomey	EMILE D. ZINSOU, president	Senegal	LEOPOLD SENGHOR, president
Equatorial Guinea	FRANCISCO MACIAS NGUEMA, president	Sierra Leone	SIAKA STEVENS, premier
Ethiopia	HAILE SELASSIE I, emperor	Somali Republic	ABDIRASHID ALI SHERMARKE, president
Gabon	ALBERT B. BONGO, president		IBRAHIM EGAL, prime minister
Gambia	D. K. JAWARA, prime minister	South Africa	J. J. FOUCHE, president
Ghana	JOSEPH A. ANKRAH, chairman		B. J. VORSTER, prime minister
Guinea	SEKOU TOURE, president	Sudan	AHMED MAHGOUB, prime minister
Ivory Coast	FELIX HOUPHOUET-BOIGNY, president	Swaziland	SOBHUZA II, king
			MAKHOSINI DLAMINI, prime minister
Kenya	JOMO KENYATTA, president	Tanzania	JULIUS K. NYERERE, president
Lesotho	MOSHOESHOE II, king	Togo	ETIENNE EYADEMA, president
Liberia	WILLIAM V. S. TUBMAN, president	Uganda	MILTON OBOTE, president
Malagasy Rep.	PHILIBERT TSIRANANA, president	Upper Volta	SANGOULE LAMIZANA, chief of state
		Zambia	KENNETH K. KAUNDA, president

	POPULATION	CURRENCY*	OAU	EAEC
Botswana	610,000	1 rand = $1.40	X	
Burundi	3,400,000	87.5 francs = $1.00	X	
Cameroun	5,590,000	246.8 francs = $1.00	X	
Central African Rep.	1,480,000	246.8 francs = $1.00	X	
Chad	3,460,000	246.8 francs = $1.00	X	
Congo (Brazzaville)	880,000	246.8 francs = $1.00	X	
Congo (Kinshasa)	16,700,000	1 zaire = $2.00	X	
Dahomey	2,600,000	246.8 francs = $1.00	X	
Equatorial Guinea	200,000	70 pesetas = $1.00		
Ethiopia	23,800,000	2.5 Ethiopian dollars = $1.00	X	X
Gabon	478,000	246.8 francs = $1.00	X	
Gambia	350,000	1 pound = $2.40	X	
Ghana	8,340,000	1 new cedi = $1.00	X	
Guinea	3,800,000	246.8 francs = $1.00	X	
Ivory Coast	4,150,000	246.8 francs = $1.00	X	
Kenya	10,250,000	7.1 shillings = $1.00	X	X
Lesotho	910,000	1 rand = $1.40	X	
Liberia	1,125,000	1 Liberian dollar = $1.00	X	
Malagasy Rep.	6,500,000	246.8 francs = $1.00	X	
Malawi	4,200,000	1 pound = $2.40	X	
Mali	4,830,000	246.8 francs = $1.00	X	
Mauritania	1,130,000	246.8 francs = $1.00	X	
Mauritius	795,000	5.6 rupees = $1.00		
Niger	3,700,000	246.8 francs = $1.00	X	
Nigeria	61,500,000	1 pound = $2.80	X	
Rhodesia	4,660,000	1 pound = $2.80		
Rwanda	3,400,000	100 francs = $1.00	X	
Senegal	3,750,000	246.8 francs = $1.00	X	
Sierra Leone	2,475,000	1 leone = $1.20	X	
Somali Republic	2,740,000	7.1 shillings = $1.00	X	X
South Africa	19,000,000	1 rand = $1.40		
Sudan	14,770,000	1 pound = $2.85	X	
Swaziland	400,000	1 rand = $1.40		
Tanzania	12,400,000	7.1 shillings = $1.00	X	X
Togo	1,765,000	246.8 francs = $1.00	X	
Uganda	8,120,000	7.1 shillings = $1.00	X	X
Upper Volta	5,150,000	246.8 francs = $1.00	X	
Zambia	4,065,000	1 kwacha = $1.40	X	X

* US $; 1968 exchange rates

OAU—Organization of African Unity
EAEC—East African Economic Community

an action that its loyalty to the British Government would be open to question.

Zambia continued to send guerrillas across the Zambezi River into Rhodesia. The armed forces of Rhodesia seemed able to contain them. And South Africa promised military help if needed. During the year it developed that the South African Government already had paramilitary men fighting with the Rhodesian armed forces.

▶ SOUTH AFRICA

Throughout 1968, South Africa drew the hostility of other African states. The OAU was instrumental in having the nation barred from the 1968 Olympics in spite of its agreeing to field an integrated team.

In December 1967 the UN General Assembly voted 89 to 2 against the South African Government's policy of apartheid. It asked other nations not to encourage "that government" to persist in its racial policies.

In March the United Nations voted censure of the country for its defiance of the Council's January resolution demanding an end to the trial of 35 South-West Africans accused of treason.

South Africa still controls the economy, and to some extent the politics, of its neighbors. Swaziland's Prime Minister stated that South Africa would come to his aid if terrorists entered his country. Lesotho also announced that it would not allow its country to be used as a terrorist base. Later the South African Government stated that it was joining with Lesotho to develop the Oxbow Hydroelectric scheme.

Britain again decided not to sell arms to South Africa in spite of a potential market of $1,000,000,000. In return the South Africans threatened to close the Simonstown Naval Base, near Cape Town, to the British Navy.

▶ THE UNITED STATES AND AFRICA

In late 1967 and early 1968, Vice-President Humphrey and Associate Justice Thurgood Marshall visited nine African countries. The Vice-President reported to President Johnson that the United States had a great deal of goodwill in Africa. He felt that the United States should play a larger role in the continent, and that if it did not help African nations, then the communist world would.

The United States continued its aid of about $200,000,000 to ten African nations. Due to budget cuts in foreign aid these figures will probably be greatly reduced in 1969. The Peace Corps is still a major asset of the United States in Africa. Lesotho received its first group at the beginning of 1968.

▶ REGIONAL COOPERATION

The nations of the East African Economic Community, which was reborn in 1967, attended a 1968 meeting of the World Bank to discuss aid for their development on a regional basis. These nations —Uganda, Kenya and Tanzania—share many services, such as rail and ports, and plan to build on these for a common market. Zambia, Ethiopia and Somalia applied for membership in the EAEC. Burundi and the Congo (Kinshasa) expressed interest in joining.

A group called the East and Central African States met in Dar es Salaam, Tanzania, in May 1968. Here 14 heads of state met for the fourth time to discuss African problems and to create better neighborly relations.

A three-state grouping of Congo (Kinshasa), Chad and the Central African Republic was formed in April. Its aim was to establish a common-market type of organization open to all independent African states. In December, however, the Central African Republic withdrew, ending the union.

The formation of an Association of African Airlines and a Union of African News Agencies was among the intra-African attempts at regional unity. All these groups were attempting close cooperation to solve common problems in various fields.

HUGH C. BROOKS
Director, African Center
St. Johns University

EQUATORIAL GUINEA

ON October 12, 1968, after nearly two centuries of Spanish rule, Equatorial Guinea became an independent nation. This new African state comprises Rio Muni on the African mainland; Fernando Po, an island in the Bight of Biafra; and four small dependent islands.

▶ THE LAND

Rio Muni, a rectangular-shaped piece of land about the size of Vermont, is situated on the west-central coast of Africa. It is bounded on the north by Cameroun, on the east and south by Gabon and on the west by the Gulf of Guinea. With its dependent islands of Corisco, Elobey Grande and Elobey Chico, it has an area of 10,100 square miles.

Rio Muni has three ports, Benito, Kogo, and Bata, its capital. The area is quite poor, and timber, coffee and cacao are its only important exports.

Fernando Po has an area of 780 square miles. It is situated 130 miles away from Rio Muni. Fernando Po's dependent island of Annobon, which has an area of 6.5 square miles, lies 400 miles to the southwest in the South Atlantic Ocean. The capital of Fernando Po is the port town of Santa Isabel. With independence, Santa Isabel became the capital of Equatorial Guinea.

Fernando Po is much richer than Rio Muni. The people who live there have a per-capita income of $250, one of the highest in Africa. The land is very fertile, and large quantities of cacao, coffee, bananas and palm oil are exported.

▶ THE PEOPLE

About 267,000 people live in Equatorial Guinea. In Rio Muni there are 200,000 Fangs. Some 15,000 Bubis live on Fernando Po, but in their own land they are outnumbered by 45,000 Nigerians, most of whom are Ibos from Biafra. The Bubis are 90 per cent literate. This is the highest literacy rate in Africa. More than 7,000 Europeans also live in Equatorial Guinea.

▶ HISTORY AND GOVERNMENT

Fernando Po was discovered by the Portuguese in 1471. In 1778 it was ceded to Spain, which, in 1829, allowed the British Slave Trade Commission to take over administration of the island. It was occupied by the British until 1843, when the Spanish again took control. In the same year, the Spanish also occupied Rio Muni. They ruled these two territories until October 12, 1968, when independence was granted.

The President of Equatorial Guinea, Francisco Macias Nguema, is a Fang. His Vice-President, Edmundo Bosio, is from Fernando Po. Equatorial Guinea has a National Assembly with 35 deputies. Nineteen are from Rio Muni, 11 from Fernando Po and 5 from the island dependencies.

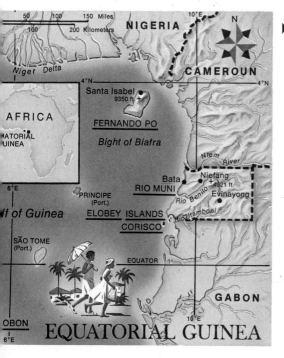

EQUATORIAL GUINEA

MAURITIUS

ON March 12, 1968, after more than a century and a half of British colonial rule, the Indian Ocean island of Mauritius became an independent nation.

▶ THE LAND

Mauritius lies in the Indian Ocean about 500 miles east of Madagascar and 20° south of the equator. With an area of only 720 square miles, Mauritius is less than two thirds the size of Rhode Island.

The island is volcanic with bare, black peaks rising from the green fields of sugarcane. There are three main groups of mountains. The highest peak, Piton de la Rivière Noire, rises to 2,711 feet.

There are a number of short, fast-flowing rivers, some of which have been harnessed for hydroelectric power.

Mauritius is roughly oval with a central plateau rising to 2,200 feet. This descends gently to the north but drops sharply to the southern and western coasts. A coral reef encloses lagoons on all sides of the island except the south.

Mauritius has three island dependencies. Rodrigues, with an area of 40 square miles, is some 350 miles east of Mauritius. Agalega, which consists of two small islets planted with coconut palms, is 580 miles north of Mauritius. The Cargados Carajos archipelago, whose chief islet, St. Brandon, is a fishing station, is about 250 miles northeast of Mauritius.

▶ CLIMATE

The climate of Mauritius is subtropical. Average temperatures range between 70° and 80°. The southeast trade winds blow from November to April. These bring heavy rains to the central plateau but leave the coasts warm and dry. Sometimes these winds bring devastating cyclones.

May to October is a period of calm or gentle southeast winds which build up rain clouds on the central plateau, producing showers nearly every afternoon. Rainfall varies from an annual 25 inches on the coasts to 175 inches in the center of the island.

▶ THE PEOPLE

At the end of 1967 the population of Mauritius was estimated at 773,573, a density of more than 1,000 persons per square mile. With a growth rate of nearly 3 per cent each year, overpopulation is the country's most serious problem. In 1966 a government family-planning program was introduced.

There were no indigenous inhabitants of Mauritius. The people who live there now are all descendants of immigrants. About two thirds of the population are of Indian origin comprising both Hindus

March 12, 1968: The British flag is lowered as Mauritius becomes an independent nation.

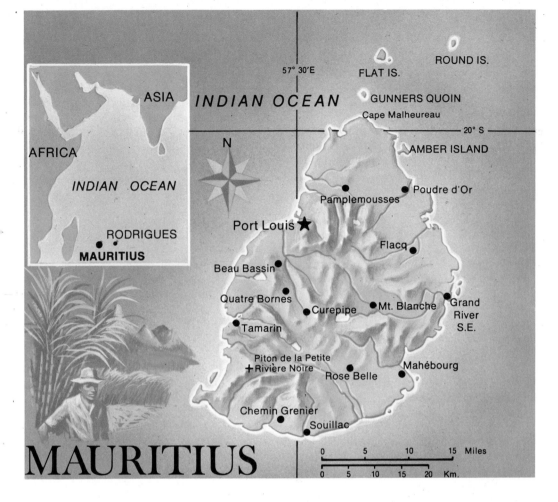

MAURITIUS

(51.3 per cent) and Muslims (16.4 per cent). About 29 per cent are classified as general population and are mostly Roman Catholics. The vast majority of these are known as Creoles and are of mixed African or Indian and European ancestry. There is considerable animosity between the Muslims and Creoles. There are also Europeans of French descent and a few Anglo-Mauritians. The remaining 3.2 per cent of the population are Chinese.

About two thirds of the population live in villages scattered throughout the island. Villages contain members of all ethnic groups except Europeans who live on their estates or in towns.

The chief town, capital and seaport is Port Louis (population 134,900) on the northwest coast. Other towns stretching up the hill toward the center of the island are Beau Bassin-Rose Hill, Quatre Bornes, Vacoas-Phoenix and Curepipe.

Mauritius has a good road system of 824 miles, four fifths of which are paved. Buses travel to all parts of the island. There are an international airport and telephone, telegraph and radio services. In 1965 a television service was introduced. By June 1966 there were 6,178 licensed sets on the island.

▶ LANGUAGE

English is the official language of Mauritius. French is widely used among the educated. The most commonly used language is Creole, a French dialect which is the lingua franca of the island. Hindi, Urdu, Tamil, Telegu, Marathi and Gujarati are among the Indian languages in use. Two Chinese dialects—Cantonese and Hakka—are also spoken.

▶ EDUCATION

Primary education in Mauritius is free but not compulsory. About 88 per cent of the children of primary-school age attend school. But because there are so many languages spoken on the island, instruction is difficult.

There are only 17 government or government-aided secondary schools, for which government scholarships are available. Students who fail to get into these schools often attend one of the 126 private secondary schools.

Mauritius also has a teachers'-training college, a technical school and a university college with faculties of agriculture, education and developmental sciences.

▶ HISTORY AND GOVERNMENT

The first Europeans to reach Mauritius were the Portuguese in the early sixteenth century. They made no attempt to settle the island, merely using it to provision their ships. However, the Portuguese greatly altered the ecology of the island by releasing pigs, goats, monkeys and, inadvertently, rats.

In 1598 the Dutch took possession of the island, naming it after Prince Maurice of Nassau. They made two attempts to settle it and to exploit the ebony forests. However, they never imported a labor force big enough to cope with the environment. It was during the Dutch occupation that the dodo, the famous flightless bird of Mauritius, was exterminated.

In 1710 the Dutch abandoned Mauritius. In 1715 the French took possession of the island, renaming it Ile de France. They imported large numbers of slaves, built a port and planted sugar, coffee and spices. During the Anglo-French wars of the eighteenth century, Ile de France became an important center for attacking British shipping in the Indian Ocean. Finally, in 1810 the British captured the island. It was formally ceded to Britain by the Treaty of Paris in 1814. The British restored its original name.

Slavery was abolished throughout the British Empire in 1833–34. In Mauritius the former slaves refused to work for their former masters. As a result, the planters turned to India for labor. Between 1835 and 1907, nearly 450,000 Indians were brought to Mauritius as indentured laborers.

During the nineteenth century and the first half of the twentieth, Mauritius was ruled by the British Colonial Service and the Franco-Mauritian planters. An elective element was introduced into the legislature in 1886, but only landowners could vote. They constituted only about 1.5 per cent of the population.

In 1947 a new constitution was introduced with a greatly extended franchise. For the first time, Indians secured a majority in the legislature. Constitutional advances throughout the 1950's and early 1960's brought Mauritians more and more self-government. In 1965 it was agreed that Mauritius should become an independent nation. A new constitution was promulgated in 1966. It provides for a legislature of 70 members with safeguards for the representation of minority communities.

Island-wide elections were held in August 1967. The Hindu-dominated Independence Party, made up of a coalition of the Labor Party, the Independent Forward Bloc and the Muslim Committee of Action, won 43 seats, mainly from the rural areas. The Opposition, Parti Mauricien Social Democrate, which did not favor independence, won 27 seats. This party is supported by most Creoles and some Chinese.

On March 12, 1968, as clashes took place between Creoles and Muslims, Mauritius became independent within the British Commonwealth. The Prime Minister is the head of the Labor Party, Sir Seewoosagur Ramgoolam.

BURTON BENEDICT
University of California, Berkeley

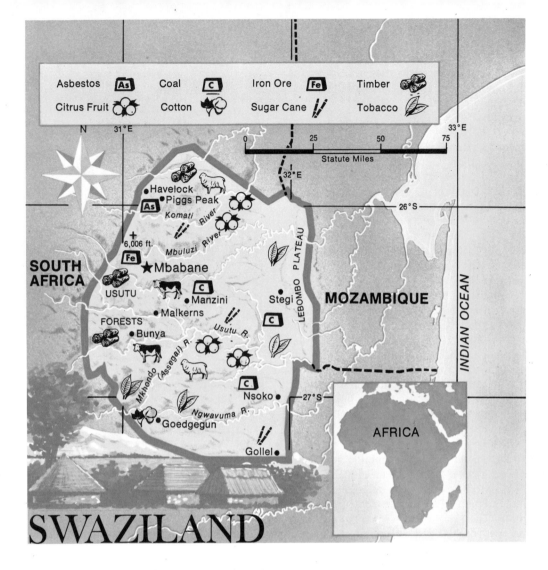

Asbestos **As**   Coal **C**   Iron Ore **Fe**   Timber

Citrus Fruit   Cotton   Sugar Cane   Tobacco

N   31°E   0   25   50   75   33°E

Statute Miles

32°E   26°S

Havelock

Piggs Peak

As

Komati River

6,006 ft.

Mbuluzi River

SOUTH AFRICA

Fe ★Mbabane

USUTU

Manzini

C

Malkerns

FORESTS

Bunya

Usutu R.

Mkhondo (Assegai) R.

C

Stegi

C

LEBOMBO PLATEAU

MOZAMBIQUE

INDIAN OCEAN

Nsoko

27°S

Ngwavuma R.

Goedgegun

Gollel

AFRICA

SWAZILAND

SWAZILAND became an independent kingdom on September 6, 1968, under the rule of King Sobhuza II. Though Swaziland remained within the British Commonwealth, its independence ended British colonial rule in Africa.

▶ THE LAND

Swaziland is an inland country about the size of New Jersey. It has an area of 6,705 square miles. It is completely surrounded by the Republic of South Africa and Portuguese Mozambique. The maximum distance from north to south is less than 120 miles, and from east to west it is less than 90 miles.

Despite its small area, Swaziland is divided into four distinct geographical regions. In the west a mountainous high veld, or grassland, consists of broken and rugged country rising to an altitude of 6,000 feet above sea level at its highest point. Although the slopes are often too steep for cultivation, and grazing is poor, the land is ideally suited for afforestation. The middle veld, with an average elevation of 2,000 to 2,500 feet, has good soil and plentiful rainfall. The low veld is characterized by gently undulating lowland, mainly between 500 and 1,000 feet in elevation. Bush vegetation is common, and cattle ranching is practiced. A fourth region, the Lubombo Plateau, overlooks the whole length of the eastern low veld. The Lubombo Plateau is mainly cattle country, but it also contains some good mixed farming.

Swaziland is one of the best-watered areas in southern Africa. Four major rivers, the Komati, Usutu, Mbuluzi and Ngwavuma, flow from west to east, cutting through the Lubombo Plateau to the Indian Ocean. The harnessing of these rivers for irrigation is of vital importance to the agricultural development of the middle veld and the low veld.

A Swazi tribesman in native dress takes part in Swaziland's independence-day ceremonies.

▶ CLIMATE

The high veld has a humid, near-temperate climate with a mean annual rainfall of 40 to 90 inches. The middle veld and the Lubombo Plateau are subtropical and drier. The low veld is almost tropical and has between 20 and 30 inches of rain annually. Most of the rain falls between October and March, but total rainfall varies widely from year to year. The mean average temperature on the high veld is just over 60° F.; that in the low veld is about 72° F.

▶ THE PEOPLE

According to the latest census (1966), the population of Swaziland was 389,492. Of this number, Europeans total about 10,000 and others (mostly Eurafricans) about 4,200. The African population is almost entirely Swazi except for about 20,000 Zulus, Tonga and Shangaans. The highest rural concentrations are in the agricultural areas of the middle veld, where 39 per cent of the population lives. About

8,000 men work outside Swaziland, mainly in South African gold or coal mines. However, this figure shows a decrease over previous years and indicates an increase of employment in Swaziland.

The two main towns of Swaziland are Mbabane, the capital, with 14,000 people, and Manzini, with 7,000.

▶ LANGUAGE

The Swazi language, Siswati, is spoken by most Africans and many Europeans and Eurafricans in Swaziland. English, however, is the official language. It is estimated that about 40 per cent of the population over nine years old is literate. But this percentage is much lower in rural areas.

▶ RELIGION

About 43 per cent of all adult Africans hold traditional animist beliefs. Almost all of the remainder of the adult population is Christian with the exception of several hundred Muslims and Hindus.

▶ HISTORY

The Swazis appear to have broken away from the main body of the southward-advancing Bantus about 1750. From this time on they were in constant conflict with the Zulus, another Bantu subgroup. Unable to match the strength of the Zulus in South Africa, the Swazis were forced to move northward in the early 1800's to the area now known as Swaziland.

The first contact with the British was in the 1840's. The tribal ruler, Mswati, from whom the Swazis are thought to have derived their name, appealed to Sir Theophilus Shepstone, the British agent-general in Natal, for assistance against the Zulus. Shepstone brought about peaceful relations between the two tribes. It was also during this period that the first Europeans settled in Swaziland.

The independence of Swaziland was guaranteed by the British and South African (Transvaal) governments in 1881 and 1884. However, because of the chaotic situation arising from the many concessions granted to Europeans by the Swazi ruler Mbandzeni, a provisional government was established in 1890. It represented the Swazis, the British and the South African Republic. In 1894, under a convention between the British and South African governments, the South African Republic was given power of protection and administration.

Swaziland continued under this form of government until the British defeated South Africa in the Boer War (1899–1902). After the war, Swaziland became a British protectorate and High Commission Territory.

The next major change came in 1963. During that year, discussions were held in London for the establishment of a Swazi constitution. In 1964, general elections were held in Swaziland for 24 members of a Legislative Council. A final constitutional review in 1967 confirmed arrangements for independence in 1968.

▶ GOVERNMENT

The Swazi constitution recognized the King as sovereign. The King, Sobhuza II, was born in 1899 and installed as Paramount (Ngwenyama) in 1921. Executive authority is vested in the king, who appoints as prime minister the elected member who commands majority support in the House of Assembly. Prince Makhosini Dlamini became Swaziland's first prime minister in 1967.

The Swaziland Parliament has two houses: a House of Assembly and a Senate. The maximum life of each Parliament is five years. The power to dissolve Parliament is vested in the king. The House of Assembly has 24 elected members and six members nominated by the king.

The franchise is universal adult suffrage with appropriate citizenship and residence qualifications.

The Senate consists of 12 members. Six are elected by the members of the Assembly, and six are appointed by the king. The king is advised on all matters regulated by Swazi law and custom by the Swazi National Council.

▶ EDUCATION

A policy of racial integration in schools was put into practice in 1963. Most schools are operated by missions with Government subsidies. The University of Botswana, Lesotho and Swaziland is located at Roma, Lesotho.

▶ ECONOMY

Swaziland is rich in minerals, especially iron ore and asbestos. With the completion of the Swaziland Railway in 1964, the export of iron ore developed rapidly and replaced asbestos as the principal mineral export. Hydroelectric-power supplies have been created, and irrigation schemes have made possible rapid expansion in the production of rice, citrus fruits and sugar. Since 1962, sugar has been Swaziland's most valuable single export. Although most Swazis are engaged in animal husbandry and subsistence agriculture, the cultivation of cash crops, such as cotton, tobacco, rice and vegetables, has also increased.

RICHARD P. STEVENS
Lincoln University

AGRICULTURE
AND FOOD

FOR the average American family around the dinner table, 1968 was another year of abundant, wholesome food. For farmers and ranchers, it was a year to swallow something harder: the realization that there is little improvement in sight for prices of the food and fiber they sell. Their political clout weakened even faster as farm families dwindled to less than 5 per cent of the United States population, and attention shifted to the problems of the cities. Sifting through the statistics, you could see farmers sorting into three groups. First, a rapidly growing number of farm families producing $20,000 or more worth of farm products a year. Second, a tenacious group of families moonlighting on the land for a little extra income, living out in the country "because it's a great place for kids to grow up" but really earning their living from a town job within a forty-mile commute. Third is the group with small, unproductive farms and little chance for outside employment: the rural poor.

▶ CROPS SET NEW RECORDS

Crop output broke records again in 1968. Production of wheat, rice and feed grains totaled about 230,000,000 tons. This was almost 2,000 pounds of grain for every person in the United States.

Corn output was 4,600,000,000 bushels, 20 per cent more than the 1962–66 average. Soybeans, which almost reached the billion-bushel total in 1967, did it with 1,100,000,000 bushels in 1968. All wheat came to a record 1,600,000,000 bushels, which sent wheat prices to rock bottom. Wheat that customarily goes for bread was being fed to livestock. Sorghum grain hit 791,000,000 bushels, spurring beef production in the High Plains.

Among the top yields announced in 1968 was a 231-bushels-per-acre corn harvest by Donald J. Storeholder, Delta, Ohio. This yield is more than twice the Illinois average, for instance.

These bumper crops brought the threat of low livestock prices as farmers converted more of the grain to meat. However, stockmen avoided a serious bust by keeping their production within bounds.

FERTILIZER OUTPUT GROWS

A surplus of something besides food piled up during the year: fertilizer. Manufacturers, eager to cash in on the growing demand, rushed into the business. Their combined efforts overstuffed the market. It will take until about 1970 for the demand to catch up. But worldwide fertilizer use will likely double by 1975, triple by 1980.

Farmers use such massive amounts of fertilizer that two firms began building pipelines from Gulf Coast areas to the Midwest. They will pump anhydrous ammonia all the way up to the Corn Belt. Ammonia is a major source of nitrogen, a key plant food.

MACHINES GET BIGGER

In response to farmers' demands, tractor makers announced several over-100-horsepower models. Oliver brought out its Model 2150, developing 131 horsepower. Ford, long a maker of small, "handy" tractors, began selling a 105-horsepower giant. Reason for it all: farm labor is expensive, power cheap. One man on a 100-horsepower tractor can do more tillage work in a day than 200 men with hand tools.

Everywhere the race was on to get rid of labor—before the high cost of labor, and losses from possible strikes, wiped out the grower himself. "Machines are expensive, but they show up in the morning," reasoned one New Jersey snap-bean grower.

In California, growers added to their fleet of mechanical tomato pickers, which have replaced thousands of Mexican bracero laborers. Other "gee-whiz" machines rolled out of the shop into production or field trials:

A cantaloupe harvester which pulls only the ripe melons off the vines.

A lettuce picker which first feels the head to see if it's fully developed.

An asparagus cutter which sizes up the edible stalk with an electric-eye beam, then cuts it off.

Most of the cherries in Michigan were "shaken down" by mechanical vibrators instead of hand pickers on ladders.

Applegrowers tried prototype catching frames, vibrators and auger-type pickers to reduce harvest labor. They also planted new orchards in narrower rows so trees would grow in thin "walls" for ease of picking.

One new crop thinner uses a simple computer you can preset to select plant size and spacing. An electronic "eye" picks out plants to be saved, and triggers a spray to kill unwanted ones.

MORE CHEMICALS ADDED

The search continued for some way to replace insecticides. Among the possibilities explored during 1968 was the release of large numbers of sterilized males of certain species, so the female's eggs will be infertile. Other possibilities were to breed good insects that prey on bad ones, and to use sound waves that destroy specific bugs at specific frequencies. Some scientists worked on chemicals that would be absorbed in plant tissue and kill or repel undesirable bugs.

Scientists probed into exotic chemicals that signal plants to grow shorter stems, drop their fruit at a preset time, accumulate more protein or oil or change shape for easier harvest. About 40 growth regulators are approved for some 100 uses. Newest is a spray that hurries apple trees to bearing maturity in 4 years instead of 8. And a new soybean chemical reduces plant size but increases the yield of beans.

BEEF FEEDERS MODERNIZE

A new term caught on big among beef feeders during 1968: *Cutability*. It measures the amount of retail meat in an animal and gives a low score to animals with excess fat. Beef men continued to work toward animals that give more lean, tender meat and less waste fat. Beef consumption per person in the United States has soared 25 per cent during the past decade.

Cattle feeding shifted more toward the Great Plains. The area's huge grain-sorghum crop and favorable weather make the region a natural for huge feedlots. On

A big cost of producing beef is the $100 or so per year to keep the cow, which produces only one calf per year. Thus scientists injected cows with hormones that produced multiple births, as shown above. Fifty-two cows had 92 calves.

February 1, Texas passed California as the No. 3 beef-feeding state, behind Nebraska (No. 2) and Iowa (No. 1).

More than 80 feedlot operators, supplying 15 per cent of the nation's fed beef cattle, opened their own market news network in September, the first of its kind.

They teletype their own selling intentions and cattle inventories to a central computer, which summarizes the market scene and relays this information back to members of the exchange. This helps pro-

ducers avoid market gluts and thus get higher average prices. The sponsoring American National Cattlemen's Association expects the network to cover half the nation's fed-beef supply eventually.

▶ DAIRYMEN EYE MARKETS

Dairymen amazed the rest of agriculture by merging several already-big marketing cooperatives into stronger units more capable of bargaining with big processors. One merger produced Milk Producers Inc., a marketing federation covering most of the Southwest. MPI began administering its own supply controls—a job that only the Federal Government has been able to handle until now.

▶ NEW IMAGE FOR HOGS

Hogs are headed into factory-type buildings that are heated in winter, cooled in summer. They're following the same trend as laying hens. Before long, hogs rooting in a pasture will be as obsolete as chickens scratching in the barnyard are today.

More pork producers turned to artificial insemination as a fast way to speed hog improvement. Semen from a few top-quality male hogs can be used on hundreds of sows.

Pork producers set out to sell more ham, pork chops and bacon. In 10 years, Americans have stepped up use of pork only 3 per cent per person. On January 1, 1968, pork producers launched a big research and promotion drive, financed by a voluntary checkoff of 5 cents per hog marketed.

Shearing sheep takes time and skill, and adds cost to your rug or sweater. In 1968 scientists announced a way to shear by feeding sheep a chemical that weakens the wool at its base for a short time. The fleece can then be rubbed off.

▶ ANIMAL HEALTH PROTECTED

American livestock remained untouched by England's tragic outbreak of foot-and-mouth disease, which claimed more than 22,000 cattle, hogs and sheep in a four-month rampage officially ending in March. A dozen American veterinarians studied the British break firsthand and returned to strengthen United States defenses against the highly infectious virus.

Drugs used to keep animals and poultry healthy are carefully tested to keep drug residues from showing up in your meat, milk and eggs. Just the same, the watchdog Food and Drug Administration tightened rules on animal antibiotics even further during 1968. Although costs of animal health protection could go up because of new restrictions, it is clear that animal products will be kept safe and wholesome.

▶ FARM EXPORTS SHRINK

Farm exports, a major winner of foreign exchange which helps the United States balance of payments, dropped 7 per cent. Farm sales abroad totaled $6,300,000,000 during the fiscal year July 1967 through June 1968. What caused the decline? Higher farm output in other countries, the unsettled international scene, and a slow-up of economic activity among several of the United States' customer nations. Also, the United States imported 5 per cent more agricultural products—$4,600,000,000 worth. Inflation and general economic expansion here caused the increase.

A large world crop of wheat drove down prices, leading to a minor trade war. The United States, under terms of an International Grains Arrangement, had agreed to sell within certain prices. But France undercut traditional United States markets by 15 to 18 cents per bushel.

▶ FARM PROGRAM EXTENDED

Preelection skirmishes between Democrats and Republicans centered on the 1965 Farm Act, the basic supply-management program. Both sides tried to trap the other into opposing a farm bill. The result:

Late in September, the House and Senate agreed on a compromise which extended the law another year, through 1970. A companion law enlarged the Food Stamp Program, which helps low-income people improve their diets through added purchases of food at ordinary retail stores.

▶ **BARGAINING STEPPED UP**

Labor can bargain for a price—why can't we? This summed up farmers' attitudes toward bargaining for a better deal in the marketplace. The American Farm Bureau Federation strengthened its 31 commodity marketing projects. The 100-year-old National Grange studied ways for farmers to take over some of the Government's role of production control and price assurance. And the militant National Farmers Organization threatened to hold products off the market until "grocery shelves are emptied." NFO did succeed in signing a 6-months contract with an Iowa packing firm to take 1,200 hogs a day at prevailing market prices.

Farmers showed positive signs that they are ready to do the specific thing needed to acquire bargaining power with big processors: Produce a standard, high-quality product in reliable supplies—but not an oversupply. And they indicated that they would rather not have the government as their spokesman along the way.

For instance, more than 100 major egg producers mapped out a national federation of regional marketing associations. Such a group could stabilize prices and sales in the egg business, which has been troubled with chronically low and unpredictable prices.

What should the United States do when foreign governments subsidize exports to us? United States policy makers puzzled this diplomatic question while the European Common Market countries paid their exporters 22 cents a pound to send us canned hams—which launched an invasion of our domestic market for canned hams. Throughout 1968, American dairymen and livestock feeders needled Congress for closer control of meat and dairy imports. But Congress stuck by the basic quota system administered by the Secretary of Agriculture.

A bill introduced late in 1968 by Montana Senator Lee Metcalf would limit distortion in the farm economy caused by "tax farmers"—high-bracket taxpayers who create tax losses in farming, then write off these losses against nonfarm income. Farm tax losses claimed by those who lost money in 1966 amounted to almost $1,000,000,000, compared with an estimated $16,000,000,000 of net farm income among those who profited.

The Farmers' Union, one of the major farm organizations, campaigned against the growing number of "corporate farms," larger units which could displace family-run farms.

The Agriculture Department released a preliminary study of 22 states showing that these states had 6,700 corporate farms. These farms held 7 per cent of the farmland and produced about 4 per cent of the farm marketings in these states. Some 71 per cent were family corporations—simply family farms organized under corporate charters to minimize finance and estate problems. Nationally there are about 19,000 corporate farms.

▶ **FARM INCOME GAINS**

Net farm income for farm operators totaled about $15,700,000,000, up about 5 per cent from a year earlier. Net per farm approached the 1966 record of $5,049, since fewer farms are sharing the total income pie. Total gross income topped $50,000,000,000, but higher production expenses chewed away a growing percentage of this gross.

Farmers earned almost as much net income from off-farm jobs and investments as they did from farming in 1967, revealed a special Census study in August of 1968. During 1968, off-farm earnings probably surpassed net farm income.

JERRY A. CARLSON
Associate Editor, *Farm Journal*

ARCHITECTURE

IN 1968, public and private clamor grew for better cities, housing, parks and schools. Real progress was made in upgrading quality of design and in getting architects involved in the problems of environment, instead of simply designing individual buildings. Many architects debated whether they could (through they knew they should) get involved with politicians, neighborhood groups and Federal officials to solve the problems of environment. Generally architects decided to accept this new involvement. Architects were finding that they could communicate the need for quality as part of the quantity of new construction that the growing population needs. Out of this struggle to create a decent environment have come new kinds of working relationships for architects and a growing role for the profession.

▶ IMPORTANT NEW TOWERS

During 1968 architects strove for taller buildings to make better use of very-high-cost land. Chicago, always a center of architectural vitality, offered a rare sight to those arriving by plane: three giant new towers. Dominant is the 100-story John Hancock Center with its unusual tapered shape. The building is an X-braced structure with giant cross girders. And it is an almost-black color. Designed by Skidmore, Owings & Merrill, this huge building will be in use 24 hours a day. It combines apartments, commercial areas, offices, restaurant and parking facilities.

Nearby is Lake Point Tower on the shore of Lake Michigan. It is the world's tallest apartment building, rising 70 stories. Designed by Schipporeit-Heinrich and essentially Y-shaped in plan, this building has a continuously curving skin of glass and aluminum. The feeling that this building is an incredibly light sheet of formed glass is heightened by the fact that the load-bearing columns are set behind the wall line. This system is almost opposite in concept to the John Hancock building in which the structure is the main design element.

Three towers: 100-story John Hancock Center, Chicago (left); 70-story Lake Point Tower, Chicago (center); 27-story Gulf Life Tower, Jacksonville, Florida (right).

The third new tower in Chicago is the gracefully curved First National Bank building. This building is 60 stories high and was designed by C. F. Murphy Associates and The Perkins & Will Partnership. Its Christmas-tree shape was dictated by the bank's need for large banking areas on the lower floors. Tenants who will rent space on the upper floors will need less interior space.

Perhaps the most interesting building of the year from an engineering point of view was the Gulf Life Tower in Jacksonville, Florida. This 27-story building, designed by Welton Becket and Associates, is the tallest precast-concrete building in the United States. The architect placed the strongest emphasis not on the vertical columns as is common, but on the horizontal beams. This solution was felt to be more expressive of the "layers" of office functions within the building. The horizontal beams extend a spectacular 42 feet beyond the pairs of vertical columns on each face of the building, creating a great sense of lightness at the corners.

▶ **DESIGN FOR THE FEDERAL GOVERNMENT**

A program was begun in the General Services Administration a few years ago to upgrade the quality of Federal Government buildings. Under this program a new building for the Department of Housing and Urban Development was completed in 1968. It was designed by Marcel Breuer, who in 1968 won the highest award of the American Institute of Architects—its Gold Medal.

The most-talked-about Federal architecture of the year was a new Federal office building and a building for the Court of Claims and Court of Customs and Patent Appeals. Both are on a historic square across the street from the White House. Architect John Carl Warnecke's solution included preserving some town houses on the square. He used red brick in the new buildings to harmonize with the town houses. The brick represented a sharp break with the traditional light-colored stone used for most official buildings in Washington.

Designed in 1968 but not yet under construction were a new art gallery for the Capitol Mall designed by Gordon Bunshaft of Skidmore, Owings & Merrill; a Department of Labor building by Brooks, Barr, Graeber & White and Pitts, Mebane, Phelps & White; an office building by Marcel Breuer and Herbert Beckhard and Nolen-Swinburne & Associates; and a National Aquarium by Kevin Roche.

▶ **COLLEGE-CAMPUS DESIGN—A NEW APPROACH**

Two new college campuses, one in New York and one in California, are good examples of a new approach to the design of building complexes that many architects would have thought most unlikely a few years ago. A huge campus for the University of California at Santa Cruz is being designed as a series of small, dense clusters spotted at intervals through the woods and meadows. Each cluster is being designed by a different architect within an agreed-upon general scheme and land plan. The overall plan was done by John Carl Warnecke, who also designed the main library. Individual college clusters have been designed by Joseph Esherick and Associates, by Campbell & Wong, by Ernest Kump, and by Wurster, Bernardi & Emmons. The central gymnasium and sports complex was designed by Charles Warren Callister.

The same team approach was adopted in developing a new campus for the Rochester (New York) Institute of Technology, which opened in September. Here architects Edward Larabee Barnes, Kevin Roche, Hugh Stubbins, Harry Weese and Lawrence Anderson each contributed a part of the total college complex. It is significant that each of these architects—each admired for his individual skill and innovative concepts —agreed to work within the limitations of a single exterior material (a distinctive brick, in this case) and a limited palette of details and shapes. The result is strikingly handsome. It is likely that the increasingly

Marcel Breuer's Housing and Urban Development building, opened in 1968.

complex architectural commissions that lie ahead in every area—urban housing and new town to name but two—would benefit from such collaborations.

▶ CONTROVERSY IN ARCHITECTURE

The architectural profession faced many controversies in 1968. Five are worth mentioning here.

The first was generated by the decision of architect Charles Luckman to sell his giant firm. The Luckman firm was responsible for the design of $100,000,000 in buildings in 1967. It was sold in 1968 to the Ogden Corporation, a holding company with diversified interests in steel, food, shipbuilding and aerospace. Luckman viewed this move as desirable since it gave his firm new capabilities and more capital. It was, however, a sharp departure from the traditional practice of the profession and was considered by some as being outside the profession's code of ethics.

The second controversy revolved around the so-called "Princeton Report." In 1966 the American Institute of Architects commissioned a $100,000 study of the state of American architectural education. The report, issued in 1968, offended many by completely refraining from the use of the words "architect" or "architecture." The report called for the inclusion of building design, engineering, landscape architecture, city planning, product styling, graphics and other design disciplines in a single profession called "environmental design." After it was released the report was rejected by a resolution of the Association of Collegiate Schools of Architecture. The matter was far from resolved and—like the Luckman merger—will doubtless echo within the profession for some years.

The three other controversies were in the area of design.

Somewhat to the embarrassment of the American Institute of Architects, the design for its own headquarters building, done by Mitchell-Giurgola Associates after a nationwide competition, was rejected by the Fine Arts Commission in Washington. After many attempts to compromise differences with the commission, the firm resigned.

There was a great stir over a proposal by developers to erect a 55-story tower designed by Marcel Breuer atop New York City's much-admired and already-crowded Grand Central Station. Numerous protests from the City Planning Commission, the Landmarks Preservation Commission and other groups were pending at the end of the year.

Perhaps the most interesting argument on design in 1968 was generated by architect John Johansen's design for a theater complex for Mummer's Theater in Oklahoma City. Johansen's concept is to express visually, as separate elements, as many parts of a building as possible. Thus the theater-in-the-round is a round building. A theater in the three-quarter round is round with a notch in it. A series of pathways or bridges placed as direct expressions of the most logical traffic pattern is used for walking about the theater complex. The water tower is the tallest element, and has large pipes leading to each of the main buildings. This kind of direct expression was, for

some, too much. For others, it was an important exploration into new design approaches.

▶ **BUILDING TECHNOLOGY**

In 1968 there was much talk about new technology but not much new technology. Great emphasis was placed by government officials, as part of the year's massive effort to create new in-city housing, on new techniques to cut costs. The much-heralded Instant Rehabilitation project, which involved the use of prefabricated kitchen-bathroom cores designed to be dropped into holes cut into tenement buildings, did not work well. Variations in floor level within the old buildings hindered the project.

The idea of using prefabricated units hoisted into place on high-rise cores gained a lot of acceptance. A small-scale prototype will soon be built in Washington. The most exciting example of this technique was proposed by architect Paul Randolph. He designed a remarkable complex of industrial, commercial and office space combined with over four thousand apartment units for New York City.

▶ **NEW KINDS OF URBAN SPACE**

Several buildings were completed in 1968 that created new kinds of space. One, the Ford Foundation building in New York, designed by Kevin Roche, generated enormous interest. Many architects and critics considered it to be one of the most beautiful buildings in the United States. Its most important feature is a garden courtyard inside the building's glass walls. The courtyard is one third of an acre in area and open to a skylight 12 stories above. All of the executive offices are placed in an L shape overlooking the garden and each other through sliding glass doors. From any point in the building the organization of the giant Ford Foundation is visibly and almost symbolically expressed.

Another kind of space, also designed by Roche, is explored in a new museum in Oakland, California. The museum covers

Garden courtyard inside the glass walls of Kevin Roche's Ford Foundation building creates new urban space.

four city blocks. It is designed as a series of stepped-back gallery spaces, separated and reached by broad and varied stairways. There are carefully landscaped pools and gardens, some atop the gallery spaces. This scheme creates not just exhibit space, but an open park and new urban core for the city.

Still another kind of space is Place Bonaventure in Montreal. Built as part of the Expo 67 development, it was not in full use until 1968. This building is a low, dense, solid mass that almost completely covers its six-acre site. Place Bonaventure was designed by the Montreal firm of Af-

fleck, Desbarats, Dimakopoulos, Lebensold & Sise. It includes a variety of exhibition and showroom space and a shopping concourse. On the upper floors there is a 400-room hotel with rooftop plazas and gardens and pools. Below street level, the giant building connects by a series of passageways to other buildings in the downtown area. It also connects to the subway and railroad stations—an out-of-weather pedestrian network most appropriate for Montreal's winter climate.

Walter F. Wagner, Jr.
Editor in Chief
Architectural Record

ASIA

THE Vietnam war continued to dominate the Asian scene in 1968. But beyond Vietnam there were many other important developments. Indeed these developments may shape the future course of Asian affairs more than the war itself. In Communist China, for example, the struggle for power seemed near an end as Communist Party Chairman Mao Tse-tung deposed his most powerful rival and former heir apparent, President Liu Shao-chi. Indonesia, one of the most populous nations of Asia, showed the first signs of recovering from the legacy of economic chaos left by the former Sukarno regime. In Japan, whose industrial production now leads the world after the United States and the Soviet Union, the ruling Liberal-Democratic Party scored an impressive triumph at the polls against its Leftist rivals. In Burma and in Cambodia, as well as in Indonesia, the Communists sustained setbacks. And India and Pakistan patched up their differences over the Rann of Kutch.

There was, however, a dark side to the picture. North Korean guerrillas tried to assassinate President Chung Hee Park of South Korea. And North Korean patrol boats seized the United States intelligence ship *Pueblo* and her 83-man crew. In Thailand, a United States military base was attacked for the first time by a band of communist guerrillas. And the Philippines reopened its claim to Sabah in Malaysian Borneo, causing tension between the two countries to stretch to the breaking point.

As for Vietnam itself, 1968 opened with a massive communist attack during the Lunar New Year truce. But the year ended on a more positive note: There was an end to American bombing of North Vietnam, and the opening of a new phase in the Paris peace talks, which had begun earlier in the year.

▶ VIETNAM WAR

On January 30, in the midst of Tet, the Vietnamese Lunar New Year, the Communists launched a massive surprise attack.

A North Vietnamese officer (left) and his men in Hue, South Vietnam, during the Tet offensive.

Ho Chi Minh, president of communist North Vietnam, sent delegates to Paris to discuss peace in Vietnam with American representatives.

North Vietnamese regulars and Vietcong irregulars struck 30 of South Vietnam's 44 provincial capitals as well as the country's largest cities, including Saigon, Hue and Danang. Scores of district capitals, airfields and military installations were hit. Communist commandos penetrated Saigon. They seized parts of the United States Embassy. They fought their way onto the grounds of the presidential palace in the heart of the capital city. And they showered rockets on Tansonnhut, a sprawling "airfield city" and American headquarters on the edge of Saigon.

Hanoi boasted that the "long-awaited offensive" would topple the South Vietnamese Government of President Nguyen Van Thieu. The dimensions of the offensive showed that the attack had been carefully prepared. However, the South Vietnamese Army, United States troops and other allies broke the attack. The Communists lost more than 38,000 of their finest troops. The South Vietnamese people failed to rise up as Hanoi had expected. And the South Vietnamese Government did not collapse.

Nevertheless, the Communists demonstrated that no part of South Vietnam was secure from their assaults. In Asia and in the United States the scope of the attack generated a crisis of confidence in American military leadership. The crisis was heightened because only a few weeks earlier General William Westmoreland, U.S. commander in Vietnam, had stated that "the end of the war begins to come into view." His strategy was also widely criticized. For, as the Communists unfolded their Tet offensive, 5,000 crack United States marines primed themselves far to the north of Saigon at Khesanh for a North Vietnamese assault that never came. Many observers felt that the marines should not have been tied down in static defense at a nonessential base.

As a result of Tet, General Westmoreland asked for 206,000 more troops. There were already 510,000 American servicemen in South Vietnam. President Johnson denied this request. During the summer General Westmoreland was appointed head of the Joint Chiefs of Staff. His deputy, General Creighton Abrams, took over as commander in Vietnam.

Meanwhile, on March 31, President Johnson declared that he would not stand for reelection. During the same speech, he announced a halt to bombing operations over most of North Vietnam. The President's actions led to the opening of peace talks in May in Paris. These talks were, however, punctuated by the "second Tet offensive." Nine provincial capitals as well as 12 district capitals in the Mekong Delta near Saigon were hit. Saigon itself was penetrated again. And a series of new raids was launched across the country by North Vietnamese and Vietcong troops. This offensive lacked the force and firepower of the January offensive. But once again, although the Communists were defeated militarily they achieved a psychological victory.

The Paris peace talks made no headway until October. In this month, North Vietnam agreed to recognize the South Vietnamese Government at the negotiations and to reduce attacks on urban centers. In return, on October 31, President Johnson ordered a complete halt to American bombing of North Vietnam. He also accepted the seating of the South Vietnamese National Liberation Front (the Vietcong) at the conference table. However, the talks were delayed when South Vietnamese negotiator Nguyen Cao Ky refused to accept Vietcong equality at the bargaining table.

▶ LAOS AND CAMBODIA

During 1968 the United States continued to feud with Cambodia. The United States accused the Cambodians of allowing the Vietcong and North Vietnamese to use their territory as a staging area and a sanctuary. Prince Norodom Sihanouk, Cambodia's chief of state, accused the United States of bombing his country. In January, United States Ambassador to India Chester Bowles visited Cambodia in an effort to improve relations. But matters worsened in July, when the Cambodians seized an American patrol boat with 11 U.S. and one South Vietnamese servicemen aboard. The ship had accidentally entered Cambodian waters. The men were released by Cambodia in December.

Despite his support of the Vietcong and North Vietnamese, Prince Sihanouk fought hard against a communist insurgency in his own country. He accused the Communists of trying to overthrow his neutralist Government.

Across the border in Laos, the communist Pathet Lao, aided by North Vietnamese troops, launched an offensive during the early part of the year. They succeeded in encircling several important towns held by Government troops.

▶ THAILAND

For the first time in almost ten years of benevolent military rule, Thailand was given a new constitution. As a result, more than ten political parties emerged. And the Thai press became outspoken on issues it would never have discussed before. Elections were scheduled for February 1969. An ominous note was introduced, however, when guerrillas in northeast Thailand, where the Communists have sought to gain a foothold, attacked a United States Air Force base. Two planes were wrecked. A Thai guard was killed, and four Americans were wounded. This assault took place near Udron, and marked the first time an American base in Thailand had been attacked.

▶ THE PHILIPPINES CLAIMS SABAH

In September 1968 the Philippines rekindled its claim to Sabah, a territory in Malaysian Borneo. As a result, on September 19, Malaysia broke diplomatic relations with the Philippines. The Philippine claim to Sabah is based on a nineteenth-century document. Then, in December, Malaysia and the Philippines restored diplomatic relations. The two countries agreed to hold off the Sabah dispute for one year. Bilateral talks on the Sabah issue will begin after 1969.

▶ KOREA: THE OTHER FRONT

On January 21, North Korean commandos slipped across the demilitarized zone between North and South Korea and infiltrated Seoul. Their goal: to assassinate South Korean President Chung Hee Park and several of his cabinet ministers. This attempt failed but two days later the Communists moved again. Four Soviet-made patrol boats intercepted and seized the 906-ton electronic intelligence ship the USS *Pueblo*. The Communists claimed that the ship had intruded into their territorial waters off Wonsan. The United States denied the charge and insisted on the return of the vessel and her crew. The Communists, however, demanded an American apology and an admission that the ship had indeed violated their territorial waters. In December the U.S. signed a document apologizing to North Korea; the 82 crewmembers, as well as the body of one seaman who had been killed when the ship was seized, were released. The U.S. repudiated the document before it was signed.

In April, Presidents Park and Johnson conferred in Hawaii. Mr. Johnson reaffirmed United States determination to repel any communist attack on South Korea. The South Koreans were especially alarmed about this possibility because they had dispatched almost 50,000 troops to South Vietnam to assist the allied effort.

During the fall and winter, North Korea sent increased numbers of guerrilla units into South Korea.

▶ **INDIA AND PAKISTAN**

India and Pakistan agreed to accept the arbitration of a three-power commission with respect to their claims to the Rann of Kutch. In 1965 the two nations had engaged in bitter fighting over this desolate salt marsh.

The commission, composed of Swedish, Yugoslavian and Iranian representatives, awarded 90 per cent of the area to India. Pakistan received 317 square miles of the area claimed by India. Although many Indians opposed the agreement, Indian Prime Minister Indira Gandhi pledged to "honor our commitment." Friends of both India and Pakistan, as an editorial in the *Washington Post* expressed it, "leapt quickly to the hope that the two countries could go on from Kutch to Kashmir by the arbitration procedure."

The Kashmir dispute has poisoned relations between the two countries since 1948. Twice they have gone to war over it. In January 1968, in a conciliatory gesture, India released from prison Sheik Mohammed Abdullah, the "Lion of Kashmir" and its most popular leader. He revisited Kashmir and was widely cheered when he declared that the people of the world should force India and Pakistan to come to an agreement so that Kashmir could have peace at last. Pakistan has accepted a United Nations proposal for a plebiscite in Kashmir, but Indian leaders have balked.

Crewmen of the captured U.S. intelligence ship "Pueblo" at a news conference in North Korea. Ship commander Lloyd Bucher is second from right.

HEADS OF GOVERNMENT

Afghanistan	MOHAMMED ZAHIR SHAH, king NOOR AHMAD ETEMADI, prime minister	Malaysia	TUNKU ABDUL RAHMAN, prime minister
Bhutan	JIGME WANGCHUK, king	Maldive Is.	MOHAMMED FARID DIDI I, sultan IBRAHIM NASIR, prime minister
Burma	NE WIN, chief of state	Mongolia	ZHAMSARANGIN SAMBU, chief of state
Cambodia	PRINCE NORODOM SIHANOUK, chief of state		YUMZHAGIN TSEDENBAL, premier
Ceylon	DUDLEY SENANAYAKE, prime minister	Nepal	MAHENDRA BIR BIKRAM SHAH DEVA, king
China (Communist)	CHOU EN-LAI, premier MAO TSE-TUNG, Communist Party chairman		SURYA BAHADUR THAPA, prime minister
China (Nationalist)	CHIANG KAI-SHEK, president	Pakistan Philip- pines	MOHAMMAD AYUB KHAN, president FERDINAND E. MARCOS, president
India	ZAKIR HUSAIN, president INDIRA GANDHI, prime minister	Singapore	YUSOF BIN ISHAK, president LEE KUAN YEW, prime minister
Indonesia	SUHARTO, chief of state	Thailand	BHUMIBOL ADULYADEJ, king
Japan	HIROHITO, emperor EISAKU SATO, prime minister		THANOM KITTIKACHORN, prime minister
N. Korea	KIM IL SUNG, premier	N. Viet- nam	HO CHI MINH, president PHAM VAN DONG, premier
S. Korea	CHUNG HEE PARK, president CHUNG IL KWON, prime minister	S. Viet- nam	NGUYEN VAN THIEU, president NGUYEN CAO KY, vice-president
Laos	SAVANG VATTHANA, king SOUVANNA PHOUMA, premier		

	POPULATION	ARMED FORCES	CURRENCY*	ASPAC	CO-LOMBO PLAN
Afghanistan	16,000,000	75,000	45 Afghani = $1.00		X
Bhutan	750,000	20,000	. . .		X
Burma	26,000,000	137,500	4.8 kyat = $1.00		X
Cambodia	6,500,000	49,000	35 riels = $1.00		X
Ceylon	12,000,000	. . .	5.9 rupees = $1.00		X
China (Communist)	792,000,000	2,761,000	2.46 yuan = $1.00		
China (Nationalist)	13,500,000	528,000	40 new Taiwan dollars = $1.00	X	
India	520,000,000	1,033,000	7.5 rupees = $1.00		X
Indonesia	112,700,000	340,000	320 new rupiahs = $1.00		X
Japan	101,000,000	250,000	362 yen = $1.00	X	X
North Korea	13,000,000	384,000	2.6 won = $1.00		
South Korea	30,000,000	620,000	274 won = $1.00	X	X
Laos	2,800,000	65,000+	240 kip = $1.00		X
Malaysia	10,000,000	33,800	3.1 Malaysian dollars = $1.00	X	X
Maldive Islands	101,000	. . .	6 rupees = $1.00		X
Mongolia	1,200,000	17,500	4 tugrik = $1.00		
Nepal	10,500,000	20,000	10.1 rupees = $1.00		X
Pakistan	110,000,000	324,000	4.8 rupees = $1.00		X
Philippines	35,000,000	30,000	3.9 pesos = $1.00	X	X
Singapore	2,050,000	4,700	3.1 straits dollars = $1.00		X
Thailand	33,000,000	141,500	20.8 baht = $1.00	X	X
North Vietnam	19,000,000	447,000	3.5 dong = $1.00		
South Vietnam	17,000,000	410,000++ 325,000+++	118 piastres = $1.00	X	X

* US $; 1968 exchange rates
+ Royal Lao Forces
++ Regular forces
+++ Paramilitary forces

ASPAC—Asian and Pacific
Council; with Australia,
New Zealand
Colombo Plan—with Austra-
lia, Canada, New Zea-
land, United Kingdom,
United States

Internally, both India and Pakistan suffered internal disorders. In India there were communal riots between Muslims and Hindus. In Pakistan, President Ayub Khan faced political opposition for the first time. His chief critic was former Air Force commander Mohammad Asghar Khan. He emerged as a likely candidate to oppose Ayub in elections scheduled for January 1970. Pakistani students joined the opposition, and in November there were student riots in several major cities.

▶ INDONESIA

For the first time since the communist-backed regime of President Sukarno was overthrown by the Army in 1965, Indonesia showed dramatic signs of economic and political rehabilitation. Rampant inflation was halted. And a general housecleaning of the corrupt, overstaffed bureaucracy was undertaken. General Suharto, head of the Government, was also installed as president by the Parliament.

In June, Suharto reshuffled his Cabinet. He installed a new Government dominated by civilians, most of whom are economists, technical experts and professors.

Indonesia was also buoyed by the failure of the Communists to regroup their shattered forces on Java. During an anticommunist drive in August, Government forces killed or captured more than two thousand members of the outlawed Indonesian Communist Party. They also thwarted a communist insurgency along the Malaysian-Indonesian border on Borneo.

▶ COMMUNIST CHINA

During 1968 there were signs that the Great Proletarian Cultural Revolution was at last becoming a spent force. The Cultural Revolution had been set in motion in late 1965 by Communist Party Chairman Mao Tse-tung. Its major purpose was to cover a massive purge of Mao's opponents in the ruling Communist Party. Indeed, from late 1965 through the end of 1968, more than half of the members of the Communist Party Central Committee were ousted from their positions. Foremost among those purged was Liu Shao-chi, president of Communist China. In October he was stripped of all his party and government posts.

An indication that the great purge was coming to an end was the fact that all of China's provinces during 1968 finally came under the control of the Revolutionary Committees which began appearing late in 1967. These committees, set up by Mao, are to administer the country until the

An Indian protests World Court decision giving part of the Rann of Kutch to Pakistan.

As part of Communist China's Cultural Revolution, students pay homage to Mao.

Leftist Japanese students, who most frequently demonstrate against the U.S., clash here with police while protesting the Soviet invasion of Czechoslovakia.

Government is handed back to a "rectified" (purged) Communist Party. Despite the control of these committees, there was some violence during 1968, especially in the spring and summer. Hundreds of people who opposed Mao were executed in various parts of the country. This turmoil and unrest seriously hampered the Chinese economy. Industrial production was below that of the pre-Cultural Revolution days.

▶ **JAPAN**

Japan's influence in Asian affairs increased noticeably during 1968. Tokyo undertook its first moves in a campaign to win a permanent seat in the United Nations Security Council. This would give Japan the same veto rights as are held by Great Britain, China, France, the Soviet Union and the United States.

Japan's growing economic and political power was underlined by its agreement to help finance Indonesia's economic recovery and by its successful struggle to regain control of Iwo Jima. This island, which was the scene of a bloody World War II battle, as well as other islands in the Bonin group, was returned to Japan by the United States on June 26.

In July the Liberal-Democratic administration headed by Premier Eisaku Sato won a stunning victory at the polls. It won 137 of the 250 seats in the House of Councillors, the upper house of the Japanese Diet (parliament). Sato's victory was interpreted as a rebuff to the anti-American Socialist Party, which advocates repeal of the mutual-defense treaty between Japan and the United States. Mr. Sato favors permitting this pact to continue automatically when its ten-year term expires in 1970.

Despite his victory in the elections, Mr. Sato had to contend with violent anti-American demonstrations held by students who oppose the stationing of American troops in Japan. These students also protested against the bringing to Japan of American soldiers wounded in Vietnam.

ARNOLD C. BRACKMAN
Author, *Southeast Asia's Second Front*

AUSTRALIA AND NEW ZEALAND

AUSTRALIA began 1968 with a new prime minister. On January 10, less than a month after the tragic drowning of Harold Holt, John Grey Gorton was sworn in as his successor (see page 115). On the world scene, Gorton continued Holt's policy of cooperation with the United States in Vietnam. To cement U.S.–Australian relations he traveled to the United States to confer with President Johnson. But, at the same time, he asserted that he would not increase the number of Australian troops in South Vietnam. Both Australia and New Zealand prepared to tackle the problems that will arise when Great Britain withdraws its forces from South Asia. This will be accomplished by 1971.

On the economic front, Australia and New Zealand made dramatic gains during 1968. Discoveries of vast mineral deposits paved the way for a bright economic future for Australia. And New Zealand made considerable headway in decreasing unemployment and remedying the financial problems that had plagued it during 1967.

After almost half a century of Australian administration, first as a League of Nations mandate and then as a United Nations trust territory, the tiny island of Nauru was granted independence on January 31 (see page 118).

▶ **AUSTRALIA**

Australia earned a new label during 1968: the "boom country." A vital role in Southeast Asia, new mineral and oil discoveries and a buoyant economy made 1968 one of Australia's most progressive and exciting years.

Foreign Trade

In 1968, Australia was the twelfth-ranked trading nation in the world. Its export earnings in fiscal 1967–68 reached $3,000,000,000 and are expected to exceed $5,000,000,000 by the mid-1970's.

Total exports to the United States increased from $144,000,000 in 1960–61 to $360,000,000 in 1967–68. The United States was Australia's third-largest buyer of goods, after Japan and Great Britain.

Australia's mining boomed in 1968 in nickel and bauxite production and in coal exports.

The Mining Boom

The mining boom of 1968 was unique in Australian history. The finding of bauxite at Weipa, Queensland, and at the Darling Range in Western Australia in the past few years led to the development of two large aluminum complexes to handle the raw material.

Queensland's booming coal-export trade with Japan continued to expand in 1968. This trade will result in the building of a new township, railway and port within three years. The partners in the project, which will cost $100,000,000, are the Utah Development Company of the United States and the Mitsubishi Shoji Kaisha of Japan.

In 1964, Australia was unknown on the world nickel scene. In 1968 it was the third-largest nickel producer. Deposits of high-grade nickel developed in 1968 in Western Australia will eventually be enough to meet the needs of Canada and Japan.

Oil continued to be the exciting news of 1968, and New South Wales joined Queensland, Victoria and Western Australia in oil research and exploration. The New South Wales government granted permits to five companies to explore the continental shelf for oil and natural gas. The spectacular find of oil in Bass Strait (off Victoria) stimulated this interest in the continental shelf.

Australia negotiated iron-ore contracts with Japan worth $3,000,000,000. The contracts call for Australia to export 364,-000,000 tons of lump ore and pellets over the next 25 years.

A vital link was forged with the United States when the Australian Atomic Energy Commission agreed to cooperate with the United States Plowshare Program. Under this program, nuclear explosions will be used to excavate and create harbors and to facilitate mining operations.

Defense

Australia continued to support United States involvement in Vietnam during 1968. With 8,000 troops fighting in South Vietnam, Australia spent $76,354,000 on defense as compared with only $3,000,000 in 1964–65.

Spectacular oil find in Bass Strait has spurred on oil research and exploration in Australia with giant offshore oil drilling rigs.

No issue since the conscription controversy of World War I has more divided the Australian people than the question of Australia's cooperation with the United States in the Vietnam war. As in the United States, the main protests came from individual church leaders, university teachers and students, peace groups and some women's organizations.

A major political controversy flared in 1968 over the United States F-111 fighter-bomber. At Fort Worth, Texas, in September 1968, Australian Defense Minister Allen Fairhall formally accepted Australia's first F-111. Twenty-three more aircraft, valued at $274,000,000, were to be delivered. But when the plane developed faults, the Labor Opposition pressured the Australian Government to cancel the purchase of the additional planes.

Prime Minister Gorton's aim is to make the "aboriginal citizens economically independent."

The Aborigines

In 1968, Australia faced up to the problems of its minority citizens—the aborigines. Until 1967 each of Australia's states had enacted its own laws concerning the aborigines. In 1967, however, in a referendum, the Federal Government won the right to control aboriginal affairs. When he assumed the office of prime minister, John Gorton promptly expressed his desire to make the "aboriginal citizens economically independent."

Australia has about eighty thousand aborigines. A few have graduated from universities. Others have made their mark in various fields, such as sports. One such example is Lionel Rose, who won the world boxing bantamweight title in 1968. However, most aborigines have a standard of living far below that of other Australians. Many aborigines are now fighting, in various ways, to improve the lot of their people.

In Australia's Northern Territory, aborigines of the Gurindji tribe, who work at a large cattle station, staged a two-year strike to win higher wages and to obtain land for hunting. In 1968 this matter was settled when William C. Wentworth, minister for aboriginal affairs, granted the Gurindjis one thousand acres of land for their own use. This action by Wentworth, as well as the Federal assumption of powers

	HEAD OF GOVERNMENT	POPULATION	ARMED FORCES	CURRENCY*
AUSTRALIA	JOHN G. GORTON, prime minister	12,050,000	84,300	1 A dollar = $1.13
NAURU	HAMMER DeROBURT, chief of state	6,055	. . .	. . .
NEW ZEALAND	KEITH J. HOLYOAKE, prime minister	2,756,000	13,170	1 NZ dollar = $1.13

*US $; 1968 exchange rates

previously held by the individual states, seems to point the way to economic and political progress for the aborigines. This, hopefully, would lessen the appeal of the few younger aborigines who have called for more militant action after studying American Negro groups.

Papua-New Guinea

Papua-New Guinea continued to make important economic gains during the year. The output of coffee, tea and peanuts was increased. New finds of gold- and copper-bearing ore as well as natural gas and oil meant good economic prospects for this Australian territory.

In October 1968 the Australian Government announced a $1,000,000,000 program to develop Papua-New Guinea over the next five years. The basic aim is to double the territory's export earnings by 1972 and to make the economy self-sufficient by 1980. This should eventually lead to independence. The program, the first of its kind, will expand industry, communications services, health services and tourism. The keynote is increased ownership and participation by the 2,300,000 natives, who now have 12 elected members in the 94-seat House of Assembly in Port Moresby.

Territory Administrator David Hay has stated that the people of Papua–New Guinea can have independence whenever they want it. Many observers feel, however, that because of the islanders' lack of a sense of nationhood (700 different languages are spoken in the territory), independence is probably ten to twenty years away.

▶ NEW ZEALAND

The highlights of 1968 were New Zealand's economic recovery and its shift away from Great Britain and toward the United States in the area of national defense.

Economy

In 1968, New Zealand overcame many of its economic problems of the previous year. Increased exports and a booming tourist trade helped correct the nation's balance-of-payments deficit. Income from exports was nearly $930,000,000. Of this amount, $61,000,000 worth of goods was exported to Australia.

It was evident that the Australian-New Zealand Free Trade Agreement, as well as the November 1967 devaluation of the New Zealand dollar, helped the economy.

Defense

New Zealand has only a small defense force of 13,170 men. Thus a major concern of New Zealanders is the defense of their country when British military forces are withdrawn from Malaysia and Singapore. This is scheduled to take place no later than 1971.

On June 10–11, at Kuala Lumpur, Malaysia, Prime Minister Keith Holyoake met with representatives from Australia, Great Britain, Malaysia and Singapore to discuss this problem and to work out alternative defense measures for the area.

Holyoake and his Government made clear that they would place major reliance on the Anzus Treaty, the mutual-defense treaty between Australia, New Zealand and the United States. Early in 1968, New Zealand began to shift from the purchase of British military hardware to that produced by the United States.

In addition to the Kuala Lumpur meeting, Prime Minister Holyoake hosted several important conferences during the year. He was chairman of the 13th Southeast Asia Treaty Organization meeting in Wellington, New Zealand, on April 2–3. This was followed by a separate meeting, on the following day, of those countries fighting in South Vietnam: Australia, New Zealand, the Philippines, Thailand, South Korea, the United States and South Vietnam. New Zealand now has 550 troops stationed in South Vietnam.

In mid-October, Prime Minister Holyoake flew to the United States for a conference with President Johnson.

GEOFFREY L. GRIFFITH
Associate Editor
Daily Mirror (Sydney)

ON December 17, 1967, the turbulent seas off Australia's southeastern coast took the life of Prime Minister Harold Holt. Australia was left leaderless, and the coalition Government was in disarray. The man chosen to lead the Liberal Party, preserve a coalition with the Country Party, and serve as Australia's prime minister was John Grey Gorton. He was sworn in on January 10, 1968, three weeks after Holt disappeared in the surf off Portsea, Victoria.

The new Prime Minister, a lean six-footer with the face of a pugilist (the legacy of war injuries), came on the international scene with a colorful history. He is an Oxford graduate, a former fighter pilot, and an orchardist. He was a parliamentarian for 17 years. In Parliament, Gorton gained a reputation for political flair, impulsiveness, and Right-Wing tendencies, though he describes himself as "slightly left of center."

Some of the tales about John Gorton are fiction, including the one that he fought for Generalissimo Franco during the Spanish Civil War. But there is enough exciting fact in his background to make up for it.

▶ EARLY YEARS

John Gorton was born September 9, 1911, near Kerang in northern Victoria, where his father owned an orange orchard. For his early schooling he went to Geelong Grammar School, an exclusive educational institution where Prince Charles, heir to the British throne, studied.

Leaving school in 1930, young Gorton spent a year working in his father's citrus groves during the Depression, then went on to Oxford. He graduated in 1936, majoring in history, economics and political science.

While studying at Brasenose College, Oxford, Gorton went on a holiday to Spain —the basis for the Franco myth. In Spain Gorton met an American named Bettina Brown of Bangor, Maine, a student at the Sorbonne. They were married in 1935, and the following year, after graduating, returned to Australia, where Gorton took over the orchard from his ailing father.

▶ MILITARY CAREER

In 1940 Gorton enlisted in the Royal Australian Air Force. He had learned to fly while at Oxford, and during World War II he served as a fighter pilot.

Gorton was lucky to survive the war. He was shot down twice and shipwrecked once. He was first shot down over the Timor Sea and parachuted into a Dutch plantation on a small island in the Netherlands East Indies. The marooned pilot lived for days on turtle eggs and fish before being rescued. In a later dogfight over Singapore, where he was stationed as a flight lieutenant with a Hurricane squadron, Gorton was again shot down. He suffered severe facial injuries which later required extensive plastic surgery. As he describes it, in typical Gorton prose, "my face got rather mixed up with the instrument panel, with lasting effects upon my beauty."

Gorton was evacuated from Singapore, but his ship was torpedoed and he spent 24 hours bobbing about on a makeshift raft in the Java Sea north of Batavia (Jakarta). The Australian corvette HMAS *Ballarat* rescued the man who from 1958 to 1963 would be minister for the Navy; and in 1944 Gorton was medically discharged from service.

IMPORTANT DATES IN THE LIFE OF JOHN G. GORTON

1911 Born near Kerang in northern Victoria, September 9.

1935 Married Bettina Brown.

1936 Graduated from Oxford.

1940– Pilot in the Royal Australian Air Force
1944 during World War II.

1949 Elected senator for Victoria in general elections, December 10.

1968 Elected Liberal Party leader, January 9. Sworn in as prime minister, January 10. Wins House of Representative seat once held by Harold Holt, February 24.

POLITICAL CAREER

After World War II, Gorton returned to the fruitgrowing business. In 1948 he switched his allegiance from the Country Party to the larger Liberal Party, and in the following year he made his debut as a politician—and lost. Gorton unsuccessfully challenged the Country Party candidate for a Victoria Legislative Council seat and was beaten by a mere 400 votes in a Country Party stronghold. In the general elections of December 10, 1949, however, Gorton was elected to Federal Parliament as a Liberal senator from the state of Victoria. He was then 38 years old.

In the next decade and a half Gorton moved up through the ranks. Under Prime Minister Robert Menzies he was variously minister for the Navy, acting minister for external affairs and chairman of the first consultative meeting under the Antarctic Treaty. When Menzies moved to increase Federal involvement in education (1963), Gorton was named "minister assisting the prime minister."

In 1966 Harold Holt became prime minister and brought Gorton into the inner Cabinet as head of the new Department of Education and Science. Gorton held this post until his own elevation to the prime-ministership.

PRIME MINISTER

Gorton was not a well-known national figure when Harold Holt died. He was seventh in cabinet seniority and had been leader of the Liberal Party in the Upper House for only three months. In fact when his name was released as the successful candidate for the prime-ministership, a voice in the crowd outside the caucus room was heard to say, "John who?"

Nevertheless, in his bid for the leadership—in a spirited, American-style race thitherto foreign to Australian politics—Gorton projected an image of a sophisticated, dashing man of action. He also came across as something of an enigma.

Well-educated and well-read, Gorton admits that he is not interested in the theater or the arts. He plays bridge and tennis; loves "mucking about in the garden"; like his predecessor adores swimming; reads everything from scientific reports to mysteries; and enjoys television Westerns.

His wife went to a university after their three children had grown up. (Both sons are lawyers, and the daughter is a computer programer.) Mrs. Gorton learned Indonesian at the Australian National University in Canberra and graduated with a Bachelor of Arts in oriental studies in 1965.

The prime-ministership of Harold Holt marked a new era of close ties with the United States. To an extent Gorton has continued that policy. He has said, however, that "I believe in the American alliance as being of enormous importance to Australia . . . but we can't give a blank check to the future."

Gorton has confirmed the Australian commitment in Vietnam, though he has balked at increasing the number of Australian troops in Vietnam. He has also been criticized editorially as being the only Allied leader who still believes a military victory possible in that country.

Long before assuming the prime-ministership, Gorton was in favor of closer ties with Asian nations. This policy has gained added importance with the planned withdrawal of British forces from that area.

Gorton has also toyed with the idea of an "Australian fortress" defense concept and the institution of an Israeli-type Army.

On the home front, Australia's new Prime Minister is in favor of increased old-age pensions. He would also like to see an increase in government-supported health services.

Gorton also leans toward federalization of government in a country which has state governments similar to those in the United States. Yet he believes that at the national level, the prime minister's power should be decentralized.

DERRYN HINCH
Foreign Correspondent
The Sydney Morning Herald (Australia)

NAURU

THE 5,263-acre phosphate island of Nauru is one of the smallest nations in the world. It is also probably the richest nation per capita. Administered by the Australian Government, Nauru was a United Nations Trust Territory from November 1, 1947, until January 31, 1968, when it became a fully independent nation.

▶ THE LAND

Nauru is located 26 miles south of the equator and midway between Honolulu, Hawaii, and Sydney, Australia. Its nearest neighbor is Ocean Island, another body of phosphate 190 miles to the east. The pear-shaped atoll is only 12 miles in circumference. Above its narrow beach of white sand is a belt of land, 150 to 300 yards wide, which produces coconut palms and some breadfruit, pandanus, mango, papaw and poinciana trees. Here and around tiny Buada Lagoon are the island's only inhabitable areas.

Rising steeply to 200 feet above sea level is a central plateau of valuable phosphate rock formed from ancient deposits of marine organisms on coral reefs. A third of the area, from which more than 37,000,000 tons of phosphate have already been mined, is an eerie bed of sharp coral pinnacles, some 50 feet tall.

Nauru is surrounded by a shelf of coral, which ends in a sheer drop to ocean depths. The island has no natural harbors and only one beach safe for swimmers.

▶ CLIMATE

Nauru's tropical climate is tempered by easterly trade winds during the dry season. From November to February, westerly winds bring an average of 80 inches of rain. The rain has varied, however, from a low of 12.29 inches to a record high of 181.76 inches. Because of this uncertain rainfall and because of brackish wells, the island's fresh water is shipped in from Australia.

▶ THE PEOPLE

Of the nation's 6,055 inhabitants, there are 3,200 Nauruans, 1,314 other Pacific islanders, 1,100 Chinese and 441 Australians and New Zealanders. The Melanesians, recruited chiefly from neighboring Gilbert and Ellice Islands, and the Chinese are not citizens but indentured laborers. They were brought to Nauru by European mineowners to work the phosphate fields.

Nauruans are predominantly Polynesian, mixed through the years with Micronesians and Melanesians. They are a short, stout people with brown skin, heavy features and thick black hair. The Nauruans adopted Christianity from the early missionaries. Two thirds are Congregationalists, and one third are Catholics.

Although Nauru has only one university graduate, a dentist who got his degree in 1964 in Australia, its people are 95 per cent literate. The island has had a free-and-compulsory, primary-and-secondary educational system for more than forty years. Nauruan (a written language) and English are spoken.

There are no taxes on Nauru. Medical care, and even the movies are free for Nauruans. A proud and gentle people, their origin is obscure, but leaders avow that they have always lived on their isolated island.

▶ HISTORY

The first European to discover Nauru was Captain John Fearn. He arrived in a whaling ship in November 1798 and named the atoll Pleasant Island. Nauru was then a matriarchy, and was ruled by a queen as late as the 1840's.

With the arrival of the white man, who introduced the gun, and the Gilbertese, who introduced alcohol made from fermented coconuts, the natural balance of power among Nauru's 12 tribes was upset. A bloody "Ten Years' War" ensued. Only occupation by the Germans in 1888, it is

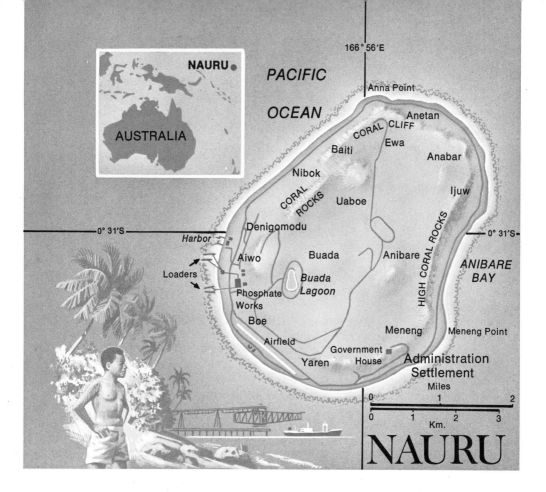

said, prevented the Nauruans from self-extermination.

Phosphate was discovered on the island by New Zealander Albert Ellis at the turn of the century. Under an agreement with Germany, which had annexed the island, the Pacific Phosphate Company, formed by Ellis and his brother, began mining operations in 1907.

In 1914, at the start of World War I, the Australian warshsip H.M.A.S. *Melbourne* captured Nauru. Under the Nauru Island Agreement of 1919, Nauru became a mandate territory under the League of Nations. Britain, Australia and New Zealand were the mandate powers, but Australia alone administered the island.

Without consulting the Nauruans, the three governments purchased phosphate rights from the Pacific Phosphate Company, and established the British Phosphate Com-

missioners to work the mines. After 1921, however, Nauruan ownership of the land was acknowledged. The Nauruans were paid a halfpenny a ton royalties.

By 1939, when they were receiving eight cents a ton, the people of Nauru began to realize that at the rate of a million tons of phosphate a year now being hauled away, their island would soon disappear. For the first time, questions of rehabilitation of the land or relocation of its people arose.

World War II brought new threats of disaster to the little atoll. Early in the war Nauru was shelled by a German raider. In 1942 the Japanese bombed the island. A Free French destroyer evacuated most of the foreigners. Those who elected to remain with the Nauruans destroyed the phosphate works. Six months later the Japanese occupied the island. When 15 of their planes were blown up during an Allied air attack, the Japanese executed five of the seven Europeans, including the Australian administrator.

Many Nauruans were put into Japanese labor battalions. Some 1,200—including Head Chief Timothy Detudamo and a young schoolteacher named Hammer De-Roburt—were exiled to Truk Island in the Carolines, 1,000 miles away. By the time World War II ended in 1945, 463 of the deportees had died of starvation, disease, bombing and Japanese brutality. The 737 survivors returned to their battered island on January 31, 1946. The 591 kinsmen who greeted them were suffering from disease and malnutrition.

Australian control had been resumed in 1945. And in 1947 Nauru became a United Nations trust territory administered by Australia.

The Council of Chiefs, a powerless and largely hereditary body formed in 1927, was replaced by the Nauru Local Government Council after the first elections were held in December 1951. It was headed by Detudamo.

Under strong leadership, the Nauruans began their drive for control of the phosphate industry and for self-government. After sixty years of foreign rule, only one position of importance—that of native-affairs officer—was held by a native. The visit of a United Nations mission in 1953 resulted in agitation for more self-rule. On the death of Detudamo, the same year, Raymond Gadabu was elected head chief. The 1955 elections brought young DeRoburt to the helm of the council.

In 1955, also, the British Phosphate Commissioners decided to increase the rate of phosphate production. This made the quest for a new home for the Nauruans all the more imperative. Locations in Australia and New Zealand, suggested by the Australian Government and the UN, were rejected. An island minority settled on a white mainland, reasoned the Nauruans, would lead to racial extinction. In 1962 a delegation headed by DeRoburt went to Australia for further talks on the subject.

Several islands were inspected, and two—Fraser and Curtis—were considered. The Nauruans later rejected these two islands when it was learned that Australian citizenship went along with the move.

When the production of phosphate was raised in 1964 to 2,500,000 tons per year (again without consulting the people), and royalties had risen to only 37 cents a ton, discussions broke down. The Nauruans decided to stay and rehabilitate their homeland. The first step toward self-government was achieved on January 31, 1966, when the Legislative Council was inaugurated.

In June 1967 an agreement was reached between Nauru and Britain, Australia and New Zealand on control of the phosphate operation. On July 1, 1970, the operation will become the Nauru Phosphate Corporation. More than one hundred Nauruans are now taking on-the-job training in mine administration preparatory to the take-over.

Following this agreement, Head Chief DeRoburt flew to the United States. He persuaded the United Nations to vote for an end to the trusteeship. The Nauru Independence Act of 1967 had already been passed by the Australian Parliament, and January 31, 1968, was agreed upon as Nauru's "Day of Deliverance."

▶ GOVERNMENT

Nauru's Legislative Council was empowered to establish a 36-member Constitutional Convention to draft, with Australian help, a constitution for the island. On Independence Day, a Council of State was elected by the Legislative Council. It in turn elected Chief DeRoburt as its chairman. Until a ministerial government is set up, this body will have full executive authority. The power to make laws for the new republic is invested in a Legislative Assembly elected by the people.

▶ ECONOMY

Nauru, which has no political parties, feels that it is too small and too remotely located to join the United Nations, although it is better able to pay UN dues than some

Two young Nauruans proudly display their country's new flag.

of the larger nations. Debt-free, it has always been self-supporting.

At the present rate of excavation, the nearly 60,000,000 tons of remaining phosphate will be exhausted in 30 years, and 80 per cent of the island will have been dug up. But by that time, an investment fund of $400,000,000 will have been built up. This will give the Nauruans an annual income of $24,000,000.

Part of this money will be used to restore the land. Negotiations are already under way to purchase a ship that will bring soil back to the country to rehabilitate the waste areas. Part of the money will also be used to develop alternative industries and for much-needed housing.

With money in the bank and the reins of government in their own hands for the first time in eighty years, Nauru has an excellent chance to survive. And although the tiny Pacific island is no paradise, its white-starred, royal-blue flag flies high over the land of the frangipani blossoms, and a long-suffering people on a once-dying island face the future with new hope and pride.

ERA BELL THOMPSON
International Editor, *Ebony* Magazine

CANADA

CANADIANS began a voyage of discovery in 1968. As the man to lead them they chose Pierre Elliott Trudeau, a relative newcomer to the political scene. With a style previously unknown to Canadian politics, Trudeau won leadership of the Liberal Party at a convention in April and became the country's 15th prime minister since Confederation. After taking over from retiring Prime Minister Lester B. Pearson, Trudeau called a general election for June 25.

His plea to the voters: "let's take a bit of a chance"; his unorthodox parliamentary dress (sport coat, ascot and sandals); and his appeal to the younger generation produced a startling victory for the Liberals. Canada had its first majority Government since 1962. In the 264-seat Parliament, the Liberals won 155 seats compared with 127 in the last House. Progressive Conservatives, under new leader Robert Stanfield, fell from 94 seats to 72. The New Democrats won 22 seats. And the Creditistes, a Quebec-based party, won 14 seats.

The son of a wealthy French-Canadian lawyer and a mother of Scottish ancestry, Pierre Elliott Trudeau personifies the ideally bicultural Canadian. He is fluent in both English and French. He is a lawyer, a world traveler and independently wealthy. At 49, he is still a bachelor.

In 1967, Trudeau had been a member of parliament for only two years. Yet in April of that year, he was named minister of justice. He had first attracted attention as a parliamentarian when he steered through Parliament three unpopular measures: stricter gun-control legislation and reforms of laws against abortion and homosexuality.

▶ QUEBEC

Trudeau had been in office just five months when the worrisome problem of Quebec was compounded by the sudden death of Quebec Premier Daniel Johnson, leader of the Union Nationale Party. Johnson, who had suffered a heart attack in

At the Liberal Party convention in April, Pierre Elliott Trudeau wins the leadership and becomes Canada's 15th prime minister.

July, had just returned to work when he died at 53.

Johnson's influence in national affairs was extremely significant. The House of Commons, for the first time in history on the death of a provincial premier, immediately adjourned as a mark of respect. In announcing Johnson's death to Parliament, Prime Minister Trudeau said that "death could not have chosen a more inopportune moment to strike down this great Canadian." Johnson had been premier of Quebec for only two years. But his steadying influence had helped create new hope that French Canada's cultural and economic aspirations could be accommodated within the Confederation of Canada.

His belief that Quebec should enjoy special status is held by his successor, former provincial Justice Minister Jean-Jacques Bertrand, 52. But there is concern that the nationalist wing of the party may oust him at a leadership convention in 1969.

Bertrand indicated that he will continue the cooperation and accord reached between France and Quebec on such matters as education and culture. And he was invited to make a state visit to Paris for talks with President de Gaulle.

Separatism

The move by some of the six million French Canadians in Quebec to separate from the rest of Canada took on new dimensions. René Lévesque, who defected from the Quebec Liberal Party in 1967, became the leader of a new political group, Le Parti Québecois. Chief aim of the party is a French-only republic linked with Canada in an economic union. With 20,000 members, the party at a founding convention in Quebec City in October hammered out a platform calling for heavy government intervention in business, industry and health services.

Le Parti Québecois brings together Lévesque's old Sovereign movement and the Ralliement Nationale group. The latter group is headed by Gilles Grégoire, a former member of the Federal Parliament.

Separatist. René Lévesque, head of Le Parti Québecois, wants a Republic of Quebec linked with Canada in an economic union.

Le Parti Québecois refused to consider a merger with the oldest separatist party, Rassemblement pour l'Indépendance Nationale (RIN) headed by Pierre Bourgault. Lévesque broke off talks with Bourgault after the RIN staged an anti-Trudeau demonstration in Montreal on the eve of the Federal elections in June. After the founding of Le Parti Québecois, however, the RIN disbanded, and most of its members joined the new separatist group.

Many observers felt the separatist-spawned violence helped ensure a majority Government for Trudeau, who, despite hurtling bottles containing paint and gasoline, continued to sit in a reviewing stand along the route of the traditional St. Jean-Baptiste Day parade.

Language

There are seven areas in Canada outside of Quebec where French-Canadian minorities exceed 10 per cent of the population. These areas, three in Ontario, two in Nova Scotia, and one each in New Brunswick and Manitoba, will now be bilingual. If passed, the Official Languages Act states that criminal courts, Federal government offices, and transportation agencies must provide information and hearings in both English and French. In introducing the bill to Parliament, Prime Minister Trudeau said the Government expects a trend to more bilingual districts throughout the country.

While Parliament was encouraging bilingualism, one small Quebec community took steps to eliminate gradually the teaching of English in its schools. At St. Leonard, a suburb of Montreal, the phasing out of English was ordered by the school board. This order came despite protests of non-French residents, who make up over 40 per cent of the population. Behind the move is the fear that an influx of new Canadians will make some Quebec cities predominantly English. A recent Government survey showed that of 620,435 immigrants who settled in the province between 1945 and 1966, 80 per cent have opted for English schooling. In Montreal the figure is 90 per cent.

▶ PARLIAMENT

Late in 1967, Prime Minister Lester B. Pearson set April 1968 as the date of his retirement from political life. But a series of events in the House of Commons almost upset his schedule.

Pearson was on a Jamaican holiday in February when the opposition parties combined to defeat the ruling Liberal Party 84-82 on a bill to impose a 5 per cent surcharge on income tax.

Tory leader Robert Stanfield called for the Government to resign. But Pearson, who cut short his holiday, denied the defeat was a vote of no confidence in the Government. Later he placed a confidence motion before the House. The Liberals won 138–

Moderate. Quebec Premier Jean-Jacques Bertrand wants special status for Quebec within Canada.

119. A watered-down bill levying a 3 per cent surcharge on personal and corporation taxes was passed in March. (In October, Canadians learned that, starting January 1, 1969, they would be taxed an extra 2 per cent to pay for new welfare and educational programs.)

Although Parliament sat for seven months, the only major legislation passed was a new divorce bill. Under the old law, adultery was the only ground for divorce. Now Canadians can obtain a divorce for desertion, bigamy, insanity, alcoholism, lengthy imprisonment, mental cruelty and marriage breakdown. The law, effective July 2, brought an estimated increase of 600 per cent in divorce applications.

▶ THE FAR NORTH

Less than a month after his election victory, Prime Minister Trudeau set out on a journey to Canada's Arctic which he

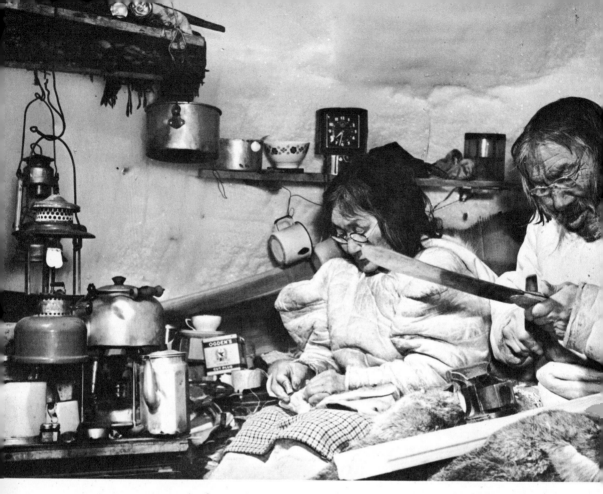

Some 1,600 families will move from igloos to prefabricated houses as part of a program to better living conditions for Canada's 13,000 Eskimos.

described as "stepping into Canada's future." In a week he covered 9,780 miles by air, visiting communities in the Yukon and Northwest Territories. At one settlement, Eureka, he was only 600 miles from the North Pole. His trip helped point up the problems of Canada's minority groups, the Indians and Eskimos.

Canada's 13,000 Eskimos, living in isolated communities across the top of the nation, are still trying to cope with the encroachment of the white man. Unemployment in many places reaches 65 per cent. This is because the younger generation has abandoned the traditional forms of Eskimo livelihood for welfare and Family Allowance payments. Squalid living conditions have helped to produce an infant-mortality

rate of 95 per 1,000 births. This is four times the national rate. Trudeau saw the first steps being taken to provide better living conditions: a program to move 1,600 families from igloos and tar-paper shacks to plywood prefabricated houses that rent for as little as $2.00 a month.

He also promised that Eskimos will be trained and hired for work on northern projects including PanArctic Oils Ltd., a consortium of 20 U.S. companies, with the Canadian Government as the chief shareholder. PanArctic is now drilling for oil on Melville Island.

Trudeau's program also includes a new Indian Act designed to help the country's 250,000 Indians achieve first-class citizenship. Jean Chrétien, minister of Indian affairs and northern development, promised the Indians a voice in designing the act. But one breakaway band of Indians, the Ermineskin Crees, have abandoned civilization for life in the wilderness of southern Alberta's Rocky Mountain foothills. Led by their chief, Robert Smallboy, a group of 200 left their comparatively prosperous reserve near Hobbema because they claimed the white man had brought drunkenness and debauchery to their reservation.

THE ECONOMY

The country's economy remained brisk despite signs of a leveling off toward the end of 1968.

The gross national product gained about 4.5 per cent. Exports to all countries were higher by 16 per cent during the first six months of 1968. And sales to the United States, sparked by the auto-trade pact and increased copper exports, were up 25 per cent.

But the labor picture and inflation still caused concern. Unemployment continued upward with 5 per cent of the work force looking for jobs. The cost-of-living index (based on a 1949 norm of 100) reached 156.4 in September. This was up from 150 for the comparable period of 1967.

The national debt rose to $16,700,000,-000, or $809 for every one of the country's 20,900,000 citizens. This was a per-capita increase of $24.

A series of strikes also hampered the economy and boosted the inflationary trend. Workers on the St. Lawrence Seaway tied up much of the Great Lakes shipping for 24 days before settling for a 19 per cent increase over 3 years.

The 20-day July-August strike of 24,000 postal workers ended only after Prime Minister Trudeau had hinted that Parliament might be called into special session to impose a settlement. The postmen agreed to a 6 per cent annual raise. To pay for the estimated $18,000,000-a-year wage increase, postal rates went up about 20 per cent.

Shipments of Western wheat from grain elevators at Fort William to eastern sea-

The 54-story Toronto-Dominion Bank Centre: tallest building in the British Commonwealth in 1968.

Expo 67 reopened in 1968 as a permanent exposition, Man and His World, with participating exhibitors from 44 foreign nations.

ports were tied up for 58 days by a strike of 1,300 Ontario grain handlers. The strike created additional hardship for prairie farmers. They had already been burdened with a surplus of 600,000,000 bushels of unsold wheat from the 1967 crop. In addition, unsettled weather conditions prevented the harvesting of much of the 1968 crop. The grain handlers, after Government intervention, settled for a pay increase of 46 per cent spread over three years.

▶ WAR ON POVERTY

Most Canadians have never known poverty. Their standard of living is one of the highest in the world. So the fifth annual report of the Economic Council of Canada came as a shock. By its standards, 27 per cent of the population are living in poverty. It defined as poor any family or individual that has to spend 70 per cent or more of income on food, clothing and shelter.

The council offered no solution to "this national disgrace." But it blamed the Government's needless duplication, lack of coordination, and fuzziness in its present antipoverty programs. It also urged immediate joint action by Prime Minister Trudeau and the ten provincial premiers to bring an end to poverty.

One of the conditions contributing to the plight of the poor, the council pointed out, is a lack of public housing in major cities. Montreal, for example, had a staggering shortage of 50,000 units. Toronto has applications from more than 10,000 families seeking public housing.

In September, Prime Minister Trudeau took the first step to help alleviate the problem. A government task force toured the country seeking ways to lower the cost of housing and to overcome a shortage estimated at 500,000 units. Parliament will act on the report early in 1969.

GOVERNMENT OF CANADA

Governor-General: ROLAND MICHENER

THE CABINET

Prime Minister: PIERRE ELLIOTT TRUDEAU

Secretary of State for External Affairs: MITCHELL SHARP

Trade and Commerce and Industry: JEAN-LUC PEPIN

Transport and Housing: PAUL T. HELLYER

National Defense: LÉO-ALPHONSE CADIEUX

Finance: EDGAR J. BENSON

Public Works: ARTHUR LAING

Indian Affairs and Northern Development: JEAN CHRÉTIEN

Justice: JOHN N. TURNER

National Health and Welfare: JOHN C. MUNRO

Fisheries: JACK DAVIS

Veterans Affairs: JEAN-EUDES DUBÉ

Secretary of State: GÉRARD PELLETIER

Defense Production: DONALD JAMIESON

Privy Council President: DONALD S. MACDONALD

Labor: BRYCE STEWART MACKASEY

Leader of the Government in the Senate: PAUL J. J. MARTIN

Forestry and Rural Development: JEAN MARCHAND

National Revenue: JEAN-PIERRE CÔTÉ

Solicitor General: GEORGE McILRAITH

Energy, Mines and Resources: JOHN J. GREENE

Manpower and Immigration: ALLAN MacEACHEN

Agriculture: HORACE A. OLSON

Postmaster General: ERIC W. KIERANS

Consumer and Corporate Affairs: RONALD BASFORD

Treasury Board President: CHARLES M. DRURY

POPULATION	ARMED FORCES	DEFENSE BUDGET *	IMPORTS *	EXPORTS *	GNP PER CAPITA *
20,906,000	101,600	$1,589,000,000	$15,000,000,000	$14,000,000,000	$2,850

* US$

PROVINCE	POPULATION	CAPITAL	PREMIER	PARTY
ALBERTA	1,520,000	Edmonton	Ernest C. Manning	Social Credit
BRITISH COLUMBIA	2,020,000	Victoria	W. A. C. Bennett	Social Credit
MANITOBA	969,000	Winnipeg	Walter Weir	Conservative
NEW BRUNSWICK	624,000	Fredericton	Louis J. Robichaud	Liberal
NEWFOUNDLAND	506,000	St. John's	Joseph R. Smallwood	Liberal
NOVA SCOTIA	760,000	Halifax	George I. Smith	Conservative
ONTARIO	7,437,000	Toronto	John P. Robarts	Conservative
PRINCE EDWARD ISLAND	110,000	Charlottetown	Alexander B. Campbell	Liberal
QUEBEC	5,955,000	Quebec	Jean-Jacques Bertrand	Union Nationale
SASKATCHEWAN	960,000	Regina	W. Ross Thatcher	Liberal

TERRITORIES	POPULATION	CAPITAL	COMMISSIONER
NW TERRITORIES	30,000	Yellowknife	Stuart M. Hodgson
YUKON	15,000	Whitehorse	James Smith

One bright spot: housing starts in 1968 totaled 180,000. However, this was partially overshadowed by continuing high mortgage interest rates, which peaked at 9 per cent.

▶ CITIES

Expo 67, Canada's centennial showpiece did not suffer the same fate as other world's fairs. When it closed in October 1967, Montreal's Mayor Jean Drapeau moved to preserve the site and all but three of the buildings, the Soviet, Yugoslav and Czech pavilions. He then launched a permanent exposition, Man and His World. It attracted 44 countries as exhibitors and a crowd of 12,500,000 during its first five-month run.

Drapeau also introduced Canada's first lottery, a monthly draw for a top prize of $100,000. He solicited $2.00 donations from all over Canada in an effort to help reduce Montreal's $32,000,000 tax deficit. The Quebec Superior Court ruled the lottery illegal. But the lottery is continuing pending an appeal.

Toronto's contribution to the centennial building boom is the 54-story Toronto-Dominion Bank Centre. At 740 feet, it is the tallest building in the British Commonwealth. But it will soon be overshadowed by a new Canadian Imperial Bank of Commerce complex. This $100,000,000 project will include a tower 766 feet high.

▶ EDUCATION

Canada did not escape the worldwide wave of student unrest. From New Brunswick to British Columbia there were demonstrations and near-violence. At Vancouver's Simon Fraser University, student power forced the resignation of the university's president. Numerous other universities granted students representation on governing boards.

In Quebec 28,000 students at ten junior colleges staged Columbia-style sit-ins to back their demands for better university facilities and increased student aid by the provincial government.

▶ POLITICS

Two provincial premiers announced retirement plans in the fall. Joseph Smallwood, who led Newfoundland into Confederation with Canada in 1949, will retire after a convention is held to choose his successor in 1969.

Ernest C. Manning, leader of the Social Credit Party, retired after 25 years as premier of Alberta.

▶ FOREIGN RELATIONS

The chilly diplomatic relations with France, which began in 1967 with President Charles de Gaulle's "Free Quebec" speech in Montreal, continued in 1968. De Gaulle did not help matters when he described French Canada as an oppressed minority deserving of self-determination.

The outburst prompted Prime Minister Trudeau to accuse France of sending "a more-or-less secret agent" to Canada in the person of Philippe Rossillon. Rossillon is head of The Committee for the Defense and Expansion of the French Language. This semisecret organization reports directly to French Premier Couve de Murville.

Canada's Department of External Affairs made public a dossier on Rossillon listing his trips to Canada. The department pointed out that whenever he visited this country there appeared to be trouble. He was in Quebec City just before Queen Elizabeth's violence-marred visit in 1964. And he was in Montreal just prior to President De Gaulle's controversial visit in 1967.

Rossillon also helped set up the Gabon conference of education ministers that resulted in Canada's suspending diplomatic relations with that African country. Gabon had invited representatives of Quebec to attend this conference, thus angering the Federal Government. Rossillon also slipped into New Brunswick where he encouraged French Canadians to visit De Gaulle and even helped draft their letter to the French President.

GUY BIRCH
News Editor, *Toronto Star*

Pierre Elliott Trudeau

ON April 6, 1968, Pierre Elliott Trudeau was elected head of Canada's ruling Liberal Party. Two weeks later, on April 20, Prime Minister Lester Pearson resigned, and Trudeau became Canada's fifteenth prime minister.

Trudeau's rise to power in the Liberal Party and the Government of Canada was unique and sensational. He had joined the Liberal Party only three years before his election as party leader, switching his allegiance from the New Democratic Party. In becoming Liberal Party leader and

prime minister, Trudeau had defeated in a leadership conference some of the outstanding Liberals of the time—men who were in Pearson's Cabinet, and who had long had their eye on the possibility of succeeding him.

Moreover, Trudeau was considered a "swinger." He was 48 years old and a man of intellect. Still, he had a youthful outlook and a magnetic appeal to the young men and women of Canada. His charismatic qualities have given rise to a Canadian phenomenon called "Trudeaumania."

Pierre Trudeau was born in Montreal on October 18, 1919. Like an earlier Prime Minister, Louis St. Laurent, Trudeau is completely at ease in Canada's chief languages, French and English. His mother, Grace Elliott, was of United Empire Loyalist descent on one side, and of French-Canadian stock on the other. His father, Charles Emile Trudeau, was a lawyer who, before his death in 1935, had made a minor fortune from a chain of automotive service stations.

Pierre studied law at the University of Montreal and then was a student at Harvard, the Sorbonne and the Institute of Political Science in Paris, and at the London School of Economics.

In 1948, his formal education completed, Trudeau decided to travel across the world. He hiked through Germany and Austria, and then used false documents to enter Poland, Hungary and Yugoslavia (where he was jailed briefly because of a fake visa). He moved on to Turkey and then into war-torn Palestine. There Arabs seized him as an Israeli spy, but he was soon released.

Trudeau then traveled to Pakistan, India, Burma, Cambodia and Vietnam. He also visited China, leaving Shanghai only a month before the Communists took over the city and completed their seizure of mainland China.

After this experience, Trudeau returned home to Canada. There he joined in the struggle of a number of young intellectuals against the Union Nationale regime of Maurice Duplessis in Quebec. He helped establish *Cité Libre,* an intellectual journal of never more than a thousand circulation, which had a remarkable influence in ending the ultraconservative Union Nationale administration.

During this period Trudeau also served as an economic adviser in the secretariat of the Privy Council in Ontario. He gave up this job when he found that being a civil servant circumscribed his freedom of political action. Trudeau began to practice law in Montreal in 1952, but his involvement in politics took up much of his time. When the Quebec Liberal Party overthrew the Union Nationale in 1960, Trudeau was a supporter of the New Democratic Party. Nevertheless, he often met for discussion of current issues with leading Quebec Liberals. These men included René Lévesque (now a former Liberal and an advocate of independence for Quebec) and Maurice Lamontagne, a minister in Pearson's Cabinet.

▶ POLITICAL CAREER

From 1961 to 1965, Trudeau was a professor at the University of Montreal. Then he went actively into politics, and in Canada's 1965 national election he successfully ran as a Liberal Party candidate for the House of Commons. Thereafter, his rise in power and influence was rapid. At first parliamentary secretary to the prime minister, he became minister of justice in 1967. The stage was set for the Liberal Party leadership.

On December 14, 1967, Lester Pearson announced that he would retire as soon as the Liberals chose a new party leader and —automatically—a new prime minister. Many leading Liberals immediately announced their candidature. Among the avowed candidates were Paul Martin, Paul Hellyer, Robert Winters, Allan Mac-Eachen, John Turner and Joseph Greene —all ministers in Pearson's Cabinet. An-

---

IMPORTANT DATES IN THE LIFE OF PIERRE ELLIOTT TRUDEAU

1919	Born in Montreal, October 18.
1943	Admitted to the bar, Quebec.
1961– 1965	Professor of law, University of Montreal.
1965	Elected to House of Commons.
1967	Appointed minister of justice and attorney general of Canada, April.
1968	Elected head of Liberal Party, April 6; prime minister of Canada, April 20; Liberal Party wins in general elections, June 25.

Throughout his 1948–49 travels in Europe, Asia and, here, in the Middle East, Trudeau often adopted the dress of the country he was visiting.

other entrant was Eric Kierans, finance minister in the former Liberal Quebec government of Jean Lesage.

Trudeau was a late entrant. He had been a cabinet minister for only a few months. Yet he was nationally known for his advocacy of more-liberal laws on divorce, abortion and homosexuality. When Trudeau announced his plans to win the party leadership, he gained the backing of most of the young Liberals as well as of several of Pearson's ministers.

▶ PARTY LEADER AND PRIME MINISTER

The Liberal Party leadership convention was held in Ottawa on April 4–6, 1968. Some 2,400 delegates assembled there to choose Pearson's successor. There was all the color and excitement of an American political convention: bands and cheerleaders, throngs of pretty girls, and behind-the-scenes maneuvering. The press, radio and television gave Trudeau extended coverage. Public-opinion polls indicated that the majority of the public favored Trudeau.

But at a party convention, their votes did not count. Trudeau's rivals had worked long and hard to win delegates strength. Trudeau's convention organization was more amateurish than the others.

On April 6 the voting continued all afternoon and into the evening. Paul Martin dropped out of the contest after the first ballot. MacEachen gave up, and asked his delegates to vote for Trudeau. Finally, on the fourth ballot, Trudeau was elected leader of the Liberal Party. Two weeks later Lester Pearson resigned, and, on his recommendation, Governor-General Roland Michener called upon the new leader to form a Government. Three days later Prime Minister Trudeau dissolved Parliament and called for a general election—even though he could have remained in office for two more years. This election was held on June 25. The Liberal Party, led by Trudeau, won 155 of the 264 seats in the House of Commons, giving Canada its first majority Government since 1962.

GEORGE LONN

CONSERVATION

AND NATURE

WHEN the history of this decade is written, 1968 may well go down as the year when the United States finally decided to lay the foundation for a national policy for the environment. The importance of such a policy can hardly be overemphasized. Indeed, many people believe that violence and lawlessness in major metropolitan areas are a result, at least in part, of the noisy, dirty and frustrating conditions under which too many people live. In a variety of ways, the major conservation organizations in the United States have contributed toward building a national policy for the environment. Such organizations are the National Wildlife Federation, The Wildlife Management Institute, The National Audubon Society, The Nature Conservancy and the Conservation Foundation, to name but a few. In 1968 these organizations stepped up their efforts to encourage intelligent management of the life-sustaining resources of the earth. They also promoted the pursuit of knowledge and appreciation of these resources.

▶ ENVIRONMENTAL DETERIORATION

About 75 per cent of the population of the United States is crowded into one per cent of the land. The problems and pressures that have resulted from this imbalance, such as the deterioration of the environment, have given the United States a challenge that it has not before faced.

Many sections of society have called for action to reduce or eliminate the contamination of the environment. The Department of the Interior, for example, entitled its 1968 yearbook *Man—An Endangered Species?*. The United States Chamber of Commerce issued a pamphlet entitled *The Need to Manage Our Environment*. The National Wildlife Federation called environmental contamination the most critical problem of the time. And many concerned congressmen proposed legislation relating to water- and air-pollution control, reclamation of mined areas and indiscriminate use of chemical pesticides.

Responding to these demands, Senator Henry M. Jackson (Washington) and Congressman George P. Miller (California) called a joint House-Senate colloquium in July to discuss a national policy for the environment. Several members of Congress, cabinet members, scientists and conservationists addressed the meeting. The consensus was that, in the long run, man cannot avoid paying the costs of using, or misusing, the environment.

The United States already has deferred payment of costs of water-pollution control. A dying Lake Erie is one among many sad and unnecessary results of this shortsightedness. Delayed control over stripmining has exacted payment in ravaged countrysides. Man-made mountains of junk, skeins of cables and utility poles, and fogs of polluted air have demanded payment through losses of public amenities.

Environmental pollution and other aspects of conservation were of particular concern to the political candidates in the 1968 election year. Both major political parties adopted platform planks that included references to water- and air-pollution control, preservation of parks and natural areas, and agriculture. The Democrats featured conservation to an important extent. One of the major factors that led to the nomination of Senator Edmund Muskie (Maine) as the Democratic vice-presidential candidate was his leadership in air- and water-pollution control and other urban problems. Presidential candidate Hubert Humphrey also laid heavy stress on his record in the Senate with respect to wilderness preservation, water-pollution control and youth conservation-corps projects.

Water-Pollution Control

In 1968, Secretary of the Interior Stewart L. Udall announced a policy of "antidegradation" with respect to Federal approval of state standards of water quality. This policy establishes three basic require-

ments. First, existing water quality cannot be reduced. Second, no waters shall be used solely or principally as waste carriers. Third, all wastes must receive the best practicable treatment or control before being discharged into interstate waters. The purpose of this policy is to designate the existing quality of water as the "quality floor" below which it will not be allowed to go. If properly carried out this policy can have an important positive bearing on the locations of industries in various parts of the United States.

In Congress, however, less than one third of the money previously authorized for Federal grants for water-pollution control was appropriated in 1968. This cutback severely hampered the construction of municipal waste-treatment plants.

Man-made mountains of junk, such as this heap of wrecked automobiles, have "polluted" the American environment.

WATER AND POWER DEVELOPMENT

In 1968 the Federal Power Commission continued to take testimony on the effects of a proposed dam on the Middle Snake River in Idaho and Oregon. In 1967 the Supreme Court had canceled Federal Power Commission approval for construction of the High Mountain Sheep Dam. The court had also remanded the case to the FPC for further study on whether any dam should be built. Meanwhile, the Department of the Interior recommended a new site eight miles upstream. However, testimony in late 1968 by conservation agencies and organizations reflected a growing feeling that potential losses to fisheries and other wildlife as well as to recreation should preclude the construction of any dam.

Congress approved a Central Arizona Project in a form that will bring Colorado River water to the interior of Arizona. The bill also authorizes dam projects in the Upper Colorado River area. Authorization for controversial dams in the Grand Canyon area was removed from the bill. But other difficulties remained. These centered on studies on the possibility of importing water to the arid Southwest, probably from the Pacific Northwest. Final decisions on water importation into this area are to be deferred for at least ten years.

NATIONAL PARKS AND RECREATIONAL AREAS

Through a burst of activity late in 1968, Congress resolved several long-standing national-park and recreation-area projects.

Additional money was provided for the Land and Water Conservation Fund. This fund is used to finance state outdoor recreational programs. It is also used to acquire Federal installations such as national parks and monuments, seashores, lakeshores, recreation areas within national forests, and facilities for protecting endangered species of wildlife. Congress recognized that the fund, which had been providing about $115,000,000 a year, was inadequate to finance both of these major efforts. It therefore authorized up to $200,000,000 a year for the next five years.

A nationwide system of scenic trails was established by Congress. The system will be initiated with the magnificent Appalachian Trail. Other trails under consideration were the Continental Divide Trail and the Pacific Coast Trails in the West, and the Potomac Heritage Trail in the East. Among those to be studied for future designation as scenic trails are the Lewis and Clark Trail, the Chisholm Trail, the Natchez Trail, the North Country Trail, the Oregon Trail, the Santa Fe Trail, the Long Trail, the Mormon Trail and several Gold Rush trails in Alaska.

The 58,000-acre Redwood National Park in California was finally established in

"Welcome aboard our annual migratory flight north. We'll be flying in our usual vee formation at an altitude of approximately 5,000 feet. We'll have scattered clouds at 4,000 feet. Visibility 11 miles with favorable tailwinds at 22 miles per hour. The temperature in Boston is 78 and it's sunny."

1968. It will cost $92,000,000. Provision was made for incorporating three outstanding state parks in this new national park.

Congress also registered important progress on other landmark legislation, including the establishment of a nationwide system of scenic rivers; the establishment of the North Cascades National Park (Washington), the Flaming Gorge National Recreation Area (Utah and Wyoming) and Apostle Islands National Lakeshore (Wisconsin).

▶ **FEDERAL LAND USE**

During 1968 the Agriculture and Interior departments considered several basic decisions regarding the use of Federal lands for grazing by private stockmen. For years the two agencies have allowed grazing at prices far lower than comparable private lands would bring in rental fees. This practice, in effect a subsidy, has been used to build the values of individual ranches. Conservationists asked that a uniform basis be used by all Federal agencies in setting fees. These fees would be based on the value of the use of the public land to the user. Livestock interests resisted these changes.

A newly hatched whooping crane at the Patuxent Wildlife Research Center in Maryland.

▶ HIGHWAYS

Secretary of the Interior Udall vetoed a proposal to build a road across the Great Smoky Mountains National Park to connect Tennessee and North Carolina. This road would have "invaded" important areas of wilderness in the park.

Two controversial highway proposals were decided by Secretary of Agriculture Orville Freeman in 1968. Right-of-way agreements necessary for the construction of a controversial highway into the Mineral King complex of the Sequoia National Park in California were approved. Some conservationists had fought against this recreational development because it posed a threat to natural resources. In another decision, Secretary Freeman denied a Colorado Department of Highways request for permission to route Interstate 70 through the Gore Range-Eagle Nest Primitive Area. The proposed route would have involved construction through national-forest wilderness.

Probably the biggest conservation setback occurred when Congress passed the Federal Aid Highway Act of 1968. Provisions in this act weaken the Highway Beautification Program by diluting billboard-removal provisions in the present law. In addition, the protection of parks, natural areas and wildlife refuges from highway construction was weakened.

▶ FISH AND WILDLIFE

Several important developments occurred in 1968 in the fields of fish and wildlife management. The growth of coho salmon and lake trout in the Great Lakes continued to be spectacular. Outstanding catches were made. However, the overpopulation of the Great Lakes by alewives now is a major problem.

For the second year, whooping-crane eggs were successfully collected and flown to the Bureau of Sport Fisheries and Wildlife's Patuxent (Maryland) Laboratory for hatching. In another area, the Army Corps of Engineers made outstanding progress in developing methods for transporting migrant salmon around dams in the Columbia and Snake River systems.

There were very poor summer water conditions in many parts of the prairie pothole country in Canada and the United States. This resulted in fewer ducks migrating down the four major continental flyways in the fall of 1968. In an attempt to assure the return of ample numbers of breeder birds in the spring of 1969, regulations were imposed on hunters.

Estuarine areas are valued as nursery grounds for fish and shellfish, as well as for waterfowl and furbearers. Recognizing this, Congress in 1968 authorized a two-year program of research on the need to protect, conserve and restore these regions. Estuaries on all coasts of the United States are now being drained, filled or otherwise damaged by water pollution and dredging.

▶ INTERNATIONAL DEVELOPMENTS

In 1968 there were several important conservation efforts on an international scale. Most important among these were the meetings held and the regulations adopted to preserve endangered species of wildlife.

A meeting held near Geneva, Switzerland, brought together a number of scientists interested in the preservation of the polar bear. All polar countries except the Soviet Union were represented.

The United States and Japan began discussing plans for a meeting which may lead to the establishment of a migratory-bird treaty similar to the one in effect between the United States and Canada and Mexico.

In accordance with recommendations of the International Whaling Commission, the United States took steps to tighten existing regulations on the taking of whales.

And in an unusual expression of international goodwill, the Bureau of Sport Fisheries and Wildlife gave the National Park Service of Portugal a pair of trumpeter swans.

DONALD J. ZINN
University of Rhode Island

ANTS AND BEES

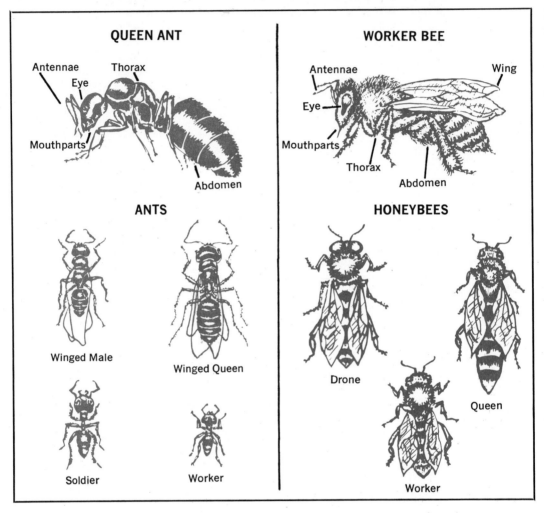

QUEEN ANT

Antennae · Eye · Thorax · Mouthparts · Abdomen

WORKER BEE

Antennae · Eye · Mouthparts · Thorax · Wing · Abdomen

ANTS

Winged Male · Winged Queen · Soldier · Worker

HONEYBEES

Drone · Queen · Worker

WHEN ants are mentioned, we immediately think of those persistent, uninvited guests in our homes or at our picnics. The name bee simply brings to mind the familiar honeybee. However, the ant and the bee world is not that simple. It comprises thousands of distinct species, most of which are noticed only by scientists.

The ways of life in this vast array of species are tremendously varied. The contrast between primitive ants and solitary bees, at one extreme, and the complex agricultural ants and honeybees, at the other, is as great as the contrast between the life of a simple Kalahari Bushman and a person living in some great urban center.

▶ **LIFE IN THE BEEHIVE AND ANT NEST**

In spite of great diversity, all ants and bees share the basic life history of most insects: an egg stage, several larval stages, (*continued on page 149*)

ANTS

ANT NESTS

LEAF CUTTER ANTS (right), also called parasol ants, sometimes form long processions as they carry bits of leaves to their underground nest. The ants use their sharp mouthparts to cut the leaves (lower right), and large colonies have been known to defoliate entire trees and shrubs.

E. S. ROSS

A TAILOR ANT NEST (below) consists of leaves fastened by a type of silk secreted by the ant larvae. Such nests are often built high in trees, sometimes 100 feet or more above the forest floor.

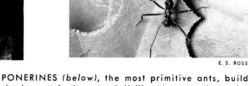

E. S. ROSS

E. S. ROSS

AN ARMY ANT BIVOUAC (below) is made up of workers who interlock their legs to form a living curtain surrounding the queen and her brood.

PONERINES (below), the most primitive ants, build simple nests in the ground. Unlike other ants, the worker ponerines, as well as the queen, sometimes lay eggs.

E. S. ROSS

CARPENTER ANTS (below) usually nest in rotting tree stumps and logs, chewing tunnels through the wood. Sometimes they invade a healthy tree or the wooden framework of a house.

E. S. ROSS

RUDOLF FREUND

LIFE IN A *FORMICA* ANT NEST

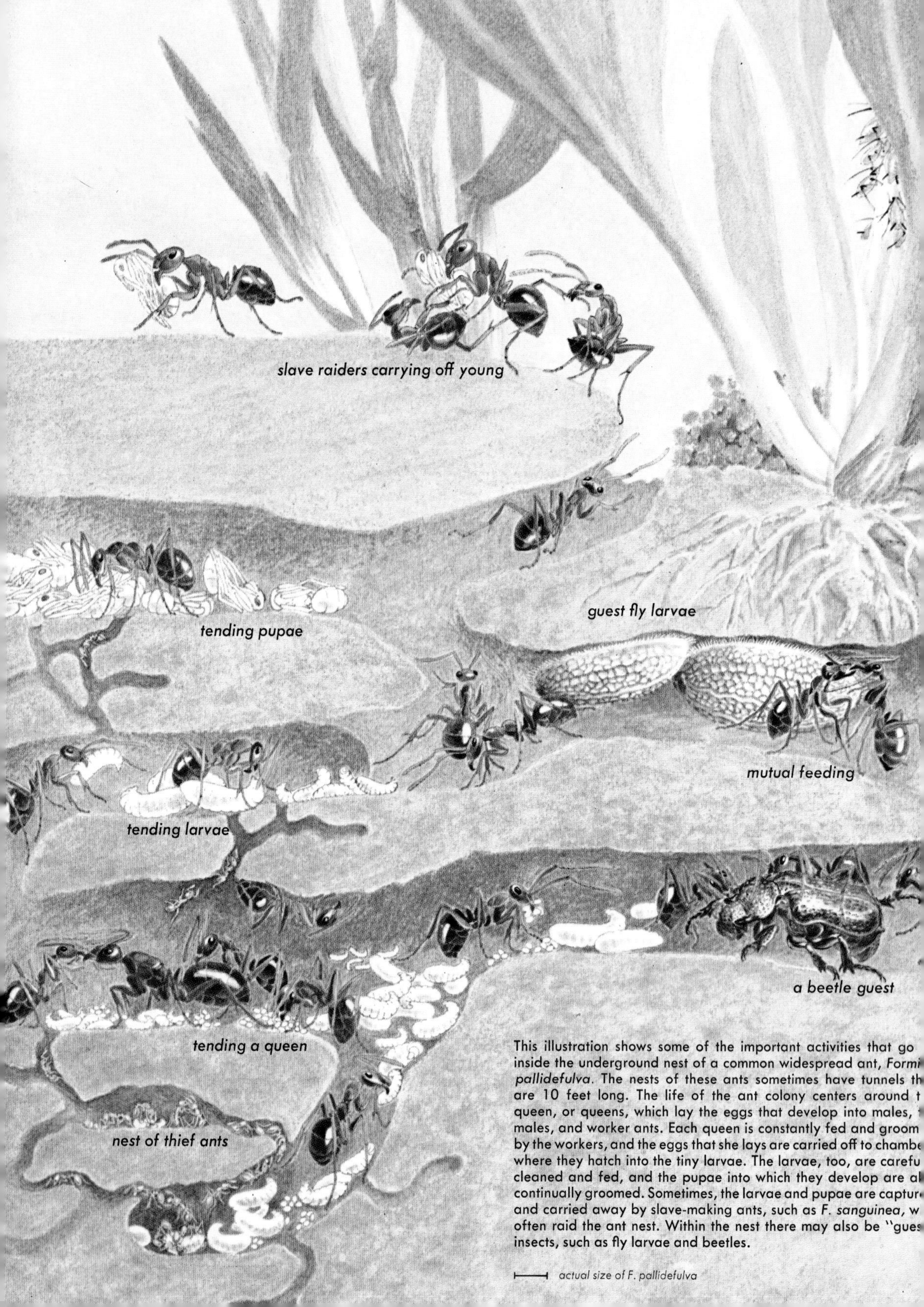

slave raiders carrying off young

tending pupae

guest fly larvae

mutual feeding

tending larvae

a beetle guest

tending a queen

nest of thief ants

This illustration shows some of the important activities that go inside the underground nest of a common widespread ant, *Formi pallidefulva*. The nests of these ants sometimes have tunnels th are 10 feet long. The life of the ant colony centers around t queen, or queens, which lay the eggs that develop into males, males, and worker ants. Each queen is constantly fed and groom by the workers, and the eggs that she lays are carried off to chambe where they hatch into the tiny larvae. The larvae, too, are carefu cleaned and fed, and the pupae into which they develop are al continually groomed. Sometimes, the larvae and pupae are captur and carried away by slave-making ants, such as *F. sanguinea*, w often raid the ant nest. Within the nest there may also be "gues insects, such as fly larvae and beetles.

⊢———⊣ actual size of F. pallidefulva

gathering honeydew from aphids

bringing in food

digging new tunnels

resting and grooming

The workers spend much of their time in housekeeping activities. Old tunnels must be maintained and new ones must be dug. Wastes must be removed along with any trace of mold or decay. The workers also clean and groom each other, and a worker with a crop full of liquid food feeds drops of it to many others. Foraging ants are constantly bringing food into the nest and these ants feed chiefly on insects and other invertebrate animals. However, the sweet honeydew se-creted by many types of insects, including aphids, scale insects, and even some butterfly larvae, is also a highly relished food. Some-times, workers climb high in trees and shrubs to find honeydew pro-ducers. The workers are also always ready to defend the colony against intruders, and if the colony is disturbed, they move the young to the safety of deeper tunnels.

ILLUSTRATION BY ARABELLE WHEATLEY

OTHER FORMICINE ANTS

A *Formica fusca* ant (right) feeds an obligatory slave-maker, *Polyergus*, who can no longer feed herself.

An allegheny mound ant, *F. exsectoides*, helps a callow emerge from its cocoon. Only some formicine ants build cocoons.

A queen carpenter ant, *Camponotus*, tends her first brood inside a cavity she has made in a tree.

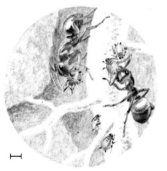

The cornfield ant, *Lasius*, tends root aphids for their sweet honeydew.

DR. THOMAS EISNER

GATHERING AND STORING FOOD

HONEY ANT REPLETES (left) are workers whose swollen abdomens store honeydew. Repletes cannot walk but must remain suspended from the ceiling of their underground nest.

E. S. ROSS

THE HARVESTER ANT (above) gathers seeds and stores them in its underground nest. If the seeds get wet and start to sprout, they are promptly discarded.

E. S. ROSS

CARNIVOROUS ANTS feed on many animals, even other ants. (Above) Army ants attack a leaf cutter soldier. (Below) Formicine ants work together to drag a dead worm snake into their underground nest.

E. S. ROSS

CATTLE-TENDING ANTS obtain honeydew by cultivating aphids (above), leaf-hoppers (below), and other insects that secrete the sweet liquid.

E. S. ROSS

E. S. ROSS

BEES

SOME COMMON KINDS OF BEES

EDWARD S. ROSS

Honeybee

EDWARD S. ROSS

Leaf-cutter bee

Alkali bee
EDWARD S. ROSS

EDWARD S. ROSS

Bumblebee

(Above) Parasitic bee
EDWARD S. ROSS

(Below) Large carpenter bee

Euglossa bee

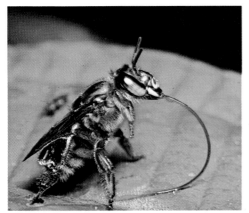

EDWARD S. ROSS

ALEXANDER B. KLOTS

145

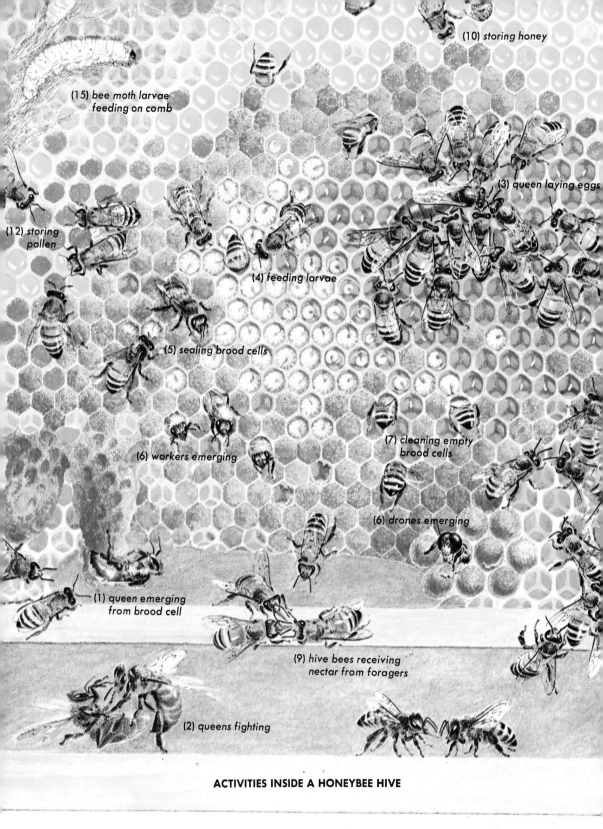

(10) *storing honey*

(15) *bee moth larvae feeding on comb*

(3) *queen laying eggs*

(12) *storing pollen*

(4) *feeding larvae*

(5) *sealing brood cells*

(7) *cleaning empty brood cells*

(6) *workers emerging*

(6) *drones emerging*

(1) *queen emerging from brood cell*

(9) *hive bees receiving nectar from foragers*

(2) *queens fighting*

ACTIVITIES INSIDE A HONEYBEE HIVE

Life Cycle: The colony's largest member is the queen, who, after emerging (1) and perhaps killing a rival queen (2), deposits her eggs in empty brood cells (3). Larvae that hatch are fed by workers (4), who cap the cells with beeswax before the larvae pupate (5). The adults emerge (6) and the cells are cleaned (7) before new eggs are laid. **Gathering and Storing Food:** Scout bees indicate a new food source to foragers

(11) capping honey cells

(8) scout performing honey dance

(16) building new comb cells

(14) ejecting drones

(13) fanning and guarding the hive entrance

ILLUSTRATION BY ARABELLE WHEATLEY

by performing a "honey dance" (8). Foragers from the field transfer nectar to hive bees (9), who convert it into honey and store it in cells (10) that are then capped with wax (11). Field bees store pollen (12). **Other Activities:** Workers ventilate the hive by fanning their wings (13), and others eject useless drones (14). Parasitic bee-moth larvae feed on the comb (15), but new comb cells are quickly built (16).

ACTIVITIES OUTSIDE THE NEST

(Left) Eucerine bees, like many other solitary bees, spend the night clinging to a leaf or stem by their mouthparts. Sometimes, they come back to the same plant night after night.

EDWARD S. ROSS

(Below) Burrowing bees, as well as many other types of bees, are covered with feathery hairs that are well adapted for collecting pollen. The pollen, together with some flower nectar, is then placed inside individual nest, or brood, cells where it later serves as food for the young larvae.

(Below) A leaf-cutter bee uses its scissorlike mouthparts for cutting off a strip of leaf. The rolled-up leaf strip will then be used for lining the leaf-cutter's underground nest.

EDWARD S. ROSS

ALEXANDER B. KLOTS

WALTER DAWN

(Right) A honeybee that has been sucking nectar from a zinnia pauses for a few moments to clean off its mouthparts.

a resting, or pupal, stage and the adult stage.

Most insects never see their offspring. Their eggs are just laid in a place where the hatched larvae can find food. From then on they shift for themselves, and only a few survive to become adults. In the case of ants and bees, however, the young are sheltered from most hazards in hives or burrows or nests built by the adults.

Not all bee nests have a queen. Primitive female bees produce their own eggs and are solely responsible for the care of the young. But in all ant nests and in the hives of socially advanced bees, eggs are laid only by a queen. Most of the resultant larvae are destined to become "workers." These are sexually underdeveloped females incapable of producing eggs. However, each worker has a normal mother instinct and goes about such tasks as nest building, nest defense and food gathering. The workers also take care of their mother's offspring as though they were their own.

An ant or bee nest may be likened to an imaginary human household in which a very prolific mother produces one baby after another but doesn't have to care for them. Many of these babies grow up as stay-at-home spinster daughters selflessly devoting their lives to the care and feeding of a steady production of younger sisters and a few brothers.

▶ STARTING A NEW NEST

Ant and honeybee queens may live for a number of years. In addition, many workers of the prior year survive the winter. Thus the next year's economy starts off with a strong labor force.

Each year, an ant nest produces a number of fully sexed males and females. Under special climatic conditions, these ants take a mating flight and pair off. The queen ants then establish new colonies. With honeybees, however, a new colony starts from a swarm of bees led off from the parent hive by the old queen. Her role in the original hive is assumed by one of her daughter queens.

▶ HOW ANTS GATHER FOOD

Ants are really special kinds of wasps which have flourished over the ages because of social habits. By dividing up different jobs, and producing offspring by assembly-line methods, a great number of cooperating individuals accumulate. The key to such cooperation is the ants' practice of exchanging food from mouth to mouth.

Certain ants of the nest forage for food and store it in their crop, or "social stomach." On returning to the nest, the forager passes portions on to the nest workers and larvae. In return for such attention, the worker receives a delectable body secretion exuded by the ant larvae.

The food habits of ants are very diverse. They eat such things as insects, sweets exuded by plants, aphids and scale insects. They also eat the fungus that grows on a rotting leaf compost gathered by the ants. Some ants even capture slaves to gather this compost and to perform other tasks around the nest.

▶ HOW BEES GATHER FOOD

Bees evolved from a higher branch of the wasp family. The essential difference between wasps and bees lies in their choice of food. Almost all wasps are carnivorous: they eat many types of insects. In contrast, bees only gather nectar and pollen for their larvae. For this reason, the bodies of bees are densely covered with hairs: the whole insect functions as a brush for gathering pollen. The only "hairless" bees are parasites. Instead of gathering their own food stores, these bees lay their eggs in the fully provisioned nests of other bees.

Because of their interest in flowers, bees are very important in pollination. The attractiveness of flowers is largely an advertisement to lure bees. Man could perhaps survive without ants, but his world would have far less floral beauty and fewer crops if there were no bees.

EDWARD S. ROSS
Curator, Department of Entomology
California Academy of Sciences

ECONOMY

U.S.A.
$11.4 BILLION

BELGIUM·GREAT BRITAIN
ITALY·NETHERLANDS
SWITZERLAND
WEST GERMANY
$13.6 BILLION

DOLLARS IN FOREIGN

GOLD POOL

ANNUAL
PRODUCTION
$1.5 BILLION

LONDON MARKET

At the end of 1967 and during 1968 the United States and its Western allies suffered three grave monetary crises. In November 1967, economic pressures forced the British to devalue the pound. A year later the French franc was almost devalued. But the gold crisis of March 1968 was by far the gravest crisis of the three. This is because world trade depends upon the stability and value of the U.S. dollar; devaluation of the dollar would cause worldwide financial chaos. Behind this crisis was U.S. policy of keeping the price of gold at $35 an ounce. To increase the price of gold would be the same as devaluing the dollar. In the past two decades Americans have spent billions of dollars in other countries. They have given away and lent many billions more. Foreigners, on the other hand, have spent, lent or invested much less money in the U.S. This deficit in the U.S. international balance of payments kept piling up: $35,700,000,000 worth of American money was in the hands of foreigners in 1968. If they cashed in their dollars, there would not be

THE year 1968 was a time of troubles for the United States dollar. Inflation, reflected by the prices people pay, rose at the highest rate since Korean war days. An even more serious development was the loss of confidence in the dollar throughout the world. It resulted in a gold crisis that threatened the whole world money system. However, as the year progressed, confidence in the dollar was largely restored. And United States business and industry advanced to new heights.

The Government in Washington made historic decisions to deal with the ailing U.S. dollar and with the national economic problems related to it. This was done against a background of political and social upheaval as dramatic as any the nation has experienced.

The year opened with a special message by President Lyndon B. Johnson aimed at meeting the critical deficit in the United States' balance of international payments. This deficit was worrying financial experts all over the world. The President's program called for increased Federal taxes and a hold-down on government expenditures. It also called for price and wage restraint. The President ordered a reduction in the flow of money American business was investing in foreign operations. He also proposed restrictions on spending abroad by American tourists, the encouragement of foreign tourism and investment to bring money into the United States, and increased United States exports.

To understand the need for such a sweeping program, it is necessary to take a glimpse at the major economic developments which had been taking place in the world prior to 1968.

▶ BALANCE-OF-PAYMENTS DEFICIT: THE ROOTS

Since the end of World War II the United States has given billions of dollars in aid to restore war-torn Europe and to help underdeveloped countries strengthen their economies. As this money was poured into foreign lands, the dollar balances of these countries grew. American business investment overseas rose too. So both Government and private capital flowed out of the United States. The United States in

enough gold to make payment. Indeed before the peak of the gold crisis the U.S. only had reserves of $11,400,000,000. Thus, as people began to worry about the stability of the dollar, speculators and investors began to trade them in for gold. But the U.S. stood firm, as did its six allies in the London gold pool. To ease pressure on the dollar, the gold-pool nations set up a two-tier system which keeps the official price of gold at $35 an ounce, but which allows the open-market price to fluctuate.

effect became the bank for the world. As it kept increasing its liabilities, U.S. gold reserves eventually began to fall. This is because under the world monetary setup, the United States is pledged to convert dollars into gold, if a foreigner wants gold. Gold really is the only universally acceptable international money. And it is the anchor for the system of fixed foreign-exchange rates that has been responsible for so much of the world's economic trade and growth since World War II.

Thus the United States suffered from a deficit in its balance of payments. That is, more dollars were going abroad than were returning. At the same time, the national budget was facing large deficits. For the fiscal year 1968, the budget deficit was more than $25,000,000,000. This was the largest deficit since World War II. New and expensive domestic social and welfare programs and the cost of the Vietnam war created the huge deficit.

Federal deficits had to be met with huge borrowings. This put heavy pressure on the money markets. So interest rates on the borrowing rose sharply.

In January 1967, President Johnson had called for increased taxes to meet the revenue needs. In August 1967 he made a specific request for a 10 per cent surcharge on income taxes. For the rest of 1967, Congress was locked in debate over the proposed surtax increase.

▶ THE GOLD CRISIS

In November of 1967, Great Britain had devalued the pound sterling, in the hope of improving its trade position. This, along with deficits the United States had been running in its international-payments balance, brought gold markets under heavy pressure from speculators. They thought the United States would have to devalue the dollar. Such a move would raise the price of gold from its rate of $35 an ounce, and make money for anybody holding gold.

As long as confidence in the dollar was high, foreign banks and foreign investors were willing to keep large reserves of dollars. But they saw persistent deficits. They saw growing inflation. They saw increasing demands on the dollar. And they were afraid that United States policy makers would not make the tough decisions necessary to guard the dollar's soundness. As a result, they wanted gold for their greenbacks.

All this was why the United States had to take some drastic action to reassure the world that the dollar was really as good as gold. In his New Year's Day message, 1968, President Johnson declared that the need to bring the balance of payments into equilibrium "is a national and international responsibility of the highest priority." The President also assured the world that "The dollar will remain convertible into gold at $35 an ounce, and our full gold stock will back that commitment."

Still the world had its doubts. It wasn't that foreigners thought the United States was going broke. Economically it is the richest nation on earth. But foreign investors, bankers and speculators still weren't sure Americans had the determination to put their fiscal house in order. They knew too that foreign-held dollars exceeded U.S. gold reserve by billions of dollars. So the rush on gold persisted. A wave of speculative buying mounted. Emergency steps became necessary.

First, Congress approved a measure to remove the 25 per cent requirement of gold backing on the nation's currency. This freed more than $10,000,000,000 of the country's gold stock for use to meet the rush on gold by foreigners.

Then, the United States, together with six other leading Western nations, established what was called the two-tier price system for gold. Under this system, the $35-an-ounce gold price would be maintained for all intergovernmental transactions, but the free-market price for individual buyers would be allowed to fluctuate according to supply and demand.

Next, one of the most decisive moves in history to free the world of its dependence on gold was taken in Stockholm, Sweden, in March. The major financial powers of the West met and decided to set up what was called Special Drawing Rights—a kind of paper gold—in the International Monetary Fund. These Special Drawing Rights would supplement gold. They could be used in financing world trade. Congress approved the move in June.

The gold crisis was ended at least for the time being. But it warned the United States Government policy makers that broader domestic decisions were needed to show the world that the United States could manage its fiscal and economic affairs wisely.

It was ironic that the French, who led the way in putting pressure on the American dollar and the British pound early in the year, suffered their own grave monetary problems in the fall. It was even more ironic that the United States and Great Britain were among those who went to the aid of the battered French franc. Because of growing inflation caused in part by

Gold was officially valued at $20.67 per fine ounce through 1933. The price was then raised to $35 per ounce. On January 1, 1968, the U.S. gold stock totaled $12,003,000,000. By the end of March, as a result of the gold crisis, the U.S. gold stock was down to $10,703,000,000.

U.S. GOLD STOCK

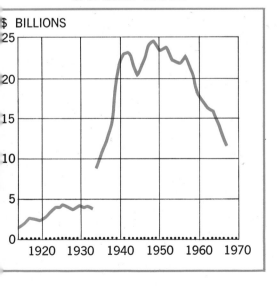

Congressman Wilbur Mills, chairman of the House Ways and Means Committee, insisted that a cut in Federal spending accompany President Johnson's 10 per cent tax surcharge.

higher wages won by French workers during the nationwide strikes in May, and because of the great strength of the West German mark, speculators began to trade in their francs for marks. In a short period of time, French reserves of gold and United States dollars declined by almost $3,000,-000,000. Only a $2,000,000,000 loan by Western banks and a severe austerity program imposed by French President Charles de Gaulle saved the franc from devaluation. West Germany, with its strong monetary system, helped by trying to decrease German exports to France.

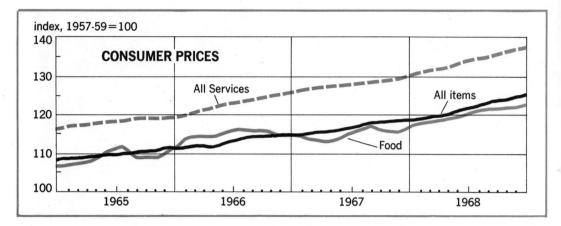

index, 1957-59 = 100

CONSUMER PRICES

All Services

All items

Food

1965   1966   1967   1968

Consumer prices reached an all-time high in 1968.

▶ **FIGHTING INFLATION**

Renewed pressure was put on Congress to approve the tax surcharge. Powerful lawmakers, led by Chairman Wilbur Mills of the tax-writing House Ways and Means Committee, insisted that the President's proposal for a tax surcharge must be accompanied by a substantial cutback in Federal spending.

Income-Tax Surcharge

Finally the administration agreed. In late June the Revenue and Expenditure Control Act of 1968 was passed. The law imposed a 10 per cent surtax on individuals and corporations and accelerated the tax payments by corporations. The new law also extended the Federal excise-tax rate on automobiles and restored the excise tax on telephone service. It called for a reduction in Federal expenditures of $6,000,000,000 during fiscal year 1969. And it limited the filling of vacancies in government-employee jobs.

When the law was passed, it was considered an act of political courage in an election year. Moreover, it was thought that it would brake the business boom and reduce the budget deficit. It was thought also that the tax hike would bring down interest rates, fight inflation, and show foreigners that the United States could practice fiscal restraint.

Discount Rates Increased

Before the tax increase was passed, the Federal Reserve Board had taken steps to try to brake the inflationary economy. The Federal Reserve Board runs the monetary affairs of the country and sets the money supply. It had jacked up the discount rate in successive moves to 5½ per cent. This is the rate member commercial banks have to pay to borrow funds from the Federal Reserve System. The discount rate placed upward pressure on commercial-bank interest rates, and it makes borrowing much more expensive.

Enactment of the tax surcharge took some of the pressure off interest rates, which had risen to the highest level since commercial banks agreed to a uniform standard in setting rates in the 1930's. It meant a reduction in Federal financing requirements. But in midyear it became increasingly apparent that the tax rise-spending cut had done little to cool the economy. Inflation hung on. And the economy seemed to move ahead through summer and fall at nearly the same pace as it had during the booming first half of the year.

As a result, the Federal Reserve Board, which had lowered the discount rate to 5¼ per cent in August, again increased it to 5½ per cent. This led the major banks to increase their interest rates on business

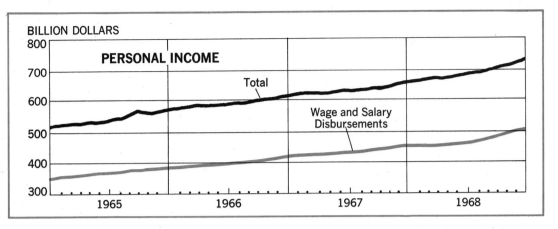

BILLION DOLLARS

PERSONAL INCOME

Total

Wage and Salary Disbursements

800
700
600
500
400
300

1965 1966 1967 1968

With almost full employment, personal income was up in 1968.

loans to 6¾ per cent. It was expected that these increases would force up rates on home mortgages.

▶ THE SPENDING SPREE

There were several reasons for the booming economy. One major reason was consumer spending. Employment was high and unemployment was about as low as it could get. Incomes were high. New labor contracts assured wage boosts of 6 to 8 per cent. Federal Government employees got a sizable pay raise. Added to this were increases in social-security benefits and in the Federal minimum wage, which ripples up through the economy making other wages rise. Personal income was rising at the strong rate of about $5,000,000,000 a month. Thus it took only a couple of months to wipe out the effect of the income surtax on individuals.

Also in the first half of 1968 people were saving at a record pace. Many citizens merely cut back to levels nearer their usual saving rate. Trimming back to normal saving rates translated into more spending. This also tended to offset the tax increase.

The new-car models sold well. Auto sales hit a new record in 1968 and were a factor in the continuing economic boom.

Housing Boom and Record Auto Sales

Demand for new housing and autos, in particular, kept the economy racing along through the year. The amount of increase in installment debt during the summer marked the biggest jump in a generation. The cost of labor and construction materials forced up the price tag on new homes. And there were high interest rates on mortgages. Nevertheless, housing starts rose to about 1,500,000 in 1968.

A real housing boom began in 1968. Real-estate activity had been sluggish for a long span, so a housing spur was overdue. Americans had been moving from rural areas to the cities at the rate of about 800,-000 a year. At the same time, urban-renewal programs, which had cleared blighted and congested areas in the cities, had reduced the supply of urban housing. Housing-vacancies rates were running at the lowest rate in about a decade. Also, marriages ran high. The number of weddings approached 2,000,000 a year.

Auto sales hit a new record in 1968. The old mark was 9,300,000 cars in 1965. The 1968 sales were propelled partly by the rush of foreign-cars imports, partly by sports-car styling and availability of autos. (The steel-strike threat was resolved in the summer with a new three-year contract.)

▶ THE ECONOMY AT YEAR'S END

In spite of the dizzy buying pace through most of 1968, the fiscal reins began to take hold late in the year. The economy slowed from a gallop to a brisk trot. Still the year saw the gross national product, the total output of goods and service, reach about $860,000,000,000, compared to about $785,000,000,000 in 1967.

The balance of international payments still was in the red at the end of 1968. American imports had surged. This was partly because of foreign-car entries, the long copper strike, and steel buying as a hedge against the strike threat. The sharp rise in imports offset a gain of $1,000,000,-000 as a result of the restrictions on foreign investment by American businesses.

▶ NEW LAWS

Several new laws besides the Revenue and Expenditure Control Act had significance for business and industry in 1968. Congress passed the so-called truth-in-lending bill, which had been in the legislative mill for several years. Under this law, lenders and retail creditors must disclose in writing the amount of finance charges on credit purchases both in dollars and in terms of annual percentage rate.

Congress also put through laws to ensure greater safety for natural-gas pipelines, to set up a system of Federal inspection of poultry and to guard against radiation from appliances.

Congress passed the most far-reaching housing bill in twenty years with new programs to help the poor buy their own homes. It also enacted an open-housing bill to bar racial discrimination in the sale or rental of housing.

▶ THE STOCK MARKET

The stock markets in 1968 were swamped with the record volume of shares bought and sold. Neither the New York Stock Exchange nor the American Stock Exchange had expected the volume of transactions to reach such peaks until the 1970's. Through most of the year the exchanges had to close down one day a week in order to keep up with the flood of paper work. Stock indexes hit record highs. Some new issues made spectacular gains. Among these were computer and technologically oriented companies.

1968 was also a year in which institutional buyers—insurance companies, pension funds and mutual funds—were heavy purchasers of shares.

Foreign investors, showing their faith in American capitalism as well as their concern over student riots in France and the Soviet invasion of Czechoslovakia, bought United States shares at a frantic rate, much higher than in prior years.

TAIT TRUSSELL
Managing Editor
Nation's Business

Betty Furness, President Johnson's special assistant for consumer affairs, explains progress being made in passing legislation to aid consumers.

Protecting the Consumer

THE dictionary defines a consumer as "one that consumes; specifically: one that utilizes economic goods." A consumer, then, is anyone who buys, borrows or uses. It is anyone who buys a loaf of bread or turns on an electric light. Indeed it might be said that every single person on earth is a consumer.

▶ **EARLY HISTORY OF CONSUMER PROTECTION**

The industrial revolution began in England in the middle of the eighteenth cen-

tury. It created problems not known to any other age in history. It also resulted in movements and legislation to protect the consumer. The consumer movement began in England in 1844 when 28 factory workers opened the Rochdale Cooperative. These workers were concerned about the very high price of food, so they began a movement to buy their own food. By pooling their money together, they were able to increase their purchasing power and to buy their food at lower prices. This idea of cooperative buying and of consumer protection soon spread across the Atlantic to the United States. Today several million Americans are active in the cooperative movement.

▶THE UNITED STATES

In the late nineteenth century in the United States, new methods of production and swifter means of transportation created many problems for the people of the growing land. These problems led to the enactment of the Postal Fraud Act of 1872, the Interstate Commerce Act of 1887 and the Sherman Antitrust Act of 1890. These acts were just the beginning. A tidal wave of reform, aimed at protecting consumers, was ushered in with Theodore Roosevelt in the early part of the twentieth century.

Theodore Roosevelt

It is to Theodore Roosevelt's administration that we owe the Pure Food and Drug Act of 1906 (upon which much subsequent legislation was built) and the Meat Inspection Act of the same year. It is to

him that we owe the first conservation program.

Woodrow Wilson

The administration of Woodrow Wilson gave the American people the Federal Trade Commission Act and the Clayton Antitrust Act of 1914. These early acts were known as reform legislation. But today we think of them as consumer legislation.

Throughout the 1920's, little new legislation was passed. But with the great depression of the 1930's, reformist legislation began again to be passed, not the least of which was social-security legislation.

Franklin D. Roosevelt

In 1933, President Franklin D. Roosevelt established the first consumer office in the Department of Agriculture. This was followed by consumer offices in other departments. During World War II and the Korean war, other such offices and committees were created to deal with wartime consumer problems. With the return to peace, these special offices and committees

---

SEVENTEEN CONSUMER BILLS ENACTED BY THE 88TH, 89TH, AND 90TH CONGRESSES

Truth-in-Securities (Enacted as Securities Exchange Act Amendment)	Enacted 1964
Federal Insecticide, Fungicide and Rodenticide Acts Amendments	Enacted 1964
Housing and Urban Development Act of 1965	Enacted 1965
Federal Hazardous Substances Act Amendments (Enacted as Child Safety Act Amendments)	Enacted 1966
Truth-in-Packaging (Enacted as Fair Packaging and Labeling Act)	Enacted 1966
National Traffic and Motor Vehicle Safety Act	Enacted 1966
Financial Institutions Supervisory Act	Enacted 1966
Wholesome Meat Act (Enacted as Meat Inspection Act Amendment)	Enacted 1967
Clinical Laboratories Improvement Act (Enacted in Parternership for Health Act)	Enacted 1967
National Commission on Product Safety	Enacted 1967
Flammable Fabrics Act Amendments	Enacted 1967
Fire Research and Safety Act	Enacted 1968
Automobile Insurance Study Act	Enacted 1968
Truth-in-Lending (Enacted as Consumer Credit Protection Act)	Enacted 1968
Interstate Land Sales Full Disclosure Act (Enacted in Housing and Urban Development Act of 1968)	Enacted 1968
Natural Gas Pipeline Safety Act	Enacted 1968
Wholesome Poultry Products Act	Enacted 1968

were abolished. The departments and agencies, however, continued their consumer programs.

In a new age of affluence, when television sets, man-made textiles and other such marvels were becoming commonplace and when credit and installment buying was used by most people in the United States, a new approach to consumer protection was needed. Thousands of frustrated citizens who did not know where or to whom to turn, either in government or in private business, were writing directly to the White House.

John F. Kennedy

In 1962, John F. Kennedy became the first president to send a special Consumer Message to Congress. He appointed the first National Consumer Advisory Council to work with him on consumer problems. This council was made up of a distinguished group of private citizens, university professors, state officials, labor leaders and others from all walks of life.

Lyndon Johnson

President Lyndon Johnson greatly expanded the consumer program begun by President Kennedy. He appointed Assistant Secretary of Labor Esther Peterson as his Special Assistant for Consumer Affairs in January 1964. He also appointed a President's Committee on Consumer Interests, in addition to the Advisory Council. This committee consists of 12 cabinet members and agency heads.

President Johnson also strongly recommended consumer legislation in four messages to Congress, in 1964, 1966, 1967 and 1968. He signed 17 consumer bills into law. Three of these laws were very important. The Meat Inspection Amendment ensured that Federal standards would be applied intrastate as well as interstate. The Truth-in-Lending Act required banks and other credit businesses to disclose the actual cost of a loan. And the Truth-in-Packaging Act required that packages clearly state contents and amounts.

The Role of the President's Special Assistant for Consumer Affairs

In 1967, President Johnson appointed me as his special assistant for consumer affairs. He asked me to work with other consumer offices within the Government and to support his overall consumer program. In this brief article, I cannot mention all that my office does. But some of our work is discussed below.

My staff and I discuss consumer problems with industry and business executives. Many industries of their own accord have taken action that will benefit their customers. We also work in cooperation with state and local consumer groups.

Within my own office, I established an Office of Consumer Education. This office works with school systems and universities throughout the United States. It encourages schools to teach consumer-education courses from kindergarten to the graduate level. It works with State Boards of Education to make such courses a requirement in school systems.

One of my jobs as special assistant is to bring my office to the people. I speak before consumer, business, labor, veteran and other groups. I appear on national television and radio programs. In short, I explain how Government is taking a real interest in consumers and their problems.

As citizens grew familiar with the program, letters began to pour in from every state. When possible, advice is given on where they can go for recourse. Other letters are referred to the proper departments or agencies. These letters aid the Federal Government in determining which are the most serious consumer problems. The Government can then take steps to help.

The problems of poor people in the United States are an increasing interest of this office. Their need for consumer education and protection is even greater than that of the rest of the people. They have less money with which to make mistakes.

BETTY FURNESS
Special Assistant to the President
for Consumer Affairs

EDUCATION

FOR American education, 1968 was a year of challenge and confrontations. The challenge was felt by educators on all levels. But it was felt most acutely by those in the urban school systems in the United States. In these systems community pressures created new demands for change in traditional structures and concepts. The confrontations brought a rash of teachers' strikes and student uprisings to the country. Out of these often jarring situations, however, came fresh hopes that a better educational process would emerge.

▶ STUDENT MILITANCY

In 1968, student militancy was a fact of academic life on many college and university campuses around the world. In the United States the most dramatic student rebellion occurred at Columbia University in the spring. A small group of students, led by the New-Left Students for a Democratic Society, occupied five campus buildings. The students demanded a greater campus role. They also challenged the university's involvement in certain defense-related activities, and other policies. These included Columbia's poor relations with the neighboring Negro community in Harlem.

The actions of the Columbia militants led to police raids to dislodge the students from the buildings. The police action in turn sparked an even greater campus revolt that brought an end to formal classes in the final weeks of the spring semester. The rebellion hastened the retirement of Columbia President Grayson Kirk and resulted in a number of university reforms. It also gave impetus to reform measures at many other colleges and universities.

▶ TEACHER MILITANCY

Teacher strikes were once a rarity. Yet in 1968 they occurred in scores of communities throughout the United States. Most of these—unlike the New York City walkouts (see below)—were over conventional issues: demands for higher salaries and for improvements in working conditions and in school conditions.

Columbia students, led by the Students for a Democratic Society, demonstrate against the university administration.

The National Education Association had long opposed teacher strikes. It called them unprofessional. But in 1968 it matched the militancy of its trade-union rival, the American Federation of Teachers. It urged its members to take to the picket lines when it felt that circumstances warranted such action. In February, NEA affiliates conducted a statewide school strike in Florida. It kept half of the state's 1,200,-000 pupils out of classes.

A bid for merger of the two national teacher organizations was made by David Selden, president of the 165,000-member AFT. But the inviation was rejected by the 1,100,000-member NEA.

▶ FEDERAL AID TO EDUCATION

President Lyndon Johnson signed into law several measures intended to help the nation's overcrowded colleges and universities. The higher-education bill authorized $7,300,000,000 through fiscal year 1971. These funds will help private and public colleges and universities build classrooms, improve libraries and expand programs for graduate students. The bill also contained a provision, bitterly opposed by many educators, to cut off Federal grants and loans to students who participate in campus disruptions. Critics viewed this as a blow to academic freedom and as punitive action that would unfairly penalize less-affluent students.

Congress also authorized over $3,000,-000,000 for a three-year period to make possible a sweeping overhaul of vocational-education programs.

▶ RESEARCH: THE FOURTH "R"

The Committee for Economic Development, an organization of prominent businessmen, called for a national effort to intensify research, innovation and evaluation in education. To lead this effort, the committee proposed that Congress create an independent, nongovernmental commission of distinguished citizens "broadly representative of the major segments of society" and comprising "persons of unques-

tioned stature as educational statesmen." In calling for this national effort, the CED said that despite important gains in recent years, American schools on the whole are not measuring up to the task of providing "the kind of education that produces rational, responsible and effective citizens."

▶ SCHOOL DESEGREGATION

The Southern Regional Council is a biracial organization that had been set up in 1944 to press for racial equality. In a recent report it conceded that there had been a "deplorable degree of failure in desegregating Southern schools." Noting that its reports in recent years were guardedly optimistic, the council said that "This time there seems almost no hope, virtually no reason to find optimistic words to say that things may improve. The mistakes of the past are repeated."

The pace of integration in the North was also very slow. Integration proposals involved busing of pupils to schools outside their neighborhood to bring about better racial balance. This stirred new controversies in Chicago, Los Angeles, San Francisco and other cities.

President Johnson's National Advisory Commission on Civil Disorders said that by 1975, if current trends continue, "80 per cent of all Negro pupils in the twenty largest cities, comprising nearly one half of the nation's Negro population, will be attending 90 to 100 per cent Negro schools."

▶ SCHOOL DECENTRALIZATION

For many years school centralization has been the goal of educators in rural America. Here the objective has been to consolidate small districts into more educationally effective administrative units. In American urban centers, however, a reverse problem—too much centralization— has developed. Here the school systems have become too large. They have become too unwieldy and too impersonal.

One of New York City's experimental districts became the center of a controversy

THE MAGNITUDE OF THE
AMERICAN EDUCATIONAL
ESTABLISHMENT (1968–69)

More than 60,400,000 Americans are engaged full-time in the nation's educational enterprise as students, teachers, or administrators. Nearly another 140,000 make education a time-consuming avocation as trustees of local school systems, state boards of education, or institutions of higher learning. The breakdown is given here:

THE TEACHERS

Public School Teachers	
Elementary	1,070,000
Secondary	856,000
Nonpublic School Teachers	
Elementary	157,000
Secondary	90,000
College and University Teachers	
Public Institutions	299,000
Nonpublic Institutions	205,000
Total Teachers	**2,677,000**

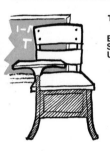

THE INSTITUTIONS

Elementary	88,556
Secondary	31,306
Universities, Colleges, and Junior Colleges	2,374
Total	**122,236**

ADMINISTRATORS AND SUPERVISORS

Superintendents of Schools	13,313
Principals and Supervisors	112,583
College and University Presidents	2,374
Other College Administrative and Service Staff	82,000
Total	**210,270**

SCHOOL DISTRICTS — 21,990

BOARD MEMBERS

Local School Board Members	110,380
State Board Members	500
College and University Trustees	25,000
Total	**135,880**

THE LEARNERS

Pupils in Elementary Schools (Kindergarten through grade 8)	
Public Schools	32,100,000
Nonpublic (Private and Parochial)	4,600,000
Total Elementary	**36,700,000**
Secondary School Students	
Public High Schools	12,800,000
Nonpublic	1,400,000
Total Secondary	**14,200,000**
College and University full- and part-time students enrolled for credit toward degrees	
Public Institutions	4,600,000
Nonpublic	2,100,000
Total Higher	**6,700,000**
Grand Total Students Enrolled	57,600,000

THE COST (IN BILLIONS)

Current Expenditures and Interest	
Elementary and Secondary Schools	
Public	$29.0
Nonpublic	3.7
Higher	
Public	9.8
Nonpublic	7.2
Capital Outlay	
Elementary and Secondary Schools	
Public	4.5
Nonpublic	0.6
Higher	
Public	2.4
Nonpublic	1.0
Total	**$58.2**

In New York City, Negro students and parents demonstrate for community control of schools in the Ocean Hill-Brownsville area of Brooklyn.

Albert Shanker, president of New York City's
United Federation of Teachers.

Rhody McCoy, unit administrator of the Ocean
Hill-Brownsville governing board.

that had city-wide impact. More than any
other local education problem, it attracted
nationwide attention.

The controversy started in the spring
of 1968. The locally-elected governing
board of the predominantly Negro Ocean
Hill-Brownsville demonstration school
district in Brooklyn tried to summarily
transfer a group of educators it considered
to be a detriment to the experimental decentralization project. The city-wide teachers'
union, the United Federation of Teachers,
charged that the local board had violated
the educators' job rights. The central Board
of Education agreed. But it was unable to
persuade the local district to reinstate the
educators. With the issue still unresolved
in September, the union—with the backing
of most of the system's supervisors—called
a series of strikes.

The strikes kept 50,000 teachers and
over a million pupils out of classes on 36
of the first 48 days of the fall term. They
ended with an uneasy truce that involved
the appointment by the state of a trustee
to oversee the Ocean Hill-Brownsville district. A special commission was set up to
assure teachers' rights throughout the New
York City school system. The bitterness
caused by the dispute, however, persisted
long after the pupils and teachers finally
returned to their schools.

Clearly the dispute fanned racial antag-
onisms throughout the city. Some observers felt that it seriously damaged the future course of school decentralization in
the city and perhaps elsewhere in the
United States. Others felt that it had pointed
up a necessary but painful lesson: that
decentralization—particularly when it involves the issue of community control—
must bring about a viable accommodation
between the proper concerns of parents and
the legitimate concerns of the professional
school staff.

LEONARD BUDER
Education Writer
The New York Times

ENTERTAINMENT

ENTERTAINMENT. What was it in 1968 for the millions who watched television, went to the theater, the movie houses and the concert halls? For theater audiences on Broadway and at playhouses all over the country, there were many fine dramas, revivals and comedies, but few good musicals. The one exception was the American tribal love-rock musical *Hair,* a smash hit off and on Broadway.

Television audiences were presented with The Year of the Widow when four series premiered featuring glamorous make-believe widows with children. The widows were Doris Day, Hope Lange, Diahann Carroll and Lucille Ball. Diahann Carroll's show was also an example of another trend in 1968—integrated shows.

For variety, viewers turned to the quick, flash, one-line comedy of *Rowan and Martin's Laugh-In.* Via television, audiences went to Mexico City and Grenoble for the Olympic Games and to Miami and Chicago for the political games. And in December, audiences viewed a "first" when President-elect Richard Nixon announced and introduced his Cabinet on television.

Music audiences found that musical events were no longer scarce. The many summer festivals, concert and opera tours and long-run symphonic engagements gave audiences music all year long.

Dance audiences have long favored *The Nutcracker* and the ballet was to be seen everywhere. Less-traditional dance also began to capture audiences. They went to see the multimedia *Astarte* and the avant-garde modern dance of Merce Cunningham and Alwin Nikolais.

Motion-picture audiences were exposed to the film-making technique of multiple images. This technique was used dramatically in *The Thomas Crown Affair* to picture the complex and split-second execution of a bank robbery.

And audiences were given a ratings system developed by the motion-picture industry to advise on the suitability of films.

Robert Joffrey's dramatic ballet "Gamelan" relates in a series of eight choreographic essays the life of the inhabitants of a never-never land.

THEATER

The cast of "Hair" on the Broadway stage.

A THEATER season may be measured in several ways: by the artistic merits of its serious drama, by the uncovering of new playwrights, by the popularity of its comedies, by the box-office success of its musicals, by its overall attendance, by its profit.

By any of these standards but one, the 1967–68 Broadway season can be called relatively successful. That one exception was in musical theater. In nine tries, Broadway was unable to produce a musical hit of its own. The only unquestioned success was *Hair,* which originated off Broadway. On the other hand, at least a dozen new dramas were met with admiration or at least respect by the critics.

▶ **DRAMA**

The best of the dramas was generally considered to be *Rosencrantz and Guildenstern Are Dead,* by Tom Stoppard. He took those two little-known and badly treated characters from Shakespeare's *Hamlet* and gave them a play of their own, a play in which they were caught in forces too large for them to control or understand. Like many of Broadway's best plays in recent seasons, *Rosencrantz and Guildenstern* was imported from London.

There were several other plays worthy of comment.

Joe Egg was about a young couple whose retarded child was both a cause and a symbol of their conflict. Peter Nichols' drama also served as the vehicle for an outstanding performance by British film star Albert Finney.

The Birthday Party, one of Harold Pinter's early plays, was revived with an American cast. It was about a man being pursued by unnamed persons for unnamed reasons. It proved again that Pinter is probably the best English-language playwright of his generation.

After the Rain took a look at what the civilization after ours might be like, as imagined by John Bowen. It was not encouraging. But it did say that there is a part of the human spirit that is hard to kill.

The season also saw an outpouring of work by leading American playwrights. Tennessee Williams' *The Seven Descents of Myrtle* once again used a Southern setting and a conflict between decadent gentility and an emerging lower class, but it was far below his best work.

TONY AWARDS

Drama: ROSENCRANTZ AND GUILDENSTERN ARE DEAD

Musical: HALLELUJAH, BABY!

Dramatic Actor: MARTIN BALSAM (*You Know I Can't Hear You When the Water's Running*)

Dramatic Actress: ZOE CALDWELL (*The Prime of Miss Jean Brodie*)

Musical Actor: ROBERT GOULET (*The Happy Time*)

Musical Actress: LESLIE UGGAMS (*Hallelujah, Baby!*)

Director of a Drama: MIKE NICHOLS (*Plaza Suite*)

Director of a Musical: GOWER CHAMPION (*The Happy Time*)

Choreography: GOWER CHAMPION (*The Happy Time*)

Scenic Design: DESMOND HEELEY (*Rosencrantz and Guildenstern Are Dead*)

Costume Design: DESMOND HEELEY (*Rosencrantz and Guildenstern Are Dead*)

Musical Score: JULE STYNE, BETTY COMDEN, ADOLPH GREEN (*Hallelujah, Baby!*)

DRAMA CRITICS CIRCLE AWARDS

Best Play: ROSENCRANTZ AND GUILDENSTERN ARE DEAD

Best Musical: YOUR OWN THING

Arthur Miller's new play *The Price* was essentially a dialogue between two brothers about the choices each one had made and the consequences of these choices. It was treated more respectfully than Williams' drama. Some critics thought it the best play of the season. Others felt it went over ground that Miller had covered better in earlier plays.

America's greatest playwright, Eugene O'Neill, was represented posthumously by *More Stately Mansions,* which was intended as part of a trilogy about an American family, and which was never completed. Despite the presence of Ingrid Bergman, Colleen Dewhurst and Arthur Hill, the drama was long and cumbersome.

The Prime of Miss Jean Brodie was an adaptation by Jay Allen of Muriel Spark's novel. It was a study of a commanding, eccentric teacher, with the title role remarkably portrayed by Zoe Caldwell.

Neil Simon, author of *Barefoot in the Park* and *The Odd Couple,* contributed the comedy hit, *Plaza Suite.* It had three one-act plays set in the famous hotel, the Plaza, with superb comic performances given by George C. Scott and Maureen Stapleton.

Other leading authors represented on Broadway were Frank D. Gilroy (*The Only Game in Town*), Robert Anderson (*I Never Sang for My Father*) and Peter De Vries (*Spofford*), whose work was adapted for the stage by Herman Shumlin.

▶ **MUSICALS**

The enormously successful *Hair* was a "tribal love-rock" musical that began the season off Broadway and then moved to a discothèque. Staged anew by Tom O'Horgan, with most of its story line eliminated, it arrived on Broadway as a hippie "environment." *Hair* overflowed the stage and overwhelmed the audiences, even those that did not like it. It was Broadway's only unquestioned musical hit.

Other musicals ranged from the fairly good to the disastrous. *George M!* relied on Joel Grey and the songs of George M. Cohan. *Golden Rainbow* was a vehicle for stars Steve Lawrence and Eydie Gorme. *The Happy Time* offered Robert Goulet and first-rate staging and scenery.

The poor crop of musicals looked all the worse compared with some of the revivals: *Brigadoon, South Pacific, The King and I* and *My Fair Lady* at the City Center, and *West Side Story* at Lincoln Center.

▶ **REPERTORY AND OFF BROADWAY**

The Repertory Theater of Lincoln Center began its season with an all-star revival of Lillian Hellman's *The Little Foxes,* directed by Mike Nichols. The cast included George C. Scott, Anne Bancroft, Margaret Leighton and E. G. Marshall. That was followed by revivals of *Saint Joan, Cyrano de Bergerac* and *Tiger at the Gates,* a program that was generally considered to be unsuccessful.

Another repertory company, the APA, had one of its best seasons, with productions of *Pantagleize, The Show-Off, Exit the King* and *The Cherry Orchard.*

Two new repertory companies had their first seasons off Broadway. The New York Shakespeare Festival's Public Theater originated the musical *Hair* and went on to exciting productions of *Hamlet, Ergo* and *The Memorandum.* The Negro Ensemble Company, predominantly black, completed a successful opening season.

The off-Broadway theater, which a few years ago was thought to be dying, maintained the vitality it had reestablished one season earlier. *Your Own Thing,* a rock musical based on *Twelfth Night,* was voted by the newspaper and magazine critics the best musical of the season, in preference to its Broadway competition. The dramatic highlight was *The Boys in the Band,* a play that deals sharply and wittily with the delicate theme of homosexuality.

▶ **REGIONAL THEATER**

The regional theater, which has been accused of failing to develop a single major new play, responded with two of them during the season.

In New Haven, Yale Drama School's repertory theater produced *We Bombed in New Haven* by Joseph Heller, the author of the novel, *Catch-22.* It was a comical tragedy that operated on two levels of reality and examined the reality of war.

The Arena Stage, in Washington, D.C., put on Howard Sackler's drama *The Great White Hope.* Based on the life of the first Negro heavyweight champion, Jack Johnson, *The Great White Hope* commented on the black man's place in American society.

Both dramas went to Broadway for the 1968–69 season, and both marked important achievements for the regional theater in the United States.

LEONARD HARRIS
CBS News

TELEVISION

Dan Rowan, Dick Martin and Goldie on "Rowan and Martin's Laugh-In."

PAST television seasons have seen cycles of The Year of the Cowboy, The Year of the Private Eye, The Year of the Fun Wars, and so on. The 1968–69 season introduced yet another cycle: The Year of the Widow.

▶ THE YEAR OF THE WIDOW

Indeed, of the new series no less than four dealt with the problems of young widows trying to build new lives for themselves—as well as for their children. Whether this trend was due to the promi-

nence of the widowhood of the former Mrs. John Kennedy or the present Mrs. Robert Kennedy or Mrs. Martin Luther King, Jr., one thing is certain. It marked the end of the trail for the television husband.

Once upon a time (remember George Burns and Gracie Allen?) there was such a thing as smart husbands and dumb wives. Then came along dumb husbands and smart wives. And now, finally, no husbands at all. *Sic transit,* apparently, not only Gloria but also Gloria's spouse.

EMMY AWARDS

Dramatic Series: MISSION: IMPOSSIBLE, CBS

Comedy Series: GET SMART, NBC

Variety Series: ROWAN AND MARTIN'S LAUGH-IN, NBC

Dramatic Program: ELIZABETH THE QUEEN, NBC

Variety Special: ROWAN AND MARTIN'S LAUGH-IN SPECIAL

Actor in a Drama: MELVYN DOUGLAS (Do Not Go Gentle into That Good Night, CBS)

Actress in a Drama: MAUREEN STAPLETON (Among the Paths to Eden, ABC)

Actor in a Dramatic Series: BILL COSBY (I Spy, NBC)

Actress in a Dramatic Series: BARBARA BAIN (Mission: Impossible)

Actor in a Comedy Series: DON ADAMS (Get Smart, NBC)

Actress in a Comedy Series: LUCILLE BALL (The Lucy Show, CBS)

News: JOHN LAURENCE and KEITH KAY ("First Cavalry" and "Con Thien" on CBS Evening News with Walter Cronkite); CRISIS IN THE CITIES (Public Broadcast Laboratory, NET)

News Documentaries: AFRICA, ABC; SUMMER '67: WHAT WE LEARNED, NBC

Cultural Documentaries: ERIC HOFFER: THE PASSIONATE STATE OF MIND, CBS; GAUGUIN IN TAHITI, CBS; JOHN STEINBECK'S "AMERICA AND AMERICANS," NBC; DYLAN THOMAS: THE WORLD I BREATHE, NET

Daytime Programing: TODAY, NBC

Sports Programing: ABC'S WIDE WORLD OF SPORTS

famed English novel *The Ghost and Mrs. Muir.* In this, a much underrated actress, Hope Lange, and her costar, Edward Mulhare, provided, by their own real medium, the otherwise very medium medium of television with its closest approach to high comedy.

Last but not least—in fact easily the most important of the new widow shows— was *Julia.* This, which featured as its widow the gorgeous Diahann Carroll, offered us a story about an all-black family. And, in color each week, it not only broke TV's color barrier but also faced up to the United States' black-and-white dilemma. The show was at first far too self-conscious. And it was hindered by overdirection of an overcute boy. But it nonetheless soon became the season's most-talked-about show. This was due to the fine acting of Miss Carroll and her costars Lloyd Nolan and Lurene Tuttle.

▶ INTEGRATED SHOWS

Integration also appeared elsewhere around the 1968–69 dial. There were no other principally black shows. But black principal characters were added to half a dozen already-running shows. The ABC network in particular came up with two new series which demonstrated complete equality of stardom. One of these was *Mod Squad,* which gave us three teen-agents, or bop cops. One of these, Clarence Williams III, played the kind of black who, even though he helps cops, will not, as he says, "fink on a soul brother."

The other interesting show was a Western called *The Outcasts.* It costarred Otis Young, a fine black actor, and, at the same time, on racial conflict pulled no cowpunches.

▶ VARIETY SHOWS

On the variety-show scene, ABC also gave us at least one that was new and different: *That's Life,* starring Robert Morse. In the average variety show, you have singers and dancers with skits and sketches. You also have guest stars and

In any case, all the shows featured very prominent widows. One of these was movie star Doris Day. Her show was perhaps the most inane, but Miss Day nonetheless managed a fine performance. Another was Lucille Ball. She not only worked too hard but also made the mistake of inserting into her show her two real children—Lucy Desiree and Desi Arnaz, Jr.

Actually, the best of the widow shows was one based on and named after the comedians with stand-up plugs and sit-down jokes. But all of them do not necessarily hang together. Indeed, most of the time they hang separately. In *That's Life,* however, they were connected to each other and indeed to the very hipbone of the show.

Elsewhere on the variety scene, the season's most popular effort was *Rowan and Martin's Laugh-In. Laugh-In* featured every kind of humor, and bore down heavily on the kind of quick flash specially tailored for TV. This show would have been better at a half hour than a full hour. And it certainly owed a great deal of its success to the fact that the Smothers Brothers had, the year before, fought the battle of the censors for them. But it nonetheless reached favorably an audience which had all but given up on TV.

In the realm of satire, *The Smothers Brothers Comedy Hour* still took first honors. This was largely due to the brothers' superb sidekick, President-unelect Pat Paulsen. In his earnest, befuddled campaign, Mr. Paulsen brought to television a quality considerably more interesting than the real thing. This was a feat shared only by the peerless Bob and Ray and their classic coverage of both the national conventions on *The Dick Cavett Show.*

▶ TALK SHOWS

The literate, sophisticated *Dick Cavett Show* was, of all the season's new talk shows, the most widely praised by the critics. Ironically it was canceled.

Obviously, since so many talk shows featured so many of the same guests over and over, the viewer's choice among them came down to the simple matter of which host he liked the best. And he lined up solidly behind either the mugging, jack-in-the-box quality of a Johnny Carson, the deep-down goodness as well as on-top funniness of a Joey Bishop, the earnest naughtiness of a Merv Griffin, or the nice-nellyism of a Mike Douglas.

In addition to these shows there were a half dozen new syndicated efforts. These ranged from a new *Steve Allen Show* to a thing called *That Show* with Joan Rivers, and from Donald O'Connor to Hugh Hefner shows. On the other hand, the heyday of the tough-guy put-downers, notably Joe Pyne and Alan Burke, seemed, in 1969, to be over.

▶ NEWS AND DOCUMENTARIES

On a more positive note, ABC won plaudits for its exclusive coverage of the 1968 Olympics. And the news department of CBS came in for praise for *60 Minutes.* This biweekly, magazine-format news show involved not only CBS regulars Mike Wallace and Harry Reasoner, but half a hundred guest columnists. NBC promptly followed suit and announced that it too would have a magazine show.

Finally, 1968–69 was the year that showed once again that TV is at its best in the unexpected, unrehearsed moment. Coverage of such sober, shocking occasions as the funeral of Dr. Martin Luther King, Jr., and the assassination and funeral of Senator Robert F. Kennedy was both moving and expert. Nonetheless, as the year progressed, public sentiment seemed to be mounting against television. It was blamed for everything from the war in Vietnam to the black-power struggle. It was accused by many of not presenting a balanced picture of the disturbances at the Democratic national convention. There was a tendency, in other words, to blame not the news but the reporting of it.

Despite this trend, two excellent documentary series appeared during the year. Both provided real understanding and sensitive treatment of American problems. One, *Of Black America,* was a seven-part series sponsored by the Xerox Corporation. It explored virtually every facet of what it means to be a Negro in the United States. The other series was the Bell Telephone Company's three-parter, *The Urban Crisis in the United States.* It explored, in equally painstaking fashion, the trouble with our American cities.

CLEVELAND AMORY
Radio and Television Commentator

MUSIC

Henry Lewis, new musical director of the 75-member New Jersey Symphony, scheduled 50 concerts for the orchestra's 1968–69 season.

IN 1968, music was a year-round activity, confirming what observers of the cultural scene have long suspected: there no longer is such a thing as the musical "season." With the many summer festivals in 1968, and music dotting the landscape from Santa Fe, New Mexico, to Lake George, New York, music lovers could, if they wished, find 52 weeks' worth of active listening.

Typical of the proliferating activities was the opening on July 19 of the Blossom Music Center in Ohio, as the new summer home of the Cleveland Orchestra.

▶ THE NEW MUSIC

Some of the things heard during 1968, both summer and winter, were quite spectacular. "The new music"—a term devised to distinguish the latest products of the avant-garde from old-fashioned "modern music"—was increasingly in evidence. The works of the new-music composers—Iannis Xenakis, Luciano Berio, Toru Takemitsu, Henri Pousseur—were strongly rhythmic, pointed and fragmented products. They were often rich in color, but fitful in melody and bereft of tonality.

Among the most admirable of the new talents was Krzysztof Penderecki. This young Polish composer made considerable impact both in Europe and the United States with two works. *Threnody for the Victims of Hiroshima* explored the widest range of string sonorities. And the *Passion according to St. Luke,* a ninety-minute work, gave a powerfully effective modern turn to a form of religious drama made famous by J. S. Bach. The *St. Luke Passion* received its American premiere in Minneapolis under the baton of Stanislaw Skrowaczewski. The *Hiroshima* piece was programed by several orchestras.

▶ SYMPHONIC MUSIC

In the symphonic world, notable changes were under way. The New York Philharmonic celebrated its 125th anniversary during the 1967–68 season, and also prepared to search for a new conductor to succeed Leonard Bernstein in 1969. The Boston Symphony announced that its departing conductor, Erich Leinsdorf, would be replaced by Pittsburgh's William Steinberg.

In 1968 a new generation of conductors came to the fore. Henry Lewis, the first Negro appointed music director of a symphony orchestra in the United States, took over the New Jersey Symphony in June. Robert Shaw began his tenure in Atlanta. André Previn proved a resounding success in Houston. And Seiji Ozawa was selected to head the San Francisco Symphony. But in Philadelphia, after 32 successful years, Eugene Ormandy continued firmly in command. In New York the 81-year-old Leopold Stokowski, a one-man bridge for the generation gap, still gave exciting, adventurous concerts with the youthful American Symphony Orchestra. Among the works he performed was *Sun-Treader,* an early twentieth-century masterpiece by American composer Carl Ruggles.

▶ OPERA

Operatically the year was not notably stimulating. The Metropolitan Opera, in its second year at New York's Lincoln Center,

recovered from the financial crisis caused by its move uptown. But the Met offered an artistically quiescent season. Critical opinion was divided on the new production by Herbert von Karajan of *Die Walküre,* which reduced the Wagnerian epic almost

Long-haired Tiny Tim, a popular singer of many voices, accompanies himself on the ukulele.

to chamber proportions. But condemnation was almost universal for a fussy and exaggerated *Carmen* staged by Jean-Louis Barrault and sung by Grace Bumbry. Critics concluded that this *Carmen* was designed more for the tired businessman than for the alert opera lover.

The New York City Opera, also at Lincoln Center, stirred up more interest than the Met. The New York City Opera's production of a modern opera, Alberto Ginastera's *Bomarzo,* seemed tame after the advance publicity of its supposed sensationalism. The company, however, reaffirmed its *expertise* in performing French opera with an exquisitely staged, beautifully sung production of Massenet's *Manon,* starring Beverly Sills.

Much of the year's operatic adventurousness was provided by summer festivals. The Santa Fe Opera, housed in a stunning new desert-style edifice, produced a strong contemporary work, Hans Werner Henze's *The Bassarids.* The Caramoor Festival at Katonah, New York, revived with distinction Monteverdi's seventeenth-century masterpiece *L'Incoronazione di Poppea.* The Lake George Opera Festival put on a wide range of works based on Shakespearean plays, including the world premiere of David Amram's *Twelfth Night.*

The seldom heard Rossini *Otello* was also performed by the Rome Opera, the most distinguished foreign troupe to visit the United States during the year.

▶ **POPULAR MUSIC**

The sounds of popular music in 1968 varied greatly. There were the falsetto and tenor voices of Tiny Tim, strumming a ukulele and tiptoeing through the tulips on the album *God Bless Tiny Tim.* There was the strong blues voice of Janis Joplin wailing above the amplified acid-rock sound of Big Brother and the Holding Company on the album *Cheap Thrills.* Critics likened Janis Joplin's voice to the blues singing of the legendary Bessie Smith.

Popular too were the songs by 21-year-old composer Jim Webb, who wrote "MacArthur Park" and the Grammy winners "Up, Up and Away" and "By the Time I Get to Phoenix."

Mozart in the Movies

The most unexpected musical development of the year was the boom in sales of a recording by Geza Anda of Mozart's Piano Concerto No. 21 in C Major. Its sudden surge to the best-seller lists was due entirely to its use as the background music in the popular Swedish movie *Elvira Madigan.* Thenceforth Mozart was to add one more claim to fame to his many musical distinctions: composer of the "Theme from *Elvira Madigan.*"

HERBERT KUPFERBERG
Music Columnist, *The Atlantic*

GRAMMY AWARDS

Record of the Year: UP, UP AND AWAY (5th Dimension, Soul City)

Album of the Year: SGT. PEPPER'S LONELY HEARTS CLUB BAND (The Beatles, Capitol)

Song: UP, UP AND AWAY

Instrumental Theme: MISSION: IMPOSSIBLE (Lalo Schifrin, Dot)

Female Vocalist: BOBBIE GENTRY ("Ode to Billie Joe," Capitol)

Male Vocalist: GLEN CAMPBELL ("By the Time I Get to Phoenix," Capitol)

Rhythm and Blues Recording: RESPECT (Aretha Franklin, Atlantic)

Country and Western: GENTLE ON MY MIND (Glen Campbell, Capitol)

Children's: DR. SEUSS: HOW THE GRINCH STOLE CHRISTMAS (Boris Karloff, MGM)

Opera: BERG: WOZZECK (Columbia)

Classical Album (tie): BERG: WOZZECK (Columbia); MAHLER: SYMPHONY NO. 8 IN E FLAT MAJOR (Columbia)

PULITZER PRIZE

Music: GEORGE CRUMB ("Echoes of Time and the River")

DANCE

Antoinette Sibley and Anthony Dowell in the Royal Ballet production of "The Nutcracker."

DANCE audiences flocked again to see England's Royal Ballet on tour in the spring of 1968. The Royal Ballet was never more brilliant in its sharp, clear style. It displayed a radiant group of young soloists along with honored guests Dame Margot Fonteyn and Rudolf Nureyev. Audiences also could not get enough of the Bolshoi Ballet. The Bolshoi arrived from the Soviet Union with a repertoire of short virtuoso pieces that dazzled the general public, yet made the critic ask for more solid fare.

▶ BALLET

American Ballet Theatre presented a successful new production of the 1841 classic *Giselle*. The lovely Italian ballerina Carla Fracci and Denmark's handsome

Erik Bruhn were outstanding in the roles of the guileless heroine and her deceitful lover. *Giselle* was staged by David Blair.

The Robert Joffrey City Center Company again toured the Northwest during the summer. The Joffrey company continued to win friends with its fine dancing, its multimedia effects in *Astarte* and its graphically startling but rather depressing *Clowns.*

The New York City Ballet offered a remarkable range of George Balanchine choreography led by the lithe, long-legged Suzanne Farrell. The New York City Ballet's audiences at Lincoln Center's State Theater were larger than ever, thanks mainly to the newly installed subscription system which at last organized audiences for dance.

Eliot Feld, the gifted 26-year-old dancer-choreographer left American Ballet Theatre to be on his own. His first two works while he was with the American Ballet Theatre, *Harbinger* and *At Midnight,* drew immediate response to the individuality of his talent. His third work was premiered by the Winnipeg Royal Ballet in early October. This work, to the Haydn Flute Concerto, will be shown by the Canadian company on its forthcoming tour of the Soviet Union.

The Nutcracker still appeared to be the omnipresent ballet. The 1892 Ivanov-Tchaikovsky ballet, first performed in St. Petersburg, has endearing qualities for both audiences and performers. In 1968 more and more companies, from Maine to Florida, from California to New York, were doing *The Nutcracker.* At Christmastime 1967 the New York City Ballet did 41 performances, as well as more during its 1968 summer season at Saratoga. Other companies also are now doing *The Nutcracker* during Easter and summer seasons.

From the audience point of view, *The Nutcracker* interests many young balletomanes, since there are many young students used onstage in the Act I Christmas party. In addition, the lady visitors in the ballet sport handsome satin crinolines and lace fichus. The gentlemen in their elegant clothes of the 1890's and the children in charming old-fashioned attire are somehow comforting in their reminder of gentler times. As for Act II, the Sugarplum Fairy is as sweetly delicious as one could wish, and that goes too for the dancers who personify cocoa, tea, marzipan, candy flowers and peppermint sticks.

▶ **MODERN DANCE**

Much less familyesque, the avant-garde continued to explore the range of nontechnique, noninhibition performances. Says talented avant-garde leader Yvonne Rainer, who appears most frequently in T-shirt, tights and sneakers, "no to spectacle . . . no to virtuosity . . . no to involvement."

Merce Cunningham, who premiered *Rainforest* and *Walkaround Time* at the Buffalo Festival of the Arts in the spring of 1968, continued to use "movement by chance." Cunningham feels that the sequence of movement is its least significant aspect. And Alwin Nikolais, whose unique company appeared in Europe and India for the first time this past year, says, "I see things best in abstract form and feel that polygamy of motion, shape, color and sound is the basic art of the theater."

All of these modern dancers, plus many others, including Martha Graham, Jose Limon, Paul Taylor and their companies, were involved in an important new venture made possible by a $485,000 grant from the Ford Foundation. The grant made possible a series of modern-dance events in the fall of 1968 at the Brooklyn Academy of Music, the Billy Rose Theater and the New York City Center of Music and Drama. A similar season was scheduled for the spring of 1969.

The purpose of this grant, says the Ford Foundation, is to find out if there are "untapped" audiences who may be ready for what contemporary modern dance has to offer. In addition to performing in the New York area, the selected companies will tour college communities around the country.

Maximiliano Zomosa and Robert Blankshine in "The Clowns."

They will spend several days in each place not only performing, but also discussing the arts in classes and lecture-demonstrations so that students may get to know the thinking of the artists. It is part of the new awareness that involvement is just as important as viewing. For education is beginning to understand that dance, presented and taught by talented persons, evokes feeling and receptivity that flow over into other areas of living.

LYDIA JOEL
Editor in Chief
Dance Magazine

MOTION PICTURES

Russian troops leave Moscow to Napoleon in the epic "War and Peace."

STANLEY KUBRICK'S *2001: A Space Odyssey* may ultimately prove to be the film event of the '68 year. A Cinerama, Super Panavision and Metrocolor production, *2001* was a lavish spectacular. It combined conventional episodic storytelling units with the more modern techniques of Kinesis. With these techniques, camera movement and subject movement were so combined as to instill physical liberation and free-fall feeling in the viewer. This may be the shape of movies to come in the future.

Lesser variations of this technique were used in two other films. The first was the Steve McQueen-Faye Dunaway film, *The Thomas Crown Affair.* In this film, an educated supercrook matched wits with a female insurance investigator. The second film was Richard Lester's *Petulia.* Here, against a San Francisco background, Julie Christie and George C. Scott played the parts of an unpredictable young matron and a world-weary doctor entangled in a hopeless affair. Both films made good use of camera work and editing combined with subject movement to create unusual effects.

Still among the films that drew the longest lines at the box offices were Mike Nichols' *The Graduate* and Roman Polanski's *Rosemary's Baby. The Graduate* was a seriocomic satire about a young man who rebels against the materialistic world of his elders. It featured Anne Bancroft and newcomers Dustin Hoffman and Katharine Ross. *Rosemary's Baby* featured Mia Farrow in an outstanding acting performance. She was ably assisted by John Cassavetes. This film was a present-day good-vs.-evil parable in which a young husband gives his wife to the devil for personal gain.

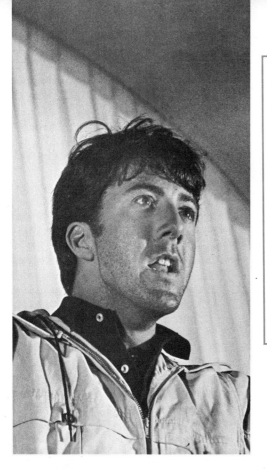

Dustin Hoffman in Mike Nichols' "The Graduate."

ACADEMY AWARDS

Motion Picture: IN THE HEAT OF THE NIGHT

Actress: KATHARINE HEPBURN (Guess Who's Coming to Dinner)

Actor: ROD STEIGER (In the Heat of the Night)

Supporting Actress: ESTELLE PARSONS (Bonnie and Clyde)

Supporting Actor: GEORGE KENNEDY (Cool Hand Luke)

Director: MIKE NICHOLS (The Graduate)

Foreign-Language Motion Picture: CLOSELY WATCHED TRAINS

Song: TALK TO THE ANIMALS (Doctor Dolittle)

Documentary Feature: THE ANDERSON PLATOON

Documentary Short: THE REDWOODS

Cartoon: THE BOX

THE EPICS

The blockbusters were with us as usual. Perhaps the biggest for all time was the two-part Russian film adaptation of the Leo Tolstoy classic *War and Peace*. The film ran for 6 hours and 13 minutes and was shown on a reserve-seat basis. Audiences had to view an afternoon and an evening performance to get it all.

Still another epic was Tony Richardson's *The Charge of the Light Brigade*. This film was not so ambitious as *War and Peace,* yet it was on an equally grand scale. Trevor Howard, Vanessa Redgrave, Sir John Gielgud and David Hemmings gave outstanding performances.

Joseph E. Levine brought to the screen the James Goldman play *The Lion in Winter.* Peter O'Toole portrayed Henry II, and Katharine Hepburn starred as his queen.

CENSORSHIP AND DARING FILMS

More than ever before, 1968's crop of films pushed back the censorship barriers until they almost seemed to have disappeared. To protect the industry's self-censorship practice, the Motion Picture Association announced that films would be rated for audience suitability. This system has long been in practice in Great Britain.

There were several very-daring films which dealt with sex in 1968. Among them were Radley Metzger's *Therese and Isabelle,* Luis Buñuel's *Belle de Jour,* and the English *Here We Go Round the Mulberry Bush.*

FAMILY FILMS

There was an abundance of family films during the year. Warner Brothers-Seven Arts production of *Heidi* was a creditable remake. And in 20th Century-Fox's *Doctor Dolittle,* Rex Harrison played the doctor who walks and talks with the animals. Straying somewhat off the beaten path of family fare, Jack Lemmon and Walter Matthau outdid themselves in the Paramount comedy *The Odd Couple,* adapted from the Neil Simon Broadway hit. Doris Day cavorted in the usual type of Doris Day film, *Where Were You When the Lights*

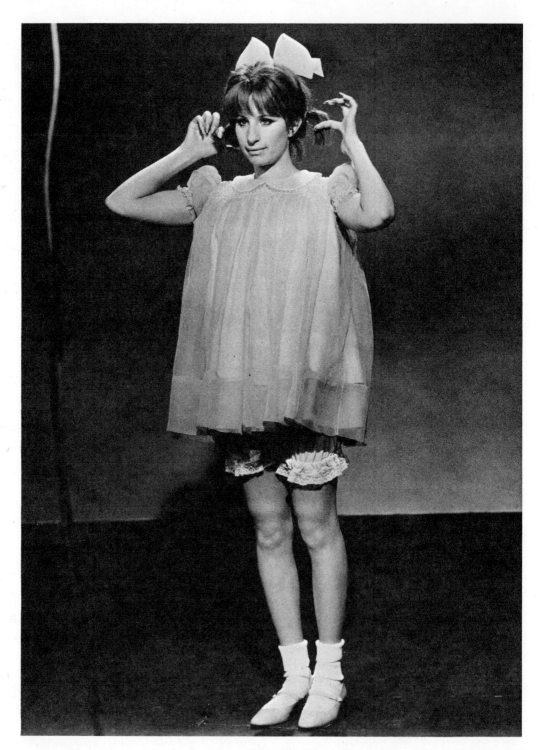

Barbra Streisand portrays Fanny Brice in "Funny Girl."

Went Out?, a series of zany antics about New York City's blackout.

Also in the comedy vein was Mel Brooks' *The Producers*. This film featured Zero Mostel as a show-business crook ably aided by Gene Wilder. Peter Sellers was on the scene, too, in *I Love You, Alice B. Toklas*. The title was somewhat catchier than the story.

Paul Newman provided film fans with a star performance in *Cool Hand Luke*. He played the part of a Southern chain-gang prisoner who keeps his indomitable spirit despite cruel and sadistic treatment by his captors. Later, Newman turned director to do *Rachel, Rachel*. His wife, Joanne Woodward, played the leading role, a schoolteacher. Elizabeth Taylor and Richard Burton were on the scene again in *Boom!*, which was more noise than quality.

▶ **MUSICALS**

Musicals were mostly adaptations of stage musicals. William Wyler's Columbia production of *Funny Girl* featured Barbra Streisand. This film and Carol Reed's *Oliver!* were among the most striking musicals. Even so, critics were quick to point out that *Funny Girl* was at its best when Miss Streisand was left alone to be her natural self. In spite of Fred Astaire, Petula Clark and the freshness of the songs, *Finian's Rainbow* was reported to be a warmed-over production.

▶ **THE NEW YORK FILM FESTIVAL**

The Sixth New York Film Festival was criticized by some as not being sufficiently international. Yet the praise that went to French and Czechoslovak films brought them almost immediately into commercial release.

In Jiri Menzel's *Capricious Summer*, three middle-aged men strove for the unattainable: youth. In Milos Forman's *The Firemen's Ball*, details of human activity at a small-town firemen's ball piled up humorously and at the same time drew an allegorical parallel to pre-July Czechoslovakia.

Jean-Luc Godard had two entries: *Two or Three Things I Know about Her* and *Weekend*. In the latter film, fiction, fantasy and documentary were blended to picturize a violent, bloody and horrifying present and future.

Most impressive was Jan Nemec's daring Czech film *Report on the Party and the Guests*. Banned in 1966 because of its comment on life under a totalitarian regime, it featured leading Czechoslovak intellectuals and artists who were part of the recent reform movement.

The American scene was represented by John Cassavetes and Norman Mailer. Cassavetes' *Faces* was an improvised, slice-of-life look at an affluent couple with their delusions, alienations and torment. In Mailer's *Beyond the Law*, detectives and suspects were pitted against each other in a made-up story to support a strong social statement.

▶ **DOCUMENTARIES**

There were four oustanding documentary presentations during the year. Eugene S. Jones' *A Face of War* was an actual account of the Vietnam fighting. *What Harvest for the Reaper* was NET's moving study of the recruitment and exploitation of migrant farm workers. David Loeb Weiss' *No Vietnamese Ever Called Me Nigger* dealt with black feelings about the Vietnam war. Alan King's *Warrendale,* made for the Canadian Broadcasting Company, was about emotionally disturbed children.

▶ **AMERICAN FILM INSTITUTE**

The American Film Institute swung into high gear in 1968. It sponsored several film-study conferences and established a $500,-000 fund for student and independent film makers. The AFI joined 12 major production companies to sponsor feature-film production. It also began a national Film Catalogue project to establish an archive of American films, and set up a scholarship program for graduate students in film production.

HAIG P. MANOOGIAN
New York University

EUROPE

FOR Europe, as for the rest of the world, 1968 was a year of turmoil, a year of change, some of it good, most of it bad. The Soviet invasion of freedom-bound Czechoslovakia seemed to throw the world back to the darkest Stalinist days of the East-West cold war. This invasion, as well as the increased presence of the Soviet fleet in the Mediterranean, heightened fears of East-West conflict as NATO warned the Soviet Union against a similar invasion of Yugoslavia, and the United States sent two naval vessels on a "show-the-flag" mission to Russia's backdoor in the Black Sea. Clearly, movement toward an East-West *détente,* which had been gaining momentum, was stalled during 1968.

Apart from the ramifications of the invasion of Czechoslovakia, the nations of Europe had other, mostly internal, problems. Throughout 1968, established institutions and social orders were challenged by young people in nearly every country from the Atlantic to the Urals. Students staged antigovernment demonstrations in Spain and Great Britain, in the Low Countries and Scandinavia, in West Germany and usually serene Switzerland, in communist Poland and Titoist Yugoslavia. In France, students almost forced President Charles de Gaulle to resign. Indeed, few nations were spared the spectacle of young people on the march or battling police.

While trying to cope with the demands of the revolutionary New-Left youth, governments, especially those of France and Great Britain, also tried to cope with increasing economic woes. Higher wages, higher prices and a huge deficit in its international balance of payments forced Britain to devalue the pound late in 1967. Similar factors, aggravated by the student-led riots and the workers' strikes in the spring of 1968, almost brought about a devaluation of the French franc in November. Eastern European nations also felt economic pressures during the year. Hardest hit was Czechoslovakia, whose already troubled economy was disrupted by the Soviet invasion.

At year's end it seemed abundantly clear that Europe would face many of the same problems in 1969.

Czechoslovak President Ludvik Svoboda, left, and Communist Party leader Alexander Dubcek were forced in August 1968 to accept Soviet occupation of their homeland.

WESTERN EUROPE

THE August 20–21 invasion of Czechoslovakia by the Soviet Union and its allies lessened hopes in Western Europe for a further easing of East-West tensions. The clatter of tanks' in Prague jarred out of key with the note of optimism that had been struck by the January Soviet-United States agreement on a draft treaty to halt the spread of nuclear weapons.

The Soviet invasion caused North Atlantic Treaty Organization nations to turn toward building their defenses. Before the Soviet invasion, at a June meeting at Reykjavik, Iceland, NATO foreign ministers had called for troop reductions by East and West. Postinvasion discussion centered on whether the shift of Soviet divisions to Czechoslovakia had tipped Europe's delicate balance of military power to favor the communist Warsaw Pact nations. Because of this fear, on November 16 the NATO Council of Ministers issued a stern warning to the Soviet Union. It said that "any Soviet intervention . . . affecting the situation in Europe or in the Mediterranean would create an international crisis with grave consequences."

In addition to the storm created by the Soviet invasion of Czechoslovakia, Western Europe was wracked by violent student demonstrations as well as by economic crises which touched almost every nation.

▶ FRANCE

On September 27, 1968, France vetoed for the third time Britain's bid for membership in the Common Market. This move decreased the harmony between France and its five partners in the European Economic Community. French relations with West Germany took a particularly bad turn in 1968. During a visit to Paris by West German President Heinrich Lübke, a German news-agency dispatch reported that West German Foreign Minister Willy Brandt had attacked De Gaulle as a man

Tens of thousands of French demonstrators jam the Champs-Elysées during the French crisis of May 1968.

"obsessed with power" blocking European unity. Denials failed to pacify De Gaulle. He angrily downgraded Lübke's scheduled official banquet to a lunch. When West German Chancellor Kurt Kiesinger later visited Paris with proposals to edge Britain nearer to Common Market membership, his reception was cool.

Riots and Strikes

President de Gaulle was preparing for a May visit to Rumania when student unrest broke out at the University of Paris campus at Nanterre. Stern measures by the Government failed to still the students' demands for drastic changes in the overcrowded, antiquated university system. Student defiance triggered widespread sympathy among the workers of France. Their living standards had been squeezed by the economic and social policies on which De Gaulle had sought to build his "New France." The end result was that ten million workers went out on strike, almost paralyzing the nation and toppling De Gaulle.

The friction between the students and the faculty at Nanterre began early in 1968. Prominent in the Nanterre clashes was a 23-year-old sociology student, German-born Daniel Cohn-Bendit, known as "Danny the Red." Because of his activities, Cohn-Bendit was threatened with expulsion from the university. He then gathered hundreds of his supporters and on May 3 marched on the Sorbonne. Authorities called the police. After evicting Cohn-Bendit and his New Left followers from the campus, police occupied the Sorbonne. Authorities ordered the school closed for the second time in its seven-century history. Only the Nazis, during World War II, had closed the Sorbonne before.

Soon after the students were ousted, fighting spread into the streets of Paris. On Monday evening, May 6, some 10,000 students clashed with police. The students ripped up streets and used the cobblestones as weapons. The police retaliated by tossing tear-gas bombs. By morning, 600 in-

French President Charles de Gaulle, who in 1968 overcame yet another series of crises.

jured students and bystanders had been treated by doctors.

Workers and the general public then became involved. They were largely sympathetic to the students, whose demands now went beyond university reform. The climax came during the evening of May 10 and the morning of May 11. Riot police stormed 30,000 students manning barricades in the Sorbonne area. In fighting that lasted from 2 A.M. to 6 A.M., at least 350 people were injured.

Faculty unions and students now aligned. Organized labor, communist and noncommunist, called for a 24-hour general sympathy strike for Monday, May 13.

French Premier Georges Pompidou hurriedly amnestied arrested students. He reopened the Sorbonne and withdrew police from the university grounds. But his actions were too little, too late. After Monday's day-long work stoppage, workers across the country refused to go back to work. De Gaulle, who had flown to Bucharest, Rumania, on May 14, cut short his visit and returned to France. He spoke to the people and called for a vote of confidence in a national referendum. But De Gaulle's prestige had plunged. The workers refused offers of substantial wage increases and a 40-hour workweek. These economic gains had been wrested by union negotiators from De Gaulle's harassed Government. Millions of workers and students shouted that "De Gaulle must go." But the President, after contemplating stepping down from office, made a sensational reversal. He decided to confront the strikers and students in a show of force—at the risk of civil war.

De Gaulle first made sure that he had the support of the Army. He then canceled the planned referendum, dissolved the National Assembly and ordered general elections. In the days before the vote, De Gaulle and his supporters stressed that the alternative to De Gaulle would be a communist dictatorship. His psychology paid off. In the voting, on June 23 and 30, the opposition parties were crushed. The Gaullist Union for the Defense of the Republic and their allied Independent Republicans won 354 seats in the 487-seat Assembly.

Firmly in control once again, De Gaulle replaced Premier Pompidou with Maurice Couve de Murville, who had been foreign minister. In October, Education Minister Edgar Faure introduced legislation that would modernize the universities and give the students a voice in university administration.

Economic Crisis

But France's troubles were far from over. The May strike had brought French workers salary increases averaging 13 per cent. This had touched off a serious inflation. As a result confidence in the stability of the French franc began to decline. Speculators began to trade in their francs for stronger currencies, particularly the German mark. France's reserves of gold, United States dollars and British pounds sterling declined from $6,000,000,000 to little more than $3,000,000,000.

As the financial drain continued, Western bankers and finance ministers met in Bonn, West Germany, to seek a solution for France and the West. Out of this meeting came a promise of $2,000,000,000 in credit for France, and an understanding that France would devalue the franc. But once again De Gaulle did just the opposite of what was expected of him. In a radio address he told his nation that he would not devalue the franc. Instead he imposed harsh austerity measures on the French people. He planned to halt the drain in reserves by cutting imports, freezing wages and prices and raising new taxes.

De Gaulle's plan seemed to work as a stopgap measure. But at the end of 1968 it was obvious that with three major international monetary crises in a year, basic changes in the world monetary system would be imperative in 1969.

▶ **GREAT BRITAIN**

In 1968 the people of Great Britain were presented with the bill for the 1967 devaluation of the pound sterling and for years of national overspending abroad. Prime Minister Harold Wilson continued plans to withdraw British forces from Asia by the early 1970's. He canceled an order for fifty F-111 fighter-bombers. And he phased out aircraft carriers and cut armed-forces strength from 429,000 to 350,000. All this was done in the name of economy.

On the domestic scene, Wilson ended free medical prescriptions, cut public construction and ordered other economies. A new budget imposed many indirect taxes, limited dividend increases and heavily taxed unearned incomes. It also set maximum wage increases at 3.5 per cent a year.

The French financial crisis in November placed new pressures on the British pound. Wilson was forced to take additional steps to cut imports and consumer spending.

Asians living in Great Britain protest a law to restrict immigration of other Asians from Kenya into the British Isles. The new law restricted the number of Asians who could go to Britain to 1,500 a year.

British Racial Tensions

When Kenya was granted independence by Great Britain in 1963, Asians living in that African country were given the choice of becoming British nationals. During 1968 many of these people were forced out of their jobs in Kenya. The jobs were then given to Kenyans. As a result, a stream of Asians, mostly Indians and Pakistanis, flooded Great Britain. An arrival rate of 3,000 monthly early in the year brought fears that 167,000 Kenyan Asians would go to Britain. A new law was then passed, and Asian immigrants were limited to less than 1,500 yearly.

In April prominent Conservative Enoch Powell called for an end to colored immigration. A national furore resulted when his supporters staged "Keep Britain White" demonstrations. A new law, however, banned discrimination in employment and housing.

▶ WEST GERMANY

In 1968 the influential *Stern* magazine published what it alleged was new evidence linking President Heinrich Lübke to the construction of concentration camps under the nazi regime during World War II. This charge had been made before—by communist East Germany. Lübke's wartime record, including twenty months of imprisonment by the Nazis, had countered the charge. Stern, however, printed a sworn affidavit from a New York handwriting expert saying that Lübke's signature had been identified on camp-construction plans that were among Nazi documents confiscated after World War II. Lübke insisted that he did not remember signing the plan.

Political Activity and Student Demonstrations

The extreme Right-Wing National Democratic Party has been labeled as neo-Nazi by the West German Government. In April elections, this party won 10 per cent of the vote and 12 of the 127 seats in the Baden-Württemberg state elections.

Demonstrations were widespread in West Germany after the attempted assassination of Leftist student leader Rudi Dutschke ("Red Rudi") on April 11.

President Heinrich Lübke of West Germany was linked to the construction of concentration camps during World War II; he denied the charges.

A Berlin policeman tries to hold back a crowd of students who rioted for several days after the shooting of student leader Rudi Dutschke.

Dutschke recovered, but two people were killed and hundreds injured in five days of bitter clashes between police and members of Dutschke's Socialist Students League. Thousands of students battled police in Berlin, Frankfurt, Munich, Cologne and other West German cities. The students also attacked the offices and buildings of publisher Axel Springer. They accused him of fostering a reactionary atmosphere in West Germany.

The Economy

The incredible strength of the West German economy was at the heart of France's monetary problems in November. As the French franc became weaker, the German mark became stronger. Germany continued to increase its exports and pile up huge reserves at such a fantastic rate that some economic experts stated that the mark should be revalued. That is, the mark should be increased in value in relation to other world currencies.

Most of the money that flowed out of France ended up in West German banks. Indeed, in a three-day period in Novem-

ber, almost $2,000,000,000 in foreign currency poured into West Germany. This forced the West to act. The meeting of bankers and finance ministers in Bonn resulted. At first an attempt was made to get West Germany to revalue the mark. But Economic Minister Karl Schiller refused. He asked why the Germans should be made to suffer for their economic success.

Germany did agree, however, to increase export prices and decrease prices on imported goods. Such a move would help cut West Germany's huge balance-of-payments surplus. West Germany also imposed restrictions that would help halt the flow of foreign money into the country. Because of their dominant economic position in Europe, many Germans could echo the headline that appeared in the newspaper *Bild Zeitung:* "Now the Germans are No. 1 in Europe."

▶ GREECE

During 1968, King Constantine remained in exile in Rome. And the military-backed Government of Greece continued its rule despite strong opposition. This Government published, on July 11, a new constitution as a basis for eventual return to civilian rule. The constitution stripped the King of many powers. It increased the independence of the armed forces. And it increased the authority of the chief executive. On September 29 the people of Greece went to the polls to vote on the new constitution. It was approved by 91.87 per cent of the people.

Seven weeks before this plebiscite, an attempt was made on the life of Premier George Papadopoulos. The would-be assassin, Alexandros Panagoulis, was caught and sentenced to death. The Government, which later commuted Panagoulis' sentence, named as the instigator of the act Andreas Papandreou. He had been released from prison at the end of 1967 and had sought asylum in the United States, where he had been a professor at the University of California. Andreas Papandreou is the son of George Papandreou, the last

elected Greek premier, who died in the fall. At his funeral, on November 3, demonstrators defied martial law to shout anti-government slogans.

United States-Greek Relations

In January the United States established relations with the Government in Athens. Later in the year it lifted its ban on the sale of arms. On October 20, Mrs. Jacqueline Kennedy, widow of the late American President, married Greek shipping magnate Aristotle Onassis on the island of Skorpios.

▶ ITALY

The Christian Democrats, who have dominated Italian politics since the end of World War II, made some gains in elections held on May 19–20. But the share of votes for the Unified Socialists, one of their partners in the Center-Left coalition Government, fell by nearly 25 per cent. And the Communists scored their biggest increase in twenty years. As a result of the vote, the Unified Socialists quit the coalition. This forced Christian Democratic Premier Aldo Moro, in office since 1963, to resign. Giovanni Leone, also a Christian Democrat, was appointed premier of an interim, minority Government. In November, however, Leone resigned in the hope that this would hasten the formation of a new Center-Left coalition Government. In December, Mariano Rumor formed a new coalition Government of Christian Democrats and Socialists. Before they agreed to rejoin the coalition, the Socialists demanded that the Christian Democrats pledge that they will bring about overdue reforms in education and social security. Lack of such reforms had resulted in student demonstrations and strikes.

▶ BELGIUM

Traditional animosity between Belgium's 5,000,000 Flemings and 3,000,000 French-speaking Walloons caused riots at the University of Louvain in January and February. This resulted in the resignation of Premier Paul Vanden Boeynants, which precipitated Belgium's longest governmental crisis. March 31 general elections failed to resolve the differences over which Vanden Boeynants and his Cabinet had split. Political negotiations continued until June 17, more than four months after Parliament's dissolution, before a Government under Premier Gaston Eyskens was formed.

▶ DENMARK

The January 21 crash of a B-52 bomber carrying four nuclear weapons sprinkled areas near Danish-governed Greenland with radioactivity. It also clouded American relations with Scandinavia.

The crash came almost on election eve in Denmark and had some effect on the results. Nevertheless, a heavy voter turnout rejected the Social Democrats, who, in a series of coalitions, had ruled Denmark for forty years. Hilmar Baunsgaard, a Radical Liberal who opposes Danish membership in NATO, replaced Jens Otto Krag as premier. Public opinion in Denmark had turned against the Social Democrats because of the nation's worsening economic situation. Taxes, prices and unemployment had all risen during the year.

▶ SWEDEN

Swedish-American relations were less than friendly during 1968 as Sweden granted sanctuary to some 180 American servicemen who had deserted in protest against the Vietnam war. U. S. Ambassador William W. Heath was recalled to Washington in March.

Despite expectations of a swing to the Right, as in Denmark, Premier Tage Erlander, in office for 22 years, and his Social Democrats were returned in September elections with an increase of 12 seats in the lower house of Parliament.

▶ FINLAND

In January elections President Urho Kekkonen was elected to his third six-year term. Premier Rafael Paasio regarded Kekkonen's reelection as a rebuff to his policies and resigned. Mauno Koivisto, former governor of the Bank of Finland, was named premier at the head of a five-party coalition Government.

▶ ICELAND

As in the case of Denmark, Iceland elected a leader who campaigned against membership in NATO. In June 30 elections, Dr. Kristjan Eldjarn was elected president. He succeeded Asgeir Asgeirsson, who had been president since 1952.

▶ PORTUGAL

Antonio de Oliveira Salazar, dictator-premier of Portugal since 1932, suffered a brain hemorrhage on September 16. President Americo Tomaz named Marcelo Caetano to succeed Salazar as premier. Caetano is a businessman, a law professor and a longtime associate of Salazar. At year's end, Salazar seemed to be improving.

▶ SPAIN

A treaty under which the United States keeps 25,000 servicemen at three air bases and a Polaris submarine station in Spain will expire in March 1969. Negotiations for renewal of the treaty were held in 1968. Spain asked the United States for military equipment that would cost $1,000,000,000 over five years. The United States, however, offered only $140,000,000 worth of goods and $100,000,000 in credits. Negotiations were still continuing at the end of the year.

The Spanish military would like to equip and train an airborne force of 3,000 men that could be flown to any part of the country to put down insurrections and disorders. Such disorder took place during August 1968 in the Basque region in the north of Spain. After the chief of secret police in one predominantly Basque province was killed, the government declared a partial state of emergency. The Basques are the majority in four Spanish provinces, and many of them have long agitated for independence.

J. J. MEEHAN
United Press International

Soviet Union and Eastern Europe

THE leaders of the Soviet Union were not sorry to see 1968 pass into history. From the point of view of the Kremlin, 1968 was a less-than-satisfactory year. It was a year in which problems and losses outweighed gains. There is every reason to suppose that the leaders of the Eastern European states loyal to Moscow—East Germany, Poland, Hungary and Bulgaria—felt much the same way about the year.

▶ SOVIET UNION

The most spectacular incident in the Soviet Union and Eastern Europe during 1968 was the invasion of Czechoslovakia. This subject is treated in full in the special article "The Soviet Bloc: Winds of Change," which begins on page 18.

Foreign Policy

Before the Soviet invasion of Czechoslovakia in August, a developing trend in Soviet foreign policy had been the movement toward improvement of relations with the United States. This took place months before President Johnson announced the halt in the bombing of North Vietnam. The most important achievement was the agreement on a treaty aimed at banning the proliferation of nuclear weapons. This agreement was achieved after many years of difficult negotiation. It was one of the major triumphs of the Johnson administration. But the ratification of the nonproliferation treaty in the United States and elsewhere was delayed by the general shock resulting from the Czechoslovak invasion. Many voices were to be heard, particularly in Europe, charging that the invasion marked a new and tougher turn of Soviet foreign policy.

Those arguing for this view pointed to the Soviet public claim that the Soviet Union was legally entitled to invade West Germany if it felt that nazi forces were being reborn there or that there was danger of aggression from that country. The Soviet press campaign against Yugoslavia and Rumania in the period following the Czechoslovak invasion also raised world fears.

This led President Johnson at one point to warn that the United States might not stand idle if another invasion took place in Europe.

Before the Czechoslovak invasion, too, the United States and the Soviet Union finally completed ratification of the Consular Treaty. This treaty is designed to give additional protection to the citizens of each country visiting the other. This treaty had been agreed upon in principle in 1933 between President Franklin D. Roosevelt and Soviet Foreign Minister Maxim Litvinov, when the United States first recognized the Soviet Union. But it took 35 years to finally complete the making of this agreement. Important too was the initiation of direct Moscow-New York City flights in mid-July with planes of the Soviet Aeroflot line and the United States Pan American Airways flying between the two cities.

On November 6, on the eve of the celebration of the 51st anniversary of the Bolshevik Revolution, the main speaker renewed the Soviet call for improvement of Washington-Moscow relations. The call was obviously directed at the newly elected President, Richard M. Nixon. Specifically the Soviet Union was interested in beginning the negotiations on a treaty that would limit the missile race. The announcement that such negotiations were about to begin had been scheduled to be announced the morning of August 21—the first morning Soviet invaders were in Czechoslovakia.

Soviet relations with many communist countries and parties left much to be desired in 1968. The international communist meeting in Budapest in late February had been called to arrange a formal world communist congress. But this meeting was boycotted by such important states as China, North Korea, North Vietnam, Albania and Cuba as well as by the significant Japanese Communist Party. Yugoslavia was not invited at all. The Rumanians walked out of the meeting. They claimed that they had been attracted there by a promise, which had been broken, that no communist party would be attacked. Later the invasion of

Young Czechoslovaks demonstrate against the Soviet invasion of their country.

Czechoslovakia further raised tempers in the communist world, drawing particularly bitter attacks on the Soviet Union from Communist China and Yugoslavia. The Chinese also charged that Soviet forces and planes on the Soviet-Chinese border were staging provocations and violating Chinese territory.

In the Middle East the Soviet Union continued to cultivate most of the Arab states. It supplied many of them—particularly Egypt and Syria—with planes, artillery and other arms needed to replace the weapons lost during the 1967 Middle East war. Large numbers of Soviet advisers were reported stationed with the Egyptian armed forces at all command levels. The growing strength of the Soviet fleet in the Mediterranean also cast the shadow of Soviet power over the Middle East. One new addition to the fleet was a Soviet aircraft carrier whose helicopters could ferry Soviet marines to any troubled area in the Middle East if desired.

Neo-Stalinism

In the Soviet Union the most significant development during 1968 was the emergence of neo-Stalinism as the dominant influence on domestic policy. Not since the last year of Stalin's life (1952–53), had the censorship and other barriers to free expression in the Soviet Union been enforced so rigidly. The struggle against possible subversion and subversives became the leading theme of major speeches. And Communist Party General Secretary Leonid I. Brezhnev took the leading role among the witch-hunters.

The impression the Soviet leaders gave was that they were frightened that the revolt of the young and the disaffected which shook so many other nations in 1968 might spread to the Soviet Union. That revolt in the West was partially responsible for Lyndon Johnson's decision not to run for reelection. And it almost toppled France's Charles de Gaulle from his primacy in Paris. The Kremlin took no chances that

An American plane flies over the Soviet Union's new 18,000-ton helicopter carrier, the "Moskva." This ship, part of the Soviet fleet in the Mediterranean, can carry a squadron of helicopters.

anything of the sort might take place in Moscow. Hence the emphasis in Soviet propaganda in 1968 was on Soviet patriotism, on the "superiority" of socialism to capitalism, and the like.

Not surprisingly in this atmosphere of enforced conformity, there was a partial rehabilitation of Joseph Stalin. And such leading nonconformist intellectuals as Yevgeny Yevtushenko and Andrei Voznesensky were kept strangely quiet most of the year.

The Economy

Not all of Soviet policy looked backward in 1968. The great area of progressive change was in the economy. By the end of 1968 most of Soviet industry had been transferred to the new economic system first introduced in 1965. In this system—whose chief sponsor has been Premier Aleksei N. Kosygin—factories are not directed in great detail. And their officials are not judged by their ability to produce more than their plans order them to manufacture. In this new system the emphasis is on selling goods rather than making them. This change means that Soviet factories are now more concerned with pleasing the buyer than they were earlier. Related to this is the new emphasis on profits, the source from which are taken the bonuses used to reward the best factory managers and workers.

Nevertheless the general conservative atmosphere in the Soviet Union had its influence on the economic reform too. It implied that there was little chance of expanding the changes so as to reduce still further the controlling grip of the central planners. In the indictment of Alexander Dubcek's Czechoslovak regime published in *Pravda* 24 hours after the invasion of Czechoslovakia, it was notable that the somewhat more daring economic reform in Prague was one of the chief targets of the Soviet attack. *Pravda* argued that Czechoslovakia's economic reform "proved" that the Prague leaders wanted to restore capitalism. There could be no doubt that this was a word of

caution to those in the Soviet Union itself who wanted to go further in freeing the economy from the still powerful remnants of Stalinist practices.

In actual production the Soviet economy did relatively well in 1968. Preliminary data suggested that gross industrial production grew about 8 or 8.5 per cent over that of 1967. Grain production—the key to the Soviet food supply—increased substantially in 1968 over the relatively poor 1967 output. The output of all grains in 1968 was officially reported to have exceeded 165,-000,000 metric tons. This implied that the Soviet Union would have more than enough grain to feed its people. And there would be enough left over to export to its friends and to add perhaps a few million tons to the stockpile. Soviet leaders feel it is necessary to have a stockpile as insurance against natural or other disaster.

Preliminary data for 1968 suggest that the Soviet Union produced over 305,000,-000 metric tons of oil and over 105,000,-000 tons of steel. For consumers, factories turned out about 800,000 motor vehicles, of which almost 300,000 were automobiles, and over 5,500,000 television sets. There was every evidence that the Soviet Union continued a high level of military production. But as usual no figures were published on the output of intercontinental missiles, hydrogen bombs and the like. There was debate in the West about how far the Soviet Union went in 1968 toward creating an anti-ballistic-missile defense system. But the rapid Soviet progress in building offensive missiles caused talk of a new "missile gap" to be an issue in the United States 1968 presidential campaign.

There was evident in 1968, however, Soviet concern about problems related to future production growth. Thus a growing shortage of workers in the major Soviet industrial centers focused new attention on the need to cut surplus working staffs in existing factories. And in agriculture, Leonid Brezhnev sketched in late 1968 ambitious new programs for increased fertilizer output and farm machinery so as to

Farm workers clean grain and load it onto trucks in the Kazakh S.S.R. During 1968 more than 165,000,000 metric tons of grain were produced in the U.S.S.R.

increase farm output very sharply by the early 1970's.

▶ EASTERN EUROPE

In Eastern Europe during 1968, political developments centered mainly on the crisis in Czechoslovakia and also the student riots in Poland in March, both described in the special article "The Soviet Bloc: Winds of Change," which begins on page 18. Related to these events was the fear that Russia might invade two nations that supported Czechoslovakia: Rumania and Yugoslavia.

Hungary

In Hungary, in 1968, the New Economic Model went into operation, trying to realize many of the objectives of the Soviet and Czechoslovak reforms. The Soviet condemnation of the Czechoslovak reform did not, however, seem to presage Hungarian abandonment of the even more radical Budapest economic changes.

Yugoslavia

The Yugoslav student disturbances in June had a very different outcome from the student unrest in Poland. Polish police met their students with clubs and water cannon. President Tito of Yugoslavia, however, made a speech declaring that the students were correct in many respects. He pledged to improve matters.

The relaxation of political tensions this brought to Yugoslavia proved very useful two months later when Czechoslovakia was invaded. That invasion solidified Yugoslav determination to defend the nation's independence. Supplies were stored in the mountains for use in possible guerrilla warfare against Soviet invaders, and arms were widely distributed among the people. Yugoslavia also drew closer to the United States. President Tito made little secret of his belief that if the Soviet Union invaded his country, he could count on U.S. help.

Rumania

Rumania, also preparing for possible Soviet invasion, began easing somewhat its formerly harsh controlled internal system. Secret-police frame-ups in the past were condemned and some victims rehabilitated. Steps were taken also to make it easier for people to get passports and to travel to foreign countries. The Rumanians continued their independent foreign policy. They

Yugoslav President Tito (center) is greeted by Czechoslovak Communist Party leader Alexander Dubcek and other Czechoslovak officials in Prague.

Young Communists from nations all over the world take part in the International Youth Festival, held in Sofia, the capital of Bulgaria, during July and August 1968. The festival is used to disseminate communist propaganda.

did, however, stop their initial strident attacks against the Czechoslovak invasion, presumably out of fear of Soviet reprisal.

Bulgaria

In Bulgaria the high spot of the year was the communist-sponsored International Youth Festival held during the summer. This brought thousands of young people from many countries to Sofia and was a success in these terms. But politically the propaganda gains were weakened by the energetic efforts of Czechoslovak young people to explain and propagate their country's point of view to the visitors.

Poland

In Poland, events during the year were dominated by the political conflict between Wladyslaw Gomulka and the "Partisan" forces seeking to bring about his downfall. Gomulka apparently enjoyed Soviet support. But his opponents appealed to nationalism and to anti-Soviet feeling.

HARRY SCHWARTZ
The New York Times

HEADS OF GOVERNMENT

EAST EUROPE

Albania	ENVER HOXHA, 1st secretary
Bulgaria	TODOR ZHIVKOV, 1st secretary
Czechoslo-vakia	LUDVIK SVOBODA, president
	ALEXANDER DUBCEK, 1st secretary
	OLDRICH CERNIK, prime minister
East Germany	WALTER ULBRICHT, 1st secretary
	WILLI STOPH, prime minister
Hungary	JANOS KADAR, 1st secretary
Poland	WLADYSLAW GOMULKA, 1st secretary
Rumania	NICOLAE CEAUSESCU, 1st secretary
U.S.S.R.	LEONID BREZHNEV, 1st secretary
	ALEKSEI KOSYGIN, premier
Yugoslavia	JOSIP BROZ TITO, president

WEST EUROPE

Austria	JOSEF KLAUS, chancellor
Belgium	BAUDOUIN I, king
	GASTON EYSKENS, prime minister
Britain	ELIZABETH II, queen
	HAROLD WILSON, prime minister
Denmark	FREDERIK IX, king
	HILMAR BAUNSGAARD, premier
Finland	URHO KEKKONEN, president
France	CHARLES DE GAULLE, president
West Germany	HEINRICH LUBKE, president
	KURT KIESINGER, chancellor
Greece	CONSTANTINE II, king (in exile)
	GEORGE PAPADOPOULOS, premier
Iceland	KRISTJAN ELDJARN, president
	BJARNI BENEDIKTSSON, premier
Ireland	EAMON DE VALERA, president
	JOHN M. LYNCH, prime minister
Italy	GIUSEPPE SARAGAT, president
	MARIANO RUMOR, premier
Luxembourg	JEAN, grand duke
	PIERRE WERNER, prime minister
Malta	GIORGIO B. OLIVIER, prime minister
Netherlands	JULIANA, queen
	PIET DE JONG, prime minister
Norway	OLAV V, king
	PER BORTEN, prime minister
Portugal	MARCELO CAETANO, premier
Spain	FRANCISCO FRANCO, chief of state
Sweden	GUSTAF VI, king
	TAGE ERLANDER, prime minister
Switzerland	WILLY SPÜHLER, president

	POPULATION	ARMED FORCES	CURRENCY*	COUNCIL OF EUROPE	EFTA	EEC
EAST EUROPE						
Albania	2,015,000	38,000	4 leks = $1.00			
Bulgaria	8,500,000	153,000	1.2 leva = $1.00			
Czechoslovakia	14,500,000	225,000	8.5 korunas = $1.00			
East Germany	17,200,000	126,000	3.4 Ostmarks = $1.00			
Hungary	10,400,000	102,000	17.4 forints = $1.00			
Poland	32,200,000	274,000	15.9 zloty = $1.00			
Rumania	19,700,000	173,000	9.4 lei = $1.00			
U.S.S.R.	236,000,000	3,220,000	1 ruble = $2.40			
Yugoslavia	20,200,000	220,000	12.5 new dinars = $1.00			
WEST EUROPE						
Austria	7,400,000	50,000	25.9 schillings = $1.00	X	X	
Belgium	9,600,000	99,000	49.9 francs = $1.00	X		X
Britain	55,500,000	350,000	1 pound = $2.40	X	X	
Denmark	4,880,000	45,500	7.5 kroner = $1.00	X	X	
Finland	4,700,000	36,400	4.2 markkas = $1.00			
France	50,400,000	505,000	5 francs = $1.00	X		X
West Germany	60,000,000	456,000	4 marks = $1.00	X		X
Greece	8,800,000	161,000	30 drachmas = $1.00	X		
Iceland	200,000	none	88 kronur = $1.00	X		
Ireland	2,900,000	13,000	1 pound = $2.40	X		
Italy	53,000,000	365,000	625 lire = $1.00	X		X
Luxembourg	335,000	560	49.9 francs = $1.00	X		X
Malta	320,000	none	1 pound = $2.40	X		
Netherlands	12,600,000	128,500	3.6 guilders = $1.00	X		X
Norway	3,825,000	35,000	7.2 kroner = $1.00	X	X	
Portugal	9,500,000	182,500	28.9 escudos = $1.00		X	
Spain	32,400,000	305,000	70 pesetas = $1.00			
Sweden	7,900,000	30,600	5.2 kronor = $1.00	X	X	
Switzerland	6,100,000	8,000	4.3 francs = $1.00	X	X	

* US $; 1968 exchange rates
EFTA—European Free Trade Association
EEC—Common Market

HOBBIES

IN 1968 a 55-year-old Liberty nickel was sold for $46,000. Two penny stamps issued in Mauritius in 1847 were sold for $380,000. And the magnificent Josiah K. Lilly collections of stamps and coins changed hands for millions of dollars. Indeed, with prices going higher and higher, it seemed to many that coin and stamp collecting were fast becoming the hobbies of the affluent. Young people, however, turned to the less-expensive craft and model hobbies during the year. Sales continued to boom in model cars and model rockets, miniature railroads and science kits. And the creatively minded turned to the arts of gold leafing and decoupage.

▶ STAMPS

THE year 1968 brought stamp collectors, both amateur and professional, one year closer to facing up to the problem that the dollar sign is proving to be a greater threat to the hobby than the postage meter, which in years past made such great inroads into the use of stamps.

Beyond any doubt, 1968 was the year of the profit motive in countries all around the world. Several stamp-auction firms announced total grosses in the millions of dollars. One collection alone, that of pharmaceutical manufacturer Josiah Lilly, of Indianapolis, was about to reach the $3,000,000 mark by itself, with more sales to take place in 1969.

More and more countries that had never issued their own stamps before (and indeed had previously admitted that they had no need for them) entered the ranks of stamp-issuing entities. Most of these did so only at the behest of promoters who would supply the stamps. A small number of these stamps were made available for postal use. But the greater amount was retained for sale to philatelists.

The various sheikdoms on the Arabian Peninsula were the sources for these issues, many of which were condemned by leading philatelic organizations. Even the names of many of these sheikdoms are unfamiliar to the general public, but philatelists, especially newer ones, find it difficult to resist the purchase of these gaudy labels. Recent additions to the ranks of stamp-issuing entities included the Trucial Oman sheikdoms

Foreign stamps pay tribute to two fallen American leaders.

of Ajman, Dibai, Fujeira, Sharjah and Umm al Qiwain.

The year also saw more omnibus issues. The phrase indicates a large number of stamps honoring the same topic, issued by many different countries. For example, though it has been five years since the assassination of President John F. Kennedy, there were nations still issuing stamps as a memorial. These stamps were intended primarily for sale to American collectors.

The Olympic Games held in Mexico City were honored by hundreds of different stamps issued by dozens of different countries, some not even participating in the Olympics competition.

The United States continued its program of issuing from 12 to twenty commemoratives each year. Since most American commemoratives were of current letter rate, 6 cents in 1968, few could complain about their frequency. Even the youngest collector, with pennies a week for spending money, was able to purchase almost every stamp issued.

Popular in 1968 were the ten 6-cent stamps presented on July 4. The series shows flags of the American forces in the Revolutionary War and in the War of 1812. And in 1968, Postmaster General W. Marvin Watson announced the first four commemoratives to be issued in 1969. They will be the 150th anniversary of Alabama statehood; the 200th anniversary of California settlement; the centenary of intercollegiate football; and the Eleventh International Botanical Congress, meeting at the University of Washington in August 1969.

During the year, a number of countries, including India, Mexico and many of the new nations of Africa, issued stamps in memory of Dr. Martin Luther King, Jr.

HERMAN HERST, JR.
Columnist, *Hobbies Magazine*

The Trucial sheikdoms issued stamps for collecting.

▶ **COINS**

The restoration of mintmarks to United States coins got the collectors' year off to a good start. The resumption of their use was considered so important that a group of hobby dignitaries was invited to the Denver mint for a January 4 ceremony marking the restoration. The return of the mintmarks once again provided collectors with ten regular coins to collect. But more important, the special mark of the newly reopened San Francisco mint ("S") was restored to those coins minted there for the first time since 1955, when this mint was closed down.

The year also saw the resumption of proof-set production, which had been halted in 1964. The minting site for proof sets was switched from Philadelphia to the San Francisco mint, and for the first time the distinctive "S" mark of the latter facility was used on such sets. Collectors responded by flooding the mint with orders for 3,000,000 proof sets. Some 2,000,000 orders were also placed for official mint sets.

Still, there is little doubt that 1968 will be recorded as the year of the silver certificate, rather than of the mintmark. For the first six months of the year—through June 24—little was heard about anything except the redemption of these notes. About $150,000,000 worth of silver certificates were turned in to the Government, and people walked away from U.S. assay offices with sacks of silver. For each $1.00 silver-certificate bill handed in, a person received $1.29 worth of silver.

Beginning June 25, the Government was no longer obligated to exchange silver for silver certificates, which, however, remained legal tender. This fact, coupled with the removal of gold backing from other U.S. circulating currency earlier in 1968, almost ended the traditional bond between United States currency and precious metals. Only the Kennedy half-dollar continued to have a 40 per cent silver content.

During the two or three years prior to 1968, coin prices were static or, in some cases, declining. In 1968, however, there was a general strengthening of prices. The stage for this switch was set in August 1967 during the American Numismatic Association's national convention. At this convention the famous McDermott specimen of the 1913 Liberty nickel was sold for $46,000. At the 1968 convention the rarest of the U.S. half eagles ($5.00 gold pieces) —the 1829 small date—changed hands for about $20,000.

With prestige coins being subjected to such healthy bidding, it is no surprise that prices have strengthened in all series, especially proof sets, commemorative halves, choice nineteenth-century coins and silver dollars. Even the modern issues have been increasing in price. This, however, can be credited, at least in part, to the Government's program of withdrawing the old silver coins from circulation for reduction to bullion form.

The biggest transaction of 1968, or any year, so far as the coin-collecting community is concerned, was the Smithsonian Institution's acquisition of the fabulous gold collection assembled by the late pharmaceutical magnate Josiah K. Lilly. This magnificent collection of 6,125 gold coins was given to the Smithsonian in return for a $5,534,808 tax credit.

Other milestones of the numismatic year included the following:

On January 18, Senator Karl E. Mundt introduced a proposal calling for the Mount Rushmore memorial to be depicted on the back of $1.00 notes.

In February, Mexico introduced a special 25-peso silver coin to commemorate its hosting of the October Olympics.

On April 23 Britain introduced 5 and 10 new-pence decimal coins.

On August 1 Canada introduced its pure-nickel 1968 dimes, quarters, halves and dollars, as it became the last of the major nations to abandon a silver-based coinage.

On September 18 the cornerstone of the new, $40,000,000 Philadelphia mint was set in place.

CLIFFORD MISHLER
Numismatic Editor, *Coins Magazine*

An artist's rendering of plastic model airplanes, which were popular with hobbyists in 1968.

CRAFT AND MODEL HOBBIES

HOBBYISTS constructed more static-plastic-model kits in 1968 than during any previous year. Static, or display, model kits ranged in types from gas-buggy cars to a supersonic transport, the prototype of which is expected to be in service in 1970. Kits are authentic copies of prototypes. For example, when the supersonic-transport scale-model kit is constructed, it is 9½ inches long, and is a carefully detailed facsimile of the aircraft, which is 318 feet long, with a wingspan of 180 feet. The scale for the model kit is thus 1/400 inches per foot. The more-usual scales for average-size airplanes are 1/48 and 1/72 scales. Plastic car-model kits, which were even more popular than airplane kits, usually are constructed in 1/25 scale. Kits that enabled the modeler to individualize or "hop up" the model were in heavy demand.

Model-Car Racing

Slot racing at home continued to be one of the most popular hobbies in 1968. Miniature car sets equipped with tiny electric motors and electric slot track afforded hours of competitive fun for thousands of hobbyists. Cars in sets are already assembled, ready to run. Other enthusiasts preferred to build their own slot-racing cars, mixing and matching parts from different model-car kits and "hopping them up" to gain competitive speeds.

Science Hobbies

Perhaps because of the increasing popularity of school science projects, out-of-school science projects interested thousands of youngsters during the year. Most sought after were various kinds of electronic kits, such as electronic-code oscillators, burglar alarms, fire alarms, audio-power amplifiers and intercoms. Also popular were magnetism, spectroscopy and polariscope kits, as well as other physics sets.

Collectors Miniature Cars

The year saw accelerated interest in miniature-scale-model collections of die-cast cars. Every type of vehicle was offered, from authentic reproductions of the horseless carriage to sleek racers, such as the Ferrari, from the 1912 Ford to an elaborate English bus. Movable parts, including steering wheels and doors, are a big feature of the miniature models. One model, a copy of a fantastic James Bond car, even has a rocket that ejects.

Model Railroading

Miniature trains, variously called "N"-gage, "postage stamp" or "micro" scale, continued to be popular in 1968. About half the size of HO-scale (⅛ of an inch to a foot), these miniature trains and layouts make it possible to construct a completely landscaped layout on a bridge table. There is even an "executive" miniature-train layout which fits snugly into an office desk drawer.

An accessory box decorated in the decoupage manner. A crest print was applied to the box and covered with many coats of a clear finish.

Radio Control

Flying model airplanes by radio control was by far the most popular scale-model-hobby sport. Thousands of dedicated followers of this hobby traveled hundreds of miles to take part in contests held almost weekly. Winners of these competitions were determined by the construction of the models and by flying skill, which is based on speed and flight realism.

Model Rocketry

Scale-model construction and the launching into "space" of model rockets attracted many hobbyists during the year. Model rocketry is an educational and spectacular sport and hobby. Most model rockets can make many flights and shoot through the air up to 2,500 feet. The hobby consists of putting the model together, lift-off, acceleration to peak altitude, parachute ejection and safe recovery.

Crafts

During 1968 the big event in jewelry making was a very sharp upsurge in the buying of small Indian bead kits. The craft was almost exclusively a hippie affair. The small Indian beads were put together in long strings of love beads.

Gold leafing, a craft dating back to the ancient Egyptians and used through the seventeenth century, came back into full bloom for handicrafters. All kinds of objects were gold leafed, from old furniture to fine statuary. The Old World art, which once required a great deal of time and care, was updated with modern materials requiring only six steps to complete: a base coat, gold-leaf adhesive, composition gold leaf, sealer, antiquing glaze and a final sealer.

The art of decoupage (pronounced day-ku-pahje) continued to be very popular in 1968. The craft involves applying a print to an object, such as a box, tray or furniture, and then getting the print to recede into the background by applying many coats of a clear finish.

WILLIAM H. VAN PRECHT
Editor, *Craft, Model &
Hobby Industry Magazine*

LATIN AMERICA

IF there was one common denominator for Latin-American developments during 1968, it must surely have been a sense of despair. 1967 had been a year of great hope that the Latin-American nations were beginning to move together to solve mutual problems. But events in 1968 were characterized by disunity and disagreement. Moreover, a number of developments suggested that the hemisphere could expect continuing, if not increasing, political instability.

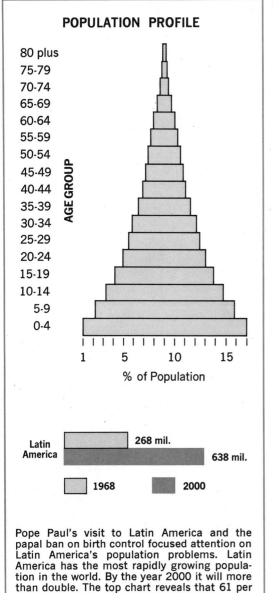

POPULATION PROFILE

AGE GROUP

80 plus
75-79
70-74
65-69
60-64
55-59
50-54
45-49
40-44
35-39
30-34
25-29
20-24
15-19
10-14
5-9
0-4

1   5   10   15

% of Population

Latin America
268 mil.
638 mil.

☐ 1968   ☐ 2000

Pope Paul's visit to Latin America and the papal ban on birth control focused attention on Latin America's population problems. Latin America has the most rapidly growing population in the world. By the year 2000 it will more than double. The top chart reveals that 61 per cent of the population is in the 0–24 age group.

▶ **POPE PAUL, BIRTH CONTROL AND OVERPOPULATION**

Pope Paul's visit to Colombia in August drew large numbers of Roman Catholic clergy and laity to that country for several religious conferences. But the Pope's earlier pronouncement on birth control left many churchmen wondering whether they could follow the Pope's lead in preaching against the use of contraceptives to limit population growth. In several surveys of Catholic Church leaders in Latin America, fully a third of them said that they were in favor of birth control despite the Pope's statement. Some of them even used the occasion of his Colombian visit to express their views.

Meanwhile, birth-control efforts went ahead in many places throughout Latin America. It was estimated, for example, that 30 per cent of young married women in Bogota, the Colombian capital, used birth-control devices to limit the size of their families. The same pattern was reported in other large metropolitan areas.

. The population of Latin America, however, was growing at the rate of 3.6 per cent per year, according to 1968 statistics. This factor affected virtually every country. Latin America has a population of about 265,000,000. Over half this population is under the age of 18. The problems of feeding, housing, clothing and educating this growing population is becoming increasingly ominous.

Many Latin-American leaders, including Chile's reformist President Eduardo Frei Montalva, spoke out on the issue, calling it "Latin America's most serious problem." There was some hope that this slowly growing concern over the population spiral

Galo Plaza Lasso, secretary-general of the OAS, criticized cuts in the Alliance for Progress.

might spur Latin America into renewing its efforts at economic and social reform which appeared to languish in 1968. The year ended with President Frei expressing his desire that 1969 be a year "to rekindle our lagging hopes."

ORGANIZATION OF AMERICAN STATES

Galo Plaza Lasso, the new secretary-general of the Organization of American States (OAS), put some of the blame for the lack of progress in Latin America on the United States. In a speech in late October, he said that "there is a profound disenchantment with the United States" throughout Latin America. He cited the recent cutbacks in Alliance for Progress funds as "symptomatic of a general downgrading of interest in Latin America" on the part of the United States. But Mr. Plaza also took issue with some of the Latin-American nations and their leaders. He stated that "some Latin Americans are resisting change."

Mr. Plaza became secretary-general of the OAS in mid-May. He immediately began efforts to reorganize the organization. During the remainder of the year, he visited each of the OAS member nations except

Cuba. (The Cuban Government is currently excluded from taking part in OAS activities.)

Mr. Plaza also made efforts to get ratification of charter changes designed to bolster the OAS. As the year ended, 11 nations had ratified the new charter. It will go into effect when 15 nations ratify it.

The OAS improved its somewhat tarnished image in 1968 with Mr. Plaza's election in February. He succeeded Dr. José A. Mora, who presided over a divided organization that was rocked by scandals in the final months of 1967. The long electoral battle to name a successor to Dr. Mora grew increasingly bitter in early 1968. The battle ended when nations supporting Mr. Plaza, a former president of Ecuador, made compromises that gave high OAS administrative posts to several Central Americans. Mr. Plaza moved quickly to heal the divisions in the OAS. He named a number of other Latin Americans to posts in the OAS secretariat.

LATIN-AMERICAN ELECTIONS

A number of Latin-American nations held elections in 1968. The first was Paraguay, a nation long governed by General Alfredo Stroessner. He was reelected for a five-year term by a sizable majority in February. However, a number of opposition parties, fielding three candidates, garnered a significant minority vote.

In May, Panama held a bitter presidential contest between former President Arnulfo Arias and David Samudio. Mr. Samudio was the candidate of the incumbent Government headed by President Marco A. Robles. After almost three weeks of vote counting and recounting, of street demonstrations and of heated arguments, Dr. Arias was named president by the National Election Tribunal. He was given a 36,000-vote plurality over Mr. Samudio. The bitterness of that campaign lingered on until Dr. Arias was inaugurated on October 1, and continued afterward until he was ousted by Panama's National Guard on October 11 (see below).

Ecuador also held a presidential election. Former President José Maria Velasco Ibarra won a fifth term by a narrow margin in a tight, three-way race. Mr. Velasco Ibarra, who had served out only one of his four former terms, took office in early September. He promised a number of social and economic reforms. Many observers wondered whether he would serve out his latest term because of continuing opposition to him among Army officers and various political groups. These groups had put forward two strong candidates in the June 2 election: Camilo Ponce Enriquez and Andres F. Cordova. And as the year ended they began mounting a variety of demonstrations against the Velasco Ibarra Government.

In Venezuela's presidential election in December, Dr. Rafael Caldera of the Christian Democratic Party won narrowly over three other candidates with 29 per cent of the vote.

Guyana held general elections in December. Prime Minister Forbes Burnham won a second five-year term. Burnham's People's National Congress won with the help of the overseas absentee vote.

▶ MILITARY SEIZURES OF POWER

The overthrow of Dr. Arias in Panama was one of two major ousters of civilian constitutional government in 1968. Both took place in October.

The first was the October 3 overthrow of Peru's President Fernando Belaunde Terry. The Army acted because of what it termed Peru's economic drift, political turmoil, and "the Government's mishandling of the IPC case." This case involved lands owned by the International Petroleum Company in northern Peru. It had become a major issue in that nation. IPC, a subsidiary of Standard Oil of New Jersey, had extracted petroleum products for over forty years. It was the largest single taxpayer in Peru. But the lands in question had been involved in disputes for nearly one hundred years. In August 1968, President Belaunde appeared to have worked out a solution. Under his

The presidency of José Maria Velasco Ibarra of Ecuador was threatened by dissidents.

plan, the lands would have reverted to Peruvian ownership, while the oil production would have been sold to the IPC refinery. The agreement came unhinged when a leading Peruvian politician, the onetime head of the country's state-owned oil enterprise, charged that a page was missing from the agreement.

After seizing power, the Peruvian military nationalized the IPC holdings, including the refinery. The military promised to consider compensation to the company against a tax bill amounting to more than the total cost of IPC's investment in Peru. Later, the nationalist-oriented Peruvian military took over a vast tract of land owned by the Cerro de Pasco Corporation. This land had been used by Cerro for agricultural purposes—to supply food to its workers. The military said that foreign investors should not be worried about future take-overs, since none were planned. But many investment groups and companies already doing business in Peru were concerned.

The ouster of Dr. Arias in Panama came on October 11. He had been in office only 11 days. The ouster was carried out by the United States-trained-and-equipped National Guard because of alleged dictatorial tendencies on the part of Dr. Arias. Twice before, Dr. Arias had been president of Panama. And twice before, he had been ousted by the National Guard. Dr. Arias took refuge for a while in the Panama Canal Zone but then left for the United States. The National Guard said that it would hold new elections "in the near future."

▶ **STUDENT UNREST**

Latin America underwent a great deal of unrest during 1968. Noteworthy was the student unrest in Mexico. This began in July and continued through August and September and into October until just before Mexico hosted the Olympic Games.

The student protest started over a variety of small nonpolitical issues. It mounted as police and Army units were used to halt the demonstrations. The students soon had a national issue: police and Army brutality. The students used this issue as the vehicle to demand a number of changes in Mexico's one-party political structure. Massive demonstrations—100,000 on August 13

The National Guard, which opposed the regime of President Robles and ousted President Arias, is a powerful force in Panamanian politics.

and 200,000 on August 27—took the protest to the Zocalo, the central plaza in Mexico City, which is the seat of government. Then, on October 2, the students and the Army engaged in a bloody clash. The students suffered major losses. These included about 40 dead, 300 injured.

The students called off their protests during the Olympics but promised to resume them afterward. There was considerable sympathy among the Mexican public for the student protest. But no major group joined with the students. President Gustavo Diaz Ordaz indicated that he would crack down heavily on student protestors. He admitted, however, that some of their complaints might well be justified.

Other student protests broke out in Brazil, Chile, Panama, Peru and Venezuela. Those in Brazil were particularly violent. The scheduled visit of Queen Elizabeth II of Great Britain to Brazil in November provided a breathing spell for the Government of Army Marshal Artur da Costa e Silva in which to work out some sort of accord with the students.

Students at the University of Mexico in Mexico City demonstrate against police brutality. The protests ended in time for the Summer Olympics.

HEADS OF GOVERNMENT

Argentina	JUAN CARLOS ONGANIA, president
Bolivia	RENE BARRIENTOS ORTUÑO, president
Brazil	ARTUR DA COSTA E SILVA, president
Chile	EDUARDO FREI MONTALVA, president
Colombia	CARLOS LLERAS RESTREPO, president
Costa Rica	JOSE JOAQUIN TREJOS, president
Cuba	OSVALDO DORTICOS TORRADO, president
	FIDEL CASTRO, premier
Dom. Rep.	JOAQUIN BALAGUER, president
Ecuador	JOSE MARIA VELASCO IBARRA, president
El Salvador	FIDEL SANCHEZ HERNANDEZ, president
Guatemala	JULIO MENDEZ MONTENEGRO, president
Guyana	FORBES BURNHAM, prime minister
Honduras	OSVALDO LOPEZ ARELLANO, president
Mexico	GUSTAVO DIAZ ORDAZ, president
Nicaragua	ANASTASIO SOMOZA DEBAYLE, president
Panama	JOSE M. PINILLA, provisional president
Paraguay	ALFREDO STROESSNER, president
Peru	JUAN VELASCO ALVARADO, president
Uruguay	JORGE PACHECO ARECO, president
Venezuela	RAFAEL CALDERA, president

	POPULATION	CURRENCY*	OAS	LAFTA	CACM
Argentina	23,370,000	350 pesos = $1.00	X	X	
Bolivia	4,000,000	11.9 pesos = $1.00	X		
Brazil	88,100,000	3.2 new cruzeiros = $1.00	X	X	
Chile	9,300,000	6.7 escudos = $1.00	X	X	
Colombia	19,500,000	16.3 pesos = $1.00	X	X	
Costa Rica	1,700,000	6.6 colons = $1.00	X		X
Cuba	8,200,000	1 peso = $1.00			
Dominican Rep.	4,000,000	1 peso = $1.00	X		
Ecuador	5,600,000	18.2 sucres = $1.00	X	X	
El Salvador	3,200,000	2.5 colons = $1.00	X		X
Guatemala	4,900,000	1 quetzal = $1.00	X		X
Guyana	700,000	2 dollars = $1.00			
Honduras	2,550,000	2 lempiras = $1.00	X		X
Mexico	47,200,000	12.5 pesos = $1.00	X	X	
Nicaragua	1,820,000	7 cordobas = $1.00	X		X
Panama	1,370,000	1 balboa = $1.00	X		
Paraguay	2,220,000	126 guaranis = $1.00	X	X	
Peru	12,500,000	38.7 sols = $1.00	X	X	
Uruguay	2,825,000	250 pesos = $1.00	X	X	
Venezuela	9,600,000	4.5 bolivars = $1.00	X	X	

* US $; 1968 exchange rates   OAS—Organization of American States; with Barbados, Haiti, Trinidad and Tobago, United States; Cuba suspended 1962
LAFTA—Latin American Free Trade Association
CACM—Central American Common Market

DEPENDENT LATIN AMERICA

	STATUS	HEADS OF GOVERNMENT	POPULATION
BR. HONDURAS	Self-governing British colony	SIR JOHN PAUL, governor	115,000
		GEORGE PRICE, premier	
FR. GUIANA	French overseas department	R. LETELLIER, prefect	40,000
SURINAM	Netherlands overseas constituent	H. DE VRIES, governor	400,000
		J. A. PENGEL, minister-president	

In December a political crisis that did not involve the students forced President Costa e Silva to assume emergency powers for one-man rule. In the crisis former President Juscelino Kubitschek was arrested, and military censorship of the press and radio was imposed.

▶ ANTI-AMERICANISM

There was considerable anti-United States fervor expressed throughout Latin America during the year. Many Latin-American leaders resented the continued United States preoccupation with Vietnam, which, they felt, turned Washington's attention away from its southern neighbors. The United States cut aid to Latin America.

Several terrorist attacks took a toll of United States officials in Latin America. In January, two military attachés in Guatemala were killed when their car was machine-gunned by members of the pro-communist Fuerzas Armadas Rebeldes. Then, in late August, John Gordon Mein, the United States ambassador to Guatemala, was killed in a similar attack. Efforts to find those responsible for the two attacks proved fruitless. In Brazil, a U.S. Army officer was killed in October.

▶ DROUGHT

A broad arc of Latin-American lands, stretching from the Caribbean down South America's Pacific coast, and then over the Andes to Argentina and Uruguay, was hit by a severe drought throughout 1968. Crop production and cattle production were off sharply. In Chile, agricultural losses totaled more than $205,000,000. In Cuba, sugar production was off at least 3,000,000 tons from the 1968 estimate. In Ecuador, the southern fourth of the nation, generally short of water, became a virtual desert. More than 75,000 persons had to migrate from their homes to better land. Only in a few locations, such as Colombia's and Brazil's usually dry northeast, did enough rainfall come to save crops and lend encouragement to continuing efforts to improve agricultural production.

▶ PLANS FOR A COMMON MARKET

In 1967, hemisphere presidents had decided to advance the idea of a hemisphere-wide common market. Three ministerial sessions were held in 1968 with the aim of furthering the presidential accord. But these failed to make any significant headway. The basic reason for this was that a number of nations began to express concern about the effects of a common market on their individual economies. However, a fourth session was called to discuss the eventual merger of the existing Central American Common Market and the Latin American Free Trade Association. Delegates from countries in the two regional groups set up a tentative merger plan.

Argentine President Juan Carlos Ongania was one of the 19 hemisphere presidents who had agreed to the idea of a common market in 1967. In 1968, however, he was a key figure in opposition to the plan. He said that he opposed placing too much authority in the hands of a supra-national organization such as a common market. He stated that "We cannot follow contradictory policies—domestically, seeking to close the gap between the government and the community so that an effective democracy may exist and, externally, transferring the power of decision to centers ever further removed from the community." To many observers, his words seemed to doom the idea of a full Latin-American common market.

There was some hope that subregional markets might take the place of the full hemisphere-wide concept. Limited progress toward forming such a grouping among South America's west-coast countries was evident during the year. But many disagreements arose among the six nations involved. These countries were Bolivia, Chile, Colombia, Ecuador, Peru and Venezuela. As the year ended, tariff and monetary disagreements stalled the efforts to form a so-called Andean bloc of countries.

JAMES NELSON GOODSELL
Latin America Editor
The Christian Science Monitor

LAW

FOR the second year in a row, an appointment to the United States Supreme Court, rather than one of the tribunal's decisions, made the biggest news in law. In June 1967 it was President Johnson's selection of Thurgood Marshall to be the Supreme Court's first Negro justice that made the headlines. Just a year later, Chief Justice Earl Warren announced his retirement. And President Johnson broke new ground once again by nominating Associate Justice Abe Fortas to be the first Jew to head the court in its 179-year history.

The choice of Fortas, plus the accompanying nomination to the high court of another longtime friend of President Johnson, U.S. Court of Appeals Judge Homer Thornberry, raised cries of "cronyism" and "lame duckism." (President Johnson had already announced his decision to leave office at the end of the year.) After a bitter and protracted Senate attack on the Fortas selection, and the threat of a filibuster, the nomination was withdrawn at Justice Fortas' request. And Chief Justice Warren remained at the court's helm.

▶ THE SUPREME COURT

Thrust into the spotlight by the Fortas controversy was the record of the "Warren Court." This name had been given—sometimes in praise, sometimes in condemnation —to the nation's highest tribunal in its 15 years under Earl Warren. During that period the Supreme Court embarked on a bold, liberal course that overturned precedents and handed down landmark decisions.

In this 15-year period the Supreme Court had declared segregation in the public schools unconstitutional. This was Chief Justice Warren's first major decision. The court had ordered the reapportionment of voting districts according to a one-man, one-vote formula. It also had given more protection to persons accused or suspected of crimes. In general, the Warren Court emphasized racial equality and personal liberties.

Earl Warren, chief justice of the Supreme Court. After the nomination of Abe Fortas was withdrawn because of opposition in the Senate, Warren announced that he would stay in his post until June 1969.

MAJOR DECISIONS OF THE SUPREME COURT IN 1968

ALCOHOLICS

Powell v. Texas (June 17) ruled 5–4 that the jailing of a chronic alcoholic for public drunkenness is not unconstitutional "cruel and unusual punishment."

BANKRUPTCY

Joint Industry Board v. United States (May 20) ruled 6–3 that a bankrupt employer's unpaid contributions to an employee's annuity fund are not wages that would give the fund a priority claim against the bankrupt estate.

CHURCH AND STATE

Board of Education v. Allen (June 10) ruled 6–3 that the New York State school-textbook-loan law which requires local school boards to buy books with state funds and lend them to parochial- and private-school students is constitutional.

Flast v. Cohen (June 10) ruled 8–1 that taxpayers can bring suits to challenge Federal expenditures on grounds that they violate the principle of separation of church and state, even though taxpayers usually cannot challenge Federal expenditures.

CIVIL RIGHTS

Brown v. Pennsylvania (May 20) let stand a lower court order that Girard College in Philadelphia admit Negro applicants.

Green v. County School Board of New Kent County; Raney v. Board of Education of the Gould School District; Monroe v. Board of Commissioners of the City of Jackson (May 27) ruled unanimously that school officials in the South cannot meet the constitutional obligation to desegregate public schools by offering "freedom of choice" plans that permit all students to pick their own schools.

Jones v. Mayer (June 17) ruled 7–2 that the Civil Rights Act of 1866 outlaws racial discrimination in all real-estate transactions.

Ferrell v. Dallas Independent School District (October 14) let stand, with Justice Douglas dissenting, a lower-court ruling that Dallas public schools could require long-haired male students to cut their hair.

COMMUNICATIONS

United States v. Southwestern Cable Co.; Midwest Television, Inc. v. Southwestern Cable Co. (June 10) ruled unanimously that the Federal Communications Commission can regulate all-cable community-antenna-television systems.

CRIMINAL LAW

Duncan v. Louisiana (May 20) ruled 7–2 that state courts grant defendants jury trials as guaranteed by the Sixth Amendment in all except trials for petty offenses.

Terry v. Ohio (June 10) ruled 8–1 that police may stop and frisk suspicious persons even if the police do not have probable cause to make an arrest.

ILLEGITIMATES

Levy v. Louisiana; Giona v. American Guarantee & Liability Insurance Co. (May 20) ruled 6–3 that a Louisiana law that barred illegitimate children and their parents from recovering damages for the wrongful death of each other was unconstitutional.

INDIANS

Menominee Tribe v. United States (May 27) ruled 6–2 that the treaty of Wolf River of 1854 gives the Menominee Indians fishing and hunting rights on their reservations in Wisconsin, and that these rights did not end in 1961 when the reservation terminated.

Puyallup Tribe v. Department of Game of Washington; Kautz v. Department of Game of Washington (May 27) ruled unanimously that the Puyallup Tribe still has fishing rights on the reservation created where the city of Tacoma is now situated, by the Treaty of Medicine Creek in 1854, but that the state of Washington may regulate the fishing.

RELIGION

Epperson v. Arkansas (November 12) ruled unanimously that the Arkansas state law ("monkey law") that makes it a crime to teach the theory of evolution in the public schools was unconstitutional.

SELECTIVE SERVICE

United States v. O'Brien (May 27) ruled 7–1 that the 1965 Selective Service Act that makes it a crime to burn a draft card was constitutional.

SELF-INCRIMINATION

Gardner v. Broderick; Uniformed Sanitation Men's Association, Inc. v. Commissioner of Sanitation (June 10) ruled unanimously that New York City cannot discharge employees for refusing to waive their privilege against self-incrimination and testify before a grand jury about alleged corruption.

TAXATION

First Agricultural National Bank of Berkshire County v. State Tax Commission (June 17) ruled 5–3 that under Federal law states may not tax a national bank.

School Desegregation

In 1968 the Supreme Court reviewed the implementation of its 1954 school-desegregation decision. The court ruled unanimously that school officials in the South could not satisfy the constitutional obligation to desegregate the public schools merely by offering "freedom of choice" plans that permitted all students to pick their own schools. The Supreme Court required public officials to take affirmative action to reduce racial imbalance in the schools. This imbalance resulted from the individual-choice system that most communities in the South were employing.

School officials were ordered to dismantle the "state-imposed dual system" and to replace it with a "unitary, nonracial school system."

Housing Bias

An almost-forgotten civil-rights law dating back to 1866 was used by the Supreme Court to prohibit racial discrimination in the sale and rental of private property. In a sweeping, 7–2 ruling the Supreme Court held that Negroes could now sue to bar discrimination in sales or rentals by private property owners. This ruling in effect established a national fair-housing statute. It went beyond the provisions of the 1968 Civil Rights Act, which did not cover private homeowners. The 1968 act also exempted rental units containing fewer than five families.

Draft-Card Burning

Resistance to the war in Vietnam continued to bring a rash of draft and civil-disobedience cases to the Federal courts. In one important decision, the Supreme Court upheld a 1965 law that made it a crime to burn or otherwise mutilate a draft card. Chief Justice Warren wrote the 7–1 opinion that supported the power of Congress to strengthen the selective-service laws. The Supreme Court reversed a lower court's ruling that declared the law against the burning of a draft card to be an unconstitutional infringement of free speech. Chief Justice Warren wrote in this decision that, "We cannot accept the view that an apparently limitless variety of conduct can be labeled 'speech' whenever the person engaging in the conduct intends thereby to express an idea."

The year's most celebrated antidraft trial took place in June. Dr. Benjamin Spock, the noted pediatrician, was convicted along with the Reverend William Sloane Coffin, chaplain of Yale University, and two oth-

---

MAJOR DECISIONS OF THE WARREN COURT

APPORTIONMENT

Baker v. Carr (1962) ruled that the court would step in to correct legislative malapportionment if the states did not act.

Reynolds v. Sims (1964) ruled that both houses of state legislatures must be apportioned on the basis of population.

Wesberry v. Sanders (1964) ruled that each Congressional district have approximately the same population.

CIVIL RIGHTS

Brown v. Board of Education (1954) outlawed public-school segregation.

Brown v. Board of Education (1955) ordered public-school officials to desegregate with "all deliberate speed."

Heart of Atlanta Motel v. United States (1964) ruled that the public-accommodations section of the 1964 Civil Rights Act that guaranteed Negroes access to hotels, motels and restaurants was legal.

CRIMINAL LAW

Mallory v. United States (1957) ruled that criminal suspects be arraigned promptly.

Mapp v. Ohio (1961) ruled that evidence obtained by illegal search and seizure could not be used in a state court.

Gideon v. Wainwright (1963) ruled that states must provide free legal counsel for indigent defendants.

Escobedo v. Illinois (1964) ruled that criminal suspect has a right to legal counsel when he is being questioned.

Miranda v. Arizona (1966) ruled that a suspect in a criminal case must be told of his right to remain silent, consult a lawyer, have a lawyer present during questioning by the police, and be provided with a lawyer if he cannot pay for one himself.

ers, of conspiracy to encourage draft evasion. They were sentenced to two-year prison terms. The verdict in a Federal court in Boston was appealed. But no decision had been reached by the end of the year.

Death Sentence

The Supreme Court applied the due-process clause of the Fourteenth Amendment in one decision. It ruled invalid a death sentence imposed by an Illinois jury from which were excluded all persons who expressed objections to the death penalty. The court held that the most that could be demanded of a prospective jury member was that he would consider all the penalties provided by state law and was not irrevocably committed to vote against the death penalty.

In another case, the Supreme Court struck down the death-penalty provision of the Federal Kidnapping Act. This provision permits imposition of the death penalty only upon defendants who assert their right to be tried by a jury. The court held that the provision discouraged a defendant from exercising his right to plead not guilty and demand a jury trial.

▶ THE TEXAS GULF SULFUR CASE

The blockbuster decision for the corporate world in 1968 was the ruling of the U.S. Court of Appeals for the Second Circuit in the Texas Gulf Sulfur case. The ruling held that officers and directors of a company cannot legally trade in their own company's shares if they have inside information not available to the public. The ruling, reversing a lower-court decision, held that some officials of the company had violated the securities law. The officials had bought stock in their own company. But they had not told the public about a major ore discovery in Canada.

The Texas Gulf decision was certain to be appealed to the Supreme Court. The decision had an immediate impact on the stock-market activities of corporate officials and on the disclosure policies of most publicly owned corporations.

▶ JURY SERVICE

A new law designed to open jury service in the Federal courts to thousands of persons who never before had the opportunity to serve went into effect at the end of the year. It provides for the selection of jurors at random from voter-registration lists. And it abolished discriminatory blue-ribbon juries and the arbitrary selection of qualified jurors by court officials.

The new law is expected to have its greatest impact in the South. Now increasing numbers of Negro voters will have the chance to be called and to serve. The law will also have an effect in other parts of the country. It will broaden the base from which prospective jurors are chosen. And it will obtain greater representation from members of lower economic groups.

▶ FEDERAL MAGISTRATES

Another new law for 1968 abolished the office of United States commissioner. Created in its place was the post of Federal magistrate. The magistrates will be given definite eight-year terms under appointment by United States district judges. They will be paid regular, set salaries rather than be compensated under the commissioners' fee system. And they are required to be lawyers. Under the new law, the magistrates will have trial jurisdiction over minor criminal offenses, supervision of pretrial proceedings, and preliminary consideration of petitions for postconviction relief.

▶ LAWYERS' SALARIES

Legal circles, especially young lawyers and law-school students, were stirred early in the year by the news that some Wall Street law firms would pay a starting salary of $15,000 a year to beginning lawyers. Comparable firms throughout the country went along with this jump of nearly 50 per cent in the salary rate. Only a relatively few new lawyers received this salary. But the increase tended to raise wages up and down the line.

MYRON KANDEL
Editor, New York Law Journal

LITERATURE

THE theme for the 1968 Children's Book Week—"Go Places with Books"—was an invitation to children and young people to explore the minds and hearts of individuals, as well as to travel via books to distant places and times.

The year 1968 marked the centenary of the publication of *Little Women* by Louisa May Alcott. Biographer Cornelia Meigs not only wrote a new introduction for the centennial edition, but she selected a charming collection of short stories for *Glimpses of Louisa* and wrote a new introduction for her redesigned Newbery Award winner, *Invincible Louisa*. Aileen Fisher's *We Alcotts* was popular with all ages as the reader saw the Alcott family through Marmee's eyes.

There were two major trends in children's books during the year. First, there was a great increase in the quantity and quality of paperbacks. Second, many books were published that were by or about Negroes. In the children's publishing field, at least, black Americans took their place as integral and natural parts of stories and illustrations.

In adult literature, book titles seemed to reflect the general state of turmoil that existed in the world during 1968. While world leaders sought solutions to the Vietnam war, crime in the streets, drug addiction and other problems, authors of both fiction and nonfiction used these problems as background for outstanding books. Noteworthy among these books were Gunnar Myrdal's *Asian Drama,* the *Report of the National Advisory Commission on Civil Disorders* and *The Walker Report: Rights in Conflict.*

ADULT LITERATURE

▶ **FICTION**

The Vietnam war continued to be one of the world's most divisive events in 1968. David Halberstam wrote about this war in *One Very Hot Day*. The story concerned a unit of soldiers seeking the Vietcong in a group of jungle villages. Though anecdotes and digressions slowed the action, they helped give a clear picture of jungle warfare and of certain types of men involved in the Vietnam conflict.

Richard Bradford made the best-seller lists with his first novel, *Red Sky at Morning*. He showed life in a small southwestern community during World War II. Then as now, people had problems, which Bradford explored with considerable humor. Humor and action made Charles Portis' second novel, *True Grit,* a delight to read. The author handled his characters with skill as he sent a 14-year-old girl of eighty years ago to avenge the murder of her father.

Among well-established novelists, John Updike enhanced his reputation with *Couples*. As he investigated changing relationships within one community, he helped readers understand more about American life.

Morris L. West and Gore Vidal continued to enjoy considerable success. West's *The Tower of Babel* capitalized on Arab-Israeli troubles, while Vidal's *Myra Breckinridge* took a look at the movie industry.

James T. Farrell has gone through a period of displeasing both readers and critics. But his latest novel, *A Brand New Life,* saw him regaining lost prestige as he worried about a couple in Chicago.

Most poets attract few readers today. Among those who should be noticed and remembered are Galway Kinnell and Carl Rakosi. In *Body Rags,* Kinnell made one see a farmhouse or an animal with new insight. Rakosi's *Amulet* was probably more difficult to understand, but it included some impressive imagery as it dealt with family relationships and nature.

▶ **NONFICTION**

Authors of nonfiction in 1968 tackled all of the world's problems. In a three-volume work called *Asian Drama,* Swedish economist Gunnar Myrdal considered politics, populations and poverty from Pakistan to Indonesia. With dozens of charts and several maps to supplement the text, he made it clear why southern Asia will long be of major concern to better-developed nations.

A much different problem attracted Erik H. Erikson. Today's young people want to "find themselves," and Erikson aided readers in understanding the problems of youth in *Identity: Youth and Crisis. The Academic Revolution,* by Christopher

---

PULITZER PRIZES

Fiction: WILLIAM STYRON (*The Confessions of Nat Turner*)

Poetry: ANTHONY HECHT (*The Hard Hours*)

History: BERNARD BAILYN (*The Ideological Origins of the American Revolution*)

Biography: GEORGE F. KENNAN (*Memoirs: 1925–1950*)

Nonfiction: WILL and ARIEL DURANT (*Rousseau and Revolution*)

NATIONAL BOOK AWARDS

Novel: THORNTON WILDER (*The Eighth Day*)

Poetry: ROBERT BLY (*The Light around the Body*)

Biography and History: GEORGE F. KENNAN (*Memoirs: 1925–1950*)

Nonfiction: JONATHAN KOZOL (*Death at an Early Age*)

Arts and Letters: WILLIAM TROY (*Selected Essays*)

Translation: HOWARD and EDNA HONG (*Soren Kierkegaard's Journals and Papers*)

Jencks and David Riesman, was also concerned with youth, as it studied the changing picture in higher education.

Race problems naturally figured in many books. In *White over Black,* Winthrop D. Jordan discussed the white man's view of the Negro during America's slave days. The book provided insight into the militant unrest of today. Covering this unrest was the *Report of the National Advisory Commission on Civil Disorders.* This book also had some historical orientation, describing past attitudes and the formation of ghettos. But it centered mostly on eight major riots and riot areas of 1967.

With a presidential election taking place in 1968, some authors were sure to write about politics. George Wallace's candidacy helped generate interest in *Gothic Politics in the Deep South* by Robert Sherrill. By concentrating on the careers of certain headline makers, the author produced a fascinating picture of a region.

Journalists seeking subjects other than world problems produced a number of outstanding biographies. Herbert Weinstock wrote *Rossini: A Biography* for the reader interested in all phases of the life of a creative person. It paid as much attention to the composer's personal adventures as to his operas. *Richard Wagner: The Man, His Mind and His Music* was Robert W. Gutman's contribution to musical biography. Marie Waife-Goldberg could call on her memories for *My Father, Sholom Aleichem.* At the same time, she gave something of her own story. Two other outstanding biographies were *Thomas Wolfe* by Andrew Turnbull and *Tolstoy* by Henri Troyat. As the bullfighter "El Cordobes," Manuel Benitez caught the fancy of a large public. Larry Collins and Dominique Lapierre caught the fancy of a large reading public by writing Benitez' biography, *Or I'll Dress You in Mourning.*

Some men prefer to tell their own stories, and in *The Double Helix* James D. Watson seemed unusually frank. As one of the 1962 Nobel Prizewinners involved in the discovery of DNA, he had a remarkable, though

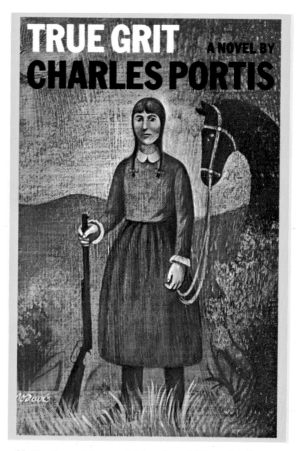

Mattie Ross, 14-year-old heroine of "True Grit."

controversial story to tell about his work.

Harold Macmillan's story of his and Britain's days during World War II also made excellent reading. *The Blast of War* left loopholes for future biographers to fill in, but it showed Macmillan as he remembered himself.

Bertrand Russell relied heavily on his correspondence in the second volume of his life—*The Autobiography of Bertrand Russell, 1914–1944*—and it's an unusual life.

Desmond Morris undertook to write the biography of all of us. In *The Naked Ape* he closely examined man as if a human being were just another animal for the microscope of the zoologist. A rather different examination of man concentrated on one phase of human behavior. This was Anthony Storr's *Human Aggression,* a study of why people perform acts of violence.

CHARLES PAUL MAY

Children's Literature

▶ REFERENCE BOOKS

A welcome addition to every home and library was *The Harcourt Brace Intermediate Dictionary* with its colorful illustrations and large, clear type. Frances Cavanah's *Freedom Encyclopedia: American Liberties in the Making* (Rand) was another of 1968's invaluable reference books.

Several excellent books on the Negro that would be useful for reference were published during the year. These included *Black on Black: Commentaries by Negro Americans* edited by Arnold Adoff (Macmillan); *Chronicles of Negro Protest: Documenting the History of Black Power* compiled by Bradford Chambers (Parents'); Julius Lester's *To Be a Slave* (Dial), a history of slavery; and Robert Goldston's *The Negro Revolution* (Macmillan). Two picture books about the tragedy of slavery were *Oh Lord, I Wish I Was a Buzzard* by Polly Greenberg (Macmillan) and *Harriet and the Promised Land* by Jacob Lawrence (Simon & Schuster).

A carefully researched and well-written book on the depression was Robert Goldston's *The Great Depression* (Bobbs).

Books about Politics

Many good books on politics were published in 1968, an election year. Besides Lee Learner Gray's revision of *How We Choose a President* (St. Martin's), other books were *We Elect a President* by David E. Weingast (Messner), Michael Dorman's *The Second Man: The Changing Role of the Vice Presidency* (Delacorte), Robert Liston's *Politics—From Precinct to Presidency* (Delacorte) and *The People's Choice: The Story of Candidates, Cam-*

paigns and Elections by Alvin Schwartz (Dutton).

To help young people analyze the issues in today's world, *Ideals and Ideologies: Communism, Socialism, and Capitalism* (World) by Harry Ellis presented an objective account of the three great "isms."

Books about Art

For years there had been a dearth of art books for children. But in 1968 many excellent books on the subject were published. There were outstanding biographies, such as Howard Greenfeld's *Marc Chagall* (Follett) and *Seven Women: Great Painters* by Frances and Winthrop Neilson (Chilton). There were also two new series: Art for Children Series (Doubleday) and Discovering Art Series (McGraw). Two delightful books on sculpture were *Looking at Sculpture* by Roberta M. Paine (Lothrop) and Marion Downer's *Long Ago in Florence: The Story of the Della Robbia Sculpture* (Lothrop).

▶ FICTION

Many of the stories for the intermediate grades were mediocre, but Beverly Cleary's *Ramona the Pest* (Morrow), John Rowe Townsend's *Pirate's Island* (Lippincott) and Eleanor Hull's *A Trainful of Strangers* (Atheneum) stood out.

While there was a dearth of quality stories for the intermediates, there was an abundance of well-written stories on subjects of interest to older boys and girls.

Short stories are not usually popular with children and teen-agers, but Paul Darcy Boles spoke directly to them in his collection *A Million Guitars* (Little).

Kristin Hunter's *The Soul Brothers and Sister Lou* (Scribners) described vividly a Negro girl in an urban ghetto struggling to discover herself and to identify with her own people. Jesse Jackson's *Tessie* (Harper) presented a real problem of a Negro girl who has won a scholarship to an all-white private school.

Many other books related directly to inner conflicts and problems of young peo-

"Drummer Hoff" adapted by Barbara Emberley.

CLICK

SULTAN

ple in today's world. Hal G. Evarts' *Smuggler's Road* (Scribners) showed character development in a boy who chose to work in a rural Mexican clinic rather than go to a reform school. Lillian Pohlmann's *Sing Loose* (Westminster) was a story of the inner struggle of a girl whose father returns from prison. Hope Campbell's *Why Join the Giraffes?* (Norton) was a delightful story of a conventional girl in an unconventional family. Girls loved Patricia Moyes' *Helter-Skelter* (Holt), a story of fun, romance and espionage that was as modern as the heroine's miniskirts.

Andre Norton's *The Zero Stone* (Viking) and John Christopher's *The Pool of Fire* (Macmillan) were two of the best science-fiction books of 1968.

Dramatic Arts

A neglected area in children's literature has been the dramatic arts. Three welcome additions were Arthur Craig de Angeli's *The Door in the Wall* (Doubleday), a dramatic version of the Newbery Award winner by his mother, Marguerite de Angeli; *The Scarlet Thread* by Mary Hays Weik

"Charley, Charlotte and the Golden Canary"

(Atheneum), a collection of five one-act plays showing how entertainers lived and were regarded by society in different periods; and Hans Baumann's *Caspar and His Friends: A Collection of Puppet Plays* (Walck).

Poetry

With the emphasis on verbal expression and creative play in work with underprivileged children, poetry came into its own in 1968. A few of the fine poetry anthologies were *I Am the Darker Brother: An Anthology of Modern Poems by Negro Americans* by Arnold Adoff (Macmillan); *The Wind Has Wings* compiled by Mary Alice Downie and Barbara Robertson (Walck) —77 poems by Canadian poets; *Piping Down the Valley Wild* edited by Nancy Larrick (Delacorte); and *Out of the Earth I Sing: Poetry and Songs of Primitive Peoples of the World* edited by Richard Lewis (Norton). The last was an unusual collection, illustrated with reproductions of primitive art. Another unusual and beautiful book was *It's Autumn!* by Sister Noemi Weygant O.S.B. (Westminster).

▶ **EASY-READING AND PICTURE BOOKS**

Many easy-reading and picture books were published during 1968. But creative, imaginative ones were few and far between. Some of the loveliest ones were the fairy and folk tales illustrated by distinguished artist Blair Lent in Hans Christian Andersen's *The Little Match Girl* (Houghton) and Arlene Mosel's *Tikki Tikki Tembo* (Holt). A delightful easy-reading book was *Ants Are Fun* by Mildred Myrick with pictures by Arnold Lobel (Harper). A few of the picture books that stood out were *Talking without Words* by Marie Hall Ets (Viking), *Spectacles* by Ellen Raskin (Atheneum), Lonzo Anderson's *Two Hundred Rabbits* illustrated by Adrienne Adams (Viking), Leo Lionni's beautiful *The Biggest House in the World* (Pantheon), and Don Freeman's *Corduroy* (Viking), a charming book for the youngest about a toy bear and a Negro girl.

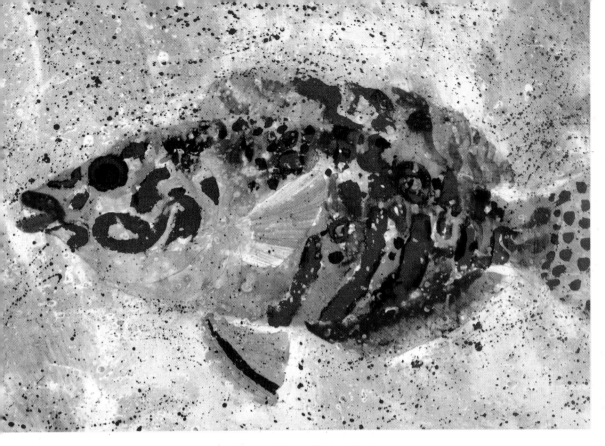

A rainbow fish from "Brian Wildsmith's Fishes."

▶FOREIGN-LANGUAGE BOOKS

There was an increase in foreign-language books and books in translation.

One of the finest books on exercise, both in text and illustration, was Rosa Demeter's *Hop Run Jump* (Day), which had been translated from Hungarian into German into English.

The interest in foreign-language books, especially Spanish, encouraged the publication of some delightful new books as well as the translation of popular English titles for the primary age. There were Lois Lenski's *El Auto Pequeño* (*The Little Auto*) and *La Granja Pequeña* (*The Little Farm*) (Walck); Robert Bright's *Mi Paraguas Rojo* (*My Red Umbrella*) (Morrow); and the Spanish translation of the Let's-Read-and-Find-Out Science Series (Crowell). All ages enjoyed Esther Hautzig's *At Home: A Visit in Four Languages* (Macmillan), which told about family life in English, French, Spanish and Russian.

▶PAPERBACK BOOKS

Many wonderful titles were added to the list of paperbacks in print. But the most exciting breakthrough was the publication of over fifty picture books with superb illustrations in color and excellent format called Peter Possum Books (Grolier). All the favorites, Beatrix Potter, Palmer Cox, Aesop, Randolph Caldecott, Howard Pyle, and many others were represented.

It seems fitting to close this brief résumé of children's books published in 1968 with the announcement that 1968 was the year of the publication of *The High King* (Holt), the fifth and last book in the series on the wonderful land of Prydain by the great American writer of fantasy, Lloyd Alexander. Many young people will eagerly be awaiting Mr. Alexander's next journey to the world of fantasy.

CAROLYN W. FIELD
Coordinator, Work with Children
Free Library of Philadelphia

MEDICINE AND HEALTH

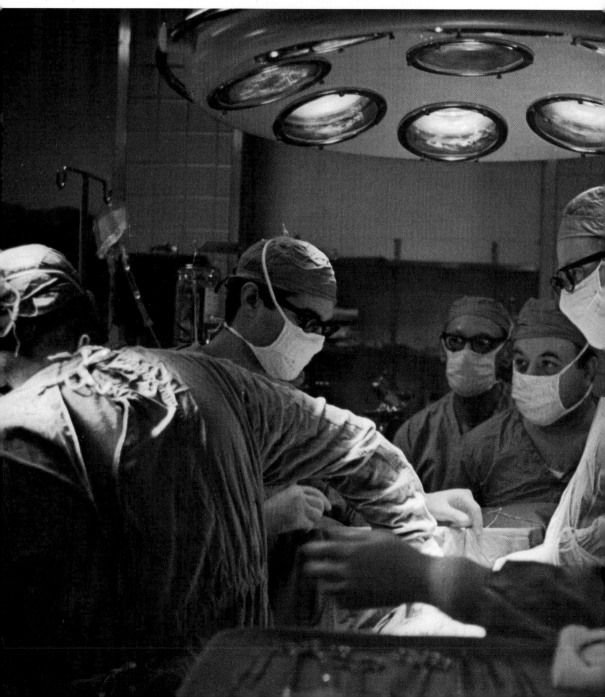

EACH year brings with it new and exciting developments in every field of endeavor. Nowhere are these developments more exciting than in the sciences. And nowhere do these developments touch man so closely as in the field of medicine. In 1968, with heart diseases once again the major cause of death in the United States, doctors and researchers made dramatic gains in the fight to control the causes of such diseases, and in the fight to cure them once they had struck. Surgical teams in all parts of the world followed the lead of Dr. Christiaan Barnard of South Africa and performed more than 100 heart transplants during 1968.

Other surgeons transplanted heart valves which were obtained from either human or animal donors. Still other medical men attacked the problem of heart diseases from a preventative angle, advising their patients to watch their diets or to strengthen their hearts through jogging or other forms of exercise.

During 1968, transplant operations were not limited to hearts. Surgeons also transplanted corneas, lungs, livers, kidneys and even pancreas glands.

In other areas of medicine, researchers perfected vaccines for German measles and mumps, and continued to work toward the day when they would find a cure for cancer. Lung cancer continued to be linked to cigarette smoking, and a new finding in 1968 linked stomach cancer to air pollution. Thus researchers sought in many ways to bring an end to environmental pollution.

From organ transplants to antismoking campaigns, the medical and allied professions sought in 1968 to build a healthier nation and to prolong life.

▶ORGAN TRANSPLANTS

By the end of 1968, more than 100 heart transplants had been performed. Although the surgical techniques had been perfected, there were, at year's end, huge gaps in the understanding of the rejection phenomenon and how best to control it. Philip Blaiberg, the South African who had received one of

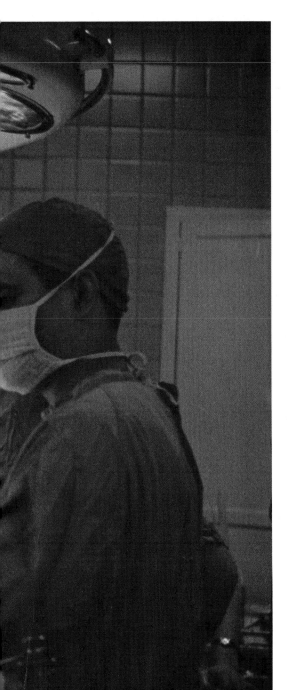

Dr. Adrian Kantrowitz and his team of surgeons perform a heart-transplant operation at Maimonides Hospital, New York City.

the first transplanted hearts, was still alive and well at the end of 1968. Yet Dr. Barnard expressed the opinion that Blaiberg's body might yet reject his new heart, and that he might have to have a second transplant operation, as had other patients.

Many physicians felt that it was more important to study those patients who had undergone transplant operations rather than to continue to do transplants when so little is known about tissue rejection. At the present time, rejection is partially controlled by the use of a substance called anti-lymphocyte globulin. This substance interferes with those blood cells (lymphocytes) which are assumed to be responsible for the rejection phenomenon.

There was another major problem involved with heart transplants. With the increasing need for heart donors, it has become important to establish more careful criteria as to when clinical death actually occurs. This is especially important since, with the help of sophisticated machinery, the heart and lungs of an individual can be kept functioning even after the individual has ceased to live. Medical consensus appears to lean heavily on the use of an elec-

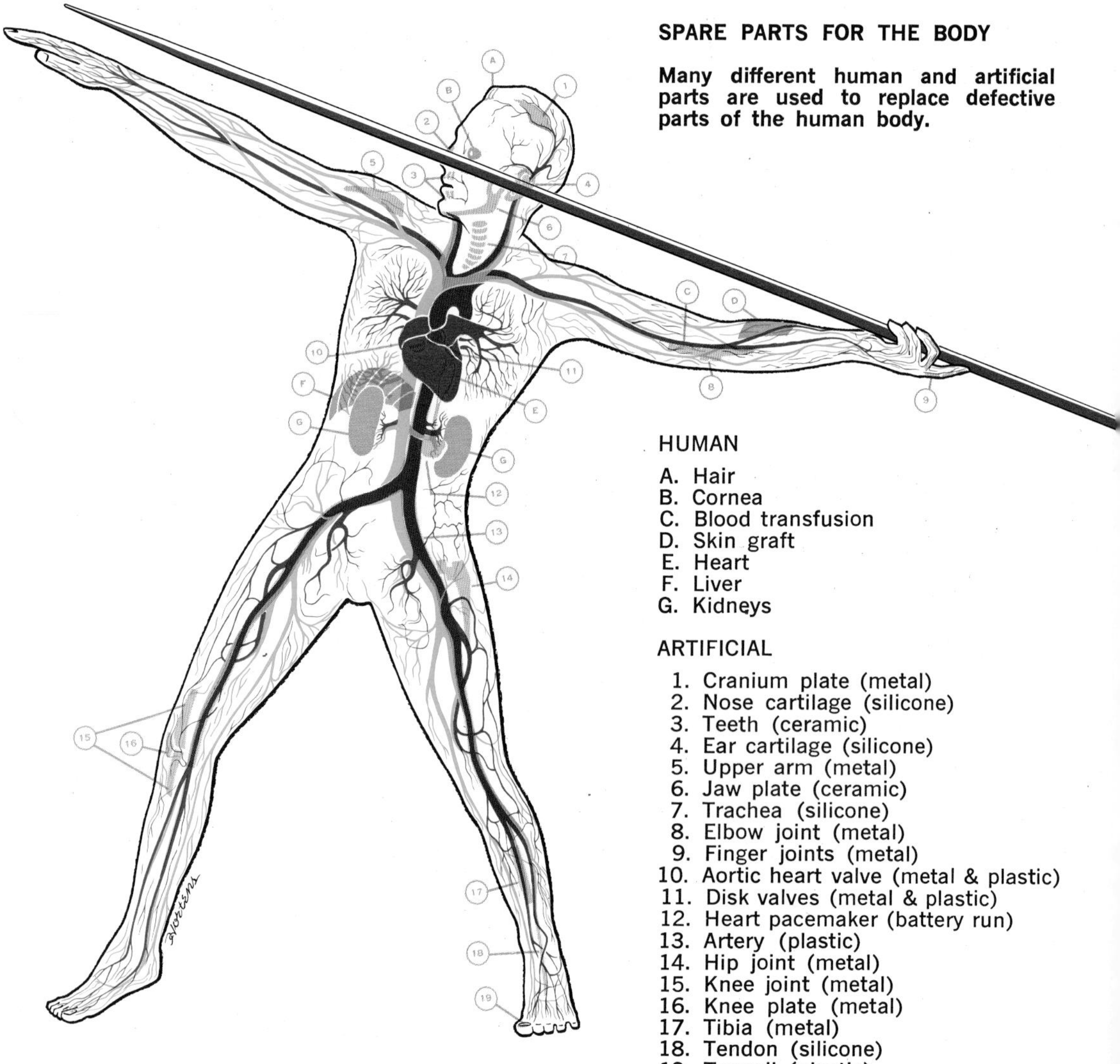

SPARE PARTS FOR THE BODY

Many different human and artificial parts are used to replace defective parts of the human body.

HUMAN

A. Hair
B. Cornea
C. Blood transfusion
D. Skin graft
E. Heart
F. Liver
G. Kidneys

ARTIFICIAL

 1. Cranium plate (metal)
 2. Nose cartilage (silicone)
 3. Teeth (ceramic)
 4. Ear cartilage (silicone)
 5. Upper arm (metal)
 6. Jaw plate (ceramic)
 7. Trachea (silicone)
 8. Elbow joint (metal)
 9. Finger joints (metal)
10. Aortic heart valve (metal & plastic)
11. Disk valves (metal & plastic)
12. Heart pacemaker (battery run)
13. Artery (plastic)
14. Hip joint (metal)
15. Knee joint (metal)
16. Knee plate (metal)
17. Tibia (metal)
18. Tendon (silicone)
19. Toenail (plastic)

troencephalogram (EEG), or brain-wave examination, as the most reliable tool to establish death. Normally the person who registers no brain wave would be regarded as dead. But as yet no official group has been set up to determine any standards. Nor has any official body reported on the various social and moral problems involved in organ transplants.

In spite of this, heart transplants were performed in 1968 with increasing frequency. Surgeons also transplanted lungs, livers, the pancreas and even a bowel. In at least one case, a surgeon attempted a multiple transplant, using a donor's lungs and heart.

▶ HEART SURGERY

In 1968 heart valves were transplanted from pig hearts and from cadavers to living recipients. The results were seemingly satisfactory, thus eliminating many of the problems that occur when artificial valves are substituted for diseased valves.

Also of great interest was the first successful repair of a congenital (one found at birth) form of heart disease called persistent *truncus arteriosus*. This form of heart defect was always thought to be incurable. Yet a team of doctors at the Mayo Clinic was able to correct the defect surgically.

▶ HEART-DISEASE STUDY

Of all the heart diseases the one that causes the greatest number of deaths among productive adult males is the heart attack. In 1968 a simultaneous study was begun by medical groups in Edinburgh, Scotland, Budapest, Hungary, and Prague, Czechoslovakia. The three groups are to study large numbers of men of coronary-attack age in the hope that such a program will yield information on the detection, prevention, treatment of heart attacks and on the rehabilitation of cardiac patients.

▶ JOGGING FOR HEALTH

1968 was the year in which patients with coronary-artery disease began to take to the road in jogging gear. It has become more

NOBEL PRIZE

Physiology and Medicine: MARSHALL W. NIRENBERG, U.S.; HAR GOBIND KHORANA, U.S.; ROBERT W. HOLLEY, U.S.

STOUFFER PRIZE

Award in Medicine: F. MERLIN BUMPUS, U.S.; WILLIAM STANLEY PEART, Britain; ROBERT SCHWYZER, Switzerland; LEONARD T. SKEGGS, U.S.

AMERICAN HEART ASSOCIATION

Blakeslee Science Reporting Awards: MATT CLARK (*Newsweek* magazine); DAVID M. CLEARY (*Philadelphia Bulletin*); RONALD KOTULAK (*Chicago Tribune*); LENNART NILSSON (*Life* magazine); RESEARCH PROJECT (NBC-TV series); DIMENSION ON HEALTH (CBS radio series)

Gold Heart Awards: MICHAEL E. DeBAKEY, Cardiovascular Research Center, Methodist Hospital, Houston; CARLETON B. CHAPMAN, Dartmouth Medical School; ROME A. BETTS, executive director, American Heart Association, 1949–68

ALBERT LASKER MEDICAL RESEARCH AWARDS

Clinical Research Award: JOHN H. GIBBON, JR., Jefferson Medical College

Basic Medical Research Award: MARSHALL W. NIRENBERG, National Heart Institute and HAR GOBIND KHORANA, University of Wisconsin; WILLIAM F. WINDLE, New York University Medical Center

Public Service Award: LISTER HILL, U.S. Senate

AMERICAN PUBLIC HEALTH ASSOCIATION

Bronfman Prizes: MOISÉS BÉHAR, Institute of Nutrition of Central America and Panama; JAMES L. GODDARD, EDP Technology; ABRAHAM LILIENFELD, Johns Hopkins University School of Hygiene and Public Health

and more commonplace to see people of all walks of life and all ages jogging up and down the streets and country lanes. Doctors now feel that this form of exercise is good for young healthy individuals, but especially for older people. A number of studies indicate that a carefully applied program of jogging is of value to selected post-heart-attack patients. The theory has been advanced that many of the diseases of middle age are related to blood-flow rates, and that as blood flow is increased, oxygen transport is improved. Jogging and other exercises increase the rate of blood flow.

▶ BLINDNESS

Less spectacular than heart transplants in 1968, but vitally important nevertheless, were the corneal transplants. In 1968 the use of a synthetic material enabled surgeons to transplant corneas in people who were blind because their own corneas were damaged, and who had undergone unsuccessful corneal transplants in the past. The synthetic material used was a layer of silicone, which helped bind the donor cornea more firmly to the recipient. With this method there was no rejection and no ultimate clouding in the transplanted cornea.

Another technique used to overcome blindness is to scrape off the damaged surface of the cornea and to suture a plastic lens in place. This procedure can be performed in a doctor's office. Thus far it has worked well.

In 1968, surgeons increasingly used cryosurgery (surgery employing freezing) to extract corneas, seal holes in the retina of the eye, and to help in correcting glaucoma.

▶ SEEKING A CURE FOR CANCER

In the field of cancer research, progress was slow but steady. Dr. Peter Medawar of the National Institute of Medical Research in Great Britain, a Nobel Prizewinner, once again emphasized the concept of the immunity aspect of cancer. This theory had been all but discarded some years ago. It was, however, recently revived and is now being restudied. At almost the same time that Dr. Medawar made his statement, a team of researchers at the National Cancer Institute in the United States reported that an antigen in melanoma cells is able to induce an antibody response in patients with malignant melanoma (a form of cancer). The inference is important in that it points up the need for research in this field. Only in this way can we get more information on how to promote antibody production and, hopefully, to establish a way to immunize people against cancer.

As to the newer advances in treatment, it has been found that certain lymphomas in children have disappeared completely with chemotherapy (the use of drugs, such as methotrexate). In leukemia, the use of a new drug, l-asparaginase, has resulted in long remissions of this disease.

At a meeting of the International Congress of Physiological Sciences, there was an encouraging report about the treatment

The new Goodyear mechanical heart, right, is much smaller than the older model and closely resembles the human heart in size and shape. When perfected and put in use, it will easily be enclosed in the body.

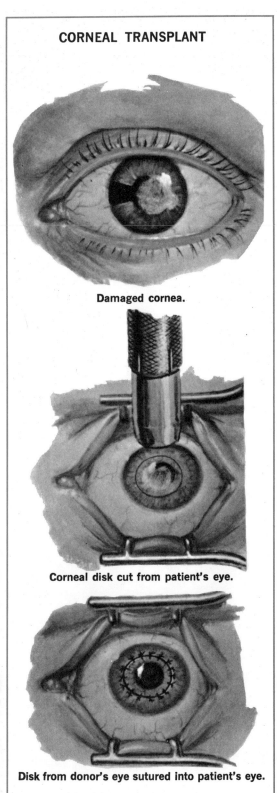

CORNEAL TRANSPLANT

Damaged cornea.

Corneal disk cut from patient's eye.

Disk from donor's eye sutured into patient's eye.

of certain tumors in experimental animals. Treatment consisted of cooling the animal, but allowing the area of the tumor to remain at normal temperatures. This causes increased blood flow to the tumor area. Using cancer-fighting drugs under these circumstances allows more of the drug to be deposited in the tumor tissue. In addition, the normal temperature of the tumor tissue causes the cancer cells in the tumor to be at a relatively higher rate of metabolism. This makes it more susceptible to drug therapy.

▶ INFECTIOUS DISEASES

Interesting developments took place in the field of infectious diseases during 1968. In South Vietnam young Americans were not only beset by all the horrors of war, but they were plagued by a resistant form of malaria. Dr. John D. Arnold, director of the Harry S. Truman Laboratory of Comparative Medicine, announced new drugs that seem to act quickly and effectively against the disease. These studies are being continued.

A vaccine to prevent rubella (German measles) is expected in one to two years, according to Dr. Paul D. Parkman of the National Institutes of Health. The vaccine has already proved effective in thousands of animals studied and in some studies with children in Taiwan. It will prove a major contribution in the protection of pregnant women against the threat of malformed children.

Mumps vaccine was finally made available in limited quantity in 1968. It should soon be available to the general public.

Immunization against a number of other diseases has been practiced for many decades. Yet it is a sad fact that in some areas society has not advanced so rapidly as has medicine. In our technically sophisticated world, smallpox, a disease which should have been wiped out, is still present and, as a matter of fact, is on the rise in some parts of the world. In East Pakistan there were 10,829 cases and 5,601 deaths in 1967. In India, in the first quarter of 1968, smallpox killed 2,329 people. The World Health Organization began a vaccination program which should wipe out smallpox by the early 1970's.

▶ **NUTRITION AND HEALTH**

In 1968 the second Western Hemisphere Nutrition Congress was held in Puerto Rico. Probably the most important concept to come out of this meeting was the possibility that malnutrition, particularly protein malnutrition, may be a chief factor in limiting the mental development as well as the physical development of children. Dr. Monckeburg, professor of pediatrics and nutrition at the University of Santiago, Chile, documented the occurrence of severe impairment of brain growth in infants who had been subjected to poor nutrition during the first months of life.

This concept has many ramifications. It will, among other things, possibly dispel the idea that there are genetic differences in various ethnic groups and that these differences account for mental attainment. Much closer to the truth is the fact that these very same ethnic groups, because of social and economic problems, are the victims of poor nutrition during pregnancy and during early infancy. It is during these important periods that malnutrition leads to a severe lag both mentally and physically. And, unfortunately, this lag is all too frequently irreversible.

▶ **HEALTH HAZARDS**

Cigarette smoking continued to be a major health hazard in 1968. A report by the United States Public Health Service suggested that smoking probably affects the heart adversely by increasing the heart's need for oxygen while reducing the ability of the blood to supply the increased need. Blood flow seems to be slower in smokers.

At the annual meeting of the American Association for the Advancement of Science, a new screening test for oral cancer indicated a higher level of positive findings among heavy cigarette smokers than among nonsmokers.

There was one encouraging note: Figures published by the Internal Revenue Service, Alcohol and Tobacco Tax Division, showed a decrease in cigarettes removed from the manufacturers' warehouses. According to Dr. Daniel Horn, director of the National Clearing House for Smoking and Health, this would indicate that there are possibly 1,500,000 fewer smokers despite the fact that there are 3,000,000 more people of smoking age.

In the field of auto safety there was much to be done. Pressure by the medical community, among others, had forced the auto manufacturers to install some safety devices in cars, and this probably has resulted in lives saved. But there should be greater efforts made toward producing a really safe automobile.

Noise pollution continued unabated in 1968. In urban centers, jet planes, helicopters, heavy-construction machinery and other city noises have been a cause of concern to many public-health workers. Stud-

American Cancer Society poster used to impress upon teen-agers the hazards of smoking.

best
tip
yet:
DON'T
START!

THE AMERICAN CANCER SOCIETY

PER-CAPITA HEALTH AND MEDICAL CARE EXPENSES

	1950	1955	1960	1963	1964	1965	1966
Total	$56.38	$76.22	$106.15	$123.76	$137.23	$147.27	$155.24
Hospital care	13.03	19.91	29.12	37.03	40.20	44.10	45.27
Physicians' services	17.22	21.07	29.80	34.32	39.83	42.65	44.42
Dentists' services	6.37	9.25	11.08	12.05	13.81	14.45	15.27
Other professional services *	2.45	3.26	4.64	4.66	4.68	4.66	4.67
Drug and drug sundries	11.38	14.45	20.20	22.10	22.81	24.34	26.06
Eyeglasses and appliances **	3.20	3.60	4.27	4.96	5.52	6.22	8.05
Nursing-home care	.73	.92	2.31	2.89	4.30	4.22	4.16
Medical-insurance payments	1.99	3.77	4.74	5.75	6.08	6.63	7.34

* Includes nurses, physical therapists, psychologists, etc.
** Includes hearing aids, orthopedic appliances, etc.

ies have shown that supposedly tolerable but above-normal noise levels can result in damage to man's hearing apparatus. A study at the Stanford Research Institute also showed alterations of brain-wave patterns among sleeping subjects when the noise level was increased. There was also a change in heart rate, respiration rate and blood pressure. All this points out the probable harmful effects of noise and points up the need to control noise.

Air pollution also continued to be an ever-increasing problem. In Buffalo, New York, a study indicated another possible bad effect of dirty air. It was found that twice as many men died of stomach cancer in the sootier areas of the city than those who lived in the areas of lower air pollution. The relationship is not so close as the relationship between air pollution and various pulmonary problems. But it does underline the fact that if this problem is not checked soon, we may yet make our planet unfit to support human life.

▶ **MEDICAL BRIEFS**

There were a number of other interesting medical advances in 1968.

In Australia a baboon was used to save the life of a girl who had a liver disease, and who was in a deep coma. The girl's blood was circulated through the baboon, which previously had had its blood replaced with blood of the same type as the patient's. The toxins in the girl's blood were removed by the baboon's liver in a six-hour period.

The young girl came out of the coma, and she has been doing well.

Dialyses machines have been used for years to remove toxins from the body. Such machines have been used especially when there has been kidney failure or poisoning due to intake of toxic agents. For many years, though, there has been only moderate success in the treatment of the latter group. Dr. H. Earl Ginn of Vanderbilt realized that most poisons taken by patients (by misake or intent) are soluble in oil. The standard dialysis solution has been a water solution. Dr. Ginn and three fellow workers simply changed the solution to an oil solution when treating patients who had taken oil-soluble poisons. The results were encouraging.

Another very encouraging development was in the treatment of Parkinsonism, a disease of blood flow through the brain. Parkinsonism causes uncontrollable tremors in the victims (usually the older age group) and sometimes results in invalidism. This unfortunate ailment has resisted all forms of treatment. In 1968, however, Dr. George C. Cotzias of Brookhaven National Laboratory made an important breakthrough. By using the drug L-dopa (short for Levodihydroxyphenyla-lanine), he was able to improve patients with the severe form of the disease. Patients with a less severe form of the disease gained virtually normal muscle control.

LEONARD I. GORDON, M.D.
Medical Consultant, *Medical Tribune*

TRANSPLANTATION

ABOUT three thousand years ago someone made the interesting observation that pieces of a tree swept by the wind against bare clefts of another tree would occasionally become joined to it and continue to grow. Farmers who tried to imitate this event were successful only with trees of identical or similar species. Tangerine and lemon trees, for example, could be linked, but pear trees and oaks could not.

The transfer and combining of different portions of plants assumed an important role in agriculture. The Romans called this maneuver *transplantation*. A synonymous term, *grafting*, probably derived from the Latin name *graphium*. This was a pencil-shaped tool used to imbed bits of the *donor* plant into the *recipient*, or *host*, plant.

Quite another sort of "transplantation" was practised as long ago as the Stone Age. In many early civilizations people actually believed that the vigor and spirit of brave foes could be transmitted by eating some of their organs. Blood was drunk to acquire health. And hearts were eaten to acquire strength. Is it not ironic that man's noble hopes and efforts to conquer disease by transplantation should have originated from such gruesome customs?

▶ THE FIRST MEDICAL TRANSPLANTATIONS

Transplantation in medicine began with surgical procedures designed to repair skin defects caused by injury. It was soon noticed that skin grafts would *take*, or fasten permanently, when obtained from the same person. But those grafts taken from other persons became detached after a few days. In the laboratory, grafting between organisms was accomplished with great difficulty and just with very primitive specimens, such as tadpoles and lizards. The prospects of ever achieving real clinical transplantation seemed bleak indeed.

▶ THE PROBLEM OF REJECTION

The *rejection* of tissues from alien sources is a natural phenomenon whereby every creature preserves its uniqueness. Rejection is brought about principally through two allied mechanisms, the *immunologic* and the *inflammatory*. Both of these vary in intensity. And the intensity depends on the characteristics of the tissues in question. If the tissues of donor and recipient resemble one another so much that rejection does not occur, prompt healing follows. *Tolerance* is then said to exist. This, however, is uncommon. Such tissue *compatibility* is directly proportional to the degree of blood-tissue relationship. Therefore tolerance is highest in identical twins, less in fraternal twins and other close kin. There is very little or no tolerance in distant family and unrelated persons.

The more complicated the cellular makeup of structures to be grafted, the greater is the chance of rejection. Simple ones, like bone and the cornea of the eye, are well tolerated. Until fairly recent years they were virtually the only tissues (except blood) that could be grafted between humans. Of course, lifeless materials, like metals and plastics, are not tissues. This is why heart valves and other devices made from synthetic substitutes can be placed inside the body without fear of rejection.

A special kind of transplantation is blood transfusion. The reason that transfusion is possible is that the red blood cells of donors and recipients are carefully screened and matched. This eliminates all risks of incompatibility.

▶ BREAKTHROUGHS IN ORGAN TRANSPLANTS

The present flurry of activity in transplantation work is a result of several major breakthroughs in research. One of these was the demonstration that the rejection of tissues can be partly held in check by various' means. X rays and certain drugs or chemical agents are used for this purpose. Another breakthrough was the development of ways to preserve organs after their removal from the body. A third was the invention of machines that can temporarily sustain life in people who are deprived of the function of impaired vital organs.

Heart Transplants

The significance of these advances can be understood by considering the situation with respect to heart transplantation. Such operations have lately evolved from the experimental to the clinical stage. When a heart is removed for grafting, its cells must be kept alive until it is stitched into its new residence. Also, the individual whose diseased heart is taken out needs a pump for a while as an artificial "heart." This pump circulates oxygenated blood throughout the rest of the body. If this were not done, he would suffer grave damage to the brain and other sensitive tissues which rely heavily on oxygen for survival. After the foreign (donor) heart is grafted into place, the tendency to rejection must be curbed. This is done with drugs, as mentioned above. At present these potent chemicals have to be given indefinitely. There are, however, side effects to these drugs. They seriously interfere with other critical processes, such as those concerned with resisting infection. However, intensive research on these problems has already produced results. There have been improvements in methods for suppressing rejection without excessively weakening other crucial body defenses.

▶ CURRENT TECHNOLOGY

What is the contemporary status of transplantation? The answer is that it is in a dynamic stage of transition. The grafting of kidneys is now being performed more often, and with rapidly increasing success rates. Hopefully, before too long, there will be similar successes with grafting of the heart, liver, lungs and other essential organs. There is steady progress in techniques for keeping tissues and organs viable for longer periods outside the body. Also, there is good headway being made toward a better understanding of the mysteries of the rejection mechanism.

▶ WHAT THE FUTURE HOLDS

Blood banks are commonplace nowadays. It can be predicted that eventually there will be "banks" for the deposit and withdrawal of a diversity of "spare parts." Human donors, however, will unavoidably always be in short supply. Thus the stored tissues and organs will doubtless be obtained more and more from suitable animals. This will come about as we learn to control the violent rejection reaction between the tissues of man and animal.

The applications of transplantation can theoretically revolutionize the art and science of medicine. For instance, an ailing organ will be separated, discarded and exchanged for a healthy one. Or it might be salvaged by intensive treatment in a bath of powerful chemical substances and then reconnected to its parent body. This body meanwhile will have been kept in a condition of "suspended animation" in special types of incubators. In other cases (as Boris Karloff did in a 1940 motion picture entitled *Black Friday!*), a brain will be transplanted into a young person who has suffered cerebral destruction from accident or sickness.

Finally, there is good reason to believe that the long-awaited cure for cancer may evolve as a by-product of unlocking the enigmas of rejection.

Incredible? Stranger than fiction? Perhaps. But these are the horizons toward which transplantation investigations will be heading gradually. Already the anticipated achievements—as well as the problems— that these fantastic undertakings will present are occupying the thoughts of physicians, philosophers, engineers, lawyers, theologians, and many other professions.

C. Walton Lillehei, M.D., Ph.D.
David Chas. Schechter, M.S., M.D.

MIDDLE EAST

WITH the major exception of the Arab-Israeli dispute, political tension in the Middle East subsided somewhat in 1968. Kurdish dissatisfaction in Iraq, the border squabble between Morocco and Algeria and the Greek-Turkish conflict over Cyprus moved out of the saber-rattling stage to the conference table. The struggle continued in Yemen between Royalists and Republicans. But the amount of bloodletting was considerably reduced as compared to 1967. In Southern Yemen the ruling National Liberation Front faced serious domestic problems. As a result it was prevented from exporting its philosophy to the Persian Gulf and southeast Arabia. The creation in the Gulf of the Federation of Arab Emirates was initiated in a relatively peaceful and orderly fashion. Political and economic developments in Turkey, Iran, Kuwait, Libya and Saudi Arabia continued to advance with a fairly large measure of success and stability.

THE SOVIET PRESENCE

The Middle East continued to experience a major change in terms of global politics. The Soviet Union enlarged its naval presence in the eastern Mediterranean to over sixty ships. This created a new power balance there. Soviet bomber squadrons have flown into Cairo and Damascus. And Soviet ships have paid courtesy calls to Arab Mediterranean ports and as far south as Iraq in the Persian Gulf. Soviet military advisers and direct Soviet military assistance have replaced the Egyptian effort in Yemen. Relations with Turkey and Iran, particularly economic relations, continued their upward spiral. Most of the Middle East states were visited by high-ranking Soviet officials in 1968.

THE ARAB-ISRAELI DISPUTE

During 1968, United Nations special envoy Gunnar Jarring tried to bring peace to the Middle East. But by year's end, because of an Israeli raid on the Beirut, Lebanon, airport, the Middle East seemed on the brink of another war.

Egyptian soldiers check out a Soviet T55 tank, a symbol of the reorganized and re-equipped United Arab Republic forces.

The arms race was escalated. The Soviet Union replaced equipment lost by the Arabs in 1967. And the United States finally agreed to supply Israel with F-4 Phantom fighter-bombers.

From the June 1967 war through October 1968, Israel demanded face-to-face discussions with the Arabs as a precondition for negotiations. Many people thus blamed Israel for the impasse in the dispute. Then in October, at the United Nations, Israeli Foreign Minister Abba Eban made a small but key concession. He stated that Israel would be willing in the initial stages of the negotiations to work through the United Nations special representative. Unfortunately this was flatly refused by Mahmoud Riad, the United Arab Republic's foreign minister. Riad announced that he would be willing to negotiate with Gunnar Jarring a timetable to put into effect the UN Middle East resolution that had been passed in November 1967. This resolution in effect called for both Israeli troop withdrawals from Arab territory occupied in June 1967 and Arab recognition of the right of every state in the area "to live in peace."

Israel contends that the UN resolution was meant as a guideline and as the basis for negotiations, not as a blueprint for action. Israel is willing to negotiate a withdrawal that will take effect when a number of other points are implemented. These points include a negotiated peace treaty and not merely the presence of peace. Israel also wants a mutual nonaggression pledge, open frontiers and freedom of navigation in the Suez Canal and Gulf of Aqaba. In addition Israel wants a conference of Middle East states and other interested parties to chart a five-year plan for the solution of the refugee problem, new arrangements for the holy places of Jerusalem, mutual recognition of sovereignty and regional cooperation.

Map illustrates the Soviet Union's presence in the Middle East through military aid and arms, trade agreements, loans and industrial projects.

The Israeli peace proposals presented in October by Abba Eban were too little too late. By June the Arab states were rearmed. They were thus prepared to make fewer compromises. And public opinion in Israel was opposed to returning all of the Arab territories. Political indecision within the U.A.R., Israel and Jordan also prevented the taking of real steps toward a settlement.

Israel

In Israel the main concern was security. For this reason Israeli leaders were unwilling to return all of the occupied territory. From the beginning Israel made it clear that its control over the Arab sector of Jerusalem was not negotiable. Israel also made quite clear that the Jordan River would be its security frontier, although the political frontier might be elsewhere.

One major problem in the dispute was that Israel's territorial intentions were by no means agreed upon inside the Israeli Cabinet itself. The coalition Government could only agree on keeping East Jerusalem. It was unable to agree on any of the other territorial issues. As the year came to a close, the long-simmering argument within the government circles over policy burst into the open. Defense Minister Moshe Dayan was for keeping as much of the Arab territories as possible. He stated that he would like to see the one million Arabs in the occupied territories integrated into the Israeli economy. His opponents, including the Prime Minister, warned that such integration would place the very survival of Israel at stake. Israel as a binational state would in time be dominated by the Arabs.

Behind much of the debate was Prime Minister Eshkol's determination to deny the premiership to his major political opponent, General Dayan. Eshkol plans to step down after the 1969 general elections.

Israeli forces pile into a helicopter for a raid into Jordan in retaliation for a Palestinian commando raid in Israeli-held Jordanian territory.

He is apparently trying to pick as his successor the Deputy Premier, Yigal Allon.

Jordan

Fierce fighting along the 64-mile cease-fire line between Israel and Jordan was repeated often during 1968. The renewed violence was largely due to the increase of Palestinian commando activity in Israeli-held Jordanian territory and in Israel itself. A series of commando raids followed by retaliatory raids by Israel into Jordan was a common occurrence.

Of all the Arab leaders, King Hussein of Jordan had spoken most insistently for a political settlement. But after the failure of the Gunnar Jarring mission in November, he declared that there was no alternative to increased military preparations. It had become clear to Hussein that if he signed a separate peace with Israel and did not get all of Jordan's territory back, and did not get the approval of the U.A.R. and the major commando groups based in Jordan, he would lose his throne. He may lose it anyway.

The major commando groups in Jordan —al-Fatah and the Palestine Liberation Organization—almost form a state within a state. These groups want to shatter Israeli hopes for peaceful coexistence in the occupied territories. And they want to prevent Jordan from making any deals with Israel. Their five thousand active members have the fervent support of most of Jordan's population which consists of displaced Palestinians who have no particular allegiance to Hussein.

Israel's determination not to return all of the territories lost by Jordan in June 1967 finally compelled Hussein to increase his cooperation with the commandos. It also forced him to seek, by year's end, closer military relations with the U.A.R., Syria and Iraq.

The United Arab Republic

By June the U.A.R. had regained the military posture it had lost during the June 1967 war. As a result, beginning in June,

military clashes and artillery duels along the Suez Canal gained in frequency and intensity. By demonstrating its new military skills against the Israelis in the Sinai, the Nasser Government hoped to regain the support and confidence of the Egyptian people and the Arab world as a whole.

Nasser in 1968 did not believe that his forces could regain the Sinai and the Gaza Strip by force. But he felt himself in a better position to harass Israel to a point short of war. This renewed confidence in the Egyptian military made it less likely that there would be a political settlement with Israel on terms acceptable to Israeli public opinion. To be sure, Egypt was still vulnerable to surprise attacks from Israel. This was demonstrated in late October by Israeli raids on three strategic targets deep inside Egypt's frontier.

At the end of 1968 the prospects for peace in the Middle East were nowhere in sight. The Middle East crisis had reached the point at which only the United States and the Soviet Union acting jointly could perhaps pressure the Arabs and the Israelis into serious negotiations for a peaceful settlement.

▶ SYRIA

Of all the Arab states involved in the June 1967 war, only Syria remained completely inflexible toward Israel. Syria insists that peace with Israel is out of the question. It insists that war must come again. In 1968, Syria also continued its policy of attacking the conservative and moderate governments of the Arab world.

One possible change in Syrian policies was indicated in late October. In that month Dr. Nureddin al-Atassi, the Syrian head of state, replaced Dr. Yussef Zayen as premier in a series of cabinet shifts. Several extreme Baathist Party ideologists were replaced by military professionals in the new Government. These men were expected to seek closer military cooperation with Jordan and Iraq. It was apparent, however, that the new Government would continue its close ties with the Soviet Union, its major source of weapons and economic assistance.

IRAQ

The changes in the Syrian Government were undoubtedly influenced by the changes in neighboring Iraq. The Iraqi Government of President Abdul Rahman Arif was overthrown in July by a bloodless military coup. It was the first Arab Government to fall since the June 1967 war.

Iraq's new military-revolutionary Command Council, with Ahmed Hassan al-Bakr as president and premier, has called for new elections. The Government of President Arif had postponed the elections due in 1968 to 1970. The new Baathist regime of Iraq includes some non-Baathist Rightists and Centrists. Whether it will forgo its ideological commitments and concentrate on its domestic problems or squander its wealth on renewed attempts to crush the Kurds and become militarily effective against Israel remains to be seen.

THE WAR IN YEMEN

The struggle in Yemen between Royalists and Republicans continued throughout 1968. In February, King Faisal of Saudi Arabia resumed military aid to the Royalists. His justification was that the Republicans were receiving aid from the Soviet Union, Syria and Southern Yemen. The year saw fierce Republican infighting, particularly in August, between rival conservative and revolutionary factions in the Army. General Hassan al-Amri, the premier, put down a mutiny in the Republican ranks which was led by Abdul Raqueed Abdul Wahab, a Leftist extremist. In September, al-Amri formed a new Cabinet. This was his sixth since the independence of the Republic of Yemen in 1962. He announced sweeping purges of the Army and Government "in the interest of national unity." His action was viewed as a victory of the moderates in the Republican camp.

The Royalists also had serious divisions within their camp. As a result they were unable to take advantage of the disunity in the Republican ranks. Early in the summer the Royalists tried to deprive Imam Mohammed al-Badr of all powers and leave him a mere figurehead. They decided to form a new six-man Imamate Council with Prince Mohammed Ben Hussein as its head. The Prince, a cousin of the Imam, was named commander in chief of the Royalist forces.

In September the Imam returned to Yemen from his exile in Saudi Arabia. He issued a Saudi-inspired call for national reconciliation. Thousands of Royalist tribesmen flocked to his side. And many threatened to defect to the Republicans if the Imam was not restored to temporal as well as religious preeminence. Prince Mohammed's position had been severely undermined by a military setback at Sana against the Republicans. As the year came to a close there was some hope that the moderate forces in both the Royalist and Republican camps would seek an end to the six-year war in Yemen.

SOUTHERN YEMEN

President Qahtan al-Shaabi of Southern Yemen supported the Yemeni Republican Government against the Royalists. And he continued to speak of a union between the sister republics. However, al-Shaabi also had his problems with the more fervent revolutionaries in the ruling National Liberation Front. On at least two occasions these revolutionaries rebelled against the Government.

Al-Shaabi's 10,000-man Army crushed the rebellions. But his future as leader remained in doubt. He must support the ambitiously socialist resolutions of the NLF and placate its revolutionary fervor. But he must also show a little realism, especially in money matters. Southern Yemen is dependent on Britain for nearly 70 per cent of its meager budget. Its only state earnings come from the British Petroleum refinery. By turning down further British assistance in order to satisfy the extremists, he found a revolt on his hands from those he was

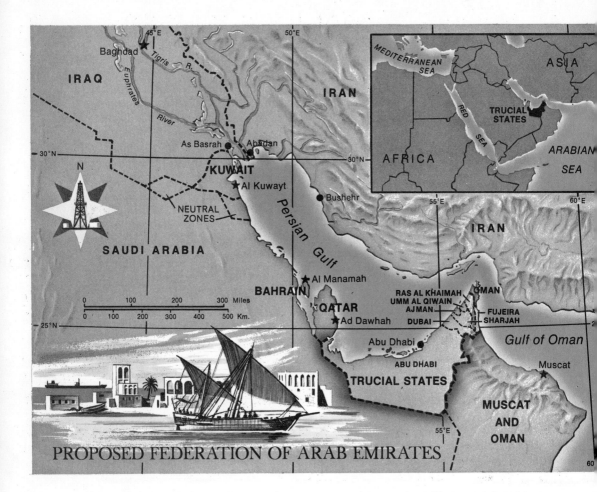

PROPOSED FEDERATION OF ARAB EMIRATES

trying to please. However, if al-Shaabi should reduce the size of the Army, which is much too large for his bankrupt country, it may overthrow him.

▶ PERSIAN GULF STATES

By the end of 1971, Britain will have pulled back its forces from the Persian Gulf. Britain's decision to do this has compelled the Arab emirates of the region to seek new ways to protect themselves. With the support of King Faisal of Saudi Arabia, they finally agreed to join in a Federation of Arab Emirates. The federation is to include Qatar, Bahrain and the seven Trucial Coast emirates. These are Abu Dhabi, Dubai, Sharjah, Ras al Khaimah, Umm al Qiwain, Ajman and Fujeira.

The total area of the federation exceeds 36,000 square miles. The population is close to 400,000. The federation has hefty oil revenues from Bahrain, Qatar and Abu Dhabi: some $300,000,000 a year. It would thus be economically viable.

The nine sheikdoms are limited in what they can do to fill the defense vacuum. Thus the greater responsibilities will fall on the two largest states in the area—Saudi Arabia and Iran—and on the richest, Kuwait. Saudi Arabia and Iran share a strong interest in keeping Egyptian influence out of the Gulf. They also fear that Russia's expanded Mediterranean fleet might come farther south.

For the moment, continued peace in the Gulf area and the success of the federation will depend in large measure on the ability of Iran and Saudi Arabia to cooperate. Iran is the most powerful of the Gulf states. It had opposed the federation ven-

HEADS OF GOVERNMENT

Algeria	HOUARI BOUMEDIENNE, premier	Morocco	HASSAN II, king
Cyprus	ARCHBISHOP MAKARIOS II, president	Muscat and Oman	SAID IBN TAIMUR, sultan
	SPYROS A. KYPRIANOU, prime minister	Saudi Arabia	FAISAL IBN ABDUL AZIZ, king
Iran	MOHAMMED RIZA PAHLEVI, shah	Southern Yemen	QAHTAN AL-SHAABI, president
	AMIR ABBAS HOVEIDA, premier	Syria	NUREDDIN AL-ATASSI, chief of state and premier
Iraq	AHMED HASSAN AL-BAKR, president and premier	Tunisia	HABIB BOURGUIBA, president
Israel	SCHNEOR ZALMAN SHAZAR, president	Turkey	CEVDET SUNAY, president
	LEVI ESHKOL, prime minister		SULEYMAN DEMIREL, premier
Jordan	HUSSEIN I, king	United Arab Rep.	GAMAL ABDEL NASSER, president
	BAHJAT AL-TALHOUNI, premier	Yemen	ABDUL RAHMAN AL-IRYANI, chief of state
Kuwait	SABAH AL-SALEM AL-SABAH, sheik		HASSAN AL-AMRI, premier
Lebanon	CHARLES HELOU, president		
	RASHID KARAMI, prime minister		
Libya	MOHAMMED IDRIS ET SENUSSI, king		
	WANIS AL-GEDDAFI, premier		

	POPULATION	ARMED FORCES	CURRENCY*	ARAB LEAGUE
Algeria	12,600,000	58,500	4.9 dinars = $1.00	X
Cyprus	610,000	. . .	1 pound = $2.40	
Iran	26,300,000	221,000	76 rials = $1.00	
Iraq	8,500,000	82,000	1 dinar = $2.80	X
Israel	2,836,000	40,000	3.5 pounds = $1.00	
Jordan	1,250,000	55,000	1 dinar = $2.80	X
Kuwait	495,000	. . .	1 dinar = $2.80	X
Lebanon	2,600,000	13,000	3.2 pounds = $1.00	X
Libya	1,800,000	6,000	1 pound = $2.80	X
Morocco	14,000,000	54,000	5 dirhams = $1.00	X
Muscat and Oman	750,000	. . .	. . .	
Saudi Arabia	6,900,000	36,000	4.5 ryals = $1.00	X
Southern Yemen	1,500,000	10,000	1 dinar = $2.40	
Syria	5,700,000	60,500	3.8 pounds = $1.00	X
Tunisia	4,600,000	17,000	1 dinar = $2.00	X
Turkey	33,000,000	514,000	9.1 lire = $1.00	
United Arab Republic	31,500,000	211,000	1 pound = $2.30	X
Yemen	5,000,000	12,000 † 40,000 ‡	1.1 rials = $1.00	X

* US $; 1968 exchange rates
† Republican Army
‡ Royalist Army

PERSIAN GULF STATES

	HEADS OF GOVERNMENT	POPULATION
Bahrain	ISA BIN SULMAN AL-KHALIFA	195,000
Qatar	AHMAD BIN ALI	75,000
Trucial States		130,000
Abu Dhabi	ZAID BIN SULTAN	
Dubai	RASHID BIN SAID	
Sharjah	KHALID BIN MOHAMMED AL-QASIMI	
Ajman	RASHID BIN HUMAID AL-NAIMI	
Umm Al Qiwain	AHMAD BIN RASHID AL-MUALLA	
Ras Al Khaimah	SAQR BIN MOHAMMED AL-QASIMI	
Fujeira	MOHAMMED BIN HAMAD AL-SHARQI	

ture because of its long-standing claim to Bahrain. This is why Bahrain is most anxious to join the federation. Iranian nationalism, however, may not be so strong as Iran's fear that the Arabian coast may fall to Arab revolutionary forces and that the Russians may gain access to ports in the Persian Gulf. A positive note was sounded in mid-November when the Shah of Iran visited Saudi Arabia and Kuwait. The Shah and King Faisal agreed to cooperate in the area and to work to exclude revolutionary forces.

▶ IRAN

In 1968, Iran continued its policy of rapidly developing the country. It also continued to maintain friendly and active relations with the United States and the Soviet Union. Iran's oil revenues are estimated to amount to $885,000,000 in 1968–69. This income plus economic and technical assistance from the Soviet Union and the United States is expected to buttress Iran's fourth 5-year development plan, which went into effect in March. The plan calls for a total investment of $10,700,000,000 and a rise in per-capita income from $220 to $304 as well as an 11.4 per cent annual growth rate in the Iranian gross national product by March 1973.

Iran also increased its investment in military preparedness. In June, during a visit with President Johnson in Washington, the Shah asked the United States to sell his country $600,000,000 worth of military equipment over a five-year period. The United States agreed, subject to annual Congressional approval.

▶ LEBANON

Lebanon is the only Arab state to enjoy parliamentary democracy. In April it completed two weeks of elections for a new 99-member Parliament. The results seemed to favor the pro-Western "Tripartite Alliance." This is an alliance of three Right-Wing parties: the Falangist Party of Pierre Gemayel, the National Liberal Party of former President Camille Chamoun and the National Bloc Party of Raymond Eddé. The Alliance won 30 seats. Its major opponent, the moderate Democratic Bloc, led by former Prime Minister Rashid Karami, won 24 seats.

Rashid Karami leaped to prominence once again after an Israeli raid on the Beirut airport on December 28, 1968. Karami, who had been premier during the June 1967 Arab-Israeli war, was recalled by President Helou. With Karami as premier, Lebanon was expected to take a strong stand against Israel and to support the other Arab nations.

▶ ARAB STATES OF NORTH AFRICA

Morocco's growth rate of 2 to 4 per cent continued to be absorbed in 1968 by an equally large increase in population. Thus, in an attempt to raise living standards, King Hassan II introduced Morocco's $1,000,000,000 five-year plan. This plan will depend heavily on foreign aid, principally from the United States. About 40 per cent of the total cost is to be financed from abroad. The plan will involve major investments in agricultural machinery and tools, irrigation and dam construction, mining equipment, mineral prospecting and hotel construction.

In 1968, Algeria and Tunisia continued to struggle with economic and political problems. Oil-rich Libya found it necessary to contract with Britain a missile-defense system in order to protect its wealth from its less-fortunate neighbors and to "support the Arab cause."

▶ TURKEY

Suleyman Demirel's ruling Justice Party continued to remain committed to NATO and the West. At the same time, Turkey tried to improve its political and economic relations with the Soviet Union and the communist states of Eastern Europe.

In June elections for 53 seats in the Senate, the Justice Party maintained its majority by winning 38 seats. Its representation in the Senate rose from 97 to 101 seats.

Two severe earthquakes in Iran on August 31 and September 1 killed thousands. The village of Kakhk lost 6,000 of its 7,000 people.

Perhaps the most significant development in Turkish foreign policy was the rapid improvement in Greek-Turkish relations. (The November 1967 crisis had nearly touched off a war between the two countries.) There was also the beginning of a breakthrough for a peaceful solution for the 15-year-old Cyprus problem. There was a flurry of meetings between Greek and Turkish diplomats in Athens and Ankara to discuss their own minority problems (the Turkish minority in Greek Thrace and the Greek minority and the Ecumenical Patriarchate in Istanbul).

▶ CYPRUS

The Cypriot and Turkish foreign ministers, attending a Council of Europe meeting in Lausanne, agreed to resume discussions on a Cyprus settlement. In an effort to get the talks going, President Makarios of Cyprus ordered the removal of roadblocks from around Turkish Cypriot enclaves. And he allowed Turkish Cypriots free movement throughout the island, even though the larger Greek Cypriot population remains barred from major Turkish Cypriot areas. Rauf Denktash, president of the Turkish Cypriot Communal Chamber, was permitted to return to Cyprus from his exile in Turkey. In June, with some assistance by the special representative of the United Nations in Cyprus, Bibiano Osorio-Tafall, talks began in Beirut, Lebanon. They then resumed in Nicosia, where they are being held alternately in the Turkish and Greek sectors of the city.

HARRY J. PSOMIADES
Queens College of the
City University of New York

MODERN LIVING

IMAGINATION and innovation marked the fashion and home-decor scenes in 1968. In fashion, men and women dressed alike and shared accessories such as chains and scarves. The Nehru jacket rose and then fell in popularity as Edwardian fashions moved center stage. Men grew sideburns and moustaches and tried on fur coats. Women peacefully settled the war of lengths by accepting all: mini, midi and maxi. And for makeup they turned to the natural look. Topless and see-through clothing failed to gain a wide following in 1968. But transparency in home decor, particularly in clear-plastic furniture, was widely used.

▶ WOMEN'S FASHIONS

The big news in 1968 was the craze for pants. The fashion newspaper *Women's Wear Daily* called Yves St. Laurent's designs citypants, saying that they were elegant enough to be worn in town, even in the finest French restaurants.

The craze for citypants and for pantsuits practically ended the question of which length—midi, mini or maxi—was the right length for coats. Any coat that looked right over pants was in fashion. Most of the country, however, settled for comfortable, conservative, knee-length and below-the-knee-length coats. Teen-agers everywhere were the exception. They remain most switched on to fashion trends, and for them the mini length remained a way of life.

Toplessness

Toplessness acquired a certain chic but no mass following. The see-through shirt was popular in the spring. One sportswear house sold eighty thousand copies of St. Laurent's organza see-through blouse. Each *couturier* showed at least one filmy, black see-through dress at the Paris collections in the fall. And for the first time the see-through dress appeared in the New York fashion shows as a matter of course. But its acceptance by the public was understandably laggard.

▶ MEN'S FASHIONS

The Nehru jacket started off strongly in the spring. But by fall men's shops reported being stuck with thousands of the high-collared jackets. Manufacturers were busy

Fashion-minded youths wear ruffle-front shirts, bell-bottom pants and Edwardian jackets.

at the end of the year adding lapels and collars to the Nehru jackets to convert them to the anticipated trend for 1969: the Edwardian jacket.

The Nehru-jacket fad ended when the shirt craze began. Shirts gaining in popularity had ruffle fronts or were turtlenecks or Russian peasant-style shirts that were worn with chains. Yves St. Laurent, Italy's Ken Scott and London's custom shirtmaker Turnbull and Asser all made colorful contributions to the men's-shirt scene.

Furs came into fashion for men in 1968. Quarterback Joe Namath of the New York Jets made headlines not only on the sports pages but on the fashion page when he posed in his new mink coat. Joe Namath was not the only man to declare his liking for warm, friendly furs. Bergdorf Goodman's ace fur designer, Emeric Partos, showed a mink tartan-plaid skating kilt for men in his winter fur show. Other designers showed a lot of practical sealskin and beaver for everyday wearing in raincoats. The fur was on the outside and was not hidden inside as a lining.

▶ **THE AMBI LOOK**

The year's most popular outfit was a shirt and a pair of flare-legged, bell-bottom pants. The outfit was worn by both men and women and was known as the "ambi" look. Department stores as well as avant-garde *boutiques* opened ambi departments or special shops for men and women dress-alikes. These shops also sold the interchangeable accessories—tunics, vests, chains and belts—popular with both sexes.

Accessories

The most imaginative accessories worn with the shirt-and-pants outfits were vests and chains. There were leather vests, embroidered vests from Pakistan, Indian fringed vests, crocheted and knitted vests, fur-lined vests, and fancy old brocade or velvet vests.

Giorgio di Sant'Angelo, who won a Coty Fashion Award for accessories, set the standard for chains. He wore at least eight or nine as well as several scarves. Chains and scarves were as important as belts to Yves St. Laurent, who visited the United

Models—teen-aged and wide-eyed or sophisticated and exotic—personify the fashion trends of the year. Teen-ager Penelope Tree (left) wears heavy lashes pasted on her lower eyelids as a trademark.

States in October for the opening in New York of a branch of his Paris *boutique,* Rive Gauche. St. Laurent started a fad for tying a scarf around the hips and adding chains on top at the waist.

Clunky shoes that looked like the shoes worn in the 1930's were very popular with women in 1968. Some of these styles, with their overly thick heels, seemed almost too heavy for comfortable walking.

Eyeglass styles for 1968 were also reminiscent of another era. Most of the year's new spectacles were rimless or had narrow, gold- or steel-rimmed frames. These replaced the supersize, plastic frames that were popular in 1967.

One fad that swept all ages was the nonhandbag handbag. Unlikely objects were used as handbags. For those who could afford them, there were the jeweled and decorated boxes that could either be held in the hand or carried by chain handles. Teen-agers substituted ingenuity for diamonds. They carried decoupage lunchboxes that they had made themselves out of ordinary metal lunchboxes by pasting on paper designs and photographs and then adding several coats of shellac.

▶ **MAKEUP AND MODELS**

The beauty business forged ahead with a return to a more natural look. There were, however, many variations of the supereyelashed eye, as launched in 1967 by Twiggy. The array of cosmetics with which to get a natural look multiplied, and

Sculptural Arco lamp is the creation of Castiglioni Brothers, an Italian design firm. The chrome lamp, which arches from its marble base into the middle of the living room, is both a sculpture and a light.

women needed guidance in choosing make-up. Consequently there was a boom in beauty consultants, and many department stores employed makeup demonstrators. Small cosmetic companies, such as Polly Bergen and Adrien Arpel, flourished when they offered an array of products with instructions on how to obtain a natural look.

At the same time, the giant beauty companies, such as Revlon, Estee Lauder, Elizabeth Arden and Helena Rubinstein, sent out barrels of gleamers and slickers for achieving high-style glimmery, or wet, looks. Rouges, highlighters and shaders were used for contouring, or sculpting, to achieve the look created by high-fashion models.

Models continued to be the glamour girls of the 1960's, and many became known by name. The personalities of

Molded-plastic furniture is portable for indoor and outdoor use and can be stacked for storage.

1968 included Penelope Tree, Veruschka, Lauren Hutton and Twiggy with long hair.

Teen-agers and Negroes became most sought after by model agencies. The number of Negro models at top New York agencies increased from token to substantial. Negro models were sought for fashion shows and magazine photography not only to accurately reflect society but also simply for their beauty.

HAIRSTYLES

Hair exploded in 1968. Girls' hair got longer, wilder and woolier. Teen-agers, who had worn straightened hair in 1967, permanented their hair to get a kinky look in 1968. There were also permanents that created Shirley Temple ringlets and Tiny Tim waves.

Men wore more hair, both real and bought, in 1968. In addition they sprouted sideburns, moustaches and beards. Theatrical-hairpiece makers found themselves in a booming business of paste-on moustaches, sideburns and hairpieces. Conservative businessmen, it was found, liked to dress the part of staid investment analysts during business hours and turn into fully bearded boulevardiers on the weekend.

HOME DECOR

Plastics dominated the home-furnishings world in 1968. Clear-plastic furniture took over from stainless steel and other metals as the material used for tables, dividers and lamps. And even a plastic automobile called Cubicar, designed by Paris' imaginative Quasar Khanh, was shown in London. Khanh's explanation was that "Transparency is part of the modern world."

Bright plastics were molded, most notably by Italian designers, into curvy armchairs, lamps and stacking tables.

Inflatable furniture of clear vinyl—chairs, lamps and tables—ballooned onto the summer scene. Inflatables could be deflated and moved to summer homes, campsites or swimming pools.

There were brilliant artistic strides in the design of lamps. The object was to show and glorify the source of light. Lamps became sculptures of light. Here again the Italians excelled in design. Globes, mushrooms, cones and spheres of light were displayed in many department stores as the lighting of the future.

Jo Ahern Zill
Fashion Editor, *Look* Magazine

PAINTING AND SCULPTURE

ARTISTS in 1968 continued to search for new materials and new forms. No style like pop art or op art seized public attention. Instead, artists explored complex and demanding ideas and sought roles for themselves in a push-button world. The notion of "fine" art was perpetually challenged. Trends of the year included walk-through and see-through sculptures; the use of an inexhaustible range of materials; the overlapping of art and technology; "participation" art which involved the spectator; and "optional" art where a viewer could change the structure and nature of an object.

▶ ENVIRONMENTAL ART

Many artists dealt with the creation of "environments," although there seemed no strict definition of the word. Marshall McLuhan, the interpreter of mass communications, defined environment as something we are not aware of. To an artist like Red Grooms, however, an environment named *Chicago,* which he exhibited as part of the United States entry at the Venice Biennale, represents a kind of puppet theater of memory. Grooms' dioramas with their large mannikins are recollections of, among other things, the puppet stage he had as a boy. For an artist such as Lucas Samaras, whose *Mirrored Room* formed part of the Second Festival of the Arts Today at the Albright-Knox Gallery in Buffalo, an environment engulfs the spectator. To Tony Martin, who showed his *Game Room* in New York, an environment makes a spectator part of the art object. In any case, environments became a conspicuous feature of the year. A 110-foot labyrinth of Dry Ice was offered as environment in Los Angeles. Other environments turned galleries into performing areas, branches of show business.

▶ SPECTATOR INVOLVEMENT

To get people actively involved in art, to goad the spectator into feeling—usually an emotion different from the response to the beauty of a flat-surface painting—was the aim of many 1968 artists.

Franz Erhard Walther, a young German who exhibited in New York in October, displayed canvases intended to link viewers into congenial groupings. Body-size hollows scooped into his canvas shapes permit four

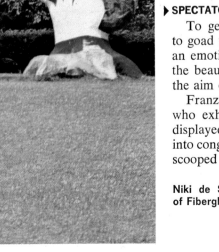

Niki de Saint-Phalle's sculptures made of Fiberglas are called "Nanas."

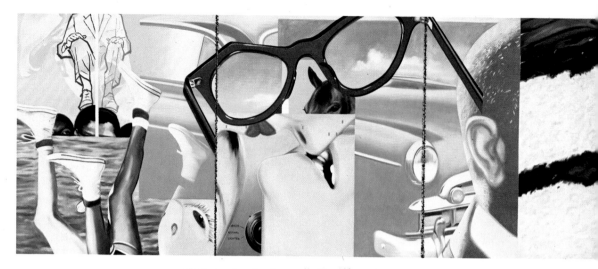

"Painting for the American Negro" by James Rosenquist.

"July White" by Jack Youngerman.

"Capillary Action II" by James Rosenquist.

people to become a part of the object, to relax and converse.

Brandeis University arranged, for late autumn, a "half-hour experience" created by the husband-and-wife team, sculptor Harris Barron and painter Ros Barron. It involved computers connected to live people. The emotional graph of the actors' blood pressure and heartbeat was translated by the machines into abstract designs projected onto screens. The Barrons felt that light shows and sound shows had previously been used for the sake of pure light or sound, and wanted to add the formal structure of theater.

▶ INTERMEDIA ART

The Barrons' "half-hour experience" and other such events demanded a sophisticated knowledge of engineering. An artist of a different order, however, mounted one of the most technologically complex exhibitions of the year at New York's Guggenheim Museum. Harold Tovish's sculpture in bronze and polished aluminum presented traditional human figures changing their expression and meaning under the impetus of strobe lights, mirror systems and concealed motors. The edge between illusion and reality, the nature of time, the mysteries of movement were some of the issues raised by Tovish's work. Nam June Paik, a Korean-born artist, was more directly concerned with technology rather than man. He exhibited black-and-white and color TV sets which could be tuned into diverse abstract shapes. Other artists prominent in 1968's intermedia were Otto Piene, who showed an environment called *Pneumatic Garden of Eden;* Tsai, a Chinese-born chemical engineer turned artist; and Gyorgy Kepes, the head of the new Center for Advanced Visual Studies at the Massachusetts Institute of Technology.

▶ A REVOLUTION IN MATERIALS

From the United States West Coast emerged a vital school of artists concerned with plastics. They often strove to give their work an industrial finish, to make it

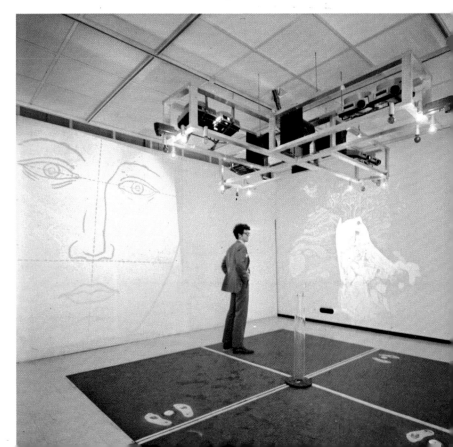

The spectator has chosen one of 1,000 possible projected images in "Game Room" by Tony Martin.

conform to the sleek burnish of customized cars and surfboards. Probably the most influential artists working in plastic were Ron Cooper, Mowry Baden, Jerrold Ballaine and DeWain Valentine.

Robert Smithson in New York exhibited geometric structures in which earth from an outdoor area was arranged and shaped. Robert Morris' chief material was industrial felt, hanging in huge swags. To be precise, most of the artists who worked in Lucite and glass belonged to "minimal" art. But in their clear, limpid forms, David Weinrib, Larry Bell and Bruce Beasley extended the "less is more" philosophy of minimalism into the materials of sculpture. There was nothing that did not constitute "material," from the human body to burned pillars of of books by John Latham.

▶ **THE MAJOR EXHIBITIONS**

Student demonstrations marred the 34th Venice Biennale, which opened in the Italian city on June 22 in an atmosphere of tension and turmoil. The prestigious West German show called Dokumenta IV at Kassel—Germany's huge contemporary-art international which tends to reappear every four years—fared better. Dokumenta highlights included the geometric signal-flag canvases of Josef Albers, Robert Rauschenberg's environmental booth (panels activated by photoelectric cells that moved with the viewer) and the slab sculpture of the young Italian, Michelangelo Pistoletto.

In the United States, Buffalo's Second Festival of the Arts Today had a fascinating historical display, "Plus by Minus: Today's Half Century." Starting with Kasimir Malevich's pioneer abstractions (1913) of two squares and a circle, the display of three hundred paintings and sculptures surveyed the major modern schools and focused attention upon the art of Buckminster Fuller and Naum Gabo.

A large Dada and surrealism exhibition opened at New York's Museum of Modern Art. The show included many items from a similar event in Paris during 1938, notably the *Rainy Taxi* of Salvador Dali.

"Light: Object and Image," at the Whitney Museum of American Art, disclosed in such pieces as Howard Jones' *Time Columns—the Sound of Light* the blending of art and science. Lights within Jones' columns were projected onto a wall which seemingly dissolved under a visual barrage of colors and lights.

▶ **POP, OP AND OTHERS**

Because art goes on, continually in a state of flux, one should not assume recently popular styles or the art of the distant past is dead. James Rosenquist, for example, whose billboard-size blowups of mundane objects relate him to pop art, had a successful exhibition at Canada's National Gallery. And Roy Lichtenstein, raising Benday dots and comic-strip scenes to the level of myth, exhibited in London and did a *Time* cover portrait of Robert Kennedy.

Victor Vasarely, whose honeycombs of ovals and handling of other forms marked him as one of the most inventive of op artists, was honored by an extensive architectural commission in the city of Grenoble, France. It was an active year for Jules Olitski, whose color-field paintings, veils of sprayed pigment, were seen in New York, London, Los Angeles and West Germany.

Among twentieth-century masters, 1968 was a year in which there was a huge Max Ernst show in Paris. During the year the sculpture of the Belgian painter, the late René Magritte, was seen in public for the first time. And at the Los Angeles County Museum, a retrospective devoted to ninety canvases by Chaim Soutine brought forth many reevaluations of this artist.

Jack Youngerman had a brilliant show of detached, cool, diamond-shaped, banner-like abstractions at Washington's Phillips Gallery. There was other art news from Washington: the opening of America's first National Portrait Gallery, part of the Smithsonian Institution. The opening, which took place in October, was clearly an event of the first cultural magnitude.

ROBERT TAYLOR
Art Editor, *Boston Globe*

OTOS THE CORNING MUSEUM OF GLASS UNLESS OTHERWISE INDICATED

Figure 1. Egyptian amphoriskos was made along the Nile River around 1500 B.C. to 1350 B.C.

THE METROPOLITAN MUSEUM OF ART, GIFT OF HENRY G. MARQUAND

Figure 2. Jug decorated with "snake-threads" of glass dates from the third-century Rhineland.

Glass as Art

GLASS was one of the first substances to be made by man. One glass charm can be dated to 7000 B.C. The earliest glass vessels, however, were made about 1500 B.C. in either Egypt or Mesopotamia. From that time to the present, man has tried to exploit the distinctive properties of glass. He has fashioned glass into useful objects as well as objects of great beauty.

(*continued on page 265*)

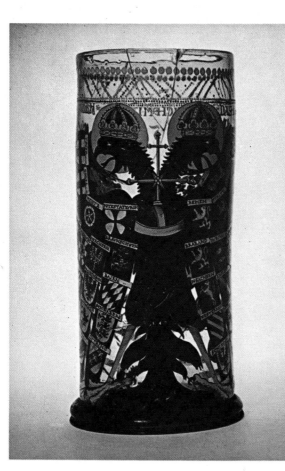

Figure 3. Enameled tankard from 1593 has the double-headed eagle of the Holy Roman Empire.

Figure 4. Small glass ornaments on the stem of this German or Netherlandish tumbler are called prunts.

Figure 5. English goblet made by George Ravenscroft about 1676–77 has stem prunts and a patterned bowl.

Figure 6. Graceful ewer of filigree glass was made in Venice in the late sixteenth or early seventeenth century.

Figure 7. Surface adornment of eighteenth-century Bohemian copper-wheel engraved goblet shows view of a city and inscriptions.

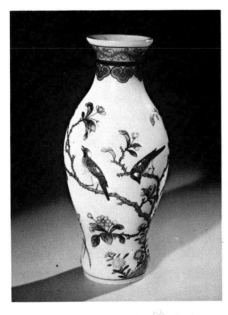

Figure 8. Opaque white glass with opaque enameled decoration was made in China in the eighteenth century.

Figure 9. Mechanical-press glassmaking produced this type of shimmering plate and goblet in Massachusetts from about 1830 to 1860.

THE METROPOLITAN MUSEUM OF ART, GIFT OF H. O. HAVEMEYER

Figure 10. Art Nouveau glass. Goblet of Favrile glass made by Louis Comfort Tiffany in 1896 combines color, line and proportion.

Figure 11. Blown-and-cut overlaid glass was made in 1962 by the Kosta Glass Works in Sweden and was designed by Mona Morales Schildt.

Figure 12. Vase engraved with a dancing ballerina was designed by Czechoslovak glass designer Pavel Hlava in 1959.

Figure 1 shows an Eighteenth Dynasty Egyptian amphoriskos (a small, ancient vase or jar). This vessel, colorfully decorated with festoons, has the simple outlines of carved hard-stone or ceramic containers made along the Nile River around 1500 B.C. to 1350 B.C. Its threaded decoration is echoed in the jug with the trefoil lip (Figure 2). This jug was made in the Rhineland around the third century A.D. Its handle, its delicately curved lip and its strong body, adorned with colorful "snake-threads" of glass left in relief, reveal a mastery in the handling of simple elements of color, line and texture. Much of the same feeling, achieved by different means, is reflected in the lacelike Venetian ewer (Figure 6).

Delicacy versus substance, practical form versus fanciful playfulness are two trends that one can follow throughout the history of glass. Many European glassmakers, in the sixteenth and seventeenth centuries, tended to favor practical shapes. A typical example is the cylindrical Bohemian *Humpen,* or tankard, (Figure 3).

When the optical properties of glass were respected, such as in the German or Netherlandish *Roemer,* or tumbler, (Figure 4), functionality was emphasized by the heavy thread wound around the foot and by the large prunts. Prunts are small glass ornaments fused to the glass vessel. Solidity and weight were emphasized at the end of the seventeenth century with the development of lead glass in England. The Germanic liking for surface adornment and capacious form appears brilliantly magnified in George Ravenscroft's lead-glass goblet (Figure 5).

Northern Europe's interest in surface adornment of glass is evident in the eighteenth-century Bohemian goblet (Figure 7). Its exquisitely precise decoration contrasts with the graceful, elegant form of the Venetian ewer (Figure 6).

Different cultures used similar techniques to create different results. For example, the heavy, opaque enameling used by a central European glassmaker on the *Humpen* (Figure 3) creates an entirely new mood when applied to an opaque white background, as on the eighteenth-century Chinese vase (Figure 8).

▶ PRESSED GLASS

The development of means for mass production in the early nineteenth century drastically altered the decorative vocabulary. For the first time, highly ornamental objects were made available at prices that almost all could afford. Pressing machines could make in seconds objects that had taken many hours if not days to create by hand. This had serious consequences for design. It subordinated the role of the glassmaker to the ingenuity of the moldmaker. Often the results were decorative (Figure 9). But as competition grew, design became more repetitive and complicated.

▶ ART NOUVEAU

A reaction against the harshness and sterility of machine-created patterns set in. Toward the end of the nineteenth century, in Europe and the United States, there was a renewal of interest in hand-produced glasses. The return to natural form was heralded by the leaders of the Art Nouveau movement in Paris. In Louis C. Tiffany this movement found one of its most talented spokesmen (see Figure 10).

▶ TWENTIETH-CENTURY GLASSMAKERS

In the twentieth century new solutions have been sought. The beauty of pure, refined materials, shaped to exploit well-understood optical properties, has been responsible for some evocative forms, such as the vase of Mona Morales Schildt (Figure 11). Other artists have found engraving best suited to evoke a mood. Some have aimed at pure sculptural precision, rendering their designs in classic, disciplined lines. Others, such as Pavel Hlava (see Figure 12), have freely sketched on the brilliant surfaces of their glass.

PAUL N. PERROT
Director, Corning Museum of Glass

PHOTOGRAPHY

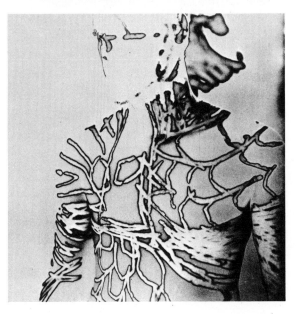

IN 1968, photography continued to make giant strides toward becoming America's first visual folk art. Television has produced a generation with the photographic image implanted in its brain and with the desire to express itself visually. Such expression was made possible by great cultural affluence and by the development of high-quality, medium-priced cameras by the Japanese.

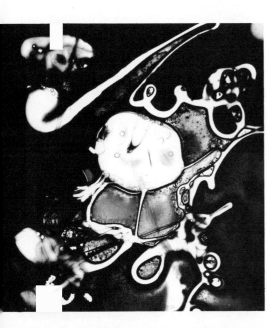

Several years ago carrying a fine camera was a mark of the snob. By 1968 it was so commonplace as to pass unnoticed. And young people were carrying cameras in order to make pictures, not merely to impress other people.

The rebellion of the young has carried over into photography, where it first expressed itself in the psychedelic image. At first this image was merely intended to be "mind blowing." Techniques were used that destroyed any relation of the image to the reality which was its source. The object was to relate pictures to the drug experience. As a result, images were made as shattered and incoherent as possible. Even so, some formal structure was necessary, for there had to be *some* coherence. This structure was borrowed intact from Art Nouveau. Photographic techniques stemmed from the experimentalists of 15

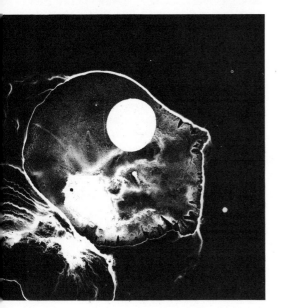

PHOTOGRAPHY IN PSYCHEDELIC ART

Psychedelic photography cannot be understood apart from psychedelic art. The former is simply the use of photographic techniques, materials and equipment to achieve the latter. Little conventional or academic use can be made of psychedelic photographs. Yet they are remarkable for their fluidity of line and brilliance of color. (The photos shown here were converted to black and white from brilliant color slides called "Lumaslides.") Technically these photographs are montages and collages. The photographer applied to photographic film combinations of different chemicals, dyes and inks. These were sometimes combined with photos of biological and astronomical subjects.

or 20 years ago. Together the borrowed structure and techniques made for images that were hostile and shattered—as if the answer to self-expression were only through total destruction of reality as we ordinarily see it.

By 1968 much of the incoherence was gone from psychedelic photography. New kinds of pictorial order were developing. Perhaps the outstanding examples of this development, which combined the feeling of youthful art with order and technical mastery of the medium, were Richard Avedon's photographs of the Beatles, published in *Look* magazine. They were dramatic and strange enough for any young person. But at the same time, they were powerfully controlled and organized.

The Beatles appeared again in a two-party essay in *Life* by Art Kane, who made no attempt to bow to psychedelic photography. Instead he applied to color photography multiple-image techniques that have long been used in black-and-white pictures. He achieved the power he wanted, not through image shattering, but through the subtlest use of the psychology of vision, of which he is the contemporary master.

In a conservative vein, one of the great pictorial coups of 1968 was Brian Brake's six-part color essay on Egypt, published in *Life*. It was in effect a super-essay. Put together, the six parts form a substantial book of high quality and interest.

▶ **PHOTOGRAPHIC BOOKS**

Among the photography annuals the 1968 *Popular Photography Annual* by Ziff-Davis was outstanding. Editor in Chief John Durniak felt that the time had come when he could risk dumping the established formulas by which annuals had been ground out for years, and attempt producing a book in which quality of image and communication was the sole criterion. The critical question was: Has public taste improved enough so that people will buy a really good annual instead of one featuring outworn photographic tricks? Since Ziff-Davis is continuing to feature quality in-stead of conformity, we can assume that the answer is yes, public taste will now support good photographic books on the popular level.

The publishing event of the year in photography was *The World of Henri Cartier-Bresson* by Henri Cartier-Bresson (New York: Viking Press, $14). Here passing in splendid review is the work of a great photographer who has had a tremendous and broadening effect on all photography, especially photojournalism, photography as art, and, strangely, cinematography.

On a lesser scale but on the same level of beauty and meaningfulness was the book *The Sweet Flypaper of Life* by Roy DeCarava and Langston Hughes. First published in 1955 by Simon and Schuster, the book was republished in late 1967 (New York: Hill and Wang, $3.50). This is a classically beautiful story of life in Harlem, with photographs by DeCarava and text by Hughes. More than any other man, DeCarava is looked to as the ideal and leader by Negro photographers, many of whom are now producing excellent work.

On the war front, *I Protest,* with pictures and text by famed war photographer David Douglas Duncan (New York: New American Library, $1.00) is worth looking into. It shows in powerful and moving photos Duncan's experience with the marines for eight days under siege at Khesanh in South Vietnam. It will particularly appeal to those who are against United States involvement in the war.

For creative spirits and darkroom experimentalists, *Darkroom Magic* by Otto Litzel (New York: Amphoto, $7.95) was a high point in 1968. Well illustrated and well written, it spells out in detail all you need to know about such things as high contrast, photoline printing, posterization and experimental use of texture screens.

For those considering photography as a profession, a must is *Professional Photography in America* edited by Oscar Katov (Professional Photographers of America, Inc., $2.95 paperback, $5.95 hard-cover).

An illustration from "The Sweet Flypaper of Life," by Roy DeCarava and Langston Hughes.

This is an unusually well-illustrated volume, in black and white and color, with pictures reflecting today's activities in various professional fields. Short, informative essays by such men as Bradford Bachrach, Yousuf Karsh, the late Ivan Dimitri, Wesley Bowman and Beaumont Newhall tell the young reader what he should expect in professional photography, and what he can do to prepare himself.

For beginners in photography, a real buy is the *1968 Invitation to Photography* by Harvey Fondiller (New York: Ziff-Davis, $1.35). An outstanding feature is David Vestal's thirty-page section on basic technique and craftsmanship, which simply and clearly tells the neophyte everything he needs to know in order to get started as a photographer.

▶ PHOTOGRAPHIC EXHIBITIONS

The major event in 1968 was in New York at The Museum of Modern Art: *Cartier-Bresson: Recent Photographs*. This was a splendidly mounted show which proved conclusively that the Grand Master of the "Decisive Moment" in picture taking has in no sense lost his touch.

Equally important, but in another way, was an exhibition in Chicago by the Exchange National Bank of their recently acquired collection of historical and contemporary photographs. The show and collection consisted of 200 photographs by 42 photographers, selected by Beaumont and Nancy Newhall, associate curators of the collection. For photographers the significance is that the bank appears to be seeing possibilities in collecting photographs as a financial investment in the same manner as paintings are collected as investments. For some of the historical photographs—work by Julia Margaret Cameron, William Henry Fox Talbot, and others—the bank paid up to $500. For contemporary work by Bill Brandt, Bruce Davidson, André Kertesz, Ansel Adams, Harry Callahan and others, prices were $50 and up. The Exchange National announced that it intended to continue its collecting until it had one of the world's greatest libraries of fine photographs.

Still on tour in 1968 was Robert Riger's superdramatic *Man in Sport* exhibition, which he designed and produced in 1967 for the Baltimore Museum of Art. With nearly 700 prints, half of them color and many of them mural size, *Man in Sport* is the most visually dramatic exhibition since Edward Steichen's *Family of Man* show at The Museum of Modern Art in New York City.

▶ NEW EQUIPMENT

In 1968 there were no dramatically new developments in cameras and equipment. However, a familiar idea was improved on considerably. It is Eastman Kodak's Instamatic camera with the do-everything, self-contained film cartridge. Originally a mere toy, the 126 camera has moved into the quality field. Outstanding examples of the new cameras are the Rolleiflex SLR 26, the Contaflex 126 SLR, Ricoh's 126 C-

"Decisive Moment" by Henri Cartier-Bresson.

Flex SLR and Kodak's own Instamatic 814. More than 30,000,000 126 cartridge-pack cameras have been manufactured since 1963, mostly simple box types selling for under $130.

Another toy with great potential was introduced in 1968: the PhotoMate Model 500 printer, manufactured by Graphic Products, Inc., a subsidiary of Transogram, Inc. It is an enlarging printer which eliminates the need for a darkroom and chemical processing. Manufactured for the 3M Company, it employs a special 3M printing paper that can be used in a room illuminated by a 60-watt bulb. The image is produced by a heat platen built into the inexpensive copier ($29.95) in sizes 4 × 5 and 5 × 7. Though the print quality is warm, slightly flat and not comparable to professional print quality, it is as good as most drugstore printing and slightly less expensive. As the printing material improves, professional enlargers will no doubt be introduced. In the meantime we have a fine toy that also serves as a visual aid for teaching some of the basic principles of photographic reproduction.

▶ MATERIALS AND PROCESSES

In this area, the most interesting development in 1968 was the Xerox Company's announcement of four new U.S. patents, including seventy claims of novelty, for a system of continuous-tone color copying. Apparently the materials will be economical and have considerable light sensitivity. At this time it appears that the color material will be only for copiers, not hand cameras or semiportable studio equipment.

To compete with GAF's Anscochrome 500 color film (ASA 500), Eastman Kodak announced a special processing service which would push the speed of High Speed Ektachrome daylight from ASA 160 to ASA 400, and Type B Ektachrome from ASA 125 to ASA 320. In professional labs the film speed of High Speed Ektachrome has been pushed for years, sometimes considerably further than ASA 400. However, there was a color

The Kodak Instamatic 814.

shift. Very conservative in such matters, the Eastman Kodak Company preferred not to announce its own speed-pushing service until it had improved the film itself, to the point that the color shift, if any, would be aesthetically negligible.

▶ TRENDS IN AMATEUR PHOTOGRAPHY

As always, the vast majority of amateur photographers see photography only as a means for recording family events. They are, however, shooting many more pictures than they did even ten years ago. There is a growing number of serious amateurs, numbering now in the thousands, who are using photography as their prime means of self-expression. Among this ever-growing and visually literate group, the dominant mode of expression seems to be an outgrowth of both surrealism and psychedelic art, which in photography have come to have their own unique expressions. The youthful notion that each person should be allowed to do "his own thing" is beginning to have a powerful and stimulative effect on amateur photography. The powerful grip of pictorial orthodoxy is being broken. For the first time, people in large numbers are really beginning to explore for themselves the remarkable self-expressive possibilities of photography.

RALPH HATTERSLEY
Contributing Editor
Popular Photography Magazine

Techniques of Photography

QUITE often the most difficult part of good photography is just seeing in a uniquely personal way. Unless you do this your pictures will be mere records that quickly bore the viewer. If you can add a "different" touch, you will soon develop a reputation as a skilled photographer. There are many ways in which you can add this "different" touch. Technical tricks, broken "rules," and visual devices are among them. Ten such ways are shown on these pages.

STOPPED ACTION. One way to capture the viewer's eye is to reveal what cannot be seen without photography's help, through stopped action. Outdoors, where light is bright enough, you can use the camera's highest shutter speeds. Indoors, electronic flash will "freeze" nearly any action. In this photo, shooting by existing light, the photographer took advantage of the action's direction, diagonal to the film plane, which requires a slower shutter speed than action that is across the plane.

PATTERNS. Obvious patterns in subject matter quickly become clichés. But by introducing unexpected patterns, you can make a photograph that stands apart from the rest. You could, for example, make a multiple portrait through a prismatic lens. Or you could sandwich your negative with a moiré-pattern screen. This nude study is unusual because of its offbeat lighting.

SIMPLICITY. Too many details tend to jade the eye. A photograph with only two or three elements grabs attention like a poster. Nature photos often become very dramatic when reduced to basics. You can achieve simplicity, as was done here, by choosing a low angle to create a background of sun and sky. Selective focus also adds to the posterlike effect.

UNCONVENTIONAL FORMAT. Too many pictures are unimaginatively printed in the format of the enlarging paper to avoid "waste" of some of the paper area. But think how effective a street scene becomes when printed as a tall, narrow vertical to emphasize the crowded feel of the street. At the other extreme, is this effective "wide-screen" illustration with excess sky and foreground cropped out to emphasize the expanse of snowy fields.

OFFBEAT POSE. Formally posed portraits are often stiff and self-conscious. Candid ones have spontaneity but are often unflattering. To avoid these pitfalls, try breaking the usual "rules" about using long-focal-length lenses to avoid distortion and not mixing informal poses with formal settings. In this double portrait, the photographer broke most of the rules and got an interesting portrait.

BLURRED ACTION. The reverse of stopped action is the purposely blurred action photo. The main action can be kept relatively sharp (as in this photo) and the rest of the picture blurred. Or the main action may be blurred, with the rest kept sharp. Use of shutter speed $\frac{1}{50}$ or longer while holding the camera still or while following the action produces this effect.

TONE CONTROL. The photographer used conventional cropping in this photo of an old farm building, but emphasized the starkness of the scene by boosting the contrast of the print. Detail is minimized, mass emphasized by printing on higher-than-normal-contrast paper. This dropped out the middle tones. Whiter whites and blacker blacks produce a slightly unreal effect.

CLOSE-UPS. The isolation and magnification of small objects is achieved in close-up photography. This photo combines techniques of simplicity, stopped action and the revelation of detail. Most interchangeable-lens cameras can, with accessories (bellows or extension tubes), focus closer than three feet. Even the simplest fixed-focus cameras can usually be fitted with inexpensive slip-on lenses for close-up work.

SHAPES AND TEXTURES. Similar to the technique of simplicity is the abstraction of the subject into shapes and textures. Here, unexciting frame buildings become fascinating because of the photographer's vision and his ability to photograph this vision rather than merely record the scene. A long-focal-length lens has flattened the roof gables into two-dimensional shapes rather than three-dimensional structures. The shadow of the round sign relieves the starkness of rectangles and triangles. And, in quasi-comic relief, there are two sea gulls—a surprise touch of life in a photographic study of plane geometry.

HUMAN INTEREST. Human interest is a picture quality that appeals to our common humanity. It can be a baby playing with his toes; a cat stopping traffic by carrying a kitten across a road; or (as here) a five-year-old acting as a museum guide for his three-year-old brother. It can be anything that ignores age, sophistication and background in reaching the viewer.

RELIGION

SEPARATE events dominated the news of the major religions in the United States in 1968. Protestantism reflected the social tensions that were felt in the 1968 presidential year. Protestant churches and clergymen during the year were involved in the civil-rights struggle, politics, poverty work and protest against the war in Vietnam. Protestant church membership, the largest in the United States, numbered about 70,000,000.

A single event occurring in July dominated the Roman Catholic world. This was the issuance by Pope Paul VI of the encyclical *Humanae Vitae* (Of Human Life). The encyclical reaffirmed the traditional ban on the use of contraceptives in marriage. As the year waned, the crisis touched off by the encyclical was still deepening. Nowhere was it graver than in the United States, where Roman Catholic Church membership was about 47,000,000.

Probably the most outstanding event for Jews and Judaism during 1968 was the twentieth anniversary of the state of Israel. Also in 1968, Jews noted that a resurgence of anti-Semitism was taking place in communist nations. The Jewish congregations in the United States included about 5,750,000 members.

▶ ROMAN CATHOLICISM

The Roman Catholic Church has been all but alone among major religious bodies in maintaining a clear doctrinal condemnation of mechanical and chemical methods of birth control. The encyclical *Casti Connubii* of Pope Pius XI in 1930 permitted Catholic couples—for certain specified reasons—to avoid unwanted pregnancies by using the rhythm method. But the same document denounced contraception in powerful language.

Before and during the Second Vatican Council (1962–65), however, some theologians and bishops began to question the doctrinal basis for the ban, the contention that contraception was "unnatural." Before his death Pope John XXIII appointed a commission to restudy the question.

Pope Paul VI enlarged the commission but would not permit full discussion of the issue by the council. He reserved the final decision to himself. During his years of silence, the debate went on. Gradually the consensus began to shift toward the progressive position. The shift accelerated after it became known that the papal commission had recommended a change in Catholic teaching. The problem of overpopulation no doubt influenced the commission. But its main argument was that the morality of birth control does not depend primarily on the method. Rather, it depends on the motive: whether a man and wife were selfish or reasonable in wanting to limit their family.

In *Humanae Vitae,* Pope Paul repeated the argument from natural law. And he made clear that he did not think the Church could alter established teaching. Almost immediately a group of theologians from colleges and universities in the United States issued a statement, in Washington, D.C. It maintained that well-instructed Catholics who honestly disagreed with the Pope were not required in conscience to obey. Eventually it was signed by more than 650 scholars in the field.

Similar views were expressed by well-known individual theologians, by lay and clerical groups and by some Catholic publications. The bishops of Germany, Belgium, Austria, Canada, the Netherlands and Scandinavia cautiously but unmistakably endorsed the "freedom of conscience" position. A survey of priests in the United States indicated that fully half of them disagreed with the encyclical. But the American bishops called for acceptance of the Pope's decision. And some among them—notably Patrick Cardinal O'Boyle of Washington, D.C.—made the issue a test of loyalty for the priests under their jurisdiction. This also appeared to be the attitude among higher officials of the Vatican.

Very quickly the focus of debate shifted from birth control to the question of the Pope's authority. His critics contended that he had gone beyond the limits of his power by imposing on a divided church a disputed philosophical conclusion without any clear foundation in the Bible. They said also that the Pope had acted contrary to the spirit of

Vatican II in taking sole responsibility for resolving the debate. Defenders of the Pope said no Catholic had a right to challenge the truth or propriety of a solemn papal decision, even if (as in this case) it was not issued as an infallible proclamation.

Inevitably the birth-control conflict added to the seriousness of other disputes, such as those over the rights of priests and the freedom of Catholic publications. The Church was becoming more sharply divided between reformers and traditionalists.

For both groups there was reason for concern in the rising number of priests leaving the ministry and entering marriage, and the continuing decline in the number of young men studying for the priesthood and young women entering convents. There was concern too for the disaffection of many of the laity, especially among the younger, more liberal and better educated. There were reports also of rising financial pressures on Catholic schools.

But 1968 was also a year of progress in moderate programs of renewal. For example, there was the formation of parish and diocesan councils and priests' associations and the improvement of religious education. No great breakthroughs were accomplished in the cause of Christian unity. But generally good relations with other churches were maintained. And it was worthy of note that the efforts of two Catholics, Eugene J. McCarthy and Robert F. Kennedy, to gain the presidency of the United States apparently caused little concern or criticism based on religion.

The crisis over birth control and papal authority overshadowed other news, such as the Pope's August visit to Bogota, Columbia, and his continuing efforts to promote peace in Vietnam and in the Middle East. The authority crisis was bound to continue. But the more-hopeful observers pointed out that the issues in contention had been certain to rise in some form, and that the Church in its long history had survived many such crises before.

ROBERT G. HOYT
Editor, *The National Catholic Reporter*

► PROTESTANTISM

Tension built up early in the year with the assassination in Memphis, Tennessee, of Dr. Martin Luther King, Jr., leading advocate of nonviolence in the civil-rights struggle and a clergyman of the American Baptist Convention. King's work had epitomized the increasing involvement of churches in what some have regarded as nonchurch business, but which a large though probably minority segment views as the essence of the mission of the church in the world. He was in Memphis to recruit public sentiment in behalf of striking Negro garbage workers when the assassin struck. King's funeral, held in Atlanta, was attended by tens of thousands, including top political notables, and was nationally televised. Reverend Ralph Abernathy became his successor as head of the Southern Christian Leadership Conference.

In August, at the national Democratic convention in Chicago, the first black American to be placed in nomination for the presidency of the United States by any major political party was also a clergyman. Reverend Channing E. Phillips, pastor of Lincoln Temple United Church of Christ of Washington, D.C., received 67½ votes.

Poverty, dramatized by the Poor People's March on Washington, in which many Protestant leaders participated, claimed the attention of the churches. Church members were beginning to question whether large church buildings and new projects should not be sacrificed to help house the poor. Many Protestant churches were sponsoring integrated low-rent housing programs.

The largest owner of nonprofit, government-subsidized housing is the American Baptist Convention. Other churches involved include the Episcopal, Methodist, United Presbyterian, African Methodist Episcopal, Presbyterian Church in the U.S., United Church of Christ, Disciples of Christ and several Lutheran denominations. A Baptist church of Wayne, Penn-

Reverend Channing E. Phillips is placed in nomination at the Democratic convention.

sylvania, mortgaged its church building for $100,000 to provide funds for inner-city work among the poor.

The Methodist Church and the Evangelical United Brethren Church merged at a Uniting Conference to form the United Methodist Church. The new church established a $20,000,000 fund to be used in helping resolve social and economic problems. The United Methodist Church also endorsed a proposal that a study commission on doctrine remove from the Methodist Church's historic Articles of Religion any derogatory references to the Roman Catholic Church. And a long-standing prohibition against the use of tobacco and alcohol by Methodist clergymen was abolished.

The ten-church Consultation on Church Union stepped up its timetable for church merger and called for formulation of a specific plan for union by 1970 at the latest. It was predicted that full agreement on union may then follow within ten years.

Conscientious objection to specific wars, as against objection to all war, gathered support among many churches. The Reverend William Sloane Coffin, Jr., Protestant chaplain at Yale University, and a United Presbyterian, was tried and convicted for counseling students to evade the draft (along with Dr. Benjamin Spock and others).

The Southern Baptist Convention in 1968 voted the most far-reaching statement on race relations and social action in its history, forcefully recommending that its churches open membership to people of all races.

Protestants from the United States played a large part in the Fourth General Assembly of the twenty-year-old World Council of Churches, which met at Uppsala, Sweden, in July. Orthodox Churches from around the world, including the Soviet Union, had full membership participation. And a score of Roman Catholic observers joined in at many levels.

KENNETH L. WILSON
Editor, *Christian Herald Magazine*

▶ **JEWS AND JUDAISM**

Celebration of the anniversary of Israel's statehood took place in the unified city of Jerusalem in June. Also of historic importance was the first meeting in Israel of the World Union of Reform Jews, which met in Jerusalem. Out of this meeting grew a confrontation between Reform and Orthodox Jews concerning worship at the Wailing Wall. Delegates to the World Union Conference who wished to pray at the wall were turned away by Orthodox Jews because men and women delegates tried to pray together. This was an affront to Orthodoxy, which maintains separation of sexes during worship. The question, which went beyond rabbinic circles, finally was to be decided by the Knesset (Israeli Parliament).

A resurgence of anti-Semitism was noted in communist countries, notably Poland and Czechoslovakia. Communist leaders, however, denied the existence of anti-Semitism in the Soviet Union or the Soviet bloc nations. And the Chief Rabbi of Moscow, Yehuda Leib Levin, was allowed to leave the Soviet Union to visit the United States, indicating to world Jewry that it was necessary to answer claims against the subjugation of Jews in communist countries.

It was thought that the anti-Semitism was tied to the increased Soviet military effort in the Middle East. During 1968 the Soviet Union trained Arab troops. They also resupplied the Arab nations with war material, replacing that which was lost to Israel during the six-day war in 1967.

An uneasy peace was maintained in the Middle East in 1968 despite sporadic artillery duels and continued attacks on Israel by Arab commandos. United Nations peace observers and truce teams under the leadership of UN envoy Gunnar Jarring continued attempts to bring Israelis and Arabs together.

Philanthropic contributions by Jews throughout the world to the United Jewish Appeal increased in 1968. The Israel Emergency Relief Fund, started in 1967,

An Orthodox Jew prays at the Wailing Wall in Jerusalem. Jews from all over the world traveled to Israel in 1968 to visit the holy places.

was continued throughout 1968. Subscriptions to Israel Bond sales provided funds needed for continued economic development in Israel, as much of the Israeli gross national product was diverted to defense. Tourism to Israel was heavy in 1968. Visiting Jews from all parts of the world taxed hotel and transportation facilities but added to Israel's income.

In the United States there was a slight drop in the elementary-grade enrollment of students in Jewish parochial schools in 1968. And in higher education, Dr. Abram Sachar retired as first president of Brandeis University to become its first chancellor. Morris Abram became president.

BERT F. KLINE
Editor, *Baltimore Jewish Times*

SCIENCE AND TECHNOLOGY

THE year 1968 was a rewarding one in most areas of scientific endeavor. In North America, anthropologists identified bone fragments as belonging to the oldest human remains ever found in the Western Hemisphere. And thousands of miles to the south, geologists discovered a fossilized fragment of the jawbone of an amphibian that lived in Antarctica more than 200,000,000 years ago, adding new evidence to the theory that this icy continent was once a much warmer place. While these scientists delved into the earth's and man's past, others sought to make the future more to man's liking. Meteorologists continued, with considerable success, their efforts to control the weather. And a Czechoslovak chemist made great strides toward developing a safe pesticide: one that would destroy harmful insects yet not adversely affect man or destroy the balance of nature. In another area of science, geneticists searched for a link between criminality and chromosomal abnormality.

Astronomers continued to scan the heavens during 1968, studying celestial objects both near and far. Icarus, a small asteroid, zoomed to within four million miles of the earth. And pulsars, those strange sources of pulsating signals far out in space, continued to intrigue and puzzle scientists.

Back on earth, technologists made great advances in applying nuclear power to peaceful uses. Huge ditches were dug with nuclear explosives, and the results so pleased scientists that they looked forward to the day when they could apply their technology to the task of creating a new canal across Central America.

In another area, an inventor introduced a simple-looking device—a friction-free roller—that he called one of the fundamentally new conceptions of the twentieth century.

FRICTION-FREE ROLLER

The traditional enemy of engineers is friction, which turns useful energy into useless heat. A new device that cuts friction to one tenth the level encountered in normal bearings moved into the final stages in 1968.

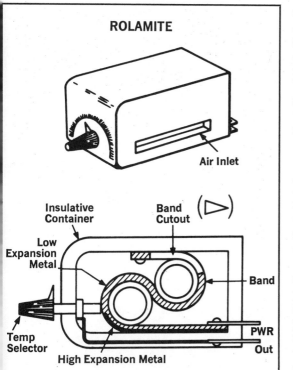

ROLAMITE

Air Inlet

Insulative Container

Band Cutout

Low Expansion Metal

Band

Temp Selector

PWR Out

High Expansion Metal

At left, inventor Donald F. Wilkes explains the concept of the low-friction Rolamite. The Rolamite may be used in many devices, including the thermostat shown here. This device for controlling a home furnace would use the "curling" action of a bimetal band to open and close a relay circuit. The curling force is counterbalanced by the band cutout, which in effect acts like a spring. As temperature drops, the spring force makes the Rolamite contact the temperature-selector screw. This turns on the furnace. Because there is little friction the thermostat would be very sensitive and accurate.

The device is called a Rolamite by its inventor, Donald F. Wilkes of the Sandia Corporation. Rolamite looks very simple. It is a boxlike rectangular cage containing an S-shaped spring which holds two rollers in place. Force applied to the assembly moves the rollers and the band at equal speeds, so that there is no sliding friction, only rolling.

The Sandia Corporation describes Rolamite as needing no lubrication, capable of being made in miniature form, and being easily made by inexpensive mass production. As such, the company said, it could be as revolutionary for engineers as the transistor was for electronics. Because Sandia works under contract to the Government, Rolamite has been made available to anyone who wants to develop a specific use for it.

▶ ANTARCTIC FOSSIL

In late 1967, scientists discovered a 2½-inch-long piece of fossilized jawbone in the bed of an ancient stream 325 miles from the South Pole. This discovery has added to the picture of an ancient Antarctica that had a semitropical climate. It has also given unexpected support to the theory that Africa, South America, India, Australia and Antarctica once formed a single giant landmass whose pieces have drifted apart over the eons.

The fossilized fragment was discovered by a group of Ohio State University geologists led by Peter J. Barrett. It was identified in 1968 by Edwin H. Colbert of the American Museum of Natural History as part of the jawbone of a labyrinthodont. The labyrinthodont was a four-foot-long amphibian which resembled a modern salamander, and which lived about 220,000,000 years ago.

Since the labyrinthodonts were warmweather animals, the discovery adds new evidence to the theory that Antarctica once had a much warmer climate. Other evidence to support this theory includes the finding of fossils of prehistoric ferns and thick seams of coal beneath the icy Antarctic surface.

The key part of the discovery, however, depends on the fact that the labyrinthodont was a freshwater animal. Until the discovery of the labyrinthodont fossil, no remnants of freshwater animals had been

Marmes Man skull fragments are believed to be 11,500 to 13,000 years old. They are the oldest human remains ever found in the Western Hemisphere.

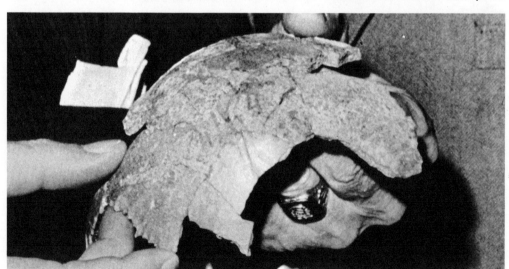

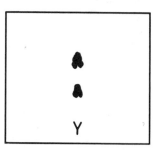

The 46 chromosomes in a normal male cell are seen in the top part of the photo (left) and are typed into pairs. The 23d pair, the sex chromosomes, has one x and one y chromosome. A genetically abnormal 23d pair has an extra y chromosome (below).

found in Antarctica. This indicated that ancient Antarctica was separated from the other continents by an impassable ocean barrier, just as it is in modern times. The existence in prehistoric Antarctica of an animal that could not have crossed such a barrier supports the view that Antarctica was once connected with other continents. This theory is now widely accepted by scientists. The Antarctic fossil adds another vital piece of evidence to the scientific jigsaw puzzle.

▶ THE OLDEST AMERICAN

Thousands of miles north of Antarctica, other bone fragments were discovered. In the state of Washington, a bulldozer uncovered some tiny pieces of bone that were identified in 1968 as the oldest human remains ever found in the Western Hemisphere.

The fragments are part of the skull of a young pre-Indian nomad who died between 11,500 and 13,000 years ago. This is about 2,000 years earlier than the date assigned to any other human bones found in the Western Hemisphere. The bones were discovered during excavations made on the ranch of Roland J. Marmes near the Palouse and Snake rivers in southern Washington. Because of this, the ancient American has been named Marmes Man.

▶ HEREDITY AND CRIME

Early criminologists believed that some people were literally "born criminals," fated to turn to crime despite themselves. In recent years this theory was largely abandoned. In 1968, however, a new discovery in genetics revived this theory, although in an updated and more subtle form.

The new discovery concerns the chromosomes, the DNA-containing bodies within each cell that determine the nature of living things. A normal human being has 46 chromosomes, or 23 pairs. Twenty-two of these pairs are identical in men and women. The 23d pair, the sex chromosomes, is different in the two sexes. Women have two x chromosomes (xx)— so-called because of their shape. Men have one x chromosome and one y chromosome (xy).

Scientists, however, have found some people who have had sex chromosomes added or subtracted. Some women have xxx or even xxxx. This often is associated with mental retardation and other disorders. Now geneticists have found a chromosomal abnormality that appears to be associated, at least in some cases, with violent crime.

The abnormality is an extra y chromosome in a man. Studies in Scotland have shown that nearly 4 per cent of the inmates in maximum-security prisons and hospitals for the criminally insane are men with this xyy abnormality. These men have a bizarre collection of symptoms. They are tall: an average of six inches taller than normal xy men. They have IQ's slightly below normal. They have a tendency to acne. And apparently they have a tendency to violence. Many of the institutionalized men with xyy chromosomes had committed murder, assault or other violent crimes.

However, scientists differ on whether xyy men are literally "born to kill." One theory is that xyy boys mature earlier, grow taller, and fail to adjust emotionally to the differences that single them out. The presence of acne, which has been linked to sex hormones, leads some scientists to believe that xyy men have abnormally high sex-hormone levels, which often leads to trouble.

Most scientists who have studied this phenomenon believe that the xyy may incline a man to violence, and that the nature of his upbringing and surroundings determines whether the tendency to violence will be fulfilled. This theory received some support from a survey taken by Dr. Park S. Gerald of Harvard University. He found that about one in every three hundred newborn boys he examined had the xyy abnormality. Such a high incidence had not been suspected.

The only way to determine the exact relationship between the xyy condition and violence, Dr. Gerald stated, would be to conduct a long-term study of several thousand xyy people. They would have to be selected as children and their lives followed into adulthood.

Some geneticists and social scientists believe the discovery of a link between the chromosomal abnormality and a personality trait may have significance beyond the

---

NOBEL PRIZES

Physics: LUIS W. ALVAREZ, U.S.
Chemistry: LARS ONSAGER, U.S.

ATOMIC ENERGY COMMISSION

Enrico Fermi Award: JOHN A. WHEELER, Princeton University

AMERICAN CHEMICAL SOCIETY

Priestley Medal: KENNETH S. PITZER, Rice University

PACIFIC SCIENCE CENTER

Arches of Science Award ($25,000): GLENN T. SEABORG

NATIONAL SCIENCE MEDALS

Medalists: KENNETH S. COLE, National Institutes of Health; ALFRED H. STURTEVANT, California Institute of Technology; HARRY F. HARLOW, University of Wisconsin; MICHAEL HEIDELBERGER, New York University; EDWIN H. LAND, Polaroid; IGOR I. SIKORSKY, Sikorsky Aircraft; PAUL J. COHEN, Stanford University; JESSE W. BEAMS, University of Virginia; FRANCIS BIRCH, Harvard; GREGORY BREIT, Yale; LOUIS P. HAMMETT, Columbia University; GEORGE B. KISTIAKOWSKY, Harvard

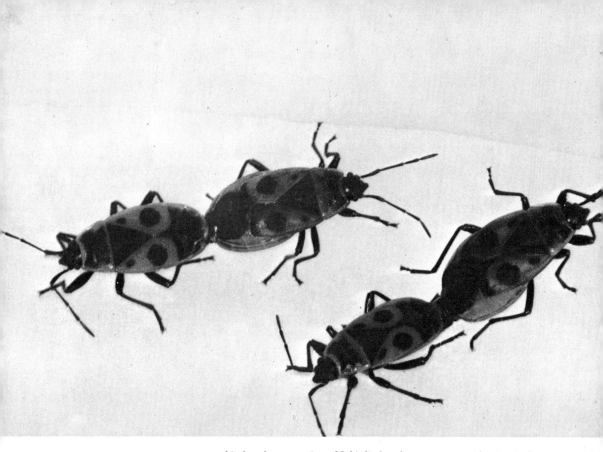

Linden bugs mating. Male linden bugs can now be treated with an artificial hormone that creates contagious sterility.

original finding. It could be, they say, that other personality traits are shaped by genetic variations that are too subtle to be detected by present-day methods. Thus the xyy discovery has become the latest chapter in the long-standing controversy over whether people are influenced more by "nature"—their inborn characteristics—or by "nurture"—their environment and upbringing.

▶ TOWARD SAFER PESTICIDES

Since Rachel Carson sounded the warning about the dangers of pesticides in her book *Silent Spring,* scientists have been searching for a substance that would kill harmful insects without harming friendly insects or higher animals. A Czechoslovak chemist reported a development that brings such a weapon closer to existence.

The chemist, Karel Slama of the Entomological Institute of the Czechoslovak Academy of Sciences, reported that he had synthesized an artificial hormone that creates contagious sterility in bugs. By treating just a few of the insects with such a substance, it is possible to stop thousands of other insects from reproducing. A few grains of the chemical made by Slama are enough to sterilize from one million to ten million linden bugs, the insects he used in his tests.

This new development was based on well-established research seeking to control insects by using their hormones. These hormones play a vital part in the complex development of insects. One of them, called the juvenile hormone, suppresses metamorphosis—the process by which a young insect, such as a caterpillar, turns

ELECTRON SCANNING MICROSCOPE

The electron scanning microscope has a magnification range from 20 to 150,000 times. Its greatest advantage is that a small object, such as a housefly, can be viewed in its entirety on a screen similar to a television screen. Changes in magnification are obtained by turning a knob.

into a mature adult, such as a butterfly. Ordinarily, production of the juvenile hormone stops so that metamorphosis can take place. Research has centered on treating the insects with juvenile hormone at just the right time, so that they never become adults.

The chemical synthesized by Slama is chemically related to the juvenile hormone, and is very powerful. In tests, a tiny amount of the chemical was applied to male linden bugs. When the males mated, the females were made sterile. The chemical was powerful enough to sterilize all the males with which these females mated. It even made sterile some of the females with which these males later mated.

The chemical appears to affect only one of the fifty families of true bugs. But its development offers hope that a truly safe insecticide, affecting only the harmful species, can come into use. The Pyrrhocoridae, the family of insects affected by the substance, include some of the most destructive enemies of the cotton plant. Because the substance affects only insects that mate with treated insects, other, harmless species are not damaged. And birds and other ani-

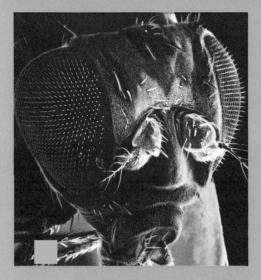

Front view of the head of a fruit fly, magnified 180 times by the electron scanning microscope.

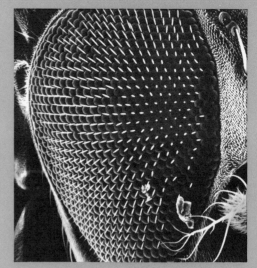

Magnified 350 times, the eye of the fruit fly is seen to contain many simple eyes.

When the fruit fly is magnified 2,240 times, the facets containing the corneal lenses are seen.

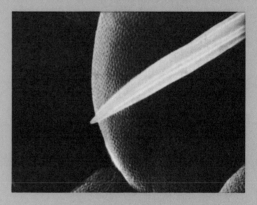

Magnified 11,200 times, each facet appears to have a substructure of humps on its surface.

mals are in no way hurt by the hormone.

Other scientists have discovered that a number of plants have developed chemicals that act like juvenile hormone, as a defense mechanism against insect predators. Use of these chemicals and of synthetic substances may enable farmers to eliminate insect pests without upsetting the delicate balance of nature.

▶ CONTROLLING THE WEATHER

In 1968, meteorologists moved two steps closer to the elusive goal of weather control. In upper New York State, scien-tists worked out a way to steer snowstorms away from the city of Buffalo and toward ski areas that welcomed them. In Sacra-mento, California, the nation's airlines suc-cessfully tested a method for clearing the skies over fogged-in airports. This will eventually cut down air-traffic delays.

The New York experiment was made by scientists from Pennsylvania State Univer-sity, Cornell Aeronautical Laboratory and the State University of New York at Al-bany. They were fighting what is called the "lake effect"—the tendency of snowstorms that form over Lake Erie to dump their snow in a narrow and heavily populated strip along the lakeshore.

In the study, the scientists first prepared a computer model of a typical storm. They then added to this model the effects of seeding the clouds with silver-iodide crystals, which can cause snowflakes to form and fall. Following the model, they then seeded a single cloud over Lake Erie. Snow from the cloud fell thirty miles away, just as the computer had predicted. The system now can be used on a large scale, according to the scientists.

The Sacramento test was under the sponsorship of the Air Transport Association, which has an obvious interest in keeping airports open. Its object was warm fog, which is responsible for 95 per cent of the aircraft delays caused by fog. While cold fog can be handled by silver-iodide seeding, the water droplets in warm fog are too warm to form snow crystals when seeded.

The Sacramento tests used two chemicals. One attracts water droplets electrically, causing them to form large drops. The other reduces surface tension on the fog droplets, making them combine. In both cases, the larger drops fall as rain, dispersing the fog. The tests were successful enough for the airlines to consider large-scale use of the method.

Other weather-modification efforts are being made in the United States and other countries. There are Soviet reports of success with a hail-prevention system which has prevented millions of dollars in damage to crops.

The U.S. Forestry Service reports that lightning-prevention tests, using cloud seeding, reduce lightning by about one third. The U.S. Department of the Interior plans a $2,000,000-a-year rainmaking program in northwestern Colorado. Step by step, man is moving closer to making the weather serve his purposes.

▶ PULSARS

Certain signals from space were so precisely timed that the British astronomers who detected them named the first known source LGM-1, for "little green men." But even after the idea that these signals were from other civilizations was dropped, the pulsars—the names given to the new phenomenon—remain one of the prime astronomical puzzles of recent years.

In 1967 and 1968, astronomers discovered at least a dozen pulsars. All have the same striking characteristics. The signals they emit are astoundingly precise. For example, the pulses emitted by the first known pulsar occur precisely every 1.337

Recording of space signals from Pulsar 1 was made at the Arecibo Ionospheric Observatory in Puerto Rico. The intervals between pulses are constant, but the intensity of each pulse varies in a one-minute cycle.

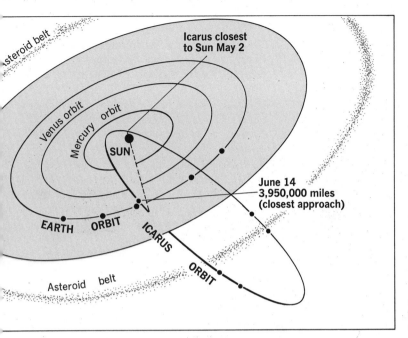

Orbit of Icarus brought the asteroid close to earth on June 14, 1968.

Within the figure:
- Asteroid belt
- Icarus closest to Sun May 2
- Venus orbit
- Mercury orbit
- SUN
- June 14 3,950,000 miles (closest approach)
- EARTH ORBIT
- ICARUS ORBIT
- Asteroid belt

seconds. The intensity of each pulse varies in a cycle lasting about a minute. The only known signals from these pulsars are radio waves, and at some frequencies the pulses are among the most powerful astronomical radio emissions known. All the pulsars thus far discovered appear to be within 50 to 300 light-years from the earth. This is relatively close by astronomical standards.

What makes the pulsars pulse? Many theories have been offered. But no single theory explains all the known facts. The theory that advanced civilizations are using the pulsars to send signals through space was ruled out early. Astronomers believe that the signals are too illogical to come from intelligent beings. Current theories center on the belief that pulsars are stars that have burned up most of their nuclear fuel and have collapsed into small and almost unbelievably dense objects.

One theory holds that the radio pulses are emitted as these stars expand and contract rapidly, emitting radio waves at each throb. Another theory is that the stellar bodies—possibly neutron stars—are spinning rapidly, with the pulses being caused

by a "lighthouse effect" as the emitting region of the star spins around toward and away from the earth.

In addition to testing their theories, astronomers are also searching for new pulsars and trying to identify the known pulsars with visible stars. They hope to get new information about the stars, including knowledge about the final stages of the process by which a star, such as the sun in our solar system fades away as it turns its matter into energy.

▶ CELESTIAL CLOSE CALL

While radio astronomers were training their telescopes on pulsars far out in space, one celestial object passed relatively close to the earth. Icarus, an asteroid less than a mile in diameter, came within 4,000,000 miles of the earth in 1968. Distant as it was, the passage was one of the closest approaches to the earth by an astronomical body. It was enough to set off a momentary panic among several hundred hippies, who fled to Colorado predicting that Icarus would hit the earth, sparing only Tibet and Boulder, Colorado, from destruction.

While the hippies fled, astronomers focused their telescopes on Icarus. They were after more information about Icarus itself and about its orbit.

Other asteroids have come closer to the earth than Icarus. The closest known approach was made by Hermes, which passed only 500,000 miles away in 1937. But Icarus' orbit brings it near the earth every 19 years. Since the orbit also carries Icarus close to the sun, astronomers hope that by measuring changes in the orbit on each approach, they can determine how the sun's gravitational field has affected Icarus.

There is also another reason for measuring the orbit. While astronomers scoffed at the hippies' fears, they are aware that asteroids have smashed into the earth in the past. Such a collision with Icarus would produce a crater 80 miles in diameter. By measuring the orbit, astronomers are attempting to determine the likelihood of such a collision.

The close approach, which occurred on June 14, also gave astronomers an opportunity to gather more information on the composition of Icarus. It is believed that the asteroids, most of which orbit the sun between Mars and Jupiter, might be remnants of a minor planet that was shattered by a collision. Photographs of Icarus made during its close passage indicate that it may be a ball of solid iron—perhaps a part of the shattered planet's core. Icarus' next approach will be in 1987. This is too far away for definite planning. Nevertheless, some astronomers are proposing a space probe that would put instruments—or men—on the asteroid to make a closer study of its characteristics.

▶ **ATOMIC PLOWSHARE**

Project Plowshare, a program for using nuclear explosives for peaceful purposes, went into high gear in 1968. Scientists made public detailed results from the

Typical sequence of events when a nuclear explosion is detonated underground (left to right). During first few microseconds the explosion creates a cavity filled with hot gases. High pressure forces the cavity to expand. As the cavity cools, some of the gases liquefy, and the molten rock runs to the bottom. The cavity roof then begins to collapse (3d diagram). Falling rock from the roof creates the chimney of broken rock which builds up to the roof.

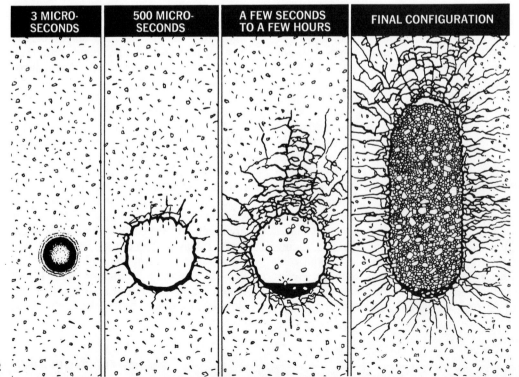

| 3 MICRO-SECONDS | 500 MICRO-SECONDS | A FEW SECONDS TO A FEW HOURS | FINAL CONFIGURATION |

world's first commercially sponsored nuclear explosion and from two cratering experiments that could lead to nuclear excavation of a new Panama Canal.

The commercial explosion was called Project Gasbuggy and was jointly sponsored by the Atomic Energy Commission and the El Paso Natural Gas Company. The explosion of a 26-kiloton nuclear device was designed to increase the flow of natural gas from formations where the rock is so permeable that the gas flows to a well slowly or not at all.

Conventionally, gas yield is increased by "shooting" the well, either by exploding nitroglycerine or by pumping in water under high pressure to fracture the rock.

Diagram shows how an underground nuclear blast could be used to extract oil from fractured shale. The nuclear blast fractures the shale, and the oil settles to the bottom of the chimney. The oil is then pumped out.

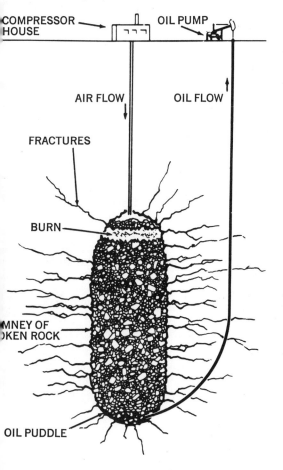

COMPRESSOR HOUSE
OIL PUMP
AIR FLOW
OIL FLOW
FRACTURES
BURN
MNEY OF)KEN ROCK
OIL PUDDLE

Conventional well shooting at the site of Project Gasbuggy would yield about 10 per cent of the available gas. Gasbuggy's supporters expect nuclear well shooting to increase that yield to 70 per cent.

The explosion, set off just before the start of 1968, created an underground "chimney" of broken rock about 360 feet high and 160 feet in diameter.

Tests did yield large amounts of gas, but the gas was contaminated with radioactivity. To be used it would have to be treated. This is an expensive project. An alternative is to use "cleaner" nuclear bombs, which is also expensive. Eventual success for Gasbuggy would have profound results for the natural-gas industry. Known gas reserves in the United States now are about 300 trillion cubic feet. If nuclear explosions could be used to free gas that is not available using conventional methods, another 317 trillion cubic feet would be freed for use.

Other peaceful uses are being planned for nuclear explosives. Potentially the most dramatic such use would be for large-scale excavation. Nuclear excavation is seriously being considered for a new, sea-level replacement for the Panama Canal. Early studies indicate that nuclear explosives could radically reduce costs.

During 1968, two nuclear-excavation tests were held. In Project Cabriolet a 2.5-kiloton nuclear explosive created a crater 360 feet in diameter and 130 feet deep. In Project Buggy-1, a series of five 1-kiloton explosives, spaced 150 feet apart, was set off simultaneously to create a ditch 300 feet wide, 80 feet deep and 900 feet long. Both explosions released very low levels of fallout. This was a tribute to the Atomic Energy Commission's program to develop low-fallout explosives for peaceful purposes.

Five other nuclear-excavation tests are scheduled to take place by 1970. A decision will then be made on whether the new canal will be dug by nuclear or conventional means.

EDWARD EDELSON

Antarctic Discoveries

In the continuing exploration of Antarctica, old whaling ships of the 1930's . . .

AT the bottom of the earth lies the frozen continent of Antarctica. The Antarctic has an area of 5,100,000 square miles, which makes it larger than the United States and Mexico combined. For centuries the giant ice continent had been unexplored. Cold weather and frozen seas prevented explorers from reaching Antarctica's shores. Many voyages were made to find the fabled southern continent, for men imagined it to be populated and to contain great riches. The earliest of these explorers instead discovered Australia and many South Pacific islands.

▶ THE DISCOVERY OF ANTARCTICA

Explorers from Spain and France discovered several of the islands within the Antarctic Convergence—the area south of 45° latitude. But it was the British navigator Captain James Cook who brought an end to the dream of an inhabited southern continent. Between 1772 and 1775, Cook sailed completely around Antarctica. Although he never sighted it, he did penetrate farther south than any man before him. And on January 17, 1773, he became the first man known to have crossed the Antarctic Circle. Cook saw great expanses of pack ice and many high icebergs. This, and the presence of numerous seabirds, led him to believe that an ice-defended land lay to the south.

Cook's exploration, plus his report of numerous seals inhabiting the southern waters, brought a flood of seal hunters to the area. It seems probable that these sealers were the first people to see Antarctica. The

. . . have given way to the more-sophisticated transport and cargo equipment of 1968.

sealers, however, tried to keep their discoveries secret to prevent others from learning of new seal colonies. The real proof that Antarctica was a continent came from an expedition led by Lieutenant Charles Wilkes of the United States Navy in 1839–40. The British naval officer James Clark Ross sailed as far south as it is possible to go by ship in 1841. He discovered the huge sea that now bears his name.

With a sea route opened, explorers from many nations headed south trying to discover the secrets of the frozen continent. In 1911 and 1912, the Geographic South Pole was reached. First to arrive was the great Norwegian explorer Roald Amundsen. Amundsen and four companions reached the Pole on December 14, 1911. One month later, January 17, 1912, Captain

Robert Scott and four other Englishmen reached the Pole only to find Amundsen's Norwegian flag flying above a deserted tent. Tragedy struck Scott and his party on their return from the Pole. Two members of the expedition died on the trail. Scott and his two remaining companions were trapped by a blizzard and froze to death in their tent, 11 miles from safety.

▶ BEGINNINGS OF THE INTERNATIONAL GEOPHYSICAL YEAR

The twentieth century brought the period of modern scientific exploration. In 1929, Rear Admiral Richard E. Byrd made the first flight over the South Pole. Three years before, Byrd had also flown over the North Pole. During Byrd's second expedition to Antarctica (1933–35), he concentrated on scientific work and used tracked vehicles more extensively than any previous expedition. An advance weather base was set up on the Ross Ice Shelf 500 miles from the South Pole in which Byrd remained alone from March 28 through August 10, 1934. No man had previously wintered so far south. Byrd's work led scientists from many countries to increase their study of the Antarctic. The culmination occurred in 1957 when 30,000 scientists representing 66 nations took part in the International Geophysical Year, a program of cooperative scientific investigation in all areas of the world. For the first time, Antarctica would be included in a world-wide study of the geophysical sciences. The geophysical sciences—which are often called earth sciences because they deal with the earth and the forces that affect it—include oceanography, meteorology, upper-atmosphere physics and glaciology.

The Antarctic program of the IGY called for scientific stations not only on the continent and offshore islands, but also on more-northerly islands and in Australia, New Zealand, South Africa and South America. This extensive coverage was designed to tie the Antarctic Continent into Southern Hemisphere and worldwide patterns of weather observation. Thus, for the first time, it was possible to make weather charts of the entire southern half of the earth. The scientific programs associated with the IGY were so successful that American scientists, with financial grants from the National Science Foundation, have participated in Antarctic research programs every year since 1956.

▶ OPERATION DEEP FREEZE AND IGY

For its logistic operations in the Antarctic, the U.S. Navy uses the nickname Deep Freeze. The Deep Freeze program was

originally intended to assist during the IGY. However, the Navy has been providing assistance to the Antarctic program every year. Deep Freeze I and II, which occurred preliminary to the IGY, saw the greatest invasion of Antarctica in history. The United States sent 19 ships and more than 4,000 men.

The IGY saw the crossing of the continent by the British Commonwealth Trans-Antarctic Expedition led by Dr. (now Sir) Vivian Fuchs. The 2,158-mile traverse allowed Fuchs and his party to map extensively the heart of the continent. In connection with the Fuchs expedition, Sir Edmund Hillary, who a few years before had been the first man (with Sherpa Tenzing) to climb Mt. Everest, led an overland party to the South Pole. Hillary became the first man to travel overland to the Pole since Amundsen and Scott made their famous treks in 1911 and 1912.

During the IGY, scientists were able to map vast areas of the continent as well as accumulate vast amounts of scientific data. They learned that Antarctica is covered with much more ice—7,000,000 cubic miles of it—than had been realized. Extensive data concerning upper-atmospheric physics was recorded. And the changes in the pull of gravity and the earth's magnetism were measured.

A further result of the IGY was a treaty signed by the United States, Soviet Union and ten other nations. The treaty, signed December 1, 1959, guarantees nonmilitarization of Antarctica and freedom of scientific investigation. The few weapons in Antarctica are used to collect specimens. There is no secrecy between nations. And representatives from countries that may be engaged in a cold war show complete cooperation in the world's coldest land. In 1968, for example, American-made scientific instruments were used by Soviet scientists at their base at Mirny to collect information on cosmic radiation. The data collected was then shared by both the Soviet Union and the United States. Antarctica today has no national boundaries and is devoted exclusively to the pursuit of science.

▶ THE UNITED STATES PROGRAM—1967–68

In 1968 the United States maintained six scientific stations in Antarctica. The largest, McMurdo Station, is located at the end of the Ross Ice Shelf a few miles from where Captain James C. Ross spent the winter aboard his ship HMS *Erebus* in 1841. McMurdo Station serves as the primary logistic facility from which are conducted air operations resupplying the inland stations and supporting field-research programs. Close to 1,100 scientific and military personnel participated in the 1967–68 program. More than half of these were stationed at McMurdo. Although

McMurdo Station, on low volcanic hills at the southern end of Ross Island, is the center for Antarctic scientific studies.

Antarctic activities: pumping tracer amounts of radioisotope iodine 131 into lake to measure currents (top left); cooking in improvised galley in a Marie Byrd Land camp (center left); collecting rocks on Mount Weaver (top right); motor tobogganing to study ice movement (bottom).

most of the work was carried out during the Antarctic summer, close to 300 people spent the bitter-cold winter isolated from the world in one of three stations: McMurdo Station, Pole Station and Byrd Station.

At the U.S. base located at the Geographic South Pole, seven scientists spent the winter in Quonset-type quarters submerged about forty feet beneath the continental ice sheet. The sun never appears in Antarctica from March through August. At the Pole, temperatures never get above 0° F. In winter, temperatures may range from −40° to −100° F. The coldest temperature on earth, −125.9° F., was recorded on August 24, 1960, at a Soviet station several hundred miles from the Pole.

Food is kept piled in tunnels beneath the ice connecting the various submerged huts. Since temperatures in the tunnels rarely get above −20° F., spoilage is no problem. Heat and electricity are supplied by gasoline-powered generators. Although Antarctica contains the world's largest supply of fresh water, it is all frozen. Drinking water is obtained by chopping ice and melting it over the hot exhaust pipes of the electric generators.

The work of the scientists occupies most of their time during the dark winter. Meteorologists take periodic readings and study the weather conditions. Because the Geographic South Pole is but several hundred miles from the Geomagnetic South Pole—the point where the magnetic lines of force come closest to the earth—scientists study solar radiation and the physics of the upper atmosphere.

Sleep and Dream Studies

At the scientific station at the South Pole, a behavioral-science laboratory was established in 1966 to conduct a three-year study of sleep-and-dream patterns of secluded Antarctic personnel. The study is expected to provide data in planning for human factors in future space explorations. The investigation, conducted by Drs. Jay T. Shurley and Chester M. Pierce of the Oklahoma Medical Research Foundation, will try to determine whether months of isolation will cause a change in an individual's psychological makeup. One preliminary theory to emerge from the study is that people who have been brainwashed may dream less than those who have not undergone mental changes.

Penguin Studies

During the 1967–68 season, Dr. David H. Thomson of the University of Wisconsin studied the Adélie penguin at the coastal station, Hallett. He tried to discover how the adult penguin can recognize its own young in a milling rookery of thousands of young penguins. It had previously been found that a penguin would feed and care for its own chicks and reject all other young birds. How these flightless birds are able to recognize their own brood is still a mystery.

Unfortunately a severe storm during the Antarctic winter of 1967 nearly destroyed one of Antarctica's largest rookeries of Adélies and the stately emperor penguin. More than one thousand chicks and adults were killed and thousands of eggs were destroyed during a storm which endangered the entire penguin population on Cape Crozier, located several miles from McMurdo. As a result of the tragedy, the National Science Foundation ordered that no emperor penguins be taken to the United States or killed for scientific or other purposes for at least a year.

Studies of penguins have not yet revealed how the adult penguin recognizes its own young.

A scientist checks the deep-core drill used to penetrate the 7,111-foot-thick Antarctic ice cap to the rock base at Byrd Station.

Deep Ice Drilling

One of the most dramatic of the Antarctic experiments came to a successful conclusion in 1968. Geologists drilled a hole through the giant ice sheet, and on January 29 struck a rock base 7,111 feet beneath the surface of the ice. This, the deepest hole ever drilled through ice, is expected to provide important information about the past condition in the frozen continent.

The hole was started at Byrd Station in late 1966 by a team of scientists under the direction of B. Lyle Hansen of the Army's Cold Regions Research and Engineering Laboratory, Hanover, N.H. As ice cores were removed from the 4½-inch-wide hole, they were labeled and placed in plastic containers and stored in sub-zero tunnels. A study of these cores will provide impor-

tant information on the rate of snow accumulation, which will indicate growth and retreat of the polar ice cap; seasonal temperature variations; average temperature, which will provide important clues to the climatic history of the Southern Hemisphere; and the physical condition of the ice and underlying rock.

Information obtained by studying the ice cores will give a picture of the continent when the lowest layers of the ice sheet were first deposited—perhaps 30,000 years ago. The Antarctic ice sheet is the largest body of ice in the world. If the giant ice sheet ever melted, it has been estimated that enough water would be added to the world's oceans to cause sea level to rise 200 feet. This rise in sea level would cover the Statue of Liberty to her nose, and flood

Fossil (top) is part of the jawbone of a labyrinthodont (reconstructed in drawing), the first land-vertebrate fossil ever found in Antarctica.

every major seaport. The Antarctic ice sheet exerts great influence on weather throughout the world.

Continental-Drift Evidence

Perhaps the most important scientific discovery was made in late December 1967. A team of geologists from Ohio State University, led by Peter Barrett of New Zealand, was studying an exposed outcropping of sedimentary layers near the upper Beardmore Glacier, 325 miles from the South Pole. One of the geologists discovered a fossil imbedded in an ancient stream bed. The small fragment was identified by Edwin H. Colbert, curator of vertebrate paleontology at the American Museum of Natural History, as part of a salamanderlike creature known as a labyrinthodont. The labyrinthodont was a four-foot-long freshwater amphibian that lived more than 200,000,000 years ago in Africa, Australia and South America.

The fossilized section of the lower jaw of a freshwater animal is the first evidence that land vertebrates once lived in Antarctica. Today all animals in Antarctica live in or by the sea. The importance of this discovery is that it provides geologists with their first concrete bit of evidence that Antarctica was once joined to a giant continent composed of Africa, South America, India and Australia. This giant continent, called Gondwana land, is thought to have split into several separate landmasses and drifted apart about 200,000,000 years ago.

Polar Traverse

Most of the scientists operate in or near one of the Antarctic bases. However, each season since 1964 a group of hearty scientists has been exploring the vast, wind-swept plateau of Queen Maud Land. This area of Antarctica nearest Africa is one of the last remaining unexplored regions of the continent. In 1967–68 a party of nine scientist-explorers, led by Norman W. Peddie of the U.S. Coast and Geodetic Survey, traveled 815 miles over the two-mile-thick ice sheet. This was the third leg of the South Pole–Queen Maud Land Traverse. The final leg of the 5,000-mile traverse was scheduled to be completed in February 1969.

The scientists traveled in large tracked vehicles called Sno-Cats. Since the men were unable to carry all their supplies with them, aircraft from McMurdo Station airdropped food and fuel to the group at predetermined meeting points. Geophysicists used special instruments to measure the thickness of the ice along the route. They also studied the characteristics of the ice sheet and bedrock interfaces. The data will be used to make subsurface topographic maps and gravity and magnetic maps. The traverse party faced severe-weather temperatures as low as −60° F. and winds of near-hurricane force.

In October 1969 another team of scientists will head for Antarctica. Its work will be part of a continuing effort to learn more about the icy continent at the bottom of the world.

BENEDICT A. LEERBURGER, JR.

SPACE

APOLLO 7 and Apollo 8, launched October 11 and December 21, restored United States confidence in its ability to attempt a lunar-landing mission in 1969.

▶ THE APOLLO PROGRAM

The enormously successful Apollo 8 flight made astronauts James Lovell, Jr., Frank Borman and William Anders the first lunar voyagers. The facts of their voyage could make a small book. But that book will scarcely be necessary, for hundreds of millions of people the world over watched at least parts of the flight on TV. They saw the launch. They saw the astronauts in flight. They saw startling TV pictures of the moon and earth. And they saw the spacecraft recovery in the Pacific, after it came down to a perfect landing on December 27. This flight paved the way for a possible lunar landing in mid-1969.

Manned space flight stirs the imagination. It whets the appetite for change in all areas of life. Indeed, many people have asked, "If the United States can send a man to the moon, why can't it bring about the social changes necessary to end its domestic turmoil?"

So the manned-space-flight program means adventure and daring. It means voyaging to other worlds. After the moon, there is Mars and Jupiter, and, then, perhaps, planets about other suns. Apollo 8, which one journalist called "a voyage for the ages," brought all this within the realm of the possible.

RECORD OF MANNED SPACE FLIGHTS

	U.S.	U.S.S.R.
Manned flights	18	10
Multiman flights	12	2
Manned hours in space	3,215	629
Men in space	32	13
Space walks	9	1
Time outside capsule	12 hrs.	10 min.
Rendezvous in space	12	2
Maneuverable spacecraft	12	1
Space linkups	7	0

A view of earth as seen by the Apollo 8 astronauts as they came from behind the moon. Moon surface is in the foreground; the earth is 240,000 statute miles away.

Apollo 8 astronauts, left to right: James Lovell, command-module pilot; William Anders, lunar-module pilot; Frank Borman, commander.

Photo of the lunar surface taken from Apollo 8. The large crater, in the foreground, Goclenius, is about 40 miles in diameter.

1. Launch, Dec. 21, 7:51 A.M. 2. Engine fires, translunar injection begins. 3. Third stage of Saturn 5 separates. 4. Mid-course correction. 5. Engine fires, places craft in lunar orbit. 6. Ten orbits of the moon. 7. Engine fires, craft heads back to earth. 8. Mid-course correction. 9. Service module jettisoned. 10. Splashdown, Dec. 27, 10:51 A.M.

APOLLO 8 LUNAR MISSION

The stage for Apollo 8 had been set two months earlier by Apollo 7. With astronauts Walter M. Schirra, Jr., Walter Cunningham and Donn Eisele aboard, the Saturn 1B/Apollo 7 lifted off at 11:03 A.M. on October 11. The spacecraft splashed down in the Atlantic Ocean at 7:11 A.M. on October 22. During this 11-day flight, the astronauts traveled some 4,500,000 miles, making 163 orbits in 260 hours. Indeed, the flight was of longer duration than a flight to the moon and back. Even though the astronauts suffered from unpleasant head colds, they ran the Apollo through more-extensive maneuvers and check-outs than had been scheduled.

Earlier in the year, on January 22, the unmanned Saturn 1B/Apollo 5 flight had partially tested a Lunar Module (LM) in orbit. And on April 4 the unmanned Saturn 5/Apollo 6 flight had exercised numerous launch and spacecraft systems. These two tests proved largely successful and paved the way for the later manned flights.

The expended Saturn-4B booster rocket as photographed from the Apollo 7 spacecraft during a rendezvous maneuver. Far below, the Atlantic Ocean and the Florida coastline are clearly visible.

Above, Apollo 7 astronauts Donn F. Eisele, left, and Walter M. Schirra, Jr., during their first TV transmission. Below, back on earth: Schirra, Eisele and Walter Cunningham.

SOVIET SPACE FLIGHTS

In the spring the Russians for the second time (previously, October 1967) demonstrated automatic rendezvous and docking of two spacecraft. Cosmos 212, launched on April 14, docked with Cosmos 213 shortly after it was launched on April 15. Both spacecraft were returned to earth by soft landing.

On April 7 the Russians sent Luna 14 toward an orbit (achieved April 10) around the moon to measure its gravitational field. This is a necessary step preparatory to a manned landing.

At least two and possibly five Russian launches in the spring and summer appeared related to manned-spacecraft development. Then, on September 15, the unmanned Zond 5 began a history-making flight around the moon and back to earth on September 21. It was recovered at sea in the Indian Ocean. Finally, after launching an unmanned Soyuz 2 on October 25, the Russians sent 47-year-old Cosmonaut Colonel Georgi T. Beregovoi into orbit in Soyuz 3 on October 26. During a four-day flight he rendezvoused twice with the Soyuz 2, but apparently attempted no docking. Both spacecraft returned safely to earth.

United States scientists believe that the Soyuz 3 might have demonstrated maneuvers that could be used in a manned lunar mission. And the Zond 5 may have demonstrated elements of a complete profile for manned flight, such as guidance and control and recovery at sea.

In November, a second Soviet craft, Zond 6, orbited the moon and returned to earth. It landed in the Soviet Union seven days after launch. The Russians stated that they used an advanced method to guide Zond 6 back to earth. The craft was slowed from 6.8 to 4.7 miles per second when it first entered the atmosphere. It then skipped back into less-dense space before once again dipping into the atmosphere, which further slowed the craft. Zond 6 carried live creatures aboard.

Soviet Cosmonaut Georgi T. Beregovoi as seen on television during his flight in Soyuz 3. He was aloft for four days.

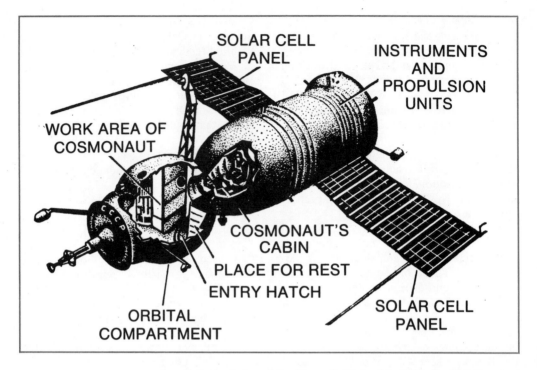

SOLAR CELL PANEL

INSTRUMENTS AND PROPULSION UNITS

WORK AREA OF COSMONAUT

COSMONAUT'S CABIN

PLACE FOR REST

ENTRY HATCH

ORBITAL COMPARTMENT

SOLAR CELL PANEL

An artist's rendering of the Soyuz 3. During his flight aboard this spacecraft, Cosmonaut Beregovoi rendezvoused twice with another craft, the Soyuz 2, and moved the Russians forward in their plans for a lunar landing.

▶ TOWARD MARS AND THE MOON

Whatever the long-range intent, the Russian flights put records on the books. They also exhibited versatile and effective technology for both manned and unmanned space missions. It has been suggested, for example, that Zond 5 followed a flight plan that could be used in a mission to Mars. In 1969 the United States and presumably the Soviet Union will launch probes to that planet. A United States Mariner spacecraft will fly past Mars and again take TV pictures of it and perhaps of one of its moons. It will also probe Mars' environment and surface with other instruments. A Russian spacecraft, following the Zond 5 pattern, might take high-resolution photographs of the planet's surface and actually return them in a capsule to earth.

Needless to say, in both lunar and planetary exploration, 1969 shapes up to be a momentous year. Mars will be probed for

the least evidence of life, upon which extraordinary events would turn. The moon will be probed for direct clues to its origin, and for the purpose of making a sound decision on setting up a lunar base.

Information already returned to earth by the Surveyor and Lunar Orbiter spacecraft indicates that the moon is a more complex body than had been previously thought. According to Orbiter data, for example, the moon has a large basin on the side facing the earth. It also has volcanic as well as meteoritic-impact features. Other results show that the moon has big "lumps" beneath its surface. And recent analyses suggest that major impact craters, such as Copernicus, expose material from tens of miles beneath the moon's surface as well as sections of the 3-mile-thick lunar crust. The astronauts who explore Copernicus may become the first men to touch the primal "stone" of a celestial body.

Some interesting lunar experiments were conducted during 1968. One such experiment utilized Surveyor 7, which was launched on January 7, landing on the moon 66½ hours later. On January 19–21, scientists at the Kitt Peak National Observatory, Arizona, and the Table Mountain Observatory, California, directed laser beams at Surveyor 7. The beams were received by the spacecraft's TV camera and transmitted back to earth. The laser tests measured the earth-moon distance with an accuracy of six inches. This is much more accurate than the standard radar measurement of the distance. This experiment entailed the first use of light to communicate over a great distance. It opens the way for many applications, some military. The Apollo astronauts who land on the moon will place laser reflectors on the Lunar Module for similar experiments.

In April, scientists at Stanford University detected further evidence of lunar volcanism. They did this by bouncing radio signals from Explorer 35, in lunar orbit, off the moon's surface to earth. These signals, in effect, map warm zones on the moon's surface. The warm zones suggest recent extrusions of lava.

Finally, Surveyor 7 itself returned over 21,000 TV pictures to earth and explored the surface of the moon with a digger claw and a chemical analyzer. It showed that the Tycho highlands differ chemically and physically from the *maria* (dark areas on the moon's surface) previously explored.

▶ EXPLORING THE SPACE ENVIRONMENT

In 1968, new satellites continued to explore and map the space environment. The largest of these, Orbiting Geophysical Observatory 5, was launched on March 4. OGO 5 ranges from 181 to 195 miles from earth. At first it deployed a record 25 experiments, but one of them failed a week after launch. It detects and measures solar and galactic cosmic rays, magnetic and electric fields, solar-wind plasma, and micrometeorites as well as other space phenomena.

Other United States scientific satellites were launched during 1968. Explorer 36, launched on January 11, transmitted geodetic data back to earth. Explorer 37, launched on March 5, returned solar-radiation data. OV 1-13 and OV 1-14 were launched on April 6 to measure radiation. OV 1-14, however, had a power failure after a week. Explorer 39 and 40, launched on August 8, are measuring upper-atmospheric density, and temperature and radiation data, respectively. And OV 2-5, OV 5-2 and OV 5-4, launched on September 26, are measuring radiation and other environmental characteristics, such as zero-*g* heat transfer.

On May 16 the United States launched ESRO-2B. This satellite was prepared by European scientists to measure solar and cosmic radiation in near-earth orbit.

The United States also kept its space weather system up to par with the launching of the meteorological satellite ESSA-7 on August 16. But it lost the advanced meteorological satellite Nimbus B in an abortive launch on May 18.

Throughout 1968 the Soviet Union launched a stream of unidentifiable satellites into stable orbit. There were 15 such launches by the end of June. Many of these undoubtedly measure the near-earth environment and make engineering tests of materials and equipment. On March 14 and on June 12, the Russians launched meteorological satellites (Cosmos 206 and 226), which take cloud-cover pictures and other weather data.

▶ SPACE ASTRONOMY

In 1968, space astronomy began its long-expected rise to prominence. NASA launched Explorer 38, the radio-astronomy satellite, on July 4. By October 8 the satellite's antennas were deployed to their full length: 750 feet each, or a total of 1,500 feet tip to tip on each full leg of an X shape. This giant cross collects low-frequency radio signals from objects in our solar system, such as Jupiter and the sun, and from sources in our galaxy, the Milky Way.

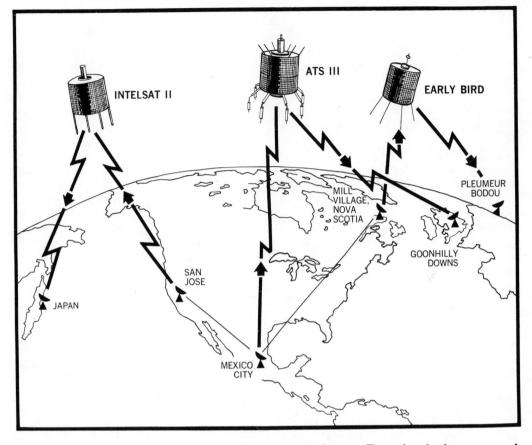

INTELSAT II

ATS III

EARLY BIRD

MILL VILLAGE, NOVA SCOTIA

PLEUMEUR BODOU

GOONHILLY DOWNS

SAN JOSE

JAPAN

MEXICO CITY

Diagram shows how communications satellites relayed color coverage of the Olympic Games in Mexico City to other areas of the world.

The Soviet Union launched a small set of ultraviolet and X-ray telescopes (Cosmos 215) into near-earth orbit in the middle of April.

The biggest event for space astronomy came with the launching of the previously trouble-plagued Orbiting Astronomical Observatory. The OAO weighs some 4,400 pounds and carries 11 telescopes.

▶ **COMMUNICATIONS SATELLITES**

Both the United States and the Soviet Union made important additions to their communication-satellite networks during the year. The United States launched eight military communication satellites with a single Titan 3-C booster on June 13. These satellites supplement the already-positioned vehicles of the initial defense-communications network.

The Soviet Union launched Molniya 1H on April 21, Molniya 1J on July 5 and Molniya 1K (the tenth in the series) on October 5 to bolster its orbital network.

The United Nations' first Space Conference on Exploration and Peaceful Uses of Outer Space was held in Vienna, Austria, the week that the Soviet Union invaded Czechoslovakia. At the conference the Soviets offered their orbital network to the world's nations as a cooperative venture under the name Intersputnik. Such a system would merely duplicate the already available U.S.-sponsored system, Intelsat.

Intelsat has welded 63 nations into an international commercial venture that in 1969 will vote its permanent form. It has within its grasp a commercial network of telephone and TV satellites that will girdle the world.

Despite the loss of a satellite launched on September 18, in preparation for the Olympics in Mexico, Intelsat delivered live color TV pictures of the games to Europe. It was able to do this with the aid of the United States Applications Technology Satellite 3, which had been launched in 1967. The Soviet Union was quick to buy distribution from the European Broadcasting Union for showing in Russia. ATS also relayed live TV pictures from Apollo 7 to Europe on October 14, during the flight.

On December 18, Intelsat 3-A was launched atop a Thor-Delta rocket. It is the first of several new communications satellites that will bring commercial communications by satellite to almost the entire world by the middle of 1969. Intelsat 3-A is the most advanced—and biggest—commercial satellite ever to be sent aloft. It will be used to relay telephone and television messages.

Military Satellites

Communication satellites have already revolutionized military operations. Late in 1968 a Titan 3-C delivered the world's largest military comsat into a synchronous orbit, 22,300 miles above the earth. This two-story, 1,600-pound satellite has a capacity equal to 10,000 two-way telephone channels. And its signal power is great enough to make useful antennas only a foot in diameter. Such antennas could be carried by a small Army unit in the field. Moreover, tanks, ships, aircraft and ground units will be able to run messages simultaneously through a satellite. This means that a central battle officer in Washington will soon have (if he does not have already) the ability to communicate directly at the same time with a helicopter, a submarine or a fighter-bomber and a squad of commanders in a ravine half the world away.

New Uses for Communications Satellites

It can now be seen that satellites can be used to route air traffic and even ground traffic. In 1968, NASA Goddard Space Flight Center used the ATS 3 satellite (22,300 miles altitude) to track a specially equipped automobile going along the Baltimore-Washington Parkway. It also located a small boat in Chesapeake Bay, an airplane in flight, and a Coast and Geodetic Survey ship, the *Discoverer,* operating in the Carribbean.

Engineers foresee combining the observational capacity of the satellite with such versatile communications to gather and distribute data on water supplies and flood control, fish movements, crop diseases, ice distribution and movement, mineral supplies and ocean conditions. In a paper given at the American Institute of Aeronautics and Astronautics annual meeting, engineer D. M. Waltz predicted that such "earth-resource" satellites would bring nearly a billion dollars in benefits by the mid-1970's. "Spacecraft could range from 150-pound vehicles carrying a single photographic system, such as a TV camera, for launch in the early 1970's, to manned spacecraft with many sophisticated sensors, for later use in the decade," noted Waltz. The Apollo 7 astronauts, it might be noted, spent their seventh day photographing hurricane Gladys in the Gulf of Mexico and tropical storm Gloria in the western Pacific.

As the ability to exploit space for commercial and military purposes grows, so does the danger. The Soyuz and Apollo spacecraft can rendezvous with lunar spaceships. But they can also rendezvous with undisclosed military spacecraft. Soon military space stations with military crews will take to orbit—unless the Soviet Union and the United States make more far-reaching agreements than the one governing the return of downed astronauts. This agreement was signed by 44 nations, including the United States and the Soviet Union, in April. Back in 1961 a psychologist remarked that space seemed to him a "powerful deepener of old ruts." In near space we confront the truth of this statement in 1969.

JOHN NEWBAUER
Editor in Chief
Astronautics & Aeronautics

MAN ON THE MOON

BECAUSE American astronauts are going to the moon, men on earth will live better. The immediate goal of the Apollo program is to land two men on the moon and return them safely to earth in this decade. But the space program, of which Apollo is a major part, will enrich our lives in many other ways. In the course of the program, new inventions are being made, new products developed. Improved manufacturing techniques and management methods are being evolved. Aids to medical research and treatment, better education and greater national security are also resulting.

▶ APOLLO REQUIREMENTS

What is needed to send men to the moon and return them safely to earth?

One requirement is a vehicle that can provide the tremendous energy needed to overcome the pull of the earth's gravity and propel an object to the moon.

Another necessity is a spacecraft in which men can live during the approximately 8 day trip. The spacecraft must be able to make a soft landing on the moon. It must be able to serve as a lunar base station. And it must be able to take off and return the men to earth. It must also be able to function in a vacuum and in temperatures as cold as $-250°$ F. and as hot as $5,000°$ F. It must protect its crew from these conditions. It must shield the astronauts from meteorites and radiation. It must be able to generate electrical power and be a communications center. It must contain systems to help astronauts solve complicated mathematical problems. In short, it must be a small, traveling world of its own for the three men aboard.

There are other requirements for a successful journey to the moon. The astronauts will need garments that will protect them from the environment on the moon's surface. They will need a system that will enable them to breathe and survive when they are exploring the moon's surface. They will need a network of stations on earth to track the course of the spacecraft and keep in touch with it by radio.

▶ LUNAR-ORBIT RENDEZVOUS

After President John F. Kennedy announced on May 25, 1961, that a manned landing on the moon was a national goal, planners considered three different methods to accomplish the mission. After more than a year of study, one method—lunar-orbit rendezvous—was selected.

With lunar-orbit rendezvous, a spacecraft would be launched from earth into lunar orbit. A section of the spacecraft would then be detached and landed on the moon. The other part of the craft would wait in orbit for the landing craft to return.

▶ THE SATURN V LAUNCH VEHICLE

The launch vehicle developed for the lunar mission is the Saturn V. It is a 3-stage rocket 281 feet high. Adding the spacecraft makes the combined height 363 feet. The Saturn V's first stage has a diameter of 33 feet, and uses five rocket engines developing a total thrust of 7,500,000 pounds. The second stage also has five engines, with a total thrust of 1,000,000 pounds. The third stage has one engine producing 200,000 pounds of thrust.

▶ THE APOLLO SPACECRAFT

The spacecraft is made up of 3 parts, or modules. The command module is the only part that will return to earth. It contains the living quarters for the three crew members and controls for in-flight maneuvers. It is cone-shaped, with a diameter at the bottom of 12.8 feet, and a height of 12 feet.

Attached behind the command module is the service module. It is a cylindrical unit 12.8 feet in diameter and 22 feet high. It contains fuel tanks, the electrical-power

(*continued on page 317*)

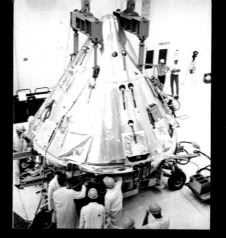

Technicians examine the Apollo 4 spacecraft command capsule before shipment from North American Rockwell in Downey, California. Notice protective covers on the hatches.

he command and service modules, with lunar module adapter ttached, is hoisted for mating to Saturn V third stage ower left). Size is shown by men on Saturn V and gantry.

Pictures on these pages courtesy of North American Rockwell Corporation Space Division

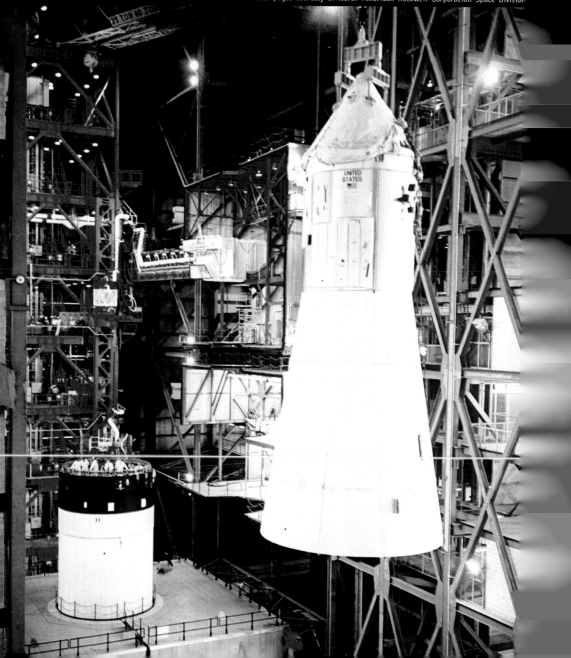

Powered by 7,500,000 pounds of thrust, the Apollo/Saturn V space vehicle begins its journey into space on November 9, 1967. The five rocket motors in the service module fired for a record 4 minutes, 40 seconds.

Photograph of the earth taken from the window of the spacecraft at an altitude of about 11,000 miles above the earth. A 70mm Maurer flight camera clicked every 10.6 seconds, producing 711 perfect photos of the earth.

Red dawn breaking over the launch site at Cape Kennedy shows the floodlighted Apollo space vehicle, 363 feet in length and weighing 310 tons, ready to be sent roaring into space (left).

Navy frogmen affix hoisting cables and an inflated ring to the command module after its landing in the Pacific Ocean. It awaits hoisting onto the recovery ship, the USS Bennington.

Charred by 5,000° temperatures but none the worse inside after its fiery reentry into the atmosphere the Apollo 4 command module is hoisted aboard the recovery ship. The flight took 8 hours, 37 minutes, 8 seconds.

equipment, a primary propulsion system for use after the launch vehicle is left behind, and small engines to control the attitude of the spacecraft and for limited maneuvering.

The third part of the spacecraft is the lunar module. After being detached from the orbiting command and service modules, it will land on the moon's surface with two of the three astronauts. It has an ascent stage and a descent stage with four spidery legs. Each stage has its own propulsion system. The lunar module has its own guidance, control, communications and environmental-control systems. For launch, it is housed in an adapter between the service module and the third stage of the Saturn V.

▶ THE FLIGHT

The flight to the moon will begin at the Kennedy Space Center in Florida. There the Apollo spacecraft will be launched by the Saturn V. The first and second stages of the launch vehicle will be discarded after their propellants have been depleted. The third-stage engine will first be fired only long enough to place itself and the spacecraft into earth orbit. After about two revolutions, while the crew checks out the spacecraft to make sure it is ready for the next step, the third-stage engine will be re-fired. This will put the spacecraft into a trajectory toward the moon. A short time later, the command and service modules will separate from the third stage, adapter and lunar module, turn around, and join the lunar module. Then springs will eject the command, service and lunar module combination away from the adapter and third-stage engine. During the journey to the moon, the service propulsion system will be fired as necessary to keep the spacecraft on course. As the spacecraft nears the moon, the service retro-engine will be fired to slow the spacecraft so that it will go into an orbit around the moon about eighty miles high.

Two of the astronauts will transfer from the command module to the lunar module.

They will then separate from the command and service modules and begin the descent to the lunar surface. The engine in the descent stage of the lunar module will enable them to slow their descent and make a soft landing.

▶ ON THE MOON

The astronauts will remain on the surface for up to one day. They will check out their craft for the return trip, explore, set up experiments, collect samples and sleep. Takeoff is accomplished with the ascent-stage engine. The descent stage is used as a launch platform.

▶ RETURN TO EARTH

The launch is timed for rendezvous and docking with the orbiting command and service modules. The two astronauts will rejoin the third in the command module, and the lunar module will be cast adrift in lunar orbit. Then the service-module engine will be fired to take the spacecraft out of lunar orbit and into a trajectory toward earth. Just before entry into the earth's atmosphere, the service module will be jettisoned. Only the command module will be lowered by parachutes into the Pacific Ocean, where ships will recover it.

▶ THE APOLLO SCHEDULE

By late in 1968, the years of ground testing and unmanned flights led to a readiness to begin a series of manned Apollo missions. In October the three-man Apollo 7 completed an 11-day, earth-orbit flight. Two months later, three other astronauts, aboard Apollo 8, made their historic journey around the moon and back. Other manned flights are planned for 1969: Apollo 9 will test the lunar module in earth orbit; Apollo 10 will test it in lunar orbit; and in July 1969, if all goes well, one of man's oldest dreams could be fulfilled when two astronauts leave their footprints on the surface of the moon.

ROBERT R. GILRUTH
Director, NASA Manned Spacecraft Center
Houston, Texas

SPORTS

NINETEEN SIXTY-EIGHT was the year in which an unknown—Lee Trevino—won golfdom's U.S. Open. It was a year in which college football provided the pros with a brilliant runner: O. J. Simpson. And it was a year in which an Army officer—Arthur Ashe—electrified the tennis world. But to millions of baseball fans it was The Year of the Tiger.

▶ BASEBALL

For 23 long, hot summers, fans of the Detroit Tigers had streamed into the charming old ball park on Michigan Avenue in Detroit, only to come away saddened and frustrated at what they saw. The Tigers had the talent, it seemed. They just couldn't win baseball games. But then, along came a brash—and often adorable —right-handed pitcher named Dennis McLain. In one wonderful summer he turned everything upside down in Detroit.

Off the baseball field, McLain wore turtleneck sweaters beneath his shiny sport jackets and played the Hammond organ in his spare time. On the field, he pitched— and he pitched. He won 11 of his first 12 games. And the Tigers opened up a big lead in the American League pennant race —and made it stand up all the way. McLain became the first pitcher to win 30 games since Dizzy Dean in 1934.

Next came the World Series against the St. Louis Cardinals. Behind Bob Gibson —another superb pitcher—they had won the National League pennant with ease. The experts said that those games matching McLain and Gibson would determine the series victor. But—as usual—the experts were not so expert. A left-hander named Mickey Lolich, who adored motorcycles, won three games for the Tigers, including the decisive seventh game against Gibson. Center fielder Jim Northrup drove in the winning runs in a 4–1 victory. But everybody's sentimental hero was Al Kaline, the Tiger right fielder. Waiting 16 years to play in a World Series, Kaline starred for the Tigers both at bat and in the field.

▶ HOCKEY

In 1967–68 the National Hockey League went through its first season of

expansion. The results were more gratifying than anybody had expected. New teams in Los Angeles, Oakland, Minneapolis–St. Paul, St. Louis, Pittsburgh and Philadelphia played like demons against their older rivals, winning almost 30 per cent of the games against them. Then came the Stanley Cup play-offs. The Montreal Canadiens had easily won the regular-season championship among the older teams. They then waltzed through their play-offs. But it was the new teams that provided the fans with some thrilling play-off hockey. The St. Louis Blues finally defeated the Minnesota North Stars in seven games for the right to meet Montreal. Everyone expected the Blues to fold up against the speedy and determined Canadiens. But instead, St. Louis pushed Montreal to the limit before losing four games by one goal—twice in overtime. Then, in the Canadiens' locker room, Toe Blake—their coach for 13 years —told his players he was retiring.

▶ **BASKETBALL**

Springtime also means 'college basketball's NCAA tournament. In January, mighty UCLA—the NCAA's defending champions and led by 7-foot 1-inch Lew Alcindor—traveled to the Astrodome in Houston to play the University of Houston. Before the largest indoor crowd ever to see a college-basketball game—52,693— Houston, paced by Elvin Hayes, pulled a stunning 71–69 upset. UCLA waited patiently, however. In the NCAA semifinals it beat Houston with ease on a superlative game from Alcindor.

The scene in professional basketball had a familiar, Boston Celtic look to it. The Celtics, led by player-coach Bill Russell, defeated Los Angeles in the National Basketball Association play-offs.

▶ **BOXING**

With Cassius Clay stripped of his boxing title—and facing a possible jail term—for

Army Lieutenant Arthur Ashe, the United States' foremost amateur tennis player, shows his serving form.

failing to report for induction into the Army, the World Boxing Association, recognized in 45 states, staged a long elimination tournament among the heavyweight contenders. Jimmy Ellis finally won the tournament by decisioning Jerry Quarry in the finals. But nobody was quite ready to call Ellis the champion. It seems that Joe Frazier, who might well be the best heavyweight of all (besides Clay), had chosen not to participate in the tournament. And he was the recognized champion in the five remaining states. Until Ellis fought Frazier, nobody could be certain who was the new heavyweight champion of the world.

▶ GOLF

In April the annual Masters Golf Tournament was held in Augusta, Georgia, as usual. But the finish was the most unusual in history. Popular Roberto de Vicenzo of Argentina tied Bob Goalby of the United States with a 277 score. But because he neglected to check his scorecard—which was in error with a 278 score—before signing his name to it, first place was awarded, by the rules, to Goalby. "I play golf all over the world for 30 years," a dejected De Vicenzo said afterward, "and now all I can think of is how stupid I am to be wrong in this wonderful tournament."

In the U.S. Open there were more surprises—the biggest of all furnished by Lee Trevino from Texas. Virtually unknown before the Open, Trevino defeated Jack Nicklaus (the defending champion) and Bert Yancey (the tournament leader for the first three days), setting a few records in the process.

▶ HORSE RACING

During the summer all Dr. Fager, the magnificent thoroughbred, did was win. And by the time the football season had arrived, Dr. Fager was a cinch for the Horse of the Year award.

▶ FOOTBALL

At the start of the college season, pro-football scouts were undecided over who was best—O. J. Simpson of Southern California, the defending national champions, or Leroy Keyes of Purdue. They had no doubts in the end. Simpson looked like collegiate football's finest runner in history. He won game after game for the Trojans almost single-handedly.

Ohio State emerged as the national champions of college football when they beat USC in the Rose Bowl 27–16. The two teams had been rated 1 and 2 throughout the season. In other bowl games it was Penn State over Kansas 15–14 in the Orange Bowl, Texas over Tennessee 36–13 in the Cotton Bowl and Arkansas over Georgia 16–2 in the Sugar Bowl.

In January 1968 the world of professional football had picked up where it left off in 1967—with the Green Bay Packers winning. On a sunny afternoon in Miami's Orange Bowl, the Packers—led by their peerless quarterback, Bart Starr—easily defeated the Oakland Raiders of the American Football League in the second annual Super Bowl game, 33–14. A few weeks later, however, Packer Coach Vince Lombardi announced that he would step down as coach and devote full time to being the club's general manager. He chose Phil Bengston, a top coaching assistant, as his replacement.

In 1968, however, the Green Bay Packers were no longer the powerhouse team of the NFL. Green Bay finished third in the Central Division with a 6–7–1 record. The strongest team in the NFL in 1968 was the Baltimore Colts. Sparked by the passing of New York Giant castoff Earl Morrall, the Colts finished with a 13–1 season. They went on to rout the Cleveland Browns 34–0 for the NFL championship.

In the AFL the New York Jets won their first league championship by defeating the Oakland Raiders 27–23. Jet star Joe Namath threw three touchdown passes.

In an upset, the New York Jets beat the Baltimore Colts 16–7 in the third Super Bowl game on January 12, 1969.

GARY M. RONBERG
Sports Illustrated

WORLD DRIVING FORMULA 1 CHAMPIONSHIP

Race	Driver	Car
South African GP	Jim Clark, Scotland	Lotus-Ford
GP of Spain	Graham Hill, Britain	Lotus-Ford
GP of Monaco	Graham Hill	Lotus-Ford
Dutch GP	Jackie Stewart, Scotland	Matra-Ford
GP of Belgium	Bruce McLaren, New Zealand	McLaren-Ford
French GP	Jackie Ickx, Belgium	Ferrari
British GP	Jo Siffert, Switzerland	Lotus-Ford
West German GP	Jackie Stewart	Matra-Ford
GP of Canada	Denis Hulme, New Zealand	McLaren-Ford
GP of Italy	Denis Hulme	McLaren-Ford
GP of United States	Jackie Stewart	Matra-Ford
GP of Mexico	Graham Hill	Lotus-Ford

World Road-Racing Champion: GRAHAM HILL

U.S. Road-Racing Champion: MARK DONOHUE

NASCAR Grand National Champion: DAVID PEARSON

USAC Stock-Car Champion: A. J. FOYT

Indianapolis 500: BOBBY UNSER (Eagle-Offenhauser)

SCCA Canadian-American Challenge Cup: DENIS HULME

SCCA Trans-American Sedan Title: MARK DONOHUE

Pitcher Denny McLain won 31 games during the season for the Detroit Tigers. He was given the Cy Young award and the AL's MVP award.

FINAL MAJOR LEAGUE STANDINGS

American League

	W	L	Pct.	GB
Detroit	103	59	.636	
Baltimore	91	71	.562	12
Cleveland	86	75	.534	16½
Boston	86	76	.531	17
New York	83	79	.512	20
Oakland	82	80	.506	21
Minnesota	79	83	.488	24
California	67	95	.414	36
Chicago	67	95	.414	36
Washington	65	96	.404	37½

National League

	W	L	Pct.	GB
St. Louis	97	65	.599	
San Francisco	88	74	.543	9
Chicago	84	78	.519	13
Cincinnati	83	79	.512	14
Atlanta	81	81	.500	16
Pittsburgh	80	82	.494	17
Los Angeles	76	86	.469	21
Philadelphia	76	86	.469	21
New York	73	89	.451	24
Houston	72	90	.444	25

LEADING BATTERS
(425 or more at bats)

American League

	AB	H	RBI	Pct.
Yastrzemski, Boston	539	162	74	.301
Cater, Oakland	504	146	62	.290
Oliva, Minnesota	470	136	68	.289
Horton, Detroit	512	146	85	.285
Uhlaender, Minnesota	488	138	52	.283
Buford, Baltimore	426	120	46	.282
Davalillo, California	519	144	31	.277
Campaneris, Oakland	642	177	38	.276
Harrelson, Boston	535	147	109	.275
F. Howard, Washington	598	164	106	.274

National League

	AB	H	RBI	Pct.
Rose, Cincinnati	626	210	49	.335
M. Alou, Pittsburgh	558	185	52	.332
F. Alou, Atlanta	662	210	56	.317
A. Johnson, Cincinnati	603	188	58	.312
Flood, St. Louis	618	186	60	.301
Jones, New York	509	151	55	.297
Beckert, Chicago	643	189	37	.294
McCovey, San Francisco	523	153	105	.293
Staub, Houston	591	172	72	.291
Clemente, Pittsburgh	502	146	57	.291

WINNING PITCHERS
(20 or more wins)

	W	L	ERA
McLain, Detroit, AL	31	6	1.93
Marichal, San Francisco, NL	26	9	2.43
Gibson, St. Louis, NL	22	9	1.12
McNally, Baltimore, AL	22	10	1.95
Tiant, Cleveland, AL	21	9	1.60

HOME RUN LEADERS
(30 or more home runs)

F. Howard, Washington, AL	44
Horton, Detroit, AL	36
McCovey, San Francisco, NL	36
Harrelson, Boston, AL	35
Allen, Philadelphia, NL	33
Banks, Chicago, NL	32

1968 WORLD SERIES RESULTS

		R	H	E	Winning/Losing Pitcher
1.	St. Louis	4	6	0	Gibson
	Detroit	0	5	3	McLain
2.	Detroit	8	13	1	Lolich
	St. Louis	1	6	0	Briles
3.	St. Louis	7	13	0	Washburn
	Detroit	3	4	0	Wilson
4.	St. Louis	10	13	0	Gibson
	Detroit	1	5	4	McLain
5.	Detroit	5	9	1	Lolich
	St. Louis	3	9	0	Hoerner
6.	Detroit	13	12	1	McLain
	St. Louis	1	9	1	Washburn
7.	Detroit	4	8	1	Lolich
	St. Louis	1	5	0	Gibson

FINAL NBA STANDINGS

Eastern Division

	W	L	Pct.
Philadelphia	62	20	.756
Boston	54	28	.659
New York	43	39	.524
Detroit	40	42	.488
Cincinnati	39	43	.476
Baltimore	36	46	.439

Western Division

	W	L	Pct.
St. Louis	56	26	.683
Los Angeles	52	30	.634
San Francisco	43	39	.524
Chicago	29	53	.354
Seattle	23	59	.280
San Diego	15	67	.183

NBA Championship: Boston

FINAL ABA STANDINGS

Eastern Division

	W	L	Pct.
Pittsburgh	54	24	.692
Minnesota	50	28	.641
Indiana	38	40	.487
Kentucky	36	42	.462
New Jersey	36	42	.462

Western Division

	W	L	Pct.
New Orleans	48	30	.615
Dallas	46	32	.590
Denver	45	33	.577
Houston	28	50	.359
Anaheim	25	53	.321
Oakland	23	55	.295

ABA Championship: Pittsburgh

COLLEGE BASKETBALL

NCAA: UCLA
National Invitation: DAYTON
NAIA: CENTRAL STATE (Wilberforce, Ohio)
National Collegiate: KENTUCKY WESLEYAN
National Junior College: SAN JACINTO (Pasadena, Texas)
Atlantic Coast Conference: NORTH CAROLINA
Big Eight: KANSAS STATE
Big Ten: OHIO STATE
Ivy League: COLUMBIA
Middle Atlantic: LA SALLE
Missouri Valley: LOUISVILLE
Pacific Eight: UCLA
Southeastern: KENTUCKY
Southern: DAVIDSON
Southwest: TEXAS CHRISTIAN
Western Athletic: NEW MEXICO
West Coast Athletic: SANTA CLARA

YACHTING

Distance Races

Newport-Bermuda: ROBIN (yawl)
Chicago-Mackinac: COMANCHE (sloop)
Los Angeles-Tahiti: ARANJI (ketch)
Victoria, B. C.-Maui, Hawaii: PORPOISE III (sloop)
Miami-Nassau: NINA (sloop)
Port Huron-Mackinac: HILARIA (yawl)
St. Petersburg-Ft. Lauderdale: RED JACKET (sloop)
San Diego-Acapulco: KIOLOA II (yawl)
Bermuda-Travemünde, W. Germany: INDIGO (yawl)
Buenos Aires-Rio de Janeiro: ONDINE III (ketch)

North American Yacht Racing Union Championships

Mallory Cup: JAMES HUNT
Adams Cup: JUNE METHOT
Sears Cup: JOHN KOLUIS
O'Day Cup: GORDY BOWERS

POWERBOATING

1968 Champion: MISS BARDAHL (Bill Schumacher, driver)
President's Cup: MISS EAGLE ELECTRIC (Warner Gardner, driver)
World Championship: MISS U.S. (Bill Muncey, driver)
Gold Cup: MISS BARDAHL (Bill Schumacher)

AMERICAN BOWLING CONGRESS CHAMPIONS

Classic Division

All-Events: JIM STEFANICH

Singles: DAVE DAVIS

Doubles: BILL TUCKER—DON JOHNSON

Team: BOWL-RITE SUPPLY (Joliet, Illinois)

Regular Division

All-Events: VINCE MAZZANTI

Singles: WAYNE KOWALSKI

Doubles: RICH STARK—WALT ROY

Team: DAVE'S AUTO SUPPLY (Philadelphia, Pennsylvania)

WOMEN'S INTERNATIONAL BOWLING CONGRESS CHAMPIONS

Division I

All-Events: SUSIE REICHLEY
Singles: NORMA PARKS
Doubles: MARY LOU GRAHAM-PAULINE STICKLER
Team: HUDEPOHL BEER (Cincinnati, Ohio)

Division II

All-Events: MAY MONROE
Singles: BEATRICE HARM
Doubles: LAMAR WARS-BETTY BEAMON
Team: JUST MADE IT (Westport, Conn.)

WORLD PROFESSIONAL CHAMPIONS

Flyweight: CHARTCHAI CHIONOI, Thailand
Bantamweight: LIONEL ROSE, Australia
Featherweight: SHO SAIJYO *, Japan
Jr. Lightweight: HIROSHI KOBAYASHI, Japan
Lightweight: CARLOS CRUZ, Dominican Republic
Welterweight: CURTIS COKES, U.S.
Jr. Middleweight: SANDRO MAZZINGHI, Italy
Middleweight: NINO BENVENUTI, Italy
Light Heavyweight: BOB FOSTER, U.S.
Heavyweight: JIMMY ELLIS *, U.S.

* WBA recognized

WESTMINSTER KENNEL CLUB

Best in Show: CH. STINGRAY OF DERRYABAH

Hound: CH. CROSS WYND'S CRACKERJACK, smooth
dachshund

Nonsporting: CH. FLAKKEE SWEEPSTAKES, Kee-
shond

Sporting: CH. CRAGMOUNT'S HI-LO, golden retriever

Terrier: CH. STINGRAY OF DERRYABAH, Lakeland
terrier

Toy: CH. DAN LEE DRAGONSEED, Pekingese

Working: CH. BAR VOM WEIHERTURCHEN, German
shepherd

INTERNATIONAL KENNEL CLUB

Best in Show: CH. SHAMROCK ACRES LIGHT BRI-
GADE

Hound: CH. BALLYKELLY COLIN, Irish wolfhound

Nonsporting: CH. TAFFY'S KID BENJAMIN, Boston
terrier

Sporting: CH. SHAMROCK ACRES LIGHT BRIGADE,
Labrador retriever

Terrier: CH. MELBEE'S CHANCES ARE, Kerry blue
terrier

Toy: CH. REBEL ROC'S STARBOARDER, miniature
pinscher

Working: CH. BOWSER WALLER, St. Bernard

FINAL NFL STANDINGS
EASTERN CONFERENCE
Century Division

	W	L	T	Pct.	PF	PA
Cleveland	10	4	0	.714	394	273
St. Louis	9	4	1	.692	325	289
New Orleans	4	9	1	.308	246	327
Pittsburgh	2	11	1	.154	244	397

Capitol Division

	W	L	T	Pct.	PF	PA
Dallas	12	2	0	.857	431	186
New York	7	7	0	.500	294	325
Washington	5	9	0	.357	249	358
Philadelphia	2	12	0	.143	202	351

WESTERN CONFERENCE
Central Division

	W	L	T	Pct.	PF	PA
Minnesota	8	6	0	.571	282	242
Chicago	7	7	0	.500	250	333
Green Bay	6	7	1	.462	281	227
Detroit	4	8	2	.333	207	241

Coastal Division

	W	L	T	Pct.	PF	PA
Baltimore	13	1	0	.929	402	144
Los Angeles	10	3	1	.769	312	200
San Francisco	7	6	1	.538	303	310
Atlanta	2	12	0	.143	170	389

NFL Championship: Baltimore

FINAL AFL STANDINGS
EASTERN DIVISION

	W	L	T	Pct.	PF	PA
New York	11	3	0	.786	419	280
Houston	7	7	0	.500	303	248
Miami	5	8	1	.385	276	355
Boston	4	10	0	.286	229	406
Buffalo	1	12	1	.077	199	367

WESTERN DIVISION

	W	L	T	Pct.	PF	PA
Oakland *	12	2	0	.857	371	179
Kansas City	12	2	0	.857	453	233
San Diego	9	5	0	.643	382	310
Denver	5	9	0	.357	264	404
Cincinnati	3	11	0	.214	215	329

AFL Championship: New York

* Won conference play-off

Heisman Trophy winner O. J. Simpson carries the ball for the University of Southern California. Simpson rushed for 1,709 yards in 1968.

COLLEGE FOOTBALL

Heisman Trophy: O. J. SIMPSON, USC
Yankee: NEW HAMPSHIRE; CONNECTICUT (tied)
Ivy League: HARVARD; YALE (tied)
Atlantic Coast: NORTH CAROLINA STATE
Southern: RICHMOND
Southeast: GEORGIA
Mid-American: OHIO UNIVERSITY
Big Ten: OHIO STATE
Big Eight: KANSAS; OKLAHOMA (tied)
Southwest: ARKANSAS; UNIV. OF TEXAS (tied)
Western Athletic: WYOMING
Pacific Eight: USC

PROFESSIONAL GOLF

U.S. Open: LEE TREVINO
Masters: BOB GOALBY
British Open: GARY PLAYER, South Africa
Canadian Open: BOB CHARLES, New Zealand
PGA: JULIUS BOROS
World Series: GARY PLAYER
U.S. National Senior Open: TOMMY BOLT
Ladies World Series: KATHY WHITWORTH
U.S. Women's Open: SUSIE MAXWELL BERNING

AMATEUR GOLF

U.S. Amateur: BRUCE FLEISHER
U.S. Women's Amateur: JOANNE GUNDERSON
    CARNER
British Amateur: MICHAEL BONALLACK, Britain

COLLEGE GOLF

NCAA Team: UNIVERSITY OF FLORIDA
NCAA Title: GRIER JONES, Oklahoma State

FINAL NHL STANDINGS

East Division

	W	L	T	Pts.	GF	GA
Montreal	42	22	10	94	236	167
Rangers	39	23	12	90	226	183
Boston	37	27	10	84	259	216
Chicago	32	26	16	80	212	222
Toronto	33	31	10	76	209	176
Detroit	27	35	12	66	245	257

West Division

	W	L	T	Pts.	GF	GA
Philadelphia	31	32	11	73	173	179
Los Angeles	31	33	10	72	200	224
St. Louis	27	31	16	70	177	191
Minnesota	27	32	15	69	191	226
Pittsburgh	27	34	13	67	195	216
Oakland	15	42	17	47	153	219

Stanley Cup: Montreal

Pro golfer Lee Trevino wins the U.S. Open with a record-equaling 72-hole total of 275.

HARNESS STAKES WINNERS

Race	Horse
Hambletonian	Nevele Pride
Yonkers Futurity	Nevele Pride
Kentucky Futurity	Nevele Pride
International Trot	Roquepine
United Nations Trot	Earl Laird
Little Brown Jug	Rum Customer
Messenger Stakes	Rum Customer
Cane Futurity	Rum Customer
International Pace	Cardinal King

THOROUGHBRED STAKES WINNERS

Race	Horse
Kentucky Derby	Dancer's Image
Preakness	Forward Pass
Belmont Stakes	Stage Door Johnny
Aqueduct Stakes	Damascus
Wood Memorial	Dancer's Image
Woodward Stakes	Mr. Right
Belmont Futurity	Top Knight
Matron Stakes	Gallant Bloom
Spinaway Stakes	Queen's Double
United Nations Hdcp	Dr. Fager
Metropolitan Hdcp	In Reality
Suburban Hdcp	Dr. Fager
Brooklyn Hdcp	Damascus

NATIONAL-FINALS RODEO

All-Around: LARRY MAHAN
Calf Riding: GLEN FRANKLIN
Steer Wrestling: JACK RODDY
Saddle Bronco Riding: SHAWN DAVIS
Bareback Bronco Riding: CLYDE VAMVORAS
Bull Riding: GEORGE PAUL
Team Roping: ART ARNOLD

COLLEGE ROWING

Intercollegiate Rowing Assn.: UNIVERSITY OF PENNSYLVANIA
Adams Cup: HARVARD
Bill Cup: RUTGERS
Blackwell Cup: PENNSYLVANIA
Childs Cup: PENNSYLVANIA
Cochrane Cup: DARTMOUTH
Compton Cup: HARVARD
Dad Vail Trophy: GEORGETOWN
Goes Trophy: CORNELL
Grimaldi Cup: HOLY CROSS
Madeira Cup: PENNSYLVANIA

BRITISH ROYAL HENLEY

Grand Challenge Cup (eights): LONDON UNIVERSITY
Thames Cup (lightweight eights): LEANDER CLUB, England
Princess Elizabeth Cup (schoolboy eights): J. E. B. STUART HIGH SCHOOL, Falls Church, Virginia

SPEED SKATING

United States Championships

Men: PETER CEFALU
Women: HELEN LUTSCH

World Championships

Men: FRED ANTON MAIER, Norway
Women: STIEN KAISER, Netherlands

1968 World Speed-Skating Records

Event	Holder	Time
1,000 meters	Ivar Eriksen, Norway	1:20.5
1,000 meters (women)	Stien Kaiser, Netherlands	1:31.0
5,000 meters	Fred Anton Maier, Norway	7:16.7
10,000 meters	Per Willy Guttormsen, Norway	15:16.1

FIGURE SKATING

United States Championships

Men: TIM WOOD
Women: PEGGY FLEMING
Pairs: CYNTHIA and RON KAUFFMAN
Dance: JUDY SCHWOMEYER—JAMES SLADKY

World Championships

Men: EMMERICH DANSER, Austria
Women: PEGGY FLEMING, U.S.
Pairs: LUDMILA and OLEG PROTOPOPOV, U.S.S.R.
Dance: DIANE TOWLER—BERNARD FORD, Britain

NATIONAL ALPINE CHAMPIONSHIPS

Men

Slalom: RICK CHAFFEE, U.S.
Giant Slalom: RICK CHAFFEE
Downhill: SCOTT HENDERSON, Canada
Combined: SCOTT HENDERSON

Women

Slalom: JUDY NAGEL, U.S.
Giant Slalom: MARILYN COCHRAN, U.S.
Downhill: ANN BLACK, U.S.
Combined: JUDY NAGEL

WORLD CUP

Men: JEAN-CLAUDE KILLY, France
Women: NANCY GREENE, Canada

NCAA CHAMPIONSHIPS

Slalom: DENNIS MC COY, University of Denver
Downhill: BARNEY PEET, Fort Lewis College
Cross-Country: CLARK MATIS, University of Colorado
Jumping: PETER ROBES, University of Wyoming
Team: WYOMING

Two-year-old thorough-bred Irish Course sits down at the starting gate. The horse was being trained in the art of the "quick break."

FINAL NORTH AMERICAN LEAGUE
SOCCER STANDINGS

EASTERN CONFERENCE

WESTERN CONFERENCE

Atlantic Division

	W	L	T	Pts.	GF	GA
Atlanta	18	7	6	174	50	32
Washington	15	10	7	167	63	53
New York	12	8	12	164	62	54
Baltimore	13	16	3	128	42	43
Boston	9	17	6	121	51	69

Lakes Division

	W	L	T	Pts.	GF	GA
Cleveland	14	7	11	175	62	44
Chicago	13	10	9	164	68	68
Toronto	13	13	6	144	55	69
Detroit	6	21	4	88	48	65

Gulf Division

	W	L	T	Pts.	GF	GA
Kansas City	16	11	5	158	61	43
Houston	14	12	6	150	58	41
St. Louis	12	14	6	130	47	59
Dallas	2	26	4	52	28	109

Pacific Division

	W	L	T	Pts.	GF	GA
San Diego	18	8	6	186	65	38
Oakland	18	8	6	185	71	38
Los Angeles	11	13	8	139	55	52
Vancouver	12	15	5	136	51	60

NASL Championship: Atlanta

Pole-vaulter Bob Seagren soars over the bar for a new indoor world record of 17′ 4¼″ in January. In the Olympics Seagren vaulted 17′ 8½″.

WORLD SWIMMING RECORDS SET IN 1968 *

Event	Holder	Time
	Men	
200-meter backstroke	Roland Matthes, East Germany	2:07.5
100-meter breaststroke	Nikolai Pankin, U.S.S.R.	1:06.2
200-meter breaststroke	Vladimir Kosinsky, U.S.S.R.	2:27.4
100-meter butterfly	Mark Spitz, U.S.	0:55.6
200-meter freestyle	Don Schollander, U.S.	1:54.3
400-meter freestyle	Ralph Hutton, Canada	4:06.5
800-meter freestyle	Mike Burton, U.S.	8:34.3
1,500-meter freestyle	Mike Burton	16:08.5
200-meter indiv'l medley	Charles Hickcox, U.S.	2:10.6
400-meter indiv'l medley	Charles Hickcox	4:39.0
440-yard indiv'l medley	Michael Holthaus, West Germany	4:46.8
400-meter freestyle relay	U.S. National team	3:32.5
	Women	
100-meter backstroke	Karen Muir, South Africa	1:06.4
110-yard backstroke	Karen Muir	1:06.7
200-meter backstroke	Karen Muir	2:23.8
220-yard backstroke	Karen Muir	2:24.1
100-meter breaststroke	Catie Ball, U.S.	1:14.2
200-meter breaststroke	Catie Ball	2:38.5
200-meter freestyle	Debbie Meyer, U.S.	2:06.7
400-meter freestyle	Debbie Meyer	4:24.5
800-meter freestyle	Debbie Meyer	9:10.4
1,500-meter freestyle	Debbie Meyer	17:31.2
1,650-yard freestyle	Angela Coughlan, Canada	18:47.8
200-meter indiv'l medley	Claudia Kolb, U.S.	2:23.5
400-meter indiv'l medley	Claudia Kolb	5:04.7
400-meter freestyle relay	Santa Clara SC	4:01.0

* January 1 to September 15, 1968

TOURNAMENT TENNIS

	U.S. Open	French Open	Wimbledon	U.S. Indoor
Men's Singles	Arthur Ashe, U.S.	Ken Rosewall, Australia	Rod Laver, Australia	Cliff Richey, U.S.
Women's Singles	Virginia Wade, Britain	Nancy Richey, U.S.	Billie Jean King, U.S.	Billie Jean King
Men's Doubles	Stan Smith-Bob Lutz, U.S.	Rosewall-Fred Stolle, Australia	John Newcombe-Tony Roche, Australia	Tom Okker, Netherlands-Tomas Koch, Brazil
Women's Doubles	Margaret Court, Australia-Maria Bueno, Brazil	Françoise Durr, France-Ann Haydon Jones, Britain	King-Rosemary Casals, U.S.	King-Casals

TRACK AND FIELD

NCAA Outdoor Team Title: SOUTHERN CALIFORNIA
NCAA Indoor Team Title: VILLANOVA
Boston Marathon: AMBROSE BURFOOT, Wesleyan
NAIA Title: PRAIRIE VIEW A & M

NAAU Indoor Title: PACIFIC COAST CLUB
NAAU Outdoor Title: SOUTHERN CALIFORNIA STRIDERS
NAAU Women's Outdoor Title: CROWN CITIES TC

SUMMER OLYMPICS

Japan's Akinori Nakayama shows his winning form on the gymnastic rings. For his outstanding performance he won a gold medal, one of Japan's 11.

DURING the month of October 1968, thousands of athletes from all over the world gathered in Mexico City to take part in the XIX Olympiad. Mexico City is 7,350 feet above sea level. Because of the rarified atmosphere, Olympic officials believed that the athletes would be hampered in their performances. But, indeed, this was not the case. In many events, new world and Olympic records were set.

▶ THE U.S. TEAM

United States athletes won 107 medals, 45 of which were gold. Runners from Kenya, because they had grown up in high-altitude conditions, excelled in the distance events. Kenya's Kipchoge Keino handed Jim Ryun, the United States' finest distance runner, a bitter defeat in the 1,500-meter race. Ryun lost by 15 meters. But nothing seemed to affect the United States sprinters. Jim Hines won the 100-meter dash, Tommie Smith the 200 and Lee Evans the 400. And American relay teams swept the 400- and 1,600-meter relays.

Americans also stood out in the field events. Bob Beamon leaped an astonishing 29 feet 2½ inches in the long jump. Dick Fosbury—captivating everybody with his unusual backward jumps—took the high jump. Bob Seagren, confident as ever, won the pole vault, and Randy Matson the shot put. Al Oerter—in one of the American's

Sixteen-year-old Debbie Meyer, winner of three gold medals in swimming events.

Czechoslovakia's Vera Caslavska, winner of four gold medals in women's gymnastics.

A happy George Forman waves an American flag after winning the Olympic heavyweight-boxing gold medal. He defeated Ionas Chepulis of Russia.

Most sports records are broken by an inch or two, a second or two. But Bob Beamon astonished spectators by breaking the Olympic long-jump record by nearly three feet.

most popular victories—claimed his fourth gold medal in the discus.

The United States swimming team—led by 16-year-old Debbie Meyer and Charles Hickcox—won 23 events, set 4 world records and 17 Olympic records. The team won 58 medals in all.

The United States basketball team successfully defended its record of never having lost a game in Olympic competition. In the finals, it handed Yugoslavia a convincing 65–50 loss.

Probably the only sour note of the games was the black-power demonstration of sprinters Tommie Smith and John Carlos. Taking the victory stand after finishing 1 and 3 in the 200-meter run, Smith and Carlos—wearing black gloves and a black scarf around their necks—held one hand high in the black-power salute and bowed their heads as the United States national anthem was played. For their actions, they were ousted from the United States team and sent home.

▶ WORLD ATHLETES

The host nation, Mexico, garnered 3 gold medals, 2 in boxing and 1 in swimming. Japanese athletes excelled in wrestling and gymnastics, winning 10 gold medals in these two fields alone. Australian men and women won 3 golds in swimming events and 2 in track. And the Canadian team took home first honors in the Grand Prix Jump equestrian team event.

But perhaps the most outstanding and popular performance was turned in by Vera Caslavska of Czechoslovakia. In gymnastics, with the predominantly Mexican and American audience cheering her on against the Russians, she won a total of 4 gold medals. The day after her astonishing feat, she married Josef Odlozil, a member of the Czechoslovak track team.

In these, the 19th Olympic Games, the United States won more medals than in any previous games. The Soviet Union, on the other hand, won fewer medals than in the 1964 Olympics held in Tokyo. But the most encouraging trend was the outstanding performance turned in by athletes from many of the smaller nations.

GARY RONBERG
Sports Illustrated

For bowing their heads and giving the black-power salute during the award ceremonies, Tommie Smith and John Carlos were ousted from the U.S. Olympic team.

19TH SUMMER OLYMPICS FINAL MEDAL STANDINGS

	Gold	Silver	Bronze
United States	45	28	34
U.S.S.R.	29	32	30
Hungary	10	10	12
Japan	11	7	7
East Germany	9	9	7
West Germany	5	10	10
Poland	5	2	11
Australia	5	7	5
Italy	3	4	9
France	7	3	5
Rumania	4	6	5
Czechoslovakia	7	2	4
Great Britain	5	5	3
Kenya	3	4	2
Mexico	3	3	3
Bulgaria	2	4	3
Yugoslavia	3	3	2
Denmark	1	4	3
Netherlands	3	3	1
Iran	2	1	2
Canada	1	3	1
Switzerland	0	1	4
Sweden	2	1	1
Finland	1	2	1
Cuba	0	4	0
Austria	0	2	2
Mongolia	0	1	3
New Zealand	1	0	2
Brazil	0	1	2
Turkey	2	0	0
Ethiopia	1	1	0
Norway	1	1	0
Tunisia	1	0	1
Belgium	0	1	1
South Korea	0	1	1
Argentina	0	0	2
Uganda	0	1	1
Pakistan	1	0	0
Venezuela	1	0	0
Cameroun	0	1	0
Greece	0	0	1
India	0	0	1
Jamaica	0	1	0
Taiwan	0	0	1

RECORDS SET AT XIX OLYMPIAD

Event	Holder	Time/Distance
Men's Track and Field		
100-meter dash	Jim Hines, U.S.	0:09.9*
200-meter dash	Tommie Smith, U.S.	0:19.8*
400-meter relay	United States	0:38.2*
400-meter run	Lee Evans, U.S.	0:43.8*
1,600-meter relay	United States	2:56.1*
800-meter run	Ralph Doubell, Australia	1:44.3
1,500-meter run	Kipchoge Keino, Kenya	3:34.9
110-meter hurdles	Willie Davenport, U.S.	0:13.3
400-meter hurdles	David Hemery, Britain	0:48.1*
High jump	Dick Fosbury, U.S.	7' 4¼"
Long jump	Bob Beamon, U.S.	29' 2½"*
Triple jump	Viktor Saneyev, U.S.S.R.	57' ¾"*
Pole vault	Bob Seagren, U.S.	17' 8½"*
Shotput	Randy Matson, U.S.	67' 4¾
Hammer	Gyula Zsivotzky, Hungary	240' 8"
Discus	Al Oerter, U.S.	212' 6½"
Javelin	Janis Lusis, U.S.S.R.	295' 7¼"
Decathlon	Bill Toomey, U.S.	8,193 pts
Women's Track and Field		
100-meter dash	Wyomia Tyus, U.S.	0:11.0*
200-meter dash	Irena Szewinska, Poland	0:22.5*
400-meter relay	United States	0:42.8*
800-meter run	Madeline Manning, U.S.	2:00.9*
80-meter hurdles	Maureen Caird, Australia	0:10.3
Long jump	Viorica Viscopoleanu, Rumania	22' 4½"*
Shotput	Margarita Gummel, East Germany	64' 4"*
Discus	Lia Manoliu, Rumania	191' 2½"
Men's Swimming		
100-meter freestyle	Michael Wenden, Australia	0:52.2*
200-meter freestyle	Michael Wenden	1:55.2
1,500-meter freestyle	Michael Burton, U.S.	16:38.9
100-meter breaststroke	Donald McKenzie, U.S.	1:07.7
100-meter butterfly	Douglas Russell, U.S.	0:55.9
100-meter backstroke	Roland Matthes, East Germany	0:58.7
200-meter backstroke	Roland Matthes	2:09.6
200-meter indiv'l medley	Charles Hickcox, U.S.	2:12.0
400-meter indiv'l medley	Charles Hickcox	4:48.4
400-meter freestyle relay	United States	3:31.7*
400-meter medley relay	United States	3:54.9*
Women's Swimming		
200-meter freestyle	Debbie Meyer, U.S.	2:10.5
400-meter freestyle	Debbie Meyer	4:31.8
800-meter freestyle	Debbie Meyer	9:24.0
100-meter breaststroke	Djurdjica Bjedov, Yugoslavia	1:15.8
200-meter breaststroke	Sharon Wichman, U.S.	2:44.4
200-meter butterfly	Ada Kok, Netherlands	2:24.7
100-meter backstroke	Kaye Hall, U.S.	1:06.2*
200-meter backstroke	Pokey Watson, U.S.	2:24.8
200-meter indiv'l medley	Claudia Kolb, U.S.	2:24.7
400-meter indiv'l medley	Claudia Kolb	5:08.5
400-meter freestyle relay	United States	4:02.5
400-meter medley relay	United States	4:28.3*

* Betters listed world record

WINTER OLYMPICS

The U.S. Olympic team marches into the Olympic stadium at Grenoble, France.

THE 1968 Winter Olympic Games in Grenoble, France, were the best and most spectacularly produced Winter Olympics of all time. They took place in the middle of this industrial, university-oriented city, set smack in the midst of the French Alps. It is said that every street in Grenoble ends in a mountain, and from the stadium built for the opening ceremony, one could see a 360° view of spectacular mountains. It was a perfect setting for the 10th Winter Games.

Jean-Claude Killy races downhill to win his third Olympic gold medal.

▶ OPENING CEREMONIES

President Charles de Gaulle of France left no stone unturned in making the Winter Olympics a two-week monument to French glory, efficiency and sportsmanship. The opening ceremonies were held in a stadium that cost $600,000 and that was used only on the day of the opening ceremonies and then torn down. Delegations of athletes from countries all over the world, each preceded by its own flag and a sign indicating the name of the country, entered the stadium. Greece, as always, led the procession. It was followed by the other nations in alphabetical order. France, the host country, came at the end. Since by tradition no political speeches are allowed, President de Gaulle, as head of the host state, was invited to "proclaim the opening of the 10th Winter Games of the modern era, revived by Baron de Coubertin in

1896." The Olympic flag was then slowly raised against a backdrop of colorfully costumed athletes and thousands of spectators. The flag consists of five circles on a white background. The blue circle stands for Europe, the yellow for Asia, the black for Africa, the green for Oceania and the red for the Americas.

To send the glad tidings of the opening of the games, a flight of pigeons was released. A three-round salvo was fired while jets flew overhead, leaving colored vapor trails. Parachutists dropped into the five linked circles drawn on the floor of the stadium. Thousands of paper Grenoble roses were dropped on the audience, as music specially composed for the games was played and sung by an enormous orchestra and choir. Alain Calmat, France's silver medalist in figure skating at the 1964 Winter Olympics, ran up an endless flight of steps, bearing a torch that had been carried from town to town from the sacred fire lit on Mount Olympus, and lit the Olympic flame, which remained ablaze for the duration of the games.

▶ THE OLYMPIC ARENA

Because the games were held in the city of Grenoble and its environs, the events were spread across three mountain ranges. Alpine skiing took place at the top of Chamrousse, east of the city. Ski jumping took place at St. Nizier, and cross-country skiing at Autrans, both west of Grenoble. Figure skating and hockey events were held in a new arena built in the center of Grenoble. Speed skaters competed in a nearby rink. The bobsledding was done at Alpe d'Huez, the luge was held at Villard de Lans—two small villages around Grenoble. It was difficult ever to feel that one was in the middle of the Olympic Games, as, for example, when they were held at tiny Squaw Valley. To aid and guide the visitors from all over the world, the authorities had provided over three hundred attractive French snow bunnies who spoke a minimum of three languages each.

▶ THE ATHLETES

As usual, a few athletes sparked all the excitement of the games. In the figure-skating competition, Peggy Fleming proved herself to be a graceful sprite on the ice as she effortlessly skated her way to the United States' only gold medal. Light and lithe, elegant and understated, her form and position won her not only first place

The U.S. scores a goal against Czech team, winners of the hockey silver medal.

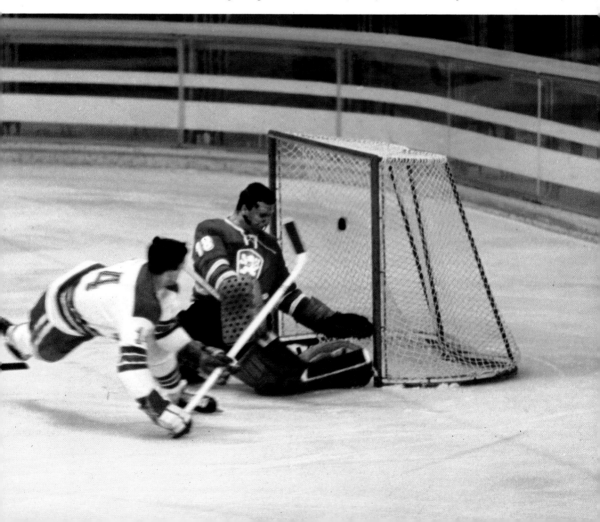

Graceful Peggy Fleming practices before going on to win the U.S.' only gold medal.

but also a place in the history of skating as one of the finest exponents of an athletic yet graceful skating form.

The Protopopovs of Russia defied the maxim that only youthful contenders can win in the Olympic Games. In their mid-thirties, this husband-and-wife team from Leningrad captured the Olympic pairs figure-skating championship with the finest performance of their career.

Perhaps the most glamorous and controversial aspect of the games centered on the skiers. Jean-Claude Killy was not only the idol of France, but the apple of every female eye. Bets were placed long before the games started that he would repeat the feat of Austria's Toni Sailer in the 1956 Olympics by winning three gold medals.

With a great deal of fanfare and what appeared to be no effort at all, he won his first two medals. When it came to the third competition, however, all of the elements seemed to work against not only Killy but the mere hope of presenting the event. Fog rolled up from the valley to envelop the skiing slopes at Chamrousse. Spectators were lucky to be able to see ten feet in front of them, let alone any of the gates that traced the side of the mountain and set the course for the slalom run. One after another the skiers raced the clock down the course. Yet the television cameras were able to record little more than a gray blur. And while millions stood by around the globe and spectators crowded the course, all unable to see the actual event, one of the greatest brouhahas in the history of all sport occurred.

Karl Schranz of Austria, shortly after starting his run, stopped to avoid hitting a policeman who had supposedly stepped out into his path of descent to replace one of the gate poles. Schranz was allowed to start over. Then it was questioned as to whether he had missed the gate before stopping. Schranz claimed that the policeman got in his way. An impartial panel disqualified Schranz and gave the medal, amid screams of protest from the Austrians, to Jean-Claude Killy, who had the next-best time.

10TH WINTER OLYMPICS FINAL MEDAL STANDINGS			
	Gold	Silver	Bronze
Norway	6	6	2
U.S.S.R.	5	5	3
France	4	3	2
Italy	4	0	0
Austria	3	4	4
Netherlands	3	3	3
Sweden	3	2	3
West Germany	2	2	3
United States	1	5	1
Finland	1	2	2
East Germany	1	2	2
Czechoslovakia	1	2	1
Canada	1	1	1
Switzerland	0	2	4
Rumania	0	0	1

▶ **FOR THE GLORY OF SPORT**

Good or bad, right or wrong, the excitement and glamor, the speed and dash, the danger and daring of the ski events, along with the bobsled, the luge, the ski jumping, hockey and speed skating and the beautiful figure skating gave viewers a continuous round of athletic excitement. Enthusiasm and youthful vigor were the order of the day everywhere. And although many a heart was broken, the spirit of the athlete was embodied in the oath spoken by one of the sportsmen at the beginning of the games: "In the name of all competitors, I promise that we will take part in these Olympic Games, respecting and abiding by the rules which govern them, in the true spirit of sportsmanship for the glory of sport and the honor of our teams."

The 10th Winter Games were the culmination of years of training for hundreds of athletes. A few achieved the highest pinnacle of athletic glory and found themselves the heroes of the day and a part of history. But when the flag had been lowered and the flame extinguished, and the participants departed for their home countries, each carried with him, if not a medal, at least that special pride and personal glory that are implied in just having been an Olympian.

DICK BUTTON
Former Olympic Gold Medalist

TRANSPORTATION

THE year 1968 began on a gloomy note for United States travelers and the transportation industry: President Lyndon B. Johnson chose New Year's Day to call for enactment of a program intended to sharply curtail travel outside the Western Hemisphere by America's free-spending tourists. Behind the President's request was the fact that payments to foreign countries for travel abroad by Americans had grown from about $1,500,000,000 in 1957 to more than $3,000,000,000 a decade later. Many more Americans traveled abroad than Europeans traveled to the United States. As a result the tourist deficit in balance of payments by the end of 1967 had reached $2,000,000,000. This was an alarming figure to economists concerned with the balance-of-payments deficit and its effect on the stability of the U.S. dollar.

President Johnson's message called on Americans to "defer for the next two years all nonessential travel outside the Western Hemisphere." Predictably, most segments of the travel industry opposed the plan. And it never received wide popular support. Some opponents saw any attempt to curb the right of the individual to travel freely as an infringement of basic democratic rights. Others saw the proposal as ineffective in curbing the dollar drain and harmful to the airline and travel industries. The plan ran into trouble in Congress, and during the course of the year was quietly dropped.

▶ **AVIATION**

The U.S. balance-of-payments deficit had an important effect on transportation developments during the year. The Boeing 707 turbojet airliner was introduced in 1958. Since that year, the sale of American jetliners to the world's airlines has brought a large volume of dollars spent abroad back to the United States. The world's airlines were still, in 1968, a very substantial market. At the very beginning of 1968, jets in service on domestic United States airlines (members of the Air Transport Association) outnumbered turboprop and pis-

Airport congestion 1968: lines of jets on the ground waiting to take off. In the air, planes in holding patterns waited to land.

ton-driven planes by 1,292 to 874. But international airlines (members of the International Air Transport Association, which includes nine U.S. airlines) had more turboprop and piston-driven planes (2,766) than pure jets (1,948). Of the 1,948 pure jets owned by IATA members, 1,558 were built by American aircraft firms. At the same time, only 77 of the 1,292 pure jets operated by members of the Air Transport Association were built abroad.

Jumbo Jets

In 1968, three major American aircraft manufacturers began an all-out effort to sell world airlines on an entirely new generation of large jet aircraft, promptly dubbed "jumbo jets." The entrant of the Boeing Company was the 747 jetliner. McDonnell Douglas Corporation and Lockheed Aircraft Corporation were represented respectively by the so-called "airbus" designs, the DC-10 and the L-1011.

Jumbo-jet design had been spurred by improvement in jet-engine technology. These improvements greatly increased the ratio of power to weight and made it possible to design bigger and bigger airplanes. With the new engines available there was strong competition between Lockheed, Boeing, the Convair Division of General Dynamics and Douglas to build a giant pure-jet freighter for the U.S. Air Force. Lockheed won the contract with its 132-ton-payload C-5. This plane was test-flown during the summer of 1968.

The C-5 is still exclusively a military plane. Lockheed has hopes, however, that the improvement in ton-mile costs a plane as big as the C-5 will bring, will provide the impetus to get the still-slumbering air-freight industry off the ground. For example, the U.S. airline industry in 1967 flew 2,350,000,000 ton-miles of freight, compared to 2,005,000,000 ton-miles in 1966. If the C-5's were operated at the ideal conditions of 500 miles per hour for 12 hours a day, 330 days a year, ten C-5's, carrying 140 tons each whenever in flight,

would be able to carry 2,077,000,000 ton-miles a year. This is more than the entire volume of the domestic air-freight industry in 1967.

Boeing lost out in the competition for the C-5 contract. It was, however, able to put its investment in jumbo-jet design to profitable use in the Boeing 747. By September 30, 1968, when the first 747 rolled out of its hangar, Boeing had sold 158 of the giant jets to 26 airlines from all over the world. The first flight of the 747 was scheduled for December 17, 1968, the 65th anniversary of the first flight of the Wright Brothers. But bad weather caused a delay in preflight tests, and the flight was put off until early 1969.

The 747 has a theoretical capacity of 490 passengers. This could be accomplished by using an all-economy-class seating arrangement of 10 passengers abreast and by sacrificing some of the amenities of travel, such as additional galleys and toilets. However, most airlines at this point are planning to put in service a dual-class cabin configuration that would have 9-abreast seating in economy class with a maximum of 362 passengers.

The pure jets of the generation of the Boeing 707 and the Douglas DC-8 increased the speed of air travel from about 300 mph to about 600 mph. Because they also had more seats, they greatly increased seat-mile capacity. The jumbo jets will not be appreciably faster than current jets. But because of their much larger size they will also increase seat-mile capacity.

The jumbo jets are a real bargain in terms of the amount of work they can do compared to the amount of air and terminal space they need. This is very important at present because the airlines are in a period of increasing air congestion and ground delays at airports. As a result, the airlines simply cannot afford *not* to buy the jumbos. Boeing sees a market of some six hundred planes for the 747 by 1975. Each will cost $20,000,000 with spare parts. Both Lockheed and McDonnell Douglas are equally optimistic about the market for the air-bus.

The Boeing 747 jumbo jet was unveiled on September 30, 1968. The 747 will probably carry a maximum of 362 passengers on most commercial flights.

The Supersonic Transport

The jumbo jets in 1968 were a success story. The main element of suspense was the uncertainty about which design would sell the most planes. The supersonic transport (SST) was a cliff-hanger of another sort.

The 1,400-mph, 130-passenger Anglo-French design, the Concorde, was scheduled to make its first test flight late in 1968. Its American competitor, the Boeing 2707, faced design problems. These involved a change from a swing-wing concept to a fixed-wing concept. Delivery for this 300-passenger, 1,800-mph plane was pushed back to 1975 at the earliest.

The United States design still offered improved seat-mile efficiency over the slower and smaller Concorde. But the economy-minded U.S. Congress in 1968 was asking whether the advantages of the American SST were worth the cost.

Airport Congestion

Events of 1968 spurred an upturn in Federal spending for air-traffic control and the national airways system. The problem had been anticipated for many years. The buildup of air traffic into the New York area, combined with the failure to build a fourth New York Jetport, made it inevitable that one day the skies over Kennedy International Airport in New York would become saturated, and aircraft en route to Kennedy would have no place to go.

On a holiday Friday in July 1968 it happened. Planes began stacking up in holding patterns waiting for clearance to land. Incoming planes from Europe, short of fuel, were diverted to such places as Niagara Falls and Boston. And planes as far away as Jacksonville and Denver went into preliminary holding patterns because there was no room for them at their destinations. Other U.S. airports inevitably were

The 1,400-mph supersonic Concorde making its taxi trials in August in France. The Concorde's test flights were planned for late in 1968.

affected, even when they had no congestion problems of their own. This was simply because New York is such an important focal point of U.S. air travel.

The problem wound up in the lap of the Department of Transportation. Through its Federal Aviation Administration, the Department of Transportation proposed schedule limitations at peak-density airports. It also proposed more-stringent performance requirements for aircraft using high-density facilities. No element in the aviation industry was entirely happy with the proposed solutions, which seemed to promise little but a winter of discontent that would erupt in new congestion in the summer of 1969. But the government proposals, though admittedly stopgap in nature, had the virtue of keeping the system running.

▶ THE RAILROADS

Because of the airport congestion, travelers within the Boston-New York-Washington supercity area wondered what had happened to the high-speed trains they had heard about. These trains were supposed to provide transportation between city centers at speeds competitive with the airlines. The Department of Transportation had originally announced that the trains would be ready for service in October 1967. The New York-Washington Metroliners of the Penn Central missed that date, then a new date scheduled for April 1968. Then they

were rescheduled when technical problems were worked out. These problems involved new-design solid-state electronic motor and controls.

In the meantime a competing design, the TurboTrain, was being prepared for testing on the tracks of the New Haven Railroad between Boston and New York. The TurboTrain is powered by self-contained gas-turbine engines rather than the external electric power of the Metroliners.

First of the high-speed trains to go into service late in 1968 was another Turbo-Train built for the Canadian National Railways. It runs between Toronto and Montreal.

Honors for high-speed performance in 1968 probably should go not to a passenger train but to a freight train: Santa Fe's Super C. This train was inaugurated in January 1968 to provide dependable 40-hour service between Chicago and Los Angeles for piggyback containers and trailers. Slow to win success in the marketplace, the Super C was an unqualified success as an operating feat. The initial run was made in 34½ hours. This broke all records for the 2,200-mile distance, including those set by the Santa Fe's crack Super Chief.

Railroad Mergers

The big news in railroading in 1968 was mergers. One merger was approved. But another was within one hour of consummation when a last-minute restraining order by a Supreme Court justice sent it back to the Interstate Commerce Commission for further hearings.

The merger that was approved was that of the New York Central Railroad into the Pennsylvania Railroad, forming the Penn Central Company.

The merger that did not take place was that of the Great Northern; the Northern Pacific; the Chicago, Burlington & Quincy; and the Spokane, Portland & Seattle railroads into the Burlington Northern Railway. This so-called Northern Lines merger was first conceived 75 years ago.. It had been eagerly sought by a cast of characters including financier J. P. Morgan and railroad builders J. J. Hill and E. H. Harriman. In 1904, however, the plan ran afoul of trust-busting President Theodore Roosevelt and the first strict application of the Sherman Antitrust Act. The 1968 setback seemed likely to be less permanent than the earlier one. Final merger of the Northern Lines is an excellent probability.

Arrivals board on the day that the skies over Kennedy International Airport became saturated and aircraft could not land.

INTERCITY TRAVEL

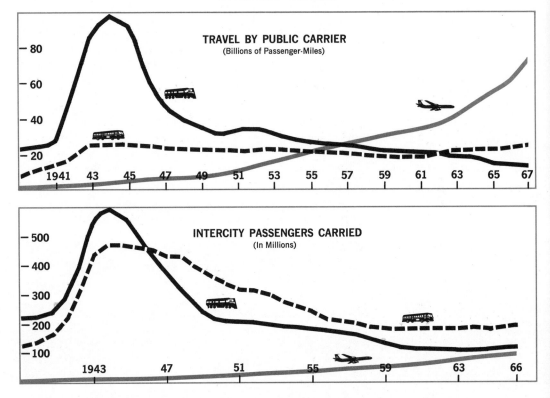

TRAVEL BY PUBLIC CARRIER
(Billions of Passenger-Miles)

80

60

40

20

1941 43 45 47 49 51 53 55 57 59 61 63 65 67

INTERCITY PASSENGERS CARRIED
(In Millions)

500

400

300

200

100

1943 47 51 55 59 63 66

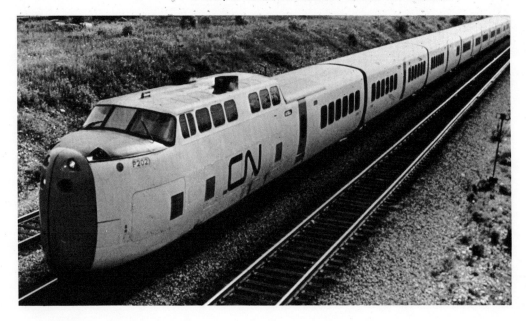

Canadian National Railways high-speed TurboTrain inaugurated a 3-hour, 59-minute run between Toronto and Montreal.

The 312,000-deadweight-ton supertanker "Universe Ireland," the world's largest tanker in 1968, carries crude oil from Kuwait to Ireland.

▶MASS TRANSPORTATION

During 1968 the Urban Mass Transportation Administration was transferred to the Department of Transportation. There was no noticeable change in policy or programs.

The billion-dollar San Francisco Bay Area Rapid Transit District, with about $900,000,000 already spent on its three-county routes and stations, ran out of money to finish the job. It waited in vain for the 1968 California legislature to come up with $144,000,000 in new funds needed before the legislature adjourned. The project is expected to resume in 1969. But there will be a delay that will put off opening of the system until August 1970 at the earliest. This is six months later than had been predicted.

▶OCEAN SHIPPING

Major events in ocean shipping in 1968 were the arrival of new containerships, for the North Atlantic trade particularly, and ever-larger tankers for moving Middle East oil to European and Japanese markets.

Tankers continued to break records in size. The 1968 record holder is the 312,000-deadweight-ton *Universe Ireland.* This ship is the first of five sister ships being built for service between Kuwait and Bantry Bay, Ireland, via the Cape of Good Hope. The *Universe Ireland* class will carry oil for the Gulf Oil Corporation. The ship is so big that it has to dock at new facilities built offshore at both terminals.

RODERICK CRAIB
Assistant Transportation Editor
Business Week magazine

UNITED NATIONS

UNITED KINGDOM

THE year 1968 was designated by the United Nations General Assembly as the International Year for Human Rights. This step was taken to commemorate the twentieth anniversary of the Universal Declaration of Human Rights. Corneliu Manescu, president of the General Assembly at the start of 1968, called on all nations to "dedicate themselves with renewed vigor to the task of securing for people the world over the full enjoyment of their human rights." In April and May, a three-week International Conference on Human Rights was held in Tehran, Iran. This conference produced encouraging statements about the rights of all members of the human family. But it could not conceal the wide gap that remains between words and deeds.

▶ SOUTH AFRICA AND RHODESIA

At United Nations headquarters in New York City, neither the General Assembly nor the Security Council was able to make any appreciable headway in lowering barriers to civil, political, economic or social equality in areas of Africa dominated by white minorities. Resolutions condemning trials, imprisonment and executions of blacks in Rhodesia, South Africa and South-West Africa were to no avail. In 1967 the Council for South-West Africa, which the UN calls Namibia, was authorized by the United Nations General Assembly to administer the area until it is ready for independence. As was expected, South Africa prevented the council members from entering South-West Africa during 1968.

Both the Security Council and the General Assembly approved comprehensive new sanctions against Rhodesia. But this attempt to moderate the Rhodesian Government's policies (aimed at subjugating the black majority) had no apparent results.

▶ THE *PUEBLO* INCIDENT

An incident that the United States regarded as a "grave threat to peace" in the Far East was put on the Security Council

At an urgent Security Council meeting, U.S. Ambassador to the UN Arthur Goldberg shows the position of the "Pueblo."

agenda in January. North Korea had seized the United States intelligence ship the *Pueblo*, and charged that she was spying within its territorial waters. The United States denied the charges. It asserted that the vessel was on the high seas, and that North Korea was guilty of piracy. United States Ambassador to the UN Arthur Goldberg was instructed to ask for an urgent meeting of the Security Council. North Korea is not a UN member. Thus the Soviet and Hungarian delegates argued the case against the United States. Other members of the council sought to lower tensions and avert American military retaliation. The Canadian delegate, George Ignatieff, proposed that the council appoint an intermediary to go to North Korea and try to work out a plan for the release of the men and the ship. By this time, however, the United States had decided to take the case to the Military Armistice Commission headquarters at Panmunjom, a village along the boundary separating North and South Korea, where it could deal alone with North Korea. Meetings were held throughout the year, and at the end of December the *Pueblo* crew members were released by the North Koreans.

▶ THE VIETNAM WAR

As 1968 opened, the Vietnam war was high on the agenda of UN Secretary-General U Thant—even though the UN can do nothing about it. At his first news conference of the year, the Secretary-General repeated what he had said throughout 1967: there could be meaningful peace talks only if the United States would unconditionally stop the bombing of North Vietnam.

In February, Thant undertook a personal mission to Moscow, London, Paris and Washington. He talked with Premier Kosygin, Prime Minister Wilson, President de Gaulle and President Johnson about the war. When he returned to United Nations headquarters, Thant declared that "It is time to call a halt . . . the world is anguished and sickened by the continued intensity and savagery of the war. It is heart-rending to witness the agony of innocent civilians who cannot possibly know what it is all about. There can be no victory, no defeat, only more suffering, more death and more destruction."

Thant also stated that he had been told that Hanoi would agree to talks as soon as there was an end to the bombing and other acts of war against North Vietnam. On March 31, President Johnson announced a partial halt to the bombing. This led to Paris meetings between representatives of North Vietnam and the United States. A total halt to the bombing was announced October 31.

▶ CHANGING U.S. AMBASSADORS

The United Nations General Assembly normally convenes in September. However, a United States presidential-election year sometimes arouses discussion about the advisability of postponing the assembly opening to avoid involvement of the UN in American political controversies.

In 1956, when General Dwight D. Eisenhower and Adlai Stevenson were the leading candidates, it was decided to postpone the assembly opening until after the American people had gone to the polls. But events would not wait. Before election day, simultaneous emergency sessions had been called to consider the Suez crisis and the Soviet invasion of Hungary.

In 1968 there was no serious consideration given to postponing the convening of the 23d General Assembly to after November 5. Nevertheless, domestic politics did have one noticeable repercussion for the United Nations: the revolving American representation. Ambassador Goldberg gave up his post in June. He had wrestled with his conscience for a year over the American bombing of North Vietnam, which he opposed. His surprise successor was former Undersecretary of State George Ball. Mr. Ball also had a reputation as being a dove on the Vietnam war issue.

Suddenly, after three months at the UN, Ball announced that he would resign and help Vice-President Hubert Humphrey fight for the presidency. At a news conference at the United States UN Mission, Ball attacked not only Republican candidate Richard Nixon but also those people who said that peace could be reached only through an end to the bombing of North Vietnam. His reference was taken as criticism of Secretary-General Thant.

Ball was replaced by *Washington Post* editor James Russell Wiggins, who had had no previous experience in diplomacy. Wiggins served only a short period of time, for in December President-elect Richard Nixon named Charles W. Yost as the U.S. ambassador to the UN. Yost took up his post after Nixon's inauguration.

▶ THE RETURN OF YAKOV MALIK

In January, after a normal tour of duty for Nikolai Fedorenko, the Soviet Union changed its head of mission. Brought back to the house on the East River was Yakov Malik, who had been associated with a major crisis and two important peace developments in the past. Malik had walked out of the Security Council at the end of 1949 when the United States first blocked Communist China's bid to replace Nationalist China. During Malik's long absence, the Security Council, in June 1950, was able to vote UN assistance to South Korea to repel North Korea's aggression. Malik soon returned to create obstacles to further UN action. But it was his speech on radio in June 1951 that first signaled the possibility of negotiating an end to the Korean war. It was Malik, too, who, in conversation with United States Representative Philip Jessup in the UN delegates' lounge, helped initiate the negotiations that led to the lifting of the Berlin blockade in 1949.

▶ THE CZECHOSLOVAK CRISIS

Malik was in the Soviet Union's chair in the Security Council on August 21, 1968, after the United States and five other members called an urgent meeting to deal with the "serious situation" in Czechoslovakia. During the night of August 20–21, that country had been invaded by hundreds of

James Russell Wiggins served as U.S. ambassador to the UN in the last months of 1968.

thousands of Soviet troops and other Warsaw Pact units.

The Soviet Union and Hungary opposed any discussion of the Czechoslovak situation in the Security Council. Discussions were, however, carried out. But on August 23, Malik vetoed a resolution condemning the armed intervention. The resolution had received ten votes for passage. Algeria, India and Pakistan had abstained. Hungary and the Soviet Union had voted no.

During the debate, the Security Council heard a statement from Czechoslovak Foreign Minister Jiri Hajek, who had been on vacation in Yugoslavia at the time of the invasion. Hajek stated that the occupation of his country was an unjustifiable act of force. He emphasized that it had not been requested by the Czechoslovak Government or any of its constitutional organs. Later, when the Czechoslovaks were forced to capitulate to Soviet demands, Hajek was removed from office. Czechoslovakia also requested that the issue of its occupation be withdrawn from the Security Council agenda "in view of the agreement which has been reached . . . during Soviet-Czechoslovak talks . . . in Moscow." Ambassador Ball told correspondents that the Soviet Union would never be allowed to forget what it had done to Czechoslovakia. But the subject was not again raised in the Security Council.

▶ NUCLEAR-WEAPONS PACT

The invasion of Czechoslovakia has blocked, at least temporarily, hopes for new cooperation between the United States and the Soviet Union. Such cooperation had been symbolized by the Treaty on the Non-Proliferation of Nuclear Weapons. This treaty had been worked on in the Geneva Disarmament Committee for four years. It had been hailed as evidence of a *détente* between East and West when it was approved by the General Assembly on June 12. President Johnson spoke before the assembly and called the treaty the most important international agreement on disarmament since the beginning of the nuclear age. Ratification by the United States, the Soviet Union, Great Britain and forty other nations would bring the pact into effect. But after the Soviet invasion of Czechoslovakia, the United States Senate decided to withhold its approval until it became known whether the Russians would allow the volatile situation in Europe to become normalized.

▶ THE MIDDLE EAST

It had been hoped that 1968 would bring some progress toward a settlement of the long-standing and complicated situation in the Middle East. UN peace efforts were handled by the Secretary-General's personal representative, Gunnar Jarring, who was on leave from his post as Swedish ambassador to Moscow.

On November 22, 1967, the Security Council had listed several principles on which peace should be built. These included the withdrawal of Israeli forces from territories occupied in the June 1967 war. The Security Council resolution also called for the end to all claims or states of belligerency, and "acknowledgement of the sovereignty, territorial integrity and political independence of every state in the area and their right to live in peace within secure and recognized boundaries free from threats or acts of force." In addition, the resolution called for freedom of navigation through international waterways (the Suez Canal and Gulf of Aqaba) and for a settlement of the refugee problem.

Gunnar Jarring labored for one year behind closed doors in the capitals of the Middle East as well as at UN headquarters. But even as he worked for peace, there were fresh outbreaks of violence between Arabs and Israelis. These outbreaks prompted the Security Council to adopt new resolutions calling on the parties to observe the cease-fire.

In an unprecedented appearance before the General Assembly's Special Political Committee, Secretary-General Thant pleaded for increased help for the Palestine refugees. As a result of the June 1967 war —the third Middle East war since 1948— the ranks of the displaced Arab refugees had swelled to well over one million. The budget for the United Nations Relief and Works Agency for 1969 has been increased from $5,000,000 to $42,500,000. This sum will be used to provide the homeless with subsistence needs.

The plight of many of the refugees would be relieved, to some extent, if they could return to the homes and refugee camps they had occupied on the West Bank of the Jordan River. But it is unlikely that this will come about before there is an overall political settlement.

▶ NEW MEMBER STATES

During 1968 the United Nations continued to attract new members. Mauritius,

Gunnar Jarring (right), the UN's special representative in the Middle East, discusses the Arab-Israeli situation with Secretary-General U Thant.

Swaziland and Equatorial Guinea swelled the General Assembly roster to 126.

▶ THE UN: ITS WORLD ROLE

In 1968, United Nations efforts to promote peace and bring an end to wars were stymied. The two major world powers continued to use force despite UN Charter injunctions against the use of such methods to settle international problems. After the 23d General Assembly convened in September 1968, Secretary-General Thant warned of the deteriorating international situation. He ascribed this deterioration to attempts to use the "strong-arm methods" of the 1930's to cope with the problems of the 1960's. He declared that "the present superior military force, on which [the great military powers] rely so heavily and are prone to use so freely, is in itself a grave and ever-present danger."

Secretary-General Thant reminded UN members that an essential role of the or-

ganization is to close the gap between the rich nations and the poor nations. He noted, however, that there were competing claims for funds by the military. Developed countries, Thant admonished, seem to have lost sight of the fact that "they could make a truly constructive contribution to their own security and to the reduction of the basic causes of unrest and insecurity by working toward the elimination of poverty and want in the world."

The Secretary-General proposed that in 1969 the foreign ministers of the United States, the Soviet Union, Great Britain and France meet to plan a summit meeting of the leaders of their countries to deal with some of their common problems. Such a meeting would provide a greater opportunity for the United Nations to carry out its major purpose: "To save succeeding generations from the scourge of war."

PAULINE FREDERICK
United Nations Correspondent, NBC News

THE UNITED NATIONS 23d SESSION

THE SECRETARIAT
Secretary-General: U Thant

THE GENERAL ASSEMBLY
President: Emilio Arenales (Guatemala)

MEMBER NATIONS AND CHIEF REPRESENTATIVES

Afghanistan	Abdul-Rahman Pazhwak	Kuwait	Muhalhel Mohamed Al-Mudha
Albania	Halim Budo	Laos	Khamking Souvanlasy
Algeria	Tewfik Bouattoura	Lebanon	Edouard A. Ghorra
Argentina	Jose Maria Ruda	Lesotho	A. S. Mohale
Australia	Patrick Shaw	Liberia	Nathan Barnes
Austria	Heinrich Haymerle	Libya	Wahbi El Bouri
Barbados	H. A. Vaughan	Luxembourg	André Philippe
Belgium	Constant Schuurmans	Malagasy Republic	Blaise Rabetafika
Bolivia	Walter Guevara Arze	Malawi	Nyemba Mbekeani
Botswana	T. J. Molefhe	Malaysia	Dato Mohd Ismail bin Mohd
Brazil	Joao Augusto de Aranjo Castro	Maldive Islands	Abdul Sattar
Britain	Lord Caradon	Mali	M. B. Kante
Bulgaria	Milko Tarabanov	Malta	Arvid Pardo
Burma	U Soe Tin	Mauritania	Abdallahi Ould Daddah
Burundi	Terence Nsanze	Mauritius	Pierre Balancy
Byelorussian S.S.R.	Guerodot G. Tchernouchtchenko	Mexico	Francisco Cuevas Cancino
Cambodia	Huot Sambath	Mongolia	Mangalyn Dugersuren
Cameroun	Michel Njine	Morocco	Ahmed Taibi Benhima
Canada	George Ignatieff	Nepal	Padma Khatri
Central African Rep.	Michel Gallin-Douathe	Netherlands	D. G. E. Middelburg
Ceylon	Hamilton S. Amerasinghe	New Zealand	N. V. Farrell
Chad	Lazare Massibe	Nicaragua	Guillermo Sevilla Sacasa
Chile	Jose Piñera	Niger	Adamou Mayaki
China	Liu Chieh	Nigeria	E. O. Ogbu
Colombia	Julio C. Turbay-Ayala	Norway	Edvard Hambro
Congo (Brazzaville)	Alphonse Ongagou	Pakistan	Agha Shahi
Congo (Kinshasa)	Théodore Idzumbuir	Panama	Aquilino Boyd
Costa Rica	Luis Dobles Sanchez	Paraguay	Miguel Solano Lopez
Cuba	Ricardo Alarcon de Quesada	Peru	Carlos Mackenhenie
Cyprus	Zenon Rossides	Philippines	Salvador P. Lopez
Czechoslovakia	Zdenek Cernik	Poland	Bohdan Tomorowicz
Dahomey	Maxime Léopold Zollner	Portugal	Duarte Vaz Pinto
Denmark	Otto Borch	Rumania	Gheorghe Diaconescu
Dominican Republic	Horacio Julio Ornes-Coiscou	Rwanda	Célestin Kabanda
Ecuador	Leopoldo Benites	Saudi Arabia	Jamil M. Baroody
El Salvador	Reynaldo Galindo Pohl	Senegal	Ibrahima Boye
Equatorial Guinea	vacant	Sierra Leone	L. A. M. Brewah
Ethiopia	Lij E. Makonnen	Singapore	T. T. B. Koh
Finland	Max Jakobson	Somalia	Abdulrahim Abby Farah
France	Armand Berard	South Africa	Matthys I. Botha
Gabon	L. M. Ntoutoume Obame	Southern Yemen	Ismail Saeed Noaman
Gambia	A. D. Camara	Spain	Jaime de Pinies
Ghana	Richard M. Akwei	Sudan	Fakhreddine Mohamed
Greece	Dimitri S. Bitsios	Swaziland	Prince Makhosini
Guatemala	Francisco Lopez Urzua	Sweden	Sverker C. Astrom
Guinea	Diallo Alpha Abdoulaye	Syria	George J. Tomeh
Guyana	Sir John Carter	Tanzania	A. B. C. Danieli
Haiti	Marcel Antoine	Thailand	Anand Panyarachun
Honduras	Humberto Lopez Villamil	Togo	Alexandre J. Ohin
Hungary	Karoly Csatorday	Trinidad and Tobago	P. V. J. Solomon
Iceland	Hannes Kjartansson	Tunisia	Mahmoud Mestiri
India	Gopalaswami Parthasarathi	Turkey	Orhan Eralp
Indonesia	Roeslan Abdulgani	Uganda	Otema Allimadi
Iran	Mehdi Vakil	Ukrainian S.S.R.	M. D. Polyanichko
Iraq	Adnan Pachachi	U.S.S.R.	Y. A. Malik
Ireland	Cornelius C. Cremin	United Arab Republic	Mohamed A. El Kony
Israel	Yosef Tekoah	United States	James Russell Wiggins
Italy	Piero Vinci	Upper Volta	Paul Rouamba
Ivory Coast	Siméon Ake	Uruguay	Pedro P. Berro
Jamaica	Keith Johnson	Venezuela	Manuel Perez Guerrero
Japan	Senjin Tsuruoka	Yemen	Mohsin Ahmed Alaini
Jordan	Muhammad H. El-Farra	Yugoslavia	Anton Vratusa
Kenya	Burudi Nabwera	Zambia	V. J. Mwaanga

THE SECURITY COUNCIL

Algeria	Pakistan
Britain *	Paraguay
China *	Senegal
Colombia	Spain
Finland	U.S.S.R. *
France *	United States *
Hungary	Zambia
Nepal	

* permanent

THE ECONOMIC AND SOCIAL COUNCIL*

Argentina	Libya
Belgium	Mexico
Britain	Norway
Bulgaria	Pakistan
Chad	Sierra Leone
Congo (Brazzaville)	Sudan
France	Tanzania
Guatemala	Turkey
India	U.S.S.R.
Ireland	United States
Jamaica	Upper Volta
Japan	Uruguay
Kuwait	Yugoslavia

* one other member to be elected in 1969

THE TRUSTEESHIP COUNCIL

Australia	France
Britain	U.S.S.R.
China	United States

THE INTERNATIONAL COURT OF JUSTICE
President: Jose Luis Bustamente (Peru)

Fouad Ammoun	Lebanon
Cesar Bengzon	Philippines
Gerald Fitzmaurice	Britain
Isaac Forster	Senegal
André Gros	France
Philip C. Jessup	United States
V. M. Koretsky	U.S.S.R.
Manfred Lachs	Poland
Gaetano Morelli	Italy
Charles Onyeama	Nigeria
Luis Padilla Nervo	Mexico
Sture Petran	Sweden
Kotaro Tanaka	Japan
Muhammed Zafrulla Khan	Pakistan

THE GENERAL ASSEMBLY COMMITTEES

Political and Security
Chairman: Piero Vinci, Italy

Special Political
Chairman: Abdulrahim Abby Farah, Somalia

Economic and Financial
Chairman: Richard Maximilian Akwei, Ghana

Social, Humanitarian and Cultural
Chairman: Erik Nettle, Austria

Trust and Non-Self-Governing Territories
Chairman: Patrick V. J. Solomon, Trinidad and Tobago

Administrative and Budgetary
Chairman: G. G. Chernushchenko, Byelo-russia

Legal
Chairman: K. Krishna Rao, India

The United Nations General Assembly

UNITED STATES

FOR the United States, 1968 was a year of momentous events—most of them bad. More sharply divided than they had been at any time in living memory, the American people pursued an uncertain course that took them through assassination, insurrection, and new strife and bitterness. And at the end of a bizarre political year, they chose as their 37th president a man who previously had been defeated in a bid for the presidency as well as for the governorship of California.

Richard M. Nixon's long-sought victory came after the most serious three-way presidential race since 1924. It was a contest in which neither Nixon nor his Democratic rival Hubert H. Humphrey generated much public enthusiasm; in which voters talked about "the lesser of two evils"; and in which third-party candidate George C. Wallace stirred the passions of a small but significant minority.

That Humphrey finally came so close to winning on November 5 was a testimony to the fortunes and misfortunes of an extraordinary year. For the Vice-President was more a survivor than a candidate of the Democratic Party. Three major Democratic names were eliminated during the year: President Johnson, whose surprise withdrawal came in the name of national unity; Robert F. Kennedy, whose brief bid was cut short by gunfire; and Eugene J. McCarthy, whose lonely quest for the nomination finally ended in Chicago.

And so the American people, who cried in 1968 for law and order, got instead more crime and violence. Americans who yearned for new leadership got two presidential candidates who represented, to many, the failures of the past. And as the President-elect prepared to assume office, Americans could have little confidence that the deep-rooted forces abroad in the land —setting blacks against whites, the affluent against the poor, and the restless young against their elders—could be pacified in the foreseeable future.

Hopes that the cold war was coming to an end and that a new era in U.S.–Soviet relations might be opening were suddenly dashed on the night of August 20–21 when the Red Army marched into Czechoslovakia. Earlier in the year, despite the tensions caused by the Vietnam war, Washington and Moscow were able to reach agreement on a proposed treaty to halt the spread of nuclear weapons. And the two superpowers were preparing to begin critical talks on limiting their arsenals of nuclear weapons.

But the dramatic invasion of Czechoslovakia brought a sudden chill to the international atmosphere and set back, at least for the present, efforts to build a more stable world peace. According to later reports, announcement of a summit meeting between President Johnson and Soviet leaders was to have been made on the very day that the Russians cracked down on their communist neighbor.

Meanwhile the Vietnam war finally moved to the conference table. But the fighting continued during the year with even greater intensity. Although President Johnson on March 31 ordered a halt to the bombing of most of North Vietnam, including the capital, Hanoi, antiwar protesters in the United States continued to press their attacks on the President's policies. Seven months later he stopped all air, naval, and artillery bombardment of the North, and announced that the Paris negotiations would be widened.

Vietnam

In his historic television address of March 31, President Johnson announced that he was ordering a stop to air and naval bombardment of "almost 90 per cent of North Vietnam's population and most of its territory." He appealed to the Hanoi regime to accept this deescalation of the conflict as an invitation to begin peace negotiations. A few days later, on April 3,

In New York City, demonstrators protest U.S. involvement in the Vietnam war.

North Vietnam accepted the President's offer and agreed to arrange for contacts with U.S. representatives. Several weeks of bickering over the site of a conference ensued, however, until at last both sides agreed on Paris.

After preliminary talks, the first official session was held on May 13 at the old Majestic Hotel, near the Arc de Triomphe. Representing the U.S. side were Ambassador W. Averell Harriman (who had successfully negotiated the limited-nuclear-test-ban treaty in 1963) and Cyrus R. Vance. Heading the North Vietnamese delegation was Minister of State Xuan Thuy.

From the very start, both delegations repeated the old accusations that the two countries had been making against each other for years. The parley dragged on for months without any apparent progress. It became clear that North Vietnam would not even discuss specific ways to end the war unless the United States first stopped all bombing of the North, with no conditions attached, But the Johnson administration insisted that the Communists must first agree to take some action of their own to reduce the level of the fighting.

At last, on October 31 (a few days before the U.S. elections), President Johnson announced a complete halt to the bombing of the North. In return, he said, Hanoi had agreed to the participation of the South Vietnamese Government at the Paris talks, while the United States was opening the conference to the National Liberation Front (Vietcong).

A snag developed immediately when the Saigon regime balked at recognizing the NLF as a separate delegation at the parley. As a result, throughout December no substantive talks were held.

On the other side of the world from the peace talks, American casualties continued to rise. By June, the number of U.S. combat deaths in Vietnam since 1961 passed 25,000. And in the same month, the bloody struggle became the longest war the United States has ever fought (exceeding the 6½

PARIS PEACE TALKS
U.S. NEGOTIATORS

W. AVERELL HARRIMAN

A former governor of New York (1955–59), Mr. Harriman has also served as U.S. ambassador to the Soviet Union (1943–46), U.S. ambassador to Britain (1946), secretary of commerce (1946–48), director of the Mutual Security Agency (1951–53), assistant secretary of state for Far Eastern affairs (1961–63) and undersecretary for political affairs (1963–65).

CYRUS R. VANCE

An experienced negotiator, Cyrus Vance mediated the Greek-Turkish dispute over Cyprus (1967) and acted as President Johnson's special envoy in Panama during anti-American riots (1964), in the Dominican Republic during the civil war (1965), and in Vietnam (1966). Previously he had served as secretary of the Army (1962–64).

An A3 Skywarrior is catapulted from the deck of the USS "Coral Sea" for bombing operations over North Vietnam. On October 31, as a prelude to expanded peace talks, President Johnson ordered a halt to such operations.

years of the American Revolution, if that war is considered to have ended with George Washington's victory over the British at Yorktown, Virginia).

In April, Defense Secretary Clark Clifford announced that a ceiling of 549,500 men had been placed on U.S. troop strength in Vietnam. He also declared that the administration would seek to transfer the main burden of the war to the South Vietnamese Government.

American forces in Vietnam got a new commander in June. General William C. Westmoreland, who became Army chief of staff, was succeeded in the Vietnam post by General Creighton W. Abrams. General Westmoreland had long been criticized by peace groups in the United States for his optimistic views on the status of the war, many of which later proved to be unfounded.

The *Pueblo* Incident

Earlier in the year, a crisis arose in the Far East when North Korean patrol boats seized a U.S. Navy intelligence ship, the *Pueblo*. The lightly armed vessel, crammed with electronic equipment, was captured with little resistance and taken to the port of Wonsan. One member of the 83-man crew was killed during the seizure of the ship.

North Korea contended that the *Pueblo* was operating within the 12-mile limit of its territorial waters. The United States denied the charge. Some congressmen demanded that the United States retaliate against North Korea with force. But President Johnson acted with restraint. He called up nearly 15,000 Navy and Air Force reservists and strengthened U.S. forces in the area. But he relied on negotiations to gain release of the ship and crew. At the end of December the *Pueblo* crew was finally released, but North Korea kept the ship.

▶ U.S.–SOVIET RELATIONS

In his final year in office, President Johnson appeared determined to achieve some basic agreements with the Soviet Union. And there were signs that the Kremlin shared his conviction that both sides would benefit from a genuine *détente* that could slow down the arms race and lessen the chances of a nuclear war.

Until the Soviet occupation of Czechoslovakia hardened the position of Washington, some progress had been made in East-West relations. The most important step was the agreement reached in the UN Disarmament Committee on a draft treaty to halt the spread of nuclear weapons. The agreement included provisions for inspection and controls. The treaty was endorsed by the UN General Assembly on June 12. And it was signed by the United States, the U.S.S.R., Britain, and 59 nonnuclear nations on July 1. At the ceremony, the President hailed the pact as "the most important international agreement since the beginning of the nuclear age."

The Soviet move against Czechoslovakia, however, stirred opposition to ratification of the treaty in the U.S. Senate. Republican presidential candidate Richard Nixon favored a delay in Senate action. And, in the rush to adjourn, consideration of the measure was laid over for the new Congress in 1969.

President Johnson announced on July 1 that the Soviets had agreed to open talks in the near future on limiting both offensive nuclear weapons and defensive antimissile systems. Foreign Minister Andrei A. Gromyko, a few days earlier, had proclaimed the Russians' willingness to enter into such discussions.

Other major steps taken in 1968 to improve U.S.–Soviet relations included ratification of a consular treaty; renewal of a cultural-exchange agreement that had expired at the end of 1967; establishment in July of the first direct airline service between New York and Moscow; and the signing of a treaty on assistance to astronauts.

Another incident that demonstrated the spirit of cooperation between the United States and the U.S.S.R. came on July 2, when the Russians promptly released an American airliner carrying 214 servicemen to Vietnam. The plane had been forced down on June 30 in the Kurile Islands, north of Japan, when it strayed into Soviet airspace.

The two countries reportedly had attained agreement on details of the all-im-

General Creighton W. Abrams, successor to General William Westmoreland as commander of United States forces in Vietnam.

portant missile talks when, literally over-
night, the Czech crisis changed the international mood. President Johnson strongly
denounced the Soviet invasion. The U.S.
State Department charged that the action
had changed the balance of power in
Europe. And the United States spear-
headed a drive in the UN Security Council
to condemn the Russians and their four
Warsaw Pact allies that took part in the
occupation. In October, speaking to the
UN General Assembly, Secretary of State
Dean Rusk warned the Soviets that any
intervention by them in West Germany
would bring a military response from the
North Atlantic Treaty Organization. (Moscow had been making threatening statements about its right to take military action
in West Germany.)

Other Developments

A monetary crisis erupted in March
when a wave of speculative buying shook
the world's gold markets. The "Gold Rush
of 1968" posed a severe threat to the stability of the dollar and caused jitters in
business circles around the world.

The gold crisis was touched off mainly
by the continuing deficit in U.S. balance
of payments and by the refusal of Congress
to approve an increase in income taxes.
This placed the dollar in a weakened position, and led many financiers to believe that
the United States could not maintain its
official gold price of $35 an ounce.

The gold-buying fever finally forced the
London market to close on March 15. Two
days later, at a meeting in Washington,
central bankers from the United States,

President Johnson is given an enthusiastic welcome during his July 6 visit to El
Salvador, where he met with the presidents of five Central American countries.

Britain, and five continental European countries agreed to establish a two-price system for the metal. Under this arrangement, the $35 price was preserved for government transactions, and a flexible price, fluctuating according to supply and demand, was set up for private dealings.

Improvements in the United States' international economic position were reported during the summer. The deficit in the balance of payments dropped in the second quarter of the year to the lowest level in two years; the trade picture brightened; and the inflow of gold in June was the largest for any month since the gold drain began in 1958.

Relations with Latin America during the year were overshadowed by developments in Asia and Europe. And there was a general feeling that the Alliance for Progress was falling far short of expectations. Galo Plaza, the new secretary-general of the Organization of American States, warned the United States in July that "the peoples of Latin America, who have looked to the Alliance for salvation, are beginning to despair." He cited the widening income and technology gap between rich and poor nations.

President Johnson traveled to El Salvador on July 6 to meet with the presidents of five Central American countries. He pledged U.S. financial support of the Central American Common Market, which has greatly stimulated trade within the region.

In the smoldering Middle East dispute, the United States lent its full support to the peace efforts of UN envoy Gunnar V. Jarring. Washington appeared to be avoiding any show of favor toward either the Israelis or the Arabs. At the same time, it kept trying to reach an understanding with the Soviets on a permanent solution to the problems remaining from the 1967 war.

▶ DOMESTIC AFFAIRS

There was little that Americans could look upon with pride and satisfaction in 1968. The murders of Dr. Martin Luther King, Jr., and Senator Robert F. Kennedy, profoundly tragic as they were, seemed to be merely symptoms of a deep disorder in the nation. Other signs that all was not well with American society were visible at every hand—in the tense black ghettos of the big cities, whose mounting troubles seemed almost beyond solution; in the student revolt that swept many university campuses across the land; in the refusal of large numbers of young people to serve in their nation's armed forces; in the soaring crime rate; in the widespread attacks on the courts; and in the growing reliance on police power to put down dissent.

Violence

About 6 P.M. on April 4, in Memphis, Tennessee, as he leaned over a second-floor balcony outside his room at the Lorraine Motel, the Reverend Dr. Martin Luther King, Jr., was struck in the neck by a sniper's bullet. An hour later he was pronounced dead at St. Joseph's Hospital.

A wave of shock and horror spread across the nation and around the world in the wake of the shooting. And in the days following, the death of this gentle champion of brotherhood and nonviolence triggered the most widespread rioting by black people ever to hit the United States.

The 39-year-old civil-rights leader had gone to Memphis to assist that city's striking sanitation workers, most of whom are Negro. The bullet that took his life was fired from a cheap rooming house nearby, according to police, and the assassin made good his escape. A nationwide manhunt was launched, and the trail eventually led to Canada and Europe. Not until June 8 (the day Senator Kennedy was buried) was a suspect in the Dr. King slaying arrested, in London. He was identified as James Earl Ray, 40, a white man who had escaped from Missouri state prison in April 1967.

The Federal Bureau of Investigation had first issued a warrant for Eric Starvo Galt, but later it announced that the name was an alias used by Ray. He was later extradited and returned to the United States, and in Memphis on July 22 he pleaded not guilty to a murder charge.

In the period following the slaying of Dr. King, sorrow, fear and anger were abroad in the land. President Johnson, declaring a national day of mourning on April 7, warned his countrymen that "the fiber and the fabric of the Republic" was being

tested. He called for a special joint session of Congress to hear his proposals for "constructive action . . . in this hour of national need" (the session was never held), and he postponed a scheduled trip to Hawaii for a conference on Vietnam.

Meanwhile thousands of black people, most of them youths, went on a rampage in cities across the nation. Scenes of looting and burning in Washington, D.C. (where for a time smoke hung over the Capitol), Baltimore, Chicago, Kansas City, Missouri, and Pittsburgh shocked and frightened all Americans. Before the fury was spent, at least 125 cities in 28 states had experienced racial disturbances. The rioting left 45 persons dead, more than 2,500 injured, and enormous property damage.

Before the rioters could be calmed, thousands of troops were called out. Nearly 36,-000 regular soldiers and marines, along with 34,000 federalized National Guardsmen, were deployed in Washington, Baltimore and Chicago, and 22,000 more regular soldiers were placed in standby positions outside the crisis cities.

Americans had hardly recovered from the death of Dr. King and its tragic aftermath when, two months later, another bright young career was cut short by an assassin's bullets. Shortly after midnight on June 5, in a crowded kitchen passageway of a Los Angeles hotel, Senator Robert F. Kennedy fell mortally wounded. He died at Good Samaritan Hospital the next day at 1:44 A.M.

The 42-year-old Senator was at the Ambassador Hotel to celebrate his victory in the California presidential primary when the fatal shots were fired. Aides of the Senator seized a young man later identified as Sirhan Bishara Sirhan, a 24-year-old Christian Arab who grew up in Jordanian Jerusalem and moved to the Los Angeles area when he was 13. Police said eight shots were fired from a .22-calibre revolver;

Atlanta, Georgia, funeral procession for Dr. King, the slain civil-rights leader.

one of the bullets penetrated the Senator's brain. Five other persons wounded in the shooting recovered.

Once again flags flew at half-staff across the country, as they had for the Senator's brother less than five years earlier. And for the next three days, Americans relived the pain and sorrow they felt at the assassination of John F. Kennedy. In the long lines of mourners outside St. Patrick's Cathedral in New York, the slow journey of the funeral train to Washington, and the nighttime burial at Arlington National Cemetery, millions of Americans experienced again the dark days of November 1963.

Within hours after Senator Kennedy's death, Congress passed an anticrime bill that included a ban on the interstate shipment of handguns. But an outcry went up from the public demanding stiffer gun-control laws. Congressmen were deluged with mail urging such action, and President Johnson pleaded for a law curbing the sales of rifles and shotguns. But the powerful, tax-exempt National Rifle Association continued to exert pressure against effective Federal control over weapons. Finally, in October, a bill restricting the interstate sale of rifles, shotguns, and ammunition was passed. But the President failed to get the registration of firearms and the licensing of gun owners that he had sought.

In appealing for stronger gun laws, President Johnson pointed out that 750,-000 Americans had been killed by firearms in this century—"far more than have died at the hands of all our enemies in all of the wars that we have fought."

The 1968 assassinations raised again the question of whether there is in fact a special

An FBI wanted poster for James Earl Ray, alias Eric Starvo Galt, the accused assassin of Martin Luther King, Jr. Ray, an escaped convict, was captured in England and returned to the United States for trial.

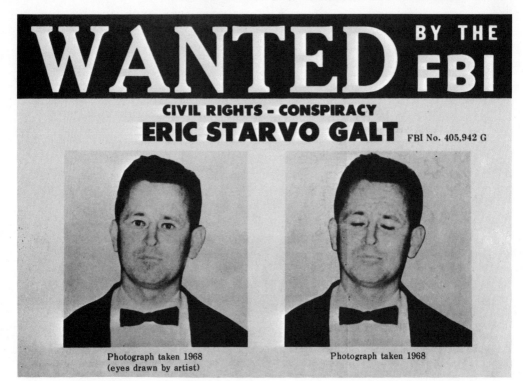

A soldier stands guard on H Street, Washington, D.C., after the slaying of Dr. Martin Luther King, Jr., touched off widespread rioting.

streak of violence peculiar to the American character. To explore the causes and nature of violence in the United States, the President on June 5 appointed a Commission on Violence, headed by Dr. Milton S. Eisenhower, a brother of former President Dwight Eisenhower.

Race Relations

An earlier commission, appointed during the devastating riots of 1967, reported its findings on February 29. The President's National Advisory Commission on Civil Disorders, headed by Illinois Gov. Otto Kerner, issued a lengthy report that blamed "white racism" for the violence that has erupted in black communities during the 1960's. The report stated: "This is our basic conclusion: Our nation is moving toward two societies, one black, one white—separate and unequal."

Reaction to the report was varied. The last statement was challenged by Vice-President Humphrey, and President Johnson himself failed to display much enthusiasm over the findings. The Kerner Report had called for a massive national program to combat poverty and the many other ills afflicting black people. But it was obvious to everyone that the necessary

Clutching rosary beads, Senator Robert F. Kennedy lies mortally wounded on the floor of the Ambassador Hotel in Los Angeles, California.

Sirhan Bishara Sirhan, the 24-year-old Jordanian immigrant accused of shooting Robert Kennedy, is taken into custody by police.

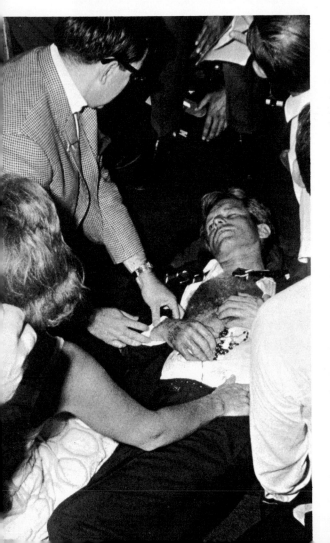

Above, the Reverend Ralph D. Abernathy, new leader of the Southern Christian Leadership Conference and the Poor People's Campaign. As part of this campaign, poor people from all over the United States converged on Washington, D.C., where they built Resurrection City (left) to dramatize the fact that too much poverty exists in the United States.

funds for an all-out effort would not be forthcoming as long as the Vietnam war drained the nation's resources.

One major attempt to dramatize the poverty that still exists in the world's richest country failed to win much success in the summer of 1968. The Poor People's Campaign, which had been conceived by Dr. King before his death, was officially opened by his widow in Washington on May 12. Led by Dr. King's successor, the Reverend Ralph D. Abernathy, the campaign was designed to prod Congress to enact programs for the impoverished. From all over the country, thousands of poor people converged on the capital, where they were sheltered in a plywood-and-canvas encampment known as "Resurrection City."

But troubles plagued the campaign from the start. Heavy rains made a quagmire of the campsite, and the program suffered from problems of leadership. Finally, on June 24, after the camp permit had expired, police moved in and cleared the site. The same day, Reverend Abernathy and 260 others were arrested for unlawful assembly on the Capitol grounds. He served 20 days in jail. Any lingering hope for a large-scale increase in aid to the poor was dispelled a few days later when President Johnson signed a tax bill requiring a $6,000,000,-000 cut in Federal spending. However, Congress did expand the food-stamp program designed to feed the hungry. And other small steps to help the poor were taken by Federal agencies.

In general, racial disturbances declined during the summer of 1968. Attorney General Ramsey Clark reported that there were only 25 major outbreaks in June, July and August, compared with 46 in the same months of 1967. And none of them approached in intensity the Newark and Detroit riots of the previous year. Clark credited effective police action for the improved record of 1968.

Turmoil in Education

From January 1, 1968, until the end of the school year in June, at least 221 major student demonstrations were staged at 101 colleges and universities in the United States. The National Student Association, which reported the figures, found that demands for black power formed the basis for 97 of the incidents. The next leading categories were demands for student power and antiwar protests.

The most serious of the student uprisings struck New York's Columbia University. On April 23–24, groups of white Leftists and blacks seized five university buildings. The students occupied the buildings until April 30, when some 1,000 city police moved in and took control. The force used by police, resulting in injuries to about 150 persons, served to intensify the students' determination to force a change in university policies, and the campus remained virtually paralyzed for the rest of the academic year.

The Vietnam war provided the vehicle for much of the student dissatisfaction with American society. In April, as part of a worldwide demonstration against the war, more than 200,000 college and high-school students cut classes in the New York area alone. Hostility toward the draft, especially after the announcement in February abolishing most graduate student deferments, was heightened during the year. In many cases the draft resisters were encouraged by clergymen and college faculty members. One of the most famous spokesmen for the antiwar movement, Dr. Benjamin Spock, was sentenced on July 10 to two years in Federal prison for conspiring to counsel draft evaders. At year's end the sentence was still under appeal.

Student unrest was not confined to higher education. In the fall, disturbances were reported at high schools and grade schools in many cities as black students and their parents demanded courses in Afro-American history and, in some cases, outright control of schools by the black community. The latter issue touched off a bitter struggle involving the teachers' union in New York City, where city-wide strikes prevented more than a million children from attending classes. Schools in other cities were closed temporarily because of tensions between white and black students.

Congress and Legislation

President Johnson's once-powerful influence over Congress faded altogether in 1968, especially after he announced plans to leave office at the end of his present term. Without strong leadership the second session of the Ninetieth Congress wrote a legislative program that emphasized economy and a generally conservative approach to foreign and domestic problems.

Although the Democrats enjoyed a numerical superiority in both houses, a coalition of Republicans and southern Democrats placed its stamp upon the election-year session. It succeeded in forcing a $6,000,000,000 reduction in Federal spending in return for passage of a tax increase, and it worked to trim nearly all of the money bills sought by the President. The lawmakers also handed President Johnson a humiliating defeat in refusing to accept his choice for a new chief justice of the Supreme Court.

On January 29, the President submitted a record budget calling for spending of $186,062,000,000 in the fiscal year 1969, and revenues of $178,108,000,000 (including income from the proposed tax surcharge). But Representative Wilbur Mills, chairman of the House Ways and Means Committee, led a campaign in Congress to reduce expenditures as part of the tax hike.

In June, Congress approved a bill that set a ceiling on spending at $180,100,000,000 and provided for a 10 per cent increase in personal and corporate income taxes, effective April 1, 1968, for individuals and the full year 1968 for businesses.

One of the most controversial bills of the session was the anticrime measure, signed on June 19. The President accepted the legislation reluctantly because of his objections to certain provisions. These included the granting of wiretapping and other eavesdropping rights to Federal, state and local law officers, and the curtailment of the rights of criminal suspects. The latter section was aimed at overturning three Supreme Court decisions of recent years that many law-enforcement agencies claimed hindered their operations.

The omnibus anticrime bill also curbed the sale of handguns and provided large Federal grants to improve local law-enforcement methods. Under strong pressure from the President and the public, Congress later approved a second bill, providing controls on the interstate sale of rifles, shotguns, and ammunition.

The slaying of Dr. King and the riots that followed spurred Congress to move quickly on the Civil Rights Act of 1968. The law's major provision was designed to bar racial discrimination in the sale and rental of about 80 per cent of all homes and apartments in the nation.

On August 1, President Johnson signed what he hailed as the "most massive housing program in all of America's history." The law authorized $5,300,000,000 in a three-year program to build more than 1,700,000 housing units. A key feature provided mortgage subsidies to help low-income families buy homes. But when it came to actually appropriating funds, the economy-minded Congress later made sharp cuts in this and other important social legislation.

Other major laws enacted in 1968 included (1) a highway bill that extends the Interstate Highway System, but that also weakens the highway-beautification program; (2) a higher-education bill authorizing $7,300,000,000 for scholarships and loans to students and for construction of new college and university buildings; (3) a "truth-in-lending" measure designed to give consumers information on finance charges for loans and credit purchases; (4) a foreign-aid appropriation of $1,750,000,000, the lowest sum in the 21-year history of the program; and (5) conservation measures that established the Redwood National Park in California and a national system of wild and scenic rivers.

Despite its budget-cutting mood, Congress approved the largest single money bill in the nation's history: $72,000,000,000 for defense. Even so, the vast sum was several billions below what the President had asked.

Supreme Court

Strong Congressional opposition to both President Johnson and the Supreme Court took a dramatic turn in 1968 when the legislative branch blocked the nomination of a new chief justice. The President, announcing on June 26 that Earl Warren was resigning after 14 years as head of the high court, selected Associate Justice Abe Fortas to succeed Warren. He also named Judge Homer Thornberry, a former congressman from Texas, to fill the seat that would be vacated by Fortas.

The announcement touched off a flurry of protests among Republicans, who, anticipating a victory in November, wanted Nixon to name the successor to Warren. They were joined by conservatives of both parties, who for years had been denouncing the liberal decisions of the Warren court.

The two factions combined in the closing days of the session to conduct a filibuster that prevented the nominations from coming to a vote. Finally, on October 2, Associate Justice Fortas asked that his name be withdrawn. Chief Justice Warren, whose resignation was dependent upon the confirmation of a successor, remained on the bench as the new term opened, along with Fortas.

Richard Nixon's political ambitions were realized on November 5, 1968, when he was elected 37th president of the United States.

Spiro T. Agnew was governor of Maryland and a political unknown when Nixon chose him to be his vice-presidential running mate.

▶THE ELECTIONS

Eight years after losing to John F. Kennedy in one of the closest presidential elections in U.S. history, and six years after a shattering defeat in the California governor's race apparently doomed him to political oblivion, Richard Milhous Nixon in 1968 at last claimed the great prize of American politics. His narrow victory over Vice-President Hubert H. Humphrey brought to a close eight years of Democratic rule, and marked only the second time since 1933 that the Republican Party controlled the White House.

The Nominations

President Johnson's announcement of March 31 that he was retiring from the political wars was but one of the shocking developments of a remarkable election year. It was a year in which nothing could be taken for granted. It was a year in which most of the old political certainties seemed to be swept away by the passions of both the Left and Right and the discontent of the Center.

The President, fearful of the growing disunity in the nation, declared in his March 31 address that "I shall not seek, and I will not accept, the nomination of my party for another term as your president." It was generally agreed that the nomination would have been his for the asking. But the mounting strength of the peace Democrats led by Senators Eugene J. McCarthy and Robert F. Kennedy undoubtedly contributed to the President's unexpected decision.

Democrats Hubert H. Humphrey and Edmund S. Muskie fought an uphill battle from the Democratic national convention in August to election day in November, narrowly losing in a close presidential race.

The announcement followed by less than three weeks Senator McCarthy's startling victory in the New Hampshire Democratic primary, the nation's first. With the help of a devoted "army" of college students and other political amateurs who were drawn to his antiwar banner, the Minnesota Senator changed the entire complexion of the 1968 campaign with that singular, personal triumph. And in so doing, he unleashed forces whose influence was felt eventually from Washington to Hanoi. (Although McCarthy polled about 42 per cent of the popular vote to 49 per cent for the President, he captured 20 of New Hampshire's 24 delegates.)

Four days after New Hampshire, Senator Kennedy was in the race for the Democratic nomination. He and Senator Mc-Carthy were united in their opposition to President Johnson's policies in Vietnam and his handling of many domestic problems. Yet the two men waged a series of heated contests in the state primaries. Senator Kennedy scored victories over his colleague in Indiana and Nebraska. Senator McCarthy prevailed in Oregon.

This brought the two contenders down to the last big primary battle of the year. And it was generally accepted that the outcome in California would determine which of the two would go on to challenge Vice-President Humphrey in Chicago. (Humphrey had entered the Democratic sweepstakes on April 27, too late to take part in the primaries.) On June 4, Senator Kennedy took California by 46 per cent to 42 per cent for McCarthy. But hours later an assassin, not the voters, put an end to Robert Kennedy's career.

On the Republican side, former Vice-President Nixon had rung up lopsided victories in one state primary after another. One of his chief rivals, Michigan Governor George Romney, dropped out even before the New Hampshire primary. His drive had failed to gain much headway. Nixon's chief threat, New York Governor Nelson A. Rockefeller, appeared to be unable to make up his mind whether to bid for the nomination. He finally entered the arena on April 30. Another Governor, Ronald Reagan of California, pursued a rather vigorous "noncandidacy" during the months preceding the national convention. Not until the delegates met in Miami Beach on August 5, did he officially toss his hat into the ring.

Senator Eugene J. McCarthy challenged President Johnson in the New Hampshire primary.

But by this time the Nixon drive was too powerful to be checked, and he easily captured the nomination on the first ballot. The vote for the main contenders was: Nixon, 692; Rockefeller, 277; Reagan, 182. The victor selected Maryland Governor Spiro T. Agnew, a relative unknown, as his vice-presidential candidate.

The Republican convention was a model of unity and order (to the point of boredom). The Democratic gathering in Chicago three weeks later proved to be one of the wildest conventions in history.

The storm flags had been flying even before the Democrats convened on August 26. Alarmed by the plans of hippies, radicals, and young McCarthy followers to stage anti-Johnson demonstrations during the convention, Chicago Mayor Richard J. Daley took elaborate precautions to preserve order. The International Amphitheatre, which housed the convention, was enclosed by a chain link fence and barbed wire. The city's entire police force was placed on 12-hour shifts. The Illinois governor called out over 5,000 National Guardsmen. And the Army sent 7,500 troops to the city for standby duty. Inside the hall, Mayor Daley set up a strong security force that maintained rigid control over the movements of the delegates, visitors and newsmen.

The violence that everyone feared did come. Trouble that simmered for several days between protesters and police flared into a bloody climax on August 28. That evening, in front of the Conrad Hilton Hotel, convention headquarters, the security force attacked some 5,000 youthful demonstrators with tear gas, clubs, rifle butts and chemical Mace.

Reports on the number of injuries suffered in the wild melee varied widely. But it is probable that hundreds of youths required medical treatment. The city reported that nearly 200 policemen were injured. This spectacle took place even as the delegates were balloting for the presidential nomination. It was witnessed by millions of television viewers throughout the nation.

A bitter controversy developed in the wake of the "Battle of Michigan Avenue." National news media charged that reporters and photographers were deliberately harassed and even beaten by the police. Mayor Daley accused the television networks of presenting a distorted account of the proceedings. And he insisted that the demonstrators were "terrorists" who intentionally provoked the police. (A poll later showed that 56 per cent of the nation's adults approved of the police action in Chicago.)

As for the convention itself, the Humphrey forces, backed by President Johnson, repelled the spirited challenge of Senator McCarthy and his supporters. The Humphrey organization, which included Mayor Daley, beat down a proposed Vietnam peace plank after a sharp floor debate and went on to clinch a first-ballot nomination for the Vice-President. The vote: Hum-

Senator Edward M. Kennedy fell heir to the Kennedy political dream when his brother Robert was killed after winning the California primary.

LOS ANGELES
bassador hotel

Chicago Mayor Richard J. Daley tried to preserve order for the Democratic national convention, but clashes between youths and police were widespread.

phrey, 1,761¾; McCarthy, 601; and Senator George S. McGovern (a late entry in the race), 146½. Senator Edmund S. Muskie of Maine was picked as Humphrey's running mate.

Feelings against the administration ran so high in Chicago that President Johnson did not make an appearance at his own party's convention. The victory of Humphrey, who as vice-president had enthusiastically defended the U.S. role in Vietnam, and the conduct of Mayor Daley and his police left large segments of the party embittered and disillusioned. For the Democrats, it was the year's low ebb.

The Balloting

It was nearly noon in New York City on November 6—the day after the election—before Richard M. Nixon could claim victory in the long and grueling 1968 presidential race. Throughout the tense night,

both Republicans and Democrats watched the returns in several big states that held the key to the final outcome. Not until Illinois swung to Nixon's column Wednesday morning did he have the necessary 270 electoral votes to assure his election as the 37th president of the United States.

The presence on the ballots of all 50 states of former Alabama Governor George C. Wallace, as well as the closeness of the balloting for Nixon and Vice-President Humphrey, produced one of the tightest races in the nation's history. When it was all over, Nixon had 301 electoral votes, Humphrey had 191 and Wallace had 46. One elector from North Carolina voted for Wallace though Nixon had won the state.

The popular vote was much closer. Of the 73,186,819 votes cast, Nixon received 31,770,237, or 43.4 per cent of the total. Humphrey got 31,270,533, or 42.7 per cent. And Wallace took 9,906,141, or 13.5

per cent. Thus Nixon received the lowest share of the total vote for a winning candidate since Woodrow Wilson defeated two rivals in 1912.

Another unusual feature of the 1968 elections was the Democratic success in the House. The victorious standard-bearer traditionally carries the House of Representatives into office with him. But the Republicans managed to pick up only five additional seats. This left the Democrats with 243 seats to 192 for the Republicans in the new Congress.

In the Senate the Republicans gained five seats, leaving the Democrats with a superiority of 58–42. (The Republicans gained a seat with the appointment of T. F. Stevens to succeed Alaska Democrat E. L. Bartlett, who died in December.)

According to the polls and other barometers, Nixon began the campaign with a wide edge over Humphrey. But in the closing days a dramatic upsurge for Humphrey and a decline in Wallace strength whittled away Nixon's apparent lead and left the outcome in doubt by Election Day.

Then President Johnson announced, virtually on the eve of election, a complete bombing halt in North Vietnam and a widening of the Paris peace talks. This

American Independent Party presidential candidate George C. Wallace and his running mate Curtis E. LeMay (above) ran on the issue of law and order and won five Deep South states.

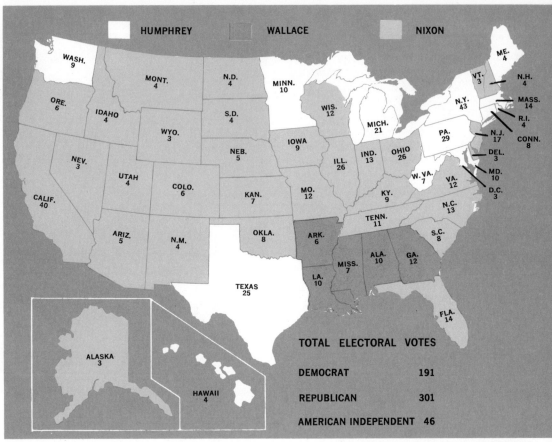

HUMPHREY	WALLACE	NIXON

TOTAL ELECTORAL VOTES

DEMOCRAT	191
REPUBLICAN	301
AMERICAN INDEPENDENT	46

One North Carolina elector voted for Wallace.

probably brought many antiwar Democrats into the Humphrey camp. At the same time, Wallace appeared to lose some support after he named (October 3) General Curtis E. LeMay, former Air Force chief of staff, as his running mate on the American Independent Party ticket.

Wallace's showing in the election was generally weaker than many observers expected and the two major parties feared. His victories were confined to five states in the Deep South. And his share of the total vote was well below the 20 per cent he had enjoyed in the early polls.

Preliminary studies of the results indicated that many potential Wallace supporters switched to Nixon in Kentucky, Tennessee and the Carolinas. This enabled the Republican to carry those states. At the same time, Humphrey seemed to benefit from Wallace defections in Pennsylvania and Michigan, which he won.

In any event, the Alabaman was frustrated in his announced intention to prevent either candidate from winning the necessary 270 electoral votes. If neither had won 270 electoral votes the decision would have been made by the House of Representatives, where Wallace hoped to compel his rivals to bargain with him. The chance that this could have happened, with all of its inherent dangers, brought a widespread demand for revision or abolition of the electoral-college system.

Principal issues in the campaign were the war in Vietnam and law and order at home. However, none of the candidates were specific on how they would deal with these and other problems. And in the end the American people's desire for a change of leadership probably was decisive.

SAL J. FODERARO
Managing Editor
The Americana Annual

UNITED STATES GOVERNMENT

President: RICHARD M. NIXON

Vice-President: SPIRO T. AGNEW

EXECUTIVE OFFICE OF THE PRESIDENT

Director of Communications: HERBERT G. KLEIN
Press Assistant: RONALD ZIEGLER
Counsel: JOHN D. EHRLICHMAN
Assistant for National Security Affairs: HENRY A. KISSINGER
Special Assistants to the President: MARTIN ANDERSON,
   ROBERT J. BROWN, PATRICK J. BUCHANAN, DWIGHT CHAPIN,
   ROBERT ELLSWORTH, H. R. HALDEMAN, BRYCE N. HARLOW,
   JAMES KEOGH, RAYMOND K. PRICE, JR.
Science Adviser: LEE A. DuBRIDGE
Bureau of the Budget: ROBERT P. MAYO, director
Council of Economic Advisers: PAUL W. McCRACKEN, chairman
Council on Urban Affairs: DANIEL P. MOYNIHAN, chief adviser
Central Intelligence Agency: RICHARD HELMS, director

THE CABINET

Secretary of State: WILLIAM P. ROGERS
Secretary of Defense: MELVIN R. LAIRD
Secretary of the Treasury: DAVID M. KENNEDY
Attorney General: JOHN N. MITCHELL
Postmaster General: WINTON M. BLOUNT
Secretary of the Interior: WALTER J. HICKEL
Secretary of Agriculture: CLIFFORD M. HARDIN
Secretary of Commerce: MAURICE H. STANS
Secretary of Labor: GEORGE P. SHULTZ
Secretary of Health, Education, and Welfare: ROBERT H. FINCH
Secretary of Housing and Urban Development: GEORGE W. ROMNEY
Secretary of Transportation: JOHN A. VOLPE

Front row, left to right: David M. Kennedy, Melvin R. Laird, Spiro T. Agnew, Richard M. Nixon, John A. Volpe, Robert Mayo, Robert H. Finch. Back row, left to right: William P. Rogers, Winton M. Blount, John N. Mitchell, Maurice Stans, George Romney, Clifford M. Hardin, George P. Shultz, Walter J. Hickel.

THE CONGRESS OF THE UNITED STATE[S]

UNITED STATES SENATE

ALABAMA
John J. Sparkman (D)
James B. Allen (D)*

ALASKA
T. F. Stevens (R)
Mike Gravel (D)*

ARIZONA
Paul Fannin (R)
Barry Goldwater (R)*

ARKANSAS
J. William Fulbright (D)**
John L. McClellan

CALIFORNIA
George Murphy (R)
Alan Cranston (D)*

COLORADO
Peter H. Dominick (R)**
Gordon Allott (R)

CONNECTICUT
Thomas J. Dodd (D)
Abraham A. Ribicoff (D)**

DELAWARE
John J. Williams (R)
J. Caleb Boggs (R)

FLORIDA
Spessard L. Holland (D)
Edward Gurney (R)*

GEORGIA
Herman E. Talmadge (D)**
Richard B. Russell (D)

HAWAII
Hiram L. Fong (R)
Daniel K. Inouye (D)**

IDAHO
Frank Church (D)**
Len B. Jordan (R)

ILLINOIS
Everett M. Dirksen (R)**
Charles H. Percy (R)

INDIANA
Vance Hartke (D)
Birch E. Bayh (D)**

IOWA
Jack Miller (R)
Harold Hughes (D)*

KANSAS
James B. Pearson (R)
Robert Dole (R)*

KENTUCKY
John S. Cooper (R)
Marlow W. Cook (R)*

LOUISIANA
Allen J. Ellender (D)
Russell B. Long (D)**

MAINE
Margaret Chase Smith (R)
Edmund Muskie (D)

MARYLAND
Joseph Tydings (D)
C. M. Mathias, Jr. (R)*

MASSACHUSETTS
Edward M. Kennedy (D)
Edward Brooke (R)

MICHIGAN
Philip Hart (D)
Robert Griffin (R)

MINNESOTA
Eugene J. McCarthy (D)
Walter Mondale (D)

MISSISSIPPI
John Stennis (D)
James O. Eastland (D)

MISSOURI
Stuart Symington (D)
T. F. Eagleton (D)*

MONTANA
Mike Mansfield (D)
Lee Metcalf (D)

NEBRASKA
Carl Curtis (R)
Roman Hruska (R)

NEVADA
Howard W. Cannon (D)
Alan Bible (D)**

NEW HAMPSHIRE
T. J. McIntyre (D)
Norris Cotton (R)**

NEW JERSEY
Clifford Case (R)
H. A. Williams (D)

NEW MEXICO
Clinton P. Anderson (D)
Joseph M. Montoya (D)

NEW YORK
Jacob K. Javits (R)**
Charles E. Goodell (R)

NORTH CAROLINA
B. Everett Jordan (D)
Samuel J. Ervin (D)**

NORTH DAKOTA
Quentin Burdick (D)
Milton Young (R)**

OHIO
Stephen Young (D)
William Saxbe (R)*

OKLAHOMA
Fred R. Harris (D)
Henry Bellmon (R)*

OREGON
Mark Hatfield (R)
R. W. Packwood (R)*

PENNSYLVANIA
Hugh Scott (R)
R. S. Schweiker (R)*

RHODE ISLAND
John O. Pastore (D)
Claiborne Pell (D)

SOUTH CAROLINA
Strom Thurmond (R)
Ernest Hollings (D)**

SOUTH DAKOTA
Karl Mundt (R)
George S. McGovern (D)**

TENNESSEE
Albert Gore (D)
Howard Baker, Jr. (R)

TEXAS
Ralph Yarborough (D)
John G. Tower (R)

UTAH
Frank E. Moss (D)
Wallace F. Bennett (R)**

VERMONT
Winston L. Prouty (R)
George D. Aiken (R)*

VIRGINIA
William Spong (D)
Harry F. Byrd, Jr. (D)

WASHINGTON
Henry M. Jackson (D)
Warren G. Magnuson (D)**

WEST VIRGINIA
Robert C. Byrd (D)
Jennings Randolph (D)

WISCONSIN
William Proxmire (D)
Gaylord A. Nelson (D)

WYOMING
Gale W. McGee (D)
Clifford Hansen (R)

* Elected November 5, 1968
** Incumbent reelected

UNITED STATES HOUSE OF REPRESENTATIVES

ALABAMA
J. Edwards (R)*
W. L. Dickinson (R)*
George Andrews (D)*
William Nichols (D)*
W. W. Flowers (D)*
John Buchanan (R)*
Tom Bevill (D)*
Robert Jones (D)*

ALASKA
H. W. Pollock (R)*

ARIZONA
John Rhodes (R)*
Morris Udall (D)*
Sam Steiger (R)*

ARKANSAS
Bill Alexander (D)
Wilbur Mills (D)*
J. Hammer-
   schmidt (R)*
David Pryor (D)*

CALIFORNIA
Don Clausen (R)*
H. T. Johnson (D)*
John Moss (D)*
R. L. Leggett (D)*
Phillip Burton (D)*
W. S. Mailliard (R)*
J. Cohelan (D)*
G. P. Miller (D)*
Don Edwards (D)*
C. S. Gubser (R)*
P. McCloskey (R)*
Burt Talcott (R)*
C. M. Teague (R)*
J. R. Waldie (D)*
John McFall (D)*
B. F. Sisk (D)*
G. M. Anderson (D)
R. B. Mathias (R)*
C. Holifield (D)*
H. A. Smith (R)*
A. F. Hawkins (D)*
J. C. Corman (D)*
Del Clawson (R)*
G. P. Lipscomb (R)*
C. E. Wiggins (R)*
Thomas Rees (D)*
E. Reinecke (R)*
Alphonzo Bell (R)*
G. E. Brown, Jr. (D)*
E. R. Roybal (D)*
C. H. Wilson (D)*
Craig Hosmer (R)*
Jerry Pettis (R)*
R. T. Hanna (D)*
James Utt (R)*
Bob Wilson (R)*
L. Van Deerlin (D)*
John Tunney (D)*

COLORADO
Byron G. Rogers (D)*
D. G. Brotzman (R)*

Frank Evans (D)*
W. N. Aspinall (D)*

CONNECTICUT
E. Q. Daddario (D)*
W. L. St. Onge (D)*
R. N. Giaimo (D)*
L. P. Weicker, Jr. (R)
J. S. Monagan (D)*
T. J. Meskill (R)*

DELAWARE
W. V. Roth, Jr. (R)*

FLORIDA
R. L. F. Sikes (D)*
Don Fuqua (D)*
C. E. Bennett (D)*
W. Chappell, Jr. (D)
Louis Frey, Jr. (R)
Sam Gibbons (D)*
James Haley (D)*
W. C. Cramer (R)*
P. G. Rogers (D)*
J. H. Burke (D)*
Claude Pepper (D)*
D. B. Fascell (D)*

GEORGIA
G. E. Hagan (D)*
Maston O'Neal (D)*
Jack Brinkley (D)*
Ben Blackburn (R)*
F. Thompson (R)*
J. J. Flynt, Jr. (D)*
J. W. Davis (D)*
W. Stuckey, Jr. (D)*
Phil Landrum (D)*
R. Stephens, Jr. (D)*

HAWAII
S. Matsunaga (D)*
Patsy Mink (D)*

IDAHO
J. A. McClure (R)*
Orval Hansen (R)

ILLINOIS
W. L. Dawson (D)*
Abner Mikva (D)
W. T. Murphy (D)*
E. J. Derwinski (R)*
J. C. Kluczynski (D)*
Dan Ronan (D)*
F. Annunzio (D)*
D. Rostenkowski (D)*
Sidney Yates (D)*
H. R. Collier (R)*
R. C. Pucinski (D)*
R. McClory (R)*
D. Rumsfeld (R)*
J. N. Erlenborn (R)*
Charlotte Reid (R)*
J. B. Anderson (R)*
L. C. Arends (R)*
Robert Michel (R)*
T. F. Railsback (R)*

Paul Findley (R)*
Kenneth Gray (D)*
W. L. Springer (R)*
George Shipley (D)*
Melvin Price (D)*

INDIANA
Ray Madden (D)*
E. F. Landgrebe (R)
John Brademas (D)*
Ross Adair (R)*
R. L. Roudebush (R)*
William Bray (R)*
John Myers (R)*
Roger Zion (R)*
Lee Hamilton (D)*
David Dennis (R)
A. Jacobs, Jr. (D)*

IOWA
Fred Schwengel (R)*
John Culver (D)*
H. R. Gross (R)*
John Kyl (R)*
Neal Smith (D)*
Wiley Mayne (R)*
W. J. Scherle (R)*

KANSAS
K. G. Sebelius (R)
Chester Mize (R)*
Larry Winn, Jr. (R)*
G. E. Shriver (R)*
Joe Skubitz (R)*

KENTUCKY
F. Stubblefield (D)*
W. H. Natcher (D)*
W. O. Cowger (R)*
M. G. Synder (R)*
Tim L. Carter (R)*
John C. Watts (D)*
Carl Perkins (D)*

LOUISIANA
F. E. Hébert (D)*
Hale Boggs (D)*
P. T. Caffery (D)
J. Waggonner (D)*
Otto Passman (D)*
J. R. Rarick (D)*
E. W. Edwards (D)*
Speedy Long (D)*

MAINE
Peter N. Kyros (D)*
W. D. Hathaway (D)*

MARYLAND
R. C. B. Morton (R)*
C. D. Long (D)*
E. A. Garmatz (D)*
George Fallon (D)*
L. J. Hogan (R)
J. G. Beall, Jr. (R)
S. N. Friedel (D)*
Gilbert Gude (R)*

MASSACHUSETTS
Silvio Conte (R)*
E. P. Boland (D)*
Philip Philbin (D)*
Harold Donohue (D)*
F. B. Morse (R)*
W. H. Bates (R)*
T. H. Macdonald (D)*
T. P. O'Neill, Jr. (D)*
J. McCormack (D)*
M. M. Heckler (R)*
James Burke (D)*
Hastings Keith (R)*

MICHIGAN
John Conyers (D)*
Marvin Esch (R)*
Garry Brown (R)*
E. Hutchinson (R)*
Gerald Ford (R)*
C. Chamberlain (R)*
D. W. Riegle, Jr. (R)*
James Harvey (R)*
G. Vander Jagt (R)*
E. A. Cederberg (R)*
Philip Ruppe (R)*
J. G. O'Hara (R)*
C. C. Diggs, Jr. (D)*
Lucien Nedzi (D)*
William Ford (D)*
John Dingell (D)*
M. W. Griffiths (D)*
W. Broomfield (R)*
J. H. McDonald (R)*

MINNESOTA
Albert Quie (R)*
Ancher Nelsen (R)*
C. MacGregor (R)*
J. E. Karth (D)*
D. M. Fraser (D)*
John Zwach (R)*
Odin Langen (R)*
John A. Blatnik (D)*

MISSISSIPPI
T. G. Abernethy (D)*
J. L. Whitten (D)*
Charles Griffin (D)*
G. Montgomery (D)*
W. M. Colmer (D)*

MISSOURI
William Clay (D)
J. W. Symington (D)
L. K. Sullivan (D)*
W. J. Randall (D)*
R. Bolling (D)*
W. R. Hull, Jr. (D)*
Durward Hall (R)*
R. H. Ichord (D)*
W. L. Hungate (D)*
Bill Burlison (D)

MONTANA
Arnold Olsen (D)*
James Battin (R)*

* Incumbent

UNITED STATES HOUSE OF REPRESENTATIVES

NEBRASKA
Robert Denney (R)*
G. Cunningham (R)*
Dave Martin (R)*

NEVADA
W. S. Baring (D)*

NEW HAMPSHIRE
Louis Wyman (R)*
J. C. Cleveland (R)*

NEW JERSEY
John E. Hunt (R)*
C. Sandman, Jr. (R)*
J. J. Howard (D)*
F. Thompson, Jr. (D)*
P. Frelinghuysen (R)*
William Cahill (R)*
W. B. Widnall (R)*
Charles Joelson (D)*
H. Helstoski (D)*
Peter Rodino, Jr. (D)*
Joseph Minish (D)*
Florence Dwyer (R)*
C. E. Gallagher (D)*
D. V. Daniels (D)*
Edward Patten (D)*

NEW MEXICO
Manuel Lujan, Jr. (R)
Ed Foreman (R)

NEW YORK
Otis G. Pike (D)*
J. R. Grover (R)*
Lester Wolff (D)*
John Wydler (R)*
A. Lowenstein (D)
S. Halpern (R)*
J. P. Addabbo (D)*
B. S. Rosenthal (D)*
J. J. Delaney (D)*
Emanuel Celler (D)*
Frank Brasco (D)*
S. Chisholm (D)
B. L. Podell (D)*
John Rooney (D)*
Hugh Carey (D)*
John M. Murphy (D)*
Edward I. Koch (D)
Adam C. Powell (D)
L. Farbstein (D)*
William F. Ryan (D)*
J. H. Scheuer (D)*
J. H. Gilbert (D)*
J. B. Bingham (D)*
Mario Biaggi (D)
R. L. Ottinger (D)*
Ogden R. Reid (R)*
M. B. McKneally (R)
H. Fish, Jr. (R)
Daniel Button (R)*
Carleton King (R)*
R. C. McEwen (R)*
A. Pirnie (R)*
H. W. Robison (R)*
* Incumbent

James Hanley (D)*
S. S. Stratton (D)*
Frank Horton (R)*
B. B. Conable, Jr. (R)*
J. F. Hastings (R)
R. D. McCarthy (D)*
H. P. Smith III (R)*
T. J. Dulski (D)*

NORTH CAROLINA
W. B. Jones (D)*
L. H. Fountain (D)*
D. N. Henderson (D)*
N. Galifianakis (D)*
Wilmer Mizell (R)
L. R. Preyer (D)
Alton Lennon (D)*
Earl B. Ruth (R)
C. R. Jonas (R)*
J. T. Broyhill (R)*
Roy A. Taylor (D)*

NORTH DAKOTA
Mark Andrews (R)*
Tom Kleppe (R)*

OHIO
Robert Taft, Jr. (R)*
D. D. Clancy (R)*
C. W. Whalen, Jr. (R)*
W. M. McCulloch (R)*
Delbert Latta (R)*
W. H. Harsha (R)*
C. J. Brown, Jr. (R)*
J. E. Betts (R)*
T. L. Ashley (D)*
C. E. Miller (R)*
J. W. Stanton (R)*
S. L. Devine (R)*
C. A. Mosher (R)*
W. H. Ayres (R)*
C. P. Wylie (R)*
Frank T. Bow (R)*
J. M. Ashbrook (R)*
Wayne Hays (D)*
M. J. Kirwan (D)*
M. A. Feighan (D)*
Louis Stokes (D)
Charles Vanik (D)*
W. E. Minshall (R)*
D. E. Lukens (R)*

OKLAHOMA
Page Belcher (R)*
Ed Edmondson (D)*
Carl Albert (D)*
Tom Steed (D)*
John Jarmon (D)*
J. N. H. Camp (R)

OREGON
Wendell Wyatt (R)*
Al Ullman (D)*
Edith Green (D)*
J. R. Dellenback (R)*

PENNSYLVANIA
W. A. Barrett (D)*
R. N. C. Nix (D)*
James Byrne (D)*
J. Eilberg (D)*
W. J. Green (D)*
Gus Yatron (D)
L. G. Williams (R)*
E. G. Biester, Jr. (R*)
G. R. Watkins (R)*
J. M. McDade (R)*
Daniel Flood (D)*
J. I. Whalley (R)*
R. L. Coughlin (R)
W. S. Moorhead (D)*
Fred Rooney (D)*
E. D. Eshleman (R)*
H. T. Schneebeli (R)*
R. J. Corbett (R)*
G. A. Goodling (R)*
Joseph Gaydos (D)
John H. Dent (D)*
John P. Saylor (R)*
A. W. Johnson (R)*
J. P. Vigorito (D)*
Frank M. Clark (D)*
Thomas Morgan (D)*
J. G. Fulton (R)*

RHODE ISLAND
F. J. St. Germain (D)*
R. O. Tiernan (D)*

SOUTH CAROLINA
L. M. Rivers (D)*
Albert Watson (R)*
W. J. B. Dorn (D)*
James R. Mann (D)
T. S. Gettys (D)*
J. L. McMillan (D)*

SOUTH DAKOTA
Ben Reifel (R)*
E. Y. Berry (R)*

TENNESSEE
J. H. Quillen (R)*
John J. Duncan (R)*
W. E. Brock III (R)*
Joe L. Evins (D)*
R. Fulton (D)*
W. R. Anderson (D)*
Ray Blanton (D)*
R. A. Everett (D)*
D. Kuykendall (R)*

TEXAS
Wright Patman (D)*
John Dowdy (D)*
J. M. Collins (R)
Ray Roberts (D)*
Earle Cabell (D)*
Olin Teague (D)*
George Bush (R)*
Bob Eckhardt (D)*

Jack Brooks (D)*
J. J. Pickle (D)*
W. R. Poage (D)*
Jim Wright (D)*
G. Purcell (D)*
John Young (D)*
E. de la Garza (D)*
Richard White (D)
Omar Burleson (D
Robert Price (R)*
George Mahon (D)
H. B. Gonzalez (D
O. C. Fisher (D)*
Bob Casey (D)*
A. Kazen, Jr. (D)*

UTAH
L. J. Burton (R)*
S. P. Lloyd (R)*

VERMONT
R. T. Stafford (R)*

VIRGINIA
T. N. Downing (D)
G. W. Whitehurst (
D. Satterfield III (
W. M. Abbitt (D)*
W. C. Daniel (D)
Richard Poff (R)*
John O. Marsh (D)
W. L. Scott (R)*
W. C. Wampler (R)
Joel Broyhill (D)*

WASHINGTON
Thomas Pelly (R)*
Lloyd Meeds (D)*
J. B. Hansen (R)
Catherine May (R
Thomas Foley (D)
Floyd Hicks (D)*
Brock Adams (D)*

WEST VIRGINIA
R. H. Mollohan (D
H. O. Staggers (D
J. M. Slack, Jr. (D
Ken Hechler (D)*
James Kee (D)*

WISCONSIN
H. C. Schadeberg
R. Kastenmeier (
V. W. Thomson (
C. J. Zablocki (D
Henry Reuss (D)*
W. A. Steiger (R)
John Byrnes (R)*
Glenn Davis (R)*
A. E. O'Konski (R
(one seat vacant)

WYOMING
John Wold (R)

New York Governor Nelson Rockefeller, a contender for the 1968 Republican presidential nomination.

GOVERNORS

ALABAMA	Albert P. Brewer (D)	MONTANA	F. H. Anderson (D)*
ALASKA	Keith H. Miller (R)	NEBRASKA	Norbert T. Tiemann (R)
ARIZONA	Jack Williams (R)**	NEVADA	Pail Laxalt (R)
ARKANSAS	Winthrop Rockefeller (R)**	NEW HAMPSHIRE	W. R. Peterson, Jr. (R)*
CALIFORNIA	Ronald Reagan (R)	NEW JERSEY	Richard J. Hughes (D)
COLORADO	John A. Love (R)	NEW MEXICO	David F. Cargo (R)**
CONNECTICUT	John N. Dempsey (D)	NEW YORK	Nelson A. Rockefeller (R)
DELAWARE	R. W. Peterson (R)*	NORTH CAROLINA	Robert W. Scott (D)*
FLORIDA	Claude Kirk, Jr. (R)	NORTH DAKOTA	William L. Guy (D)**
GEORGIA	Lester Maddox (D)	OHIO	James A. Rhodes (R)
HAWAII	John A. Burns (D)	OKLAHOMA	Dewey Bartlett (R)
IDAHO	Donald Samuelson (R)	OREGON	Tom McCall (R)
ILLINOIS	R. B. Ogilvie (R)*	PENNSYLVANIA	Raymond P. Shafer (R)
INDIANA	E. D. Whitcomb (R)*	RHODE ISLAND	Frank Licht (D)*
IOWA	Robert Ray (R)*	SOUTH CAROLINA	Robert McNair (D)
KANSAS	Robert Docking (D)**	SOUTH DAKOTA	Frank Farrar (R)*
KENTUCKY	Louie B. Nunn (R)	TENNESSEE	Buford Ellington (D)
LOUISIANA	John J. McKeithen (D)	TEXAS	Preston Smith (D)*
MAINE	Kenneth M. Curtis (D)	UTAH	Calvin L. Rampton (D)**
MARYLAND	Marvin Mandel (D)	VERMONT	Deane C. Davis (R)*
MASSACHUSETTS	Francis W. Sargent (R)	VIRGINIA	Mills E. Godwin, Jr. (D)
MICHIGAN	William G. Milliken (R)	WASHINGTON	Daniel J. Evans (R)**
MINNESOTA	Harold LeVander (R)	WEST VIRGINIA	Arch A. Moore (R)*
MISSISSIPPI	John Bell Williams (D)	WISCONSIN	Warren P. Knowles (R)**
MISSOURI	Warren E. Hearnes (D)**	WYOMING	Stan K. Hathaway (R)

* Elected November 5, 1968
** Incumbent reelected

HEMISFAIR'68

HEMISFAIR'68 made San Antonio, Texas, the most exciting and interesting place in the United States during the six months of its run (April 6–October 6). HemisFair celebrated the 250th anniversary of the founding of San Antonio, a city famed for the Alamo and renowned for its grace and beauty.

The theme of HemisFair was "Confluence of Civilizations in the Americas." The fair was meant to show how people from all over the world came to the United States and founded a new country and a new way of life. It also took a look into the future to see what it might hold for the United States and the world.

HemisFair occupied a site of 92.6 acres in the heart of downtown San Antonio. Over six million people attended the fair. They saw exhibits from more than thirty nations as well as industrial exhibits.

Altogether the buildings erected for HemisFair cost $156,000,000. Most world's-fair buildings are torn down at the closing of the exposition. But at HemisFair many buildings were built for permanent use. Among these are the theme structure, the 622-foot Tower of the Americas,

San Antonio's HemisFair'68 theme structure, the 622-foot Tower of the Americas, stands tall on the 92.6-acre downtown fairgrounds site.

Las Plazas del Mundo housed the exhibits of the many foreign nations participating in HemisFair.

a great Convention Center, the United States Pavilion, the Texas Pavilion and others.

UNITED STATES PAVILION

The United States Pavilion at Hemis-Fair consisted of two buildings: an exhibit hall and a 1,200-seat theater. In the exhibit hall were exhibits showing the people of the United States and their achievements. Across a connecting plaza, the theater showed a unique film on the largest cur-vilinear motion-picture screen in the world. The circular theater contained three sepa-rate sections. During the 23-minute film, the walls separating the sections were raised so that the three audiences merged into one. At the same time, the three separate motion pictures merged into one.

TOWER OF THE AMERICAS

The dominant structure at HemisFair was the Tower of the Americas. This 622-foot concrete tower has a rotating restau-rant and observation decks at the top. The Tower of the Americas is the tallest obser-vation tower in the Western Hemisphere. On a clear day visitors could see the hori-zon 90 miles away. Three glass-fronted elevators carried visitors to the top.

TEXAS PAVILION

The biggest exhibit building at Hemis-Fair was the Texas Pavilion, called the Institute of Texan Cultures. The building, which cost $10,000,000, contained exhibits showing the contributions made to Texas

HemisFair's hit show: "Les Poupées de Paris."

Split screens and live performers were part of HemisFair's Kino-Automat exhibit where the audience selected the plot by pushing buttons.

by pioneers from many lands. Each nationality group in Texas was represented by a separate area of exhibits. These exhibits included artifacts of all kinds, as well as pictures and sound, which presented the story of the founding and development of Texas. At the center of the Texas Pavilion, visitors could sit on the carpeted floor, and see above them, projected on nearly forty different screens, slides and movies about Texas' past, present and future.

Probably the most unique of HemisFair's exhibits was the Alexander Girard Folk Art Collection, a stunning display of over ten thousand dolls and other miniatures from countries all over the Western Hemisphere.

▶ FOREIGN EXHIBITS

Foreign exhibits at HemisFair were housed in a section called Las Plazas del Mundo—Plazas of the World. Canada, one of the large exhibitors, welcomed visitors with a display showing how Canadians live, how they are governed, and their country's place in the world. Spain displayed priceless art.

Other foreign exhibitors were Belgium, Bolivia, Colombia, France, Italy, Japan, Korea, Portugal, Panama, China, Thailand, Venezuela, Costa Rica, El Salvador, Guatemala, Honduras, Nicaragua, West Germany and Switzerland.

Mexico contributed a pavilion filled with valuable paintings and artifacts. One of the most popular attractions at HemisFair were the mariachis, who performed on a floating stage in a lagoon just outside the Mexican Pavilion.

Los Voladores de Papantla, the famous Flying Indians of Papantla, Mexico, thrilled HemisFair visitors with a daily reenactment of a 400-year-old ritual. The authentically costumed Indians performed a complete ceremony, climaxed by a rain dance performed on a 12-inch disk at the top of a 114-foot-high pole. At the end of the ceremony, four of the Indians descended from the pole, flying head down on ropes secured to their waists. The flyers made 32 turns around the pole, fanning out some thirty feet in a spectacular ritual defying death itself. The ceremony is one performed by the Totonac Indians today just as it was four hundred years ago.

▶ INDUSTRIAL PAVILIONS

The Radio Corporation of America sponsored an exhibit showing present and future use of computers as teaching aids for children. The exhibit included live demonstrations of children learning with the help of an advanced computer. A short distance away, International Business Machines showed how a computer can be connected to a loom to weave any design. Visitors drew any design they liked, and the computer commanded the loom to weave it.

The Coca-Cola Company Pavilion featured 120 puppets in a colorful and imaginative show enjoyed by children and adults alike. The Bell Telephone System sponsored a popular magic show. The Gulf Oil Corporation presented a miniature freeway where drivers could test their skills safely. General Motors, the Ford Motor Company, the Eastman Kodak Company and many other industrial exhibitors participated in HemisFair.

▶ THE FAIRGROUNDS

HemisFair was designed for people, and the walking distances from any one point of the grounds to any other point were short. "People expressways" shortened distances and made walking easier. Those who wished to ride could choose a sky-ride or a miniature monorail. A lagoon and a waterway system ran throughout the grounds, and many visitors saw HemisFair from gondolas.

HemisFair was built in an old part of San Antonio. The builders of the fair decided to restore 27 old homes and historic buildings in the grounds rather than destroy them. Old houses became restaurants, clubs and visitor centers. And an old warehouse became an exhibit hall. A carriage house became a sidewalk restaurant, while an old school served as HemisFair headquarters. The old buildings, scattered throughout the HemisFair site, offered charm and contrast to the sleek new buildings all around. The grounds were enhanced by a waterway, which included a rerouted San Antonio River, and by twenty fountains of all kinds and sizes. Sculptures, more than a hundred of them, dotted the grounds. They represented artists both recognized and new, and works in every mode from plastic to welded steel.

Food at HemisFair ranged from traditional hot dogs to exotic dishes from all corners of the world. A Mexican restaurant, two French restaurants, a Polynesian restaurant, a Philippine restaurant and many others offered food at every price and to every taste.

▶ PROUD SAN ANTONIO

World's fairs seldom produce any profit, and HemisFair closed at a loss. The underwriters of the loans used by HemisFair had to pay for the losses, but they did so gladly, because HemisFair had brought 6,384,482 people to San Antonio, and they spent $134,000,000 in San Antonio alone. But more important than the money was the fact that HemisFair did start San Antonio moving ahead, and it did focus new attention on a proud old city, and that is exactly what the supporters of the fair hoped for.

HENRY B. GONZALEZ
United States House of Representatives

WEST INDIES

THERE is no common name for the islands of the Caribbean. This indicates the great diversity of the region. West Indies, the term most widely used, and the Antilles are geographical expressions, not the names of countries. Variety and contrast are the chief characteristics of this geographical area. There are cultural, racial and political differences because for most of their history the islands were tied to different European powers.

▶ THE NORTH AMERICAN PRESENCE

Notwithstanding these differences, events of 1968 pointed to certain general trends. One of the most significant was the continued growth of the North American presence in countries that up to recently were European colonies. Clearly, the influence of the United States and Canada is gaining strength at the expense of Britain and, to a lesser extent, Holland.

The flocks of North American visitors and the flow of North American investment prove the trend. Jet planes and industrial plants have made the Commonwealth Caribbean a part of the North American coastline. Sparkling seas and sunlit beaches lie almost on the doorstep of the commuter in New York, Chicago and Toronto. In 1967 350,000 visitors contributed almost 10 per cent of Jamaica's income. In the Netherlands Antilles, 700 miles to the south, the island of Aruba reported that the total number of nights spent in deluxe hotels by tourists increased by 23 per cent. Sun and sea, natural beauty and an excellent climate may yet be the most important resources of the West Indies, outlasting the wasting bauxite of Jamaica and the diminishing oil of Trinidad and Tobago.

The story is not all tourism. In almost every country of the Commonwealth Caribbean, members of the Peace Corps and the Canadian University Service Overseas were at work during 1968. So was the North American taxpayer's dollar. An example was the announcement in January by the Canadian Government that it would put $5,000,000 into a five-year program aimed at improving airports in the eastern

Sun, sea and sand may yet be the most important resources of the West Indies.

Caribbean. This was the first step in a long-range aid program based on a survey by a team of advisers from Britain, Canada and the United States. The report emphasized that tourism could become the main support of many of the islands. Canada has already taken over some of Britain's responsibilities for aid. In 1967–68, Canada's grants to the Commonwealth Caribbean countries amounted to over $17,000,000.

▶ DEVALUATION OF THE POUND STERLING

Despite the increased North American presence, Britain remained a strong trading partner of the Commonwealth Caribbean countries. It sustained the economies of the islands with a system of preferential tariffs for agricultural products, especially sugar. The United States, however, displaced Britain as Jamaica's chief market. Bauxite and alumina exports to the United States and Canada brought this about.

It was significant that as soon as Britain devalued the pound sterling late in 1967, Jamaica and the other West Indian islands followed suit. They had to. There were, however, two exceptions: the Bahamas and the British Virgin Islands. The Bahamas have a very small nondollar trade. And the British Virgin Islands use the United States dollar as their currency. Had the other English-speaking islands not devalued, they would have lost heavily on their sales of sugar to the United Kingdom. In addition, remittances from West Indians living in Britain would have been sharply reduced in value. There was an added benefit from devaluation. Tourists found that the purchasing power of the United States and Canadian dollars was increased.

▶ INVESTMENT AND INDUSTRIALIZATION

During 1968, North American investment increased steadily. In Jamaica, Alcan Jamaica Ltd., a subsidiary of Aluminum Limited of Canada, announced that by 1969 it would increase alumina production from 815,000 to 1,100,000 long tons. Three bauxite companies, Anaconda, Kai-

Almost every island in the West Indies is overcrowded and has a very high birthrate.

ser and Reynolds, began work on a new alumina plant, the island's third. A $27,000,000 caustic-soda plant was being built. When fully completed it will be one of the largest of the kind in the world. New hotels, including one by Hilton International, were planned or being built in Tobago.

In the Netherlands Antilles the economic structure has changed. In the 1950's the oil refineries had carried the economy. These have now been automated. To pro-

	HEADS OF GOVERNMENT	POPULATION
Barbados	ERROL W. BARROW, prime minister	300,000
Haiti	FRANÇOIS DUVALIER, president	4,700,000
Jamaica	HUGH SHEARER, prime minister	1,900,000
Trinidad and Tobago	ERIC WILLIAMS, prime minister	1,100,000

	STATUS	POPULATION
Antigua	British associated state	62,000
Bahama Islands	Self-governing British colony	145,000
Bermuda	Self-governing British colony	52,000
British Virgin Islands	British colony	9,000
Dominica	British associated state	70,000
Grenada	British associated state	98,000
Guadeloupe	French overseas department	321,000
Martinique	French overseas department	331,000
Montserrat	British colony	14,000
Netherlands Antilles	Netherlands overseas constituent	211,000
Puerto Rico	U.S. commonwealth	2,800,000
St. Kitts-Nevis-Anguilla	British associated state	62,000
St. Lucia	British associated state	105,000
St. Vincent	British colony	91,000
Turks and Caicos Islands	British colony	6,300
U.S. Virgin Islands	U.S. organized	52,000

vide alternative employment, the Government has promoted tourism, improved harbors and airports and built new hotels. In a few years the tourism percentage of the national product rose from 4 per cent to 12 per cent. By 1969 the Netherlands Antilles will have 1,200 hotel rooms. A growing tourist industry means sight-seeing organizations, taxis, guesthouses, schools for training hotel personnel and the like. In addition, new industries have been promoted. Aruba has a water-desalting plant and chemical factories. And the United States Silitron Company made plans to enter into the electronic industry.

There were also signs of more American investment in the French Antilles. In September it was announced that a United States firm would build a fertilizer complex in Martinique and would export its products to other Caribbean countries.

▶ POPULATION PRESSURES

Another West Indian trend in 1968 was the growing concern of governments about overpopulation. Almost all of the islands are overcrowded. They have birthrates that range from Jamaica's 29 per 1,000 to Trinidad's 40 per 1,000. In 1968 a Puerto Rican was born every seven minutes, a Barbadian every nine minutes.

Puerto Rico, however, has two advantages: it is industrialized and it is part of the United States. It could thus siphon off its surplus population into North America. The English-speaking islands exported large numbers of skilled and semiskilled people to Britain in the 1950's. However, recent British legislation reduced the flow of West Indian immigrants. As a result, many governments set up birth-control clinics and supported family planning. This had been attempted before—by the colonial governments. But such plans had met with little success. This was partly because of opposition from the Catholic Church. Also, many people felt that birth control was a plan to kill black people. In 1968, however, black intellectuals and politicians led the attack on the high birthrate.

▶ CARIBBEAN FREE TRADE AREA

The Caribbean Free Trade Area (CARIFTA) first came into being on December

30, 1966. The agreement provided for the gradual elimination of trade quotas and tariffs between the three signatory states: Antigua, Barbados and Guyana. In 1968, CARIFTA was expanded to include many other islands of the West Indies. These are Trinidad and Tobago, St. Kitts-Nevis-Anguilla, St. Lucia, St. Vincent, Jamaica, Dominica, Grenada and Montserrat. British Honduras (Belize) is also expected to ratify the CARIFTA agreements.

With its expanded membership, CARIFTA, hopefully, will foster increased and diversified trade in the area. Some regulations of the agreement appear to imply that CARIFTA would lead at some time to a common market.

▶ **POLITICAL DEVELOPMENTS**

During 1968, political activity in the West Indies was dominated by elections in the Bahamas, Bermuda, the Dominican Republic and Puerto Rico as well as by an ill-fated attempt by Haitian exiles to invade their homeland.

Bahamas

On April 10, Lynden O. Pindling, the 38-year-old prime minister of the Bahamas, won an overwhelming victory at the polls. His Progressive Liberal Party won 29 of the 38 seats in the House of Assembly. The predominantly white United Bahamian Party won only 7 seats. This election seemed to mark the end of white domination in the Bahamas. Though most Bahamians favor this, many whites, especially businessmen, fear that Pindling will demand independence from Great Britain, a move, they say, which could result in economic chaos.

Bermuda

Against a background of racial tension and civil disturbances, the predominantly white United Bermuda Party won a surprise victory over the Left-Wing Progressive Labor Party. Walter Robinson, leader of the Progressive Labor Party, had campaigned on a platform of independence and an end to British rule. The United Bermuda Party, led by Sir Henry Tucker, won 30 of the 40 seats in the House of Assembly. This was seen as strong support for continuation of British rule.

Dominican Republic

In local elections for 77 mayoralties and 488 City Council seats, President Joaquin Balaguer's Reformist Party won handily. These results were interpreted as support and enthusiasm for the modest but important economic gains which have been made in the country since Balaguer won the presidential elections the year after the 1965 revolution.

Puerto Rico

After ruling Puerto Rico for 28 years, the Popular Democratic Party, under the leadership of Luis Muñoz Marin, was turned out of office. The winner in the November 5 elections was Louis Ferre, leader of the New Progressive Party and a strong advocate of statehood for Puerto Rico. He defeated Muñoz Marin's hand-picked candidate, Luis Negron Lopez, for the governorship. Mr. Ferre, a millionaire industrialist, stated that he will hold a new referendum in two years so that the people of Puerto Rico can vote on whether they want statehood or independence. Puerto Rico now enjoys a commonwealth status, which Governor Ferre calls a "transitory condition."

Haiti

On May 20 a relatively small force of Haitian exiles invaded their homeland. They made an unsuccessful attempt to bomb the palace of Haitian dictator François Duvalier. Most of the invaders were killed or captured. A dozen of those captured were placed on trial. President Duvalier used the event to picture Haiti as being the victim of an international conspiracy led by Britain and the United States.

PHILIP M. SHERLOCK
Vice-Chancellor
University of the West Indies

dictionary

supplement

By Bruce Bohle

A

aerobics *noun.* A program of exercises designed to promote physical fitness developed by Major Kenneth H. Cooper of the U.S. Air Force Medical Corps.

Amphibex *acronym.* Amphibious exercise.

AstroTurf (*trademark*) *noun.* Synthetic turf, or sod, made of nylon and with a high degree of resistance to hard wear. It is used both for home lawns and in sports, in stadiums housing baseball and football, on tennis courts, and on tees and greens of golf courses. The Astrodome in Houston, Texas, was the first major stadium to use it.

B

ball game. *Informal.* A competition of any kind, but often applied to a political race in the expression "new ball game" to signify the sudden appearance of open or renewed competition due to change of circumstances, where lack of competition, or one-sidedness, had seemed earlier to make the outcome a foregone conclusion.

bantam *noun.* A small grocery store that carries a limited stock made up principally of essential items having a rapid turnover. Such stores often operate during off-hours of supermarkets.

be-in *noun. Slang.* A planned happening or event devoted to activity by hippies or other nonconformists.

Ben Franklin glasses. *Slang.* Spectacles with square or rectangular lenses and a steel frame.

Bingo. A radio call used by an aircraft to report that its fuel supply is running low.

biodegradation *noun.* The purification of polluted water through the action of appropriate bacteria.

biosonar *noun.* In medicine a device for examining, by means of echo sounding, the internal organs of the human body.

bird *noun. Slang.* 1. An airplane that operates from an aircraft carrier; sometimes also a land-based military plane. 2. A missile.

bleeding heart. *Slang.* A person who shows strong liberal sympathies, especially with respect to civil rights, individual rights of the criminally accused, and the like. (So called, contemptuously, by a person whose sympathies are otherwise.)

blow one's mind (also **bend one's mind, break one's mind**). *Slang.* 1. To have a mental experience induced by a psychedelic drug. 2. To rid oneself of inhibitions related to conventional conduct and morality, sometimes with the aid of a narcotic; thus, to destroy temporarily one's conventional mind.

bolter *verb intr. Slang.* To miss the arresting cables on the flight deck of an aircraft carrier in unsuccessfully attempting to land a carrier-based plane. (Said of the pilot of such a plane.)

bombed *adj. Slang.* Stuporous as a result of indulging in alcohol or narcotics.

bug out. *Slang.* To depart.

C

cable television (also **community antenna television, CATV**). A system of subscription television in which broadcast signals are transmitted through a coaxial cable, rather than directly over the air, into the sets of subscribers. The programs presented are usually selected from standard broadcasting and relayed by special means to subcribers, who pay a fee for installation and a monthly charge for viewing. Installation consists of connecting the master cable to subscribers' receiving sets, which are conventional models. Such systems operate privately under franchises granted by the municipalities they serve. In general they offer a greater selection of programing than nonsubscription television, since they provide not only the local channels of the communities they serve but also the offerings of stations too far distant to be received with the facilities of nonsubscription television. In some cases the broadcast fare includes programs originated by operators of the system. A typical cable-television system employs a large main antenna, which is erected on a site in or near the community and so constructed as to receive distant signals with the help of microwave receiving stations located at intervals between the points of transmission and the main antenna. The antenna in turn directs the signals into a central station, which tunes and amplifies them before they are passed into the cable. The cable, located underground or strung on poles, is equipped with amplifiers to maintain the strength of the signals. The cable usually is constructed to accommodate up to twenty channels.

carotatoxin *noun.* An oxygenated hydrocarbon chemically akin to acetylene and naturally present in small amounts in carrots and celery. In pure form it is very toxic.

CAT *acronym.* Clear-air turbulence, an atmospheric condition that menaces air navigation because it cannot be foreseen or predicted.

cheap shot. *Slang.* 1. In sports, any unfair or unsportsmanlike conduct. 2. Specifically in football, an unnecessarily rough and often illegal act, as in blocking or tackling, especially after the whistle has blown to signify the end of an individual play from scrimmage.

Chemical Mace. A compound used in the form of a spray as a temporary disabling weapon, especially in controlling rioters.

chutzpah *noun.* Effrontery; audacity; impudence.

cinematheque *noun.* A nightclub that offers motion pictures together with food and drink.

Colidar *acronym.* Coherent-light radar, a ranging device.

Comsymp *acronym. Slang.* Communist sympathizer: a term of reproach.

cornerman (also **corner man**) *noun.* In basketball, a forward.

coydog *noun.* A predatory animal produced by the breeding of a coyote and a wild dog. It is about the size of a small coyote.

cryobiology *noun.* Biology in relation to the effects of chilling or freezing on living matter.

current art. *Informal.* Artistic representations, collectively, that employ specially designed artificial light in some significant way: to illuminate sculptured objects, to help create an object in space, or to create an image or abstract impression as by reflection on a wall or screen.

D

Dancercise (*trademark*) *noun.* A system of physical exercise for women that incorporates the movements of popular dance steps.

demographic edition. An edition of a publication intended for distribution to only a certain category of its subscribers.

dimethyl sulfoxide (also **DMSO**). A chemical compound derived from the lignin in wood. It is used as a solvent; for a wide variety of medical purposes, including treatment of inflammation, burns, strains, and sprains; and as an aid in promoting the growth of certain plants.

disco *noun. Slang.* A discotheque.

ditty bob. *Slang.* A Negro whose behavior is embarrassing to other Negroes: a term of contempt applied by a Negro.

domino theory. The premise or assumption that the fall of one neutral country to communist encroachment automatically leads, or tends to lead, to a progression of communist conquest, just as the fall of one domino standing on edge in a line of dominoes leads to the fall of its neighbor and so produces a chain reaction. The theory is applied especially to Southeast Asian politics.

driver *noun. Slang.* The pilot of an airplane based on an aircraft carrier.

dropout *noun. Slang.* 1. A person who withdraws from society (usually applied to hippies). 2. A person who leaves school (usually high school) before graduating.

dynametropolis *noun.* A large and dynamic city, especially one that exhibits great diversity and complexity.

dynapolis *noun.* A dynamic city; a city that exhibits continuous change, especially with respect to growth.

dystopia *noun.* An evil place: in contrast with utopia.

E

ecumenopolis *noun.* A city of the future that will cover the whole earth as a single, universal settlement.

electro-hydronic heating. Hot-water space heating that employs a number of separate units, each of which has an independent electric heating element.

electronic range. A range for home use that is employed in microwave cooking (which see). It usually comprises a conventional electric range, with broiler and surface units, and an electronic oven. The oven generally permits cooking by conventional means, by microwave or by a combination of the two.

entopia *noun.* Any place that is practicable in the sense of being capable of existence.

F

fallout *noun.* 1. By-products, considered collectively. 2. *Slang.* Consequences, usually unfortunate, that follow a major development; aftereffects.

fetology *noun.* A branch of medical science concerned with the care and treatment of the human fetus, or unborn child in the womb.

fleshprinting *noun.* An electronic process, employing electrophoresis, by means of which the protein makeup of fish is determined chemically.

flower child. *Slang.* A hippie. (Usually in the plural; as such, also **flower people, love children**.)

found object. A manufactured object, such as a shovel, discarded tin can, or refrigerator shelf, usually selected from a junkyard and mounted for artistic display, independently as an artifact of civilization or as part of a work of sculpture.

freak out (also **freak, freak freely**). *Slang.* 1. To have an emotional experience, usually one induced by a psychedelic drug and marked by the absence of conventional inhibitions with respect to behavior. Drug users often regard the experience as the achievement of individuality and freedom to be oneself, unchecked by fear of adverse reaction from others. 2. To divest oneself of responsibility. 3. To behave in a seemingly irrational way, without reference to narcotics. (Also used as a noun: **freakout** or **freak-out:** an instance of such experience or behavior.)

freedom school. A school for American Negro children in areas where public education is not operated on a wholly integrated basis.

Frescan (*trademark*) *noun.* A U.S. Navy electronic-scanning radar system.

Frescanar (*trademark*) *noun.* A U.S. Army air-defense radar system.

G

glue sniffing. The practice of inhaling the fumes of certain types of glue for its intoxicating effect.

granny glasses. *Slang.* Spectacles that have round, rectangular or octagonal lenses and a plain steel frame.

gun barrel. *Slang.* The launch tube used in firing a missile.

guru *noun. Slang.* A teacher, spiritual leader, or mentor, especially of members of the fashionable young set. (After "guru": an East Indian teacher or religious counselor.)

guru jacket. See **Nehru jacket.**

H

hangup (also **hang-up**) *noun. Informal.* 1. An emotional problem or anxiety, often considered the result of an inhibition or a repression. 2. Any problem, difficulty or dilemma. 3. An obstruction to a settlement; a dispute that prevents action; a delay; a deadlock.

head *noun. Slang.* A person who is addicted to a drug, often to a psychedelic drug. (Frequently used in combinations: **acidhead,** referring to a user of LSD 25; **pothead,** referring to a user of marijuana.)

heart transplant. See **transplant.**

heliox *acronym.* A mixture of helium and oxygen.

high binder. *Slang.* A politician who is influential, though dishonest.

Huff-Duff *acronym.* High-frequency direction finder.

I

ideopolis *noun.* A group of related universities, or a single large university comprising several divisions, which works in conjunction with other educational institutions, such as research centers.

Incaparina (*trademark*) *noun.* A vegetable mixture, especially rich in protein, used in baking and cooking and as an ingredient in beverages. It has been used widely in underdeveloped areas of Latin America.

Institute for Defense Analyses (IDA). A U.S. government-sponsored organization, made up of independent affiliates, which performs research and analysis relating to national defense and riot control. American universities are among the participating affiliates.

intermedia (also **multimedia, mixed media**) *noun.* A form of stage production that combines one or more of the traditional art forms with technological by-products, usually with the expressed purpose of creating "total theater." The principal ingredients presented in various combinations, often simultaneously, are music, dance, drama, painting, sculpture, recited poetry, and film. The artistic montage thus produced also employs any or all of the following: electronically amplified music, special sound effects, video tape, diffracted light, and unusual staging. Often the staging brings the audience into the performing area.

J

jet set. *Informal.* A group of international celebrities who regularly frequent fashionable resorts.

JOBS *acronym.* Job Opportunities in the Business Sector, a program designed to provide training and employment in private industry for the hardcore American unemployed, organized by the National Alliance of Businessmen at the request of the Federal Government. The program, jointly financed by the Government and NAB, also sought to provide summer employment for youths.

join the waxworks. *Slang.* To sit on a dais, especially at a public gathering of some importance. (Said especially of a politician.)

jumboize *verb tr.* To enlarge a ship, especially a tanker, usually either by inserting a newly built midsection between the bow and stern of an existing vessel or by joining a new fore-section to the stern of an existing ship.

jump-jet *noun.* 1. A jet airplane of the VTOL (vertical take-off and landing) type. 2. Any short-range jet airplane.

K

kicker rocket. In space exploration an auxiliary rocket that supplements a satellite's booster rocket. It is used in orbiting the satellite when the booster rocket alone cannot accomplish this task.

kinetic sculpture. A mobile, or mobiles considered collectively.

knob *noun. Informal.* A rounded, bony protuberance developed on the leg or foot of a surfer as a result of riding a surfboard while kneeling. Such growths are usually located on the forward part of the leg, shortly below the knee, or on the instep between the toes and ankle. (Usually in the plural.)

kuru *noun.* A disease of the central nervous system, usually fatal and marked by degeneration of the cerebellum, or a part of the hindbrain, and loss of muscular control. It has especially afflicted groups of primitive people of New Guinea.

L

LAMP *acronym.* Labor and Management Plan, a project for voluntary mediation of labor disputes, operative in several large American cities. The project works outside the framework of Federal and state mediation services; it operates on a local level in each instance, by involving the services of residents of each city involved.

LASH *acronym.* Lighter aboard ship: usually employed as an attributive adjective in combinations such as **LASH freighter** and **LASH vessel,** terms for merchant ships carrying barges or lighters that can be loaded and unloaded independently of the ship itself. Upon reaching a destination, such ships can discharge their cargo-filled barges or lighters, take on a new cargo load in identical prestowed barges or lighters, and set sail before the original cargo is unloaded onshore in that destination. Delays in port for loading and unloading are thus eliminated.

lidar *acronym.* Radar equipment that employs laser beams.

linecasting machine. A typesetting machine that is activated and fed by a perforated tape produced earlier by means of a computer. The machine is employed principally by large daily newspapers, and operates much more rapidly than a Linotype.

linkup (also **link-up**) *noun.* The joining, or linking, in orbital flight of two or more spacecraft launched independently and traveling independently prior to their coming together.

M

Mace. See **Chemical Mace.**

mail cover. Governmental surveillance of an individual, such as a suspect in a case involving national security or a violation of Federal law, that takes the form of scrutiny of mail sent and received by him. Usually such scrutiny involves merely noting the names of correspondents and such other information as can be gleaned from inspection of envelopes or wrappers.

make waves. *Slang.* To be active, forceful or obtrusive, especially in circumstances that call for prudence, restraint or even inaction.

maxiskirt. A skirt or dress that reaches the ankle.

meditation shirt. A one-piece dress with a short skirt, flared sleeves that extend to the midpoint of the forearms, and a high, close-fitting collar. It is worn alone or as a pants top.

member (also **club member**). *noun. Slang.* A fellow Negro.

microwave cooking. A form of cooking, employing an electronic oven, in which microwave energy penetrates the food, causing molecules to vibrate against one another so rapidly that they create the heat necessary for cooking. The heat thus originates inside the food instead of penetrating from outside, as in conventional roasting or baking. In general, microwave cooking is a much faster process than conventional cooking.

midiskirt *noun*. A skirt that reaches approximately to mid-calf.

military-industrial complex. The professional military and the aggregate of arms and munitions makers in the United States, considered collectively and, usually, as a special-interest group with great influence on American policymaking on the highest levels of government.

MIRV *acronym*. Multiple Independently targeted Reentry Vehicle: used principally as an attributive adjective, as in **MIRV warhead** (of a nuclear missile).

Mobot *acronym*. A mobile robot.

multimedia. See **intermedia.**

N

Nehru jacket (also **guru jacket**). A jacket patterned on the dress of Jawaharlal Nehru of India, and worn principally by young men and women. Its length usually extends to the mid-area of the thigh; the shoulders are angular, the skirt rather full, and the middle area of the sides constricted. The sleeves are full-length, and buttons are arranged along the single-breasted front from just below the collar, which is high, circular and close-fitting, to a point slightly below the waist.

New Left. A loose-knit association of Americans dedicated to an economic and political philosophy considerably to the left of that associated with liberalism, and dominated largely by college students, including Students for a Democratic Society, and intellectuals. The membership was active in opposing the war in Vietnam and military conscription in the United States, and sought to promote the civil-rights movement in the United States.

New Politics. 1. Politics actively involving a broad range of interested private citizens, including young people, rather than a relatively small number of professionals, and employing techniques and operating procedures not limited to, and often at variance with, those of traditional American practical politics. The campaign of Eugene McCarthy for the Democratic presidential nomination in 1968 is an example of New Politics in this broad sense. 2. Politics in which modern, highly sophisticated technology is used in an attempt to gain desired ends, and in which many older techniques identified with American traditional politics are subordinated or abandoned. The new system usually employs professional political-management firms, which organize and conduct well-financed campaigns based on a scientific appeal for votes, using data processed by computers; specially conducted polls for gaining specific information used in the campaigns; direct-mail appeals to special-interest groups determined by computers; the services of advertising and public-relations agencies; and extensive time on commercial television. Often inherent in this form of New Politics is the "creation" and presentation of a candidate, such as a successful actor or businessman, whose background is essentially non-political.

NLF *abbreviation*. National Liberation Front, the political arm of the Vietcong of South Vietnam.

O

oceanaut *noun*. An aquanaut or diver who lives and works on the floor of the ocean for extended periods.

P

pacification *noun*. In the war in Vietnam, an American program designed to make the South Vietnamese countryside secure, area by area, after it is brought under military control. The program includes clearing the area of Vietcong; making it impervious to attack or subversion; instituting civil reforms and social measures designed to improve the lot of the residents; and in general seeking to win the loyalty of the people to the national Government of South Vietnam.

pad *noun*. *Slang*. Living quarters; sometimes, short-term accommodations.

paramedical *adj*. Related to medicine, considered as a branch of knowledge and practice, but not a constituent part of medicine.

pass-along readership. That part of the public that can be presumed to read, or at least to have access to, a publication but is not among the subscribers to the given publication.

penalty killer. In ice hockey a player used especially when his team is shorthanded; that is, when one or more teammates are serving penalties.

pill, the *noun*. *Informal*. An oral contraceptive.

plastic *noun*. *Slang*. A person said to be devoted to synthetic values; generally one who lives and works in accordance with the conventional values of society for the most part, and compensates for this by being unconventional in off-hours. Sometimes, one who professes to hold unconventional views at variance with his own well-established position in society. The term is often used in combination: **plastic hippie,** a middle-class, suburban boy or girl who joins a hippie community on weekends; **plastic liberal,** one whose liberalism is more fashionable talk than a reflection of his way of making a living or of conducting his own life.

play out an option. In American professional football or basketball, to play a season for a team after the expiration of one's contract. When a player is unable to come to terms with the team that owns his services, in renewing a contract, or is otherwise dissatisfied with his present situation, he may notify the team of his intention not to sign a new contract. Under existing rules, he must then play an additional season for that team, which has an option on his services for such a one-year period by terms of the expired contract. At the end of that period, he is free to sign with any team in his league. If he elects to sign a contract with a team other than his original one, the team with which he signs must make acceptable reimbursement to the original team.

power play. In ice hockey an attempt by a team to score when it has a manpower advantage as a result of a penalty incurred by an opposition player.

provo *noun*. *Informal*. A youthful activist, typically in a large city, who rebels against the prevailing social and political order.

psychedelic art. Artistic expression, especially abstract painting, whose bizarre and very stylized pictorial quality is intended to suggest the product of a mind under the powerful influence of a hallucinatory drug. Sometimes also painting on the human torso.

Q

quantum jump. An advantage accruing from a rapid change.

R

rap *verb intr. Slang.* To talk.

ratfink *noun. Slang.* A person who is mean or contemptible; especially, one who informs on another or others.

raunchy *adj. Informal.* 1. Unclean; unhygienic. 2. Lustful.

Resurrection City. A temporary community of poor Americans in Washington, D. C., inhabited by persons who participated in the Poor People's Campaign of 1968. The settlement served as a base for the poor who marched to Washington to petition the Federal Government for relief from poverty in the United States.

S

Scanfar *(trademark) noun.* A U.S. Navy electronic-scanning radar system.

scene *noun. Slang.* The center of activity; place where things occur. Often used in **to make the scene:** to be present in such a place as a participant, usually in a fashionable activity.

Sceptron *acronym.* Spectral comparative pattern recognizer.

seeker *noun. Slang.* A person who professes devotion to the cause of finding beatitude, truth or self-expression, and who withdraws from conventional society and frequently becomes a mystic or a member of a communal group such as a hippie colony.

shootout *noun. Slang.* A gunfight.

sidewinder *noun. Slang.* A low blow, especially one struck, verbally, in a political context.

simolivac *noun.* The frothy-textured top surface of rock produced when lava emerges and cools in a vacuum, as on the moon.

skyjack *verb tr. Slang.* To hijack (an airplane).

sniffer *noun. Informal.* An electronic odor-sensing device used to detect the presence of human beings by the scent emanating from them. The machine was used by American troops in Vietnam to locate enemy guerrilla forces.

soft loan. A sum of money lent by one country to another with the provision that it be repaid on easy terms in the currency of the borrower rather than that of the lender.

soul *adj. Slang.* Of or pertaining to Negroes, their culture, institutions and the like.

space yield. The profitableness of one square foot of space accessible to customers in a supermarket.

special team. In football, especially professional football, one of several combinations of players employed as a unit in specific situations: at kickoffs; when field goals or conversions are attempted; and for punting (and returning punts). A special team usually functions for both offensive and defensive sides on such occasions, made up of men specially trained for the jobs involved.

splashdown *noun.* In space travel, the landing in water of a manned craft.

stem winder. *Slang.* A stirring speech, especially a political speech.

STOL *acronym.* Short takeoff and landing. Generally used as an attributive adjective in combinations: **STOL plane,** one with large wing surfaces and flaps that permit taking off and landing at low speeds; **STOL strip,** an airstrip for such a plane.

STOLport *noun.* An airport for craft constructed on the principle of short takeoff and landing.

Students for a Democratic Society (SDS). A nationwide organization of American college students with chapters in more than 100 schools by the late 1960's. Left-Wing in orientation and philosophy, it sought actively and sometimes violently to give students a greater voice in formulating and administering policies of the schools (and thus to achieve the goal of "participatory democracy") and to make the schools responsive to the problems of the communities in which they are located. Members also were active in the civil-rights movement in the United States, and in opposing military conscription there as part of an effort to end American involvement in the war in Vietnam.

superette *noun.* A retail food store that is organized and operated like a supermarket but is much smaller than a supermarket.

surface *verb intr. Informal.* To come to the surface, specifically, to one's attention; to emerge from hiding, obscurity, neglect, or from the state of being misplaced.

Syncom *acronym.* A synchronous communications satellite.

T

take him on the mountaintop. *Slang.* To make a promise (to someone), especially a political promise.

TEMPO *acronym.* Transportation, Employment, and Manpower Provide Opportunity, a federally financed experimental project for transporting residents of the central areas of large cities to jobs located outside or near the city limits.

tokenism *noun.* The granting of partial (token) recognition to a person or persons, such as Negroes aspiring to full civil rights; partial fulfillment of a pledge, such as a promise of genuine equality. (Used principally in American civil-rights parlance.)

top out. In high-altitude flying, to level off after reaching a peak altitude.

transplant *noun.* The surgical implanting of a bodily organ or gland, such as a heart, lung or pancreas, in a human being whose own corresponding organ or gland is defective; or a similar operation involving animals. In most operations involving persons, the implanted part comes from another human being. The part thus transplanted is taken from a recently deceased person, with legal approval, and kept in functioning condition by mechanical means, such as a respirator, in the interval between death of the donor and implant in the patient.

tuned-in *adj. Slang.* Keenly aware of, and responsive to, one's social and intellectual environment or milieu.

U

underground film. A motion picture produced with a small budget, and generally involving a director, technicians and actors who are virtually unknown or little known in the commercial cinema. Such a film is typically shown in a small, out-of-the-way theater. It is usually highly unconventional also in its choice of subject or theme, which is typically offbeat and sometimes taboo by commercial-motion-picture standards, or which is detailed more frankly or explicitly than the standard of commercial films permits; and it is often even more unconventional in its development of the theme through stress on artistic techniques unlike those employed in straightforward narrative.

uptight *adj. Informal.* 1. Conforming rigidly to conventional values, especially with respect to morality, law and order, and social responsibility; eminently respectable (though a person to whom the term is applied is often regarded with a certain contempt by users of the word in this sense). 2. Showing anxiety or concern about something. 3. Emotionally taut; tense; manifesting hostility. (Also used as a noun: a person showing such qualities.)

V

Vaicom *acronym.* Variable Image Compositor, a system used by police for making a facial sketch of a suspect from a description given by a victim or witness. It employs projected slides of various facial features to form an image, which is then photographed and copied.

vest-pocket park. A small, public park, usually in a congested urban area.

VTOL. See **jump-jet.**

W

whale *noun. Slang.* A twin-jet plane that operates from an aircraft carrier and is capable of carrying nuclear or conventional weapons and of serving as an airborne tanker, or plane employed for refueling others in flight.

whitelist *verb tr. Informal.* To mark down in a list those white persons considered unfair to Negroes and to refuse them support, commercial patronage or the like. As a noun, such a list of persons. (After "blacklist.")

Willie Fudd. *Slang.* A propeller-driven radar plane attached to an aircraft carrier.

Y

yippie *noun. Slang.* 1. (cap.) A member of the Youth International Party, which actively opposed American foreign policy, especially with relation to involvement in Southeast Asia. 2. (lower case) Any youthful and militant American activist who seeks confrontation with the establishment as a means of expressing strong disapproval of American policy, especially with respect to foreign affairs and race relations. Such persons are often affiliated with overtly nonconformist groups such as hippies or associations of radical students.

Index

A

Abdullah, Mohammed 106
Abernathy, Ralph D. 61, 371, picture 371
Aborigines, Australia, with picture 113
Abrams, Creighton W. 57, 104, 362, picture 363
Academy awards 181
Accessories 252–53, picture 253
Africa, with pictures 76–82
  government, heads of 81
   Mauritius, with map and picture 84–86
   Swaziland, with map and picture 87–89
  UN developments in 351
  See also names of countries

Agnew, Spiro T., was elected 39th vice-president of the United States on November 5, 1968. He was selected to be Richard Nixon's running mate at the Republican Convention on August 8, 1968. Agnew was born in Baltimore, Maryland, on November 9, 1918. He received his law degree from the University of Baltimore Law School. In 1966, after serving four years as Baltimore county executive, Agnew was elected governor of Maryland.
  See also 64, 70, 376, 381, pictures 374, 381

Agriculture, developments in, with pictures 90–95
  Latin American 215
  Soviet Union 197, picture 198
Airliners, with pictures 342–46
Airplanes
  model kits, with picture 206
Air pollution 136, 237
Airport congestion 345–46, pictures 343, 347
Air-traffic control 345–46, picture 343
Al-Amir, Hassan 245

Al-Badr, Imam Mohammed 245
Alcoholism
  Supreme Court decision 218
Alcott, Louisa May 223
Algeria 248
Alienation of youth 40
Alliance for Progress 365
Al-Shaabi, Qahtan 245–46
Alumina
  West Indies 392

Alvarez, Luis Walter, 57, physicist, was awarded the 1968 Nobel Prize in Physics for his work in the early 1960's on the physics of subatomic particles and their detection. Dr. Alvarez' work has been varied: he conceived X-raying the pyramid of Khafre to find hidden chambers; he devised a way of producing nuclear reactions without uranium or million-degree heat; and he designed the first bad-weather landing system for planes. Dr. Alvarez is senior physicist at the Lawrence Radiation Laboratory, at the University of California at Berkeley.

Amateur photography 271
Ambi look 252
American Ballet Theatre 177–78
American Film Institute 183
Amundsen, Roald 295

Anders, William Alison, astronaut, major, USAF, was the systems engineer on the Apollo 8 moon flight, December 21–27, 1968. In the Apollo program, Major Anders has prepared as a moon-landing-vehicle specialist. He was born on October 17, 1933, in Hong Kong, where his father, a naval officer, was stationed. In 1955 Anders graduated from the U.S. Naval Academy. He holds a master's degree in nuclear engineering from the Air Force Institute of Technology. Before joining the U.S. space program in 1963, Major

Anders piloted all-weather interceptors for the Air Defense Command.
See also 73, pictures 72, 304

Antarctica
discoveries, with pictures 294–301
Antarctic fossil, with picture 284–85
Anthropology
ancient human-bone fragments found 285
Antarctic fossil, with picture 284–85
Anti-Americanism
Latin America 215
Anti-Establishment 40
Anti-Semitism
Communist countries 280
Poland 32–33
Ants, with pictures 140–49
Apollo space program, with pictures 312–17
Apollo 8 mission 73, 303, 305, pictures 72, 302–04
Apollo 7 mission 68, 303, 305, pictures 305–06
Apportionment
Supreme Court decisions 220
Arab-Israel dispute 241–44, picture 243
Arab League 247
Arab nations
UN peace efforts 354
Architecture, with pictures 96–101
Arias, Arnulfo 59, 210, 211, 212
Armed forces
Asia 107
Europe 201
Middle East 247
Arno, Peter 53
Arnold, John D. 235
Arts
children's books about 227
dance, with pictures 177–79
glass, with pictures 261–65
HemisFair '68, 389
literature, with picture 224–25
music, with pictures 174–76
painting and sculpture, with pictures 256–60
psychedelic photography 267–68, 271, pictures 266–67
youth's influence on, 37, 44, picture 38
Asghar Khan, Mohammad 108
Ashe, Arthur, picture 320
Asia, with pictures 102–09
government, heads of 107
See also names of countries
Asian and Pacific Council 107
Assassinations
Kennedy, Robert F. 61, 366, 368, pictures 60, 365, 370
King, Martin Luther, Jr. 56, 61, 63, 366, pictures 57, 367
Association of Southeast Asia 107
Asteroid Icarus studies, with diagram, 291–92
Astronauts 68, 73, 303, 305, pictures 72, 304, 306, 307
lunar landing 317
Astronomy
Icarus, asteroid, studies of, with diagram, 291–92
pulsars 290–91
space 309
Atomic energy see **Nuclear energy**
Australia, with pictures 110–14
Gorton, John Grey 116–17, picture 115

Nauru 118–21
Authoritarianism, with picture 40
Autobiographies 225
Automation
farm machinery 92
Automobile racing 322
Automobiles
junk mountains, with picture 136
model kits 206
safety 235
sales 156, picture 155
Avedon, Richard 268
Aviation, with pictures 342–47
intercity travel, charts 348
Moscow–New York flights 195
Awards see **Prizes and awards**
Ayub Khan, Mohammad 108

B

Bahamas 394

Bailyn, Bernard, professor of history, was awarded the 1968 Pulitzer Prize for history for *The Ideological Origins of the American Revolution.* Bailyn was born in Hartford, Connecticut, on September 10, 1922, and received his doctorate from Harvard in 1953. He is now on the Harvard faculty. Bailyn has also written *The New England Merchants in the Seventeenth Century.*

Balance of payments 150–51
gold crisis 364–65
tourist deficit 343
Ball, George 352–53, 354
Ballet, with pictures 166–67, 177
Bankhead, Tallulah 73
Bankruptcy
Supreme Court decision 218
Banks and banking
gold crisis 55
Barnard, Christiaan N. 50
Barrett, Peter J. 284
Bartlett, E. L. 73, 379
Baseball 319, 323
Basketball 320, 324
Baunsgaard, Hilmar 193
Bauxite
West Indies 392
Beamon, Bob 332, picture 334
Beatles, photographic techniques used 268
Beef feeders 92–93
Bees, with pictures 140–49
Belaunde Terry, Fernando 211
Belgium 192–93
Beregovoi, Georgi T. picture 307
Bermuda 394
Bertrand, Jean-Jacques 124, picture 125
Biafra 59, 77–78, pictures 77–78
Bilingualism, in Canada 125
Biographies 225
Bird migration treaty 139
Birds
conservation 139

C

Cooke, Terence James, at 47 became spiritual leader of 1,900,000 Roman Catholics, when he was appointed archbishop of New York by Pope Paul VI in March 1968. He succeeded Francis Cardinal Spellman, who died in December 1967. Ordained in 1945, Cooke was the episcopal vicar for the Manhattan and Bronx parishes in New York City in 1966. At Christmastime 1968, Cooke, as the Vatican's military vicar in the United States, visited the U.S. armed forces in Vietnam.
See also 55, 57

Corey, Wendell, 54, stage and motion-picture actor, died on November 8, 1968. Corey appeared in *Rear Window, The Rainmaker* and *The Rack.* He was a former president of the Academy of Motion Picture Arts and Sciences.

Crumb, George, composer, was awarded the 1968 Pulitzer Prize for music for *Echoes of Time and the River.* The work was commissioned by the University of Chicago. Crumb was born in Charleston, West Virginia, on October 24, 1929, and has degrees from Mason College, the University of Illinois and the University of Michigan. Crumb presently teaches composition at the University of Pennsylvania. His other musical works include *Eleven Echoes of Autumn* and *Variozioni for Large Orchestra.*

F

Finch, Robert Hutchinson, lieutenant governor of California, was named U.S. secretary of health, education, and welfare by President-elect Nixon on December 11, 1968. Finch was born in Arizona on October 9, 1925. He received his law degree from the University of Southern California. In 1958 Finch was Vice-President Nixon's administrative assistant; in 1960 he managed Nixon's unsuccessful presidential campaign.
See *also* with picture 381

G

H

Hahn, Otto 63
Hail-prevention experiments 290
Hair, musical play 167, 170, picture 168
Hair styles 255, picture 253
Haiti 394
Hajek, Jiri 353–54
Handbag fashions 253
Handicrafts, with picture 207

Hardin, Clifford Morris, university administrator and farm economist, was named U.S. secretary of agriculture by President-elect Nixon on December 11, 1968. Hardin was born in Indiana on October 15, 1915. He received his doctorate in agricultural economics from Purdue. In 1954 he became chancellor of the University of Nebraska. Hardin edited *Overcoming World Hunger*, which deals with the threat of world famine.
    See also with picture 381

Harriman, W. Averell, with picture 361
Hassan, Ahmed 63
Health, with pictures 230–37
    livestock protection 94
Heart disease and surgery 233
Heart transplants 50, 230–34, 239, picture 230–31

Hecht, Anthony, poet, was awarded the 1968 Pulitzer Prize for poetry for *The Hard Hours*. Hecht was born in New York City in 1923. His first book, *A Summoning of Stones*, appeared in 1954 and was set to music as *A Choir of Starlings* by composer Leo Smits. In 1951 Hecht was given a literary fellowship by the American Academy in Rome. He presently teaches at the University of Rochester.

HemisFair '68, with pictures 386–89
Heredity
    chromosome abnormality linked to crime 285–86

Heymans, Corneille Jean François, 76, Belgian Nobel Prizewinner in 1938 for his work on the human respiratory and blood systems, died on July 18, 1968, in Knokke, Belgium. Heymans was director of the Institute of Pharmacodynamics and Therapeutics in Ghent, Belgium.

Hickel, Walter Joseph, governor of Alaska, was named U.S. secretary of the interior by President-elect Nixon on December 11, 1968. Hickel was born in Kansas on August 18, 1919. He went to Alaska when he was 20 years old and became a wealthy real-estate construction businessman. In 1966 Hickel was elected Alaska's first Republican governor. During the 1968 presidential campaign he was one of Nixon's campaign managers in the West.
    See also with picture 381

Highways 139
Hillary, Edmund 297
Hippie movement 37, 45, pictures 46
Hobbies, with pictures 206–07
    coins 205
    stamps, with pictures 202–04
Ho Chi Minh, picture 104

Hockey 319–20, 327
    Olympic Games, with picture 339
Hoffman, Dustin 180, picture 181
Hogs
    production developments 94
Holyoake, Keith 114
Holy Roman Empire tankard 265, picture 262
Hormones
    multiple births for cows, picture 93
Horse racing 321, 328, picture 329

Horton, Douglas, 77, Protestant church leader, former head of the Congregational Christian Churches (1938–55) and dean of the Harvard Divinity School (1955–59), died on August 21, 1968. The Reverend Dr. Horton was an ecumenical leader who was the International Congregational Council observer to the Vatican Ecumenical Council sessions (1962–65). He also was a founder of the World Council of Churches and the United Church of Christ.

Housing
    architectural design 100, picture 101
    Canada 126, 128, 130, picture 126
    consumer demand 156
    legislation 373
    Protestant involvement 279–80
    Supreme Court decision 218, 220
Human rights
    United Nations 351

Humphrey, Hubert Horatio, 38th vice-president of the United States, was defeated in his bid for the presidency of the U.S. by Richard M. Nixon. As the 1968 Democratic presidential candidate, Humphrey ran with Edmund S. Muskie. Humphrey was born in Wallace, South Dakota, on May 27, 1911. He received degrees from the Denver College of Pharmacy, the University of Minnesota and Louisiana State University. Humphrey taught at both LSU and at Macalester College in St. Paul. In 1945 he was elected mayor of Minneapolis. He was a U.S. Senator (1949–65) until tapped by Lyndon Johnson to be the Democratic vice-presidential candidate in the 1964 campaign. In the Senate, Humphrey served as majority whip (1961–64).
    See also 64–65, 70, 136, 359, 375, 377–80, picture 375

Hungarian Revolution 1956, 19–20, picture 20
Hungary 198

Hurst, Fanny, 78, novelist and short-story writer, died on February 23, 1968. She wrote *Back Street*, *Imitation of Life* and *Great Laughter*.
    See also 53

Hussein, King, Jordan 244

I

Icarus, asteroid, studies, with diagram, 291–92
Ice cores, Antarctica, with picture 300
Ice hockey see Hockey

J

Jamaica, West Indies 392

James, Howard, newspaper reporter, was awarded the 1968 Pulitzer Prize for national reporting for a series of articles, "Crisis in the Courts," in *The Christian Science Monitor*. James was born in Iowa City, Iowa, on May 28, 1935, and joined *The Monitor* as staff correspondent in 1964. He presently is chief of *The Monitor's* Midwest news bureau in Chicago.

K

Kadar, Janos 20, picture 21
Kantrowitz, Adrian 50, picture 230–31
Kashmir dispute 106

Kawabata, Yasunari, 69-year-old Japanese author, was awarded the 1968 Nobel Prize for Literature. He is Japan's first Nobelist writer. His episodic novels, *Snow Country* and the still-unfinished *The Thousand Cranes*, have been translated into eight languages including English.
  See also 69

Kennan, George F., was awarded the 1968 Pulitzer Prize for biography for his *Memoirs*. Kennan previously won the 1957 Pulitzer Prize for history for *Russia Leaves the War*. Born in Milwaukee on February 16, 1904, Kennan entered the foreign service in 1926. He served as U.S. ambassador to the Soviet Union (1952) and to Yugoslavia (1961–63). Since 1956 he has also been a professor at the Institute for Advanced Study, Princeton.

Kennedy, David Matthew, banker, was named U.S. secretary of the treasury by President-elect Nixon on December 11, 1968. Kennedy was born in Utah on July 21, 1905. He spent the first 16 years of his career with the Federal Reserve Board in Washington. Under President Johnson, Kennedy headed a commission that produced a major change in the presentation of the Federal budget. From 1959 until appointment, he was chairman of the board of the Continental Illinois National Bank & Trust Company in Chicago.

See also with picture 381

Kissinger, Henry Alfred, 45, professor of government, was appointed assistant for national security affairs in the Nixon administration. Since 1962 Kissinger has been professor of government, the Center for International Affairs, Harvard. He served as director of the Rockefeller Brothers Fund Special Studies Project (1956–58) and has been a consultant to the National Security Council, the Department of State and the U.S. Arms Control and Disarmament Agency. His books include *Nuclear Weapons and Foreign Policy* (1957) and *The Necessity for Choice: Prospects of American Foreign Policy* (1961).

Knight, John S., editorial chairman of Knight Newspapers, a chain of seven newspapers, was awarded the 1968 Pulitzer Prize for editorial writing and for his signed column "The Editor's Column." Knight was born October 26, 1894, in Bluefield, West Virginia. He became managing editor of the first of the Knight newspapers, the *Akron Beacon-Journal*, after World War I.

Kotz, Nathan K., newspaper reporter, was awarded the 1968 Pulitzer Prize for national reporting for his articles about unsanitary conditions in meat-packing plants. His reports helped passage of the Federal Wholesome Meat Act of 1967. Kotz was born in San Antonio, Texas, on September 16, 1932. He was graduated from Dartmouth and attented the London School of Economics. Kotz, a member of *The Des Moines Register*'s Washington bureau, joined the newspaper in 1958 as a government specialist.

L

Laird, Melvin Robert, U.S. Congressman from Wisconsin, was named U.S. secretary of defense by President-elect Nixon on December 11, 1968. Laird was born in Wisconsin on September 1, 1922. He was elected to the House of Representatives in 1952 after serving six years in the Wisconsin State Senate. As a member of the House Committee on Defense Appropriations, Laird was a strong critic of Secretary of Defense McNamara's defense budget and estimates of the cost of the Vietnam war. At first Laird was considered a hawk on the Vietnam issue; but by the end of 1968 he began to speak of a quick end to the Vietnam war.

See also with picture 381

Landau, Lev Davidovich, Soviet theoretical physicist and 1962 Nobel Prizewinner, died April 1, 1968, of injuries suffered in an auto accident in January 1962. Landau was born in Baku, Russia, on January 22, 1908. He studied at the Baku Economics Technicum and entered Baku University when he was 14 years old. His doctorate was earned at the University of Leningrad. In 1927 Landau introduced the "density matrix" concept of energy. Landau developed the thermodynamic theory of second-order phase transitions in solid bodies. He also developed the macroscopic theory of superfluidity of liquid helium. Landau predicted that sound waves could travel through helium at two different speeds.

LeMay, Curtis Emerson, retired Air Force general, was 1968 vice-presidential candidate of the American Independent Party and running mate of George C. Wallace. LeMay was born in Ohio on November 15, 1906. He received an engineering degree from Ohio State University and a law degree from John Carroll University. LeMay began his Air Force career in 1928. During World War II he organized and commanded

M

O

P

Q

R

Richter, Conrad, 78, author, died October 30, 1968. Richter won the 1951 Pulitzer Prize for fiction for *The Town* and the 1960 National Book Award for fiction for *Waters of Kronos.* He also wrote *Sea of Grass, Light in the Forest* and *Tacey Cromwell.*

Rogers, William Pierce, lawyer, was named U.S. secretary of state by President-elect Nixon on December 11, 1968. Rogers was born in New York on June 23, 1913. He received his law degree from Cornell University. He was first deputy attorney general and then attorney general (1957–61) in the Eisenhower administration.
See *also* with picture 381

Romney, George Wilcken, governor of Michigan, was named U.S. secretary of housing and urban development by President-elect Nixon on December 11, 1968. Romney was president of American Motors Corporation from 1954 to 1962, when he was elected governor. He was reelected for two successive terms. Romney announced his candidacy for the 1968 Republican presidential nomination late in 1967 but withdrew from the race a few days before the New Hampshire primary in March 1968. Romney was born in Mexico on July 8, 1907.

See also 53, 376, 381, picture 381

Roosevelt, Franklin D. 158
Roosevelt, Theodore 158
Rose, Lionel 113
Rosencrantz and Guildenstern are Dead 169
Rosenquist, James 260, pictures 258
Ross, James Clark 295
Rossillon, Philippe 130
Rowan and Martin's Laugh-In 173, picture 171
Rowing
    statistics 328
Royal Ballet, with picture 177
Rubella 235
Rudd, Mark, picture 45
Rumania 53, 199–200
Rusk, Dean 364

S

Sabah 105
Safety, automobiles 236
Saint-Phalle, Niki de, Nanas, picture 256–57

Sakai, Toshio, photographer, was awarded the 1968 Pulitzer Prize for feature photography for his photograph "Dreams of Better Times," which shows an American soldier asleep in the rain in Vietnam. Sakai was born in Tokyo, Japan, in 1940. He is a staff photographer with United Press International in Tokyo.

Sakharov, Andrei D. 22–24
San Antonio, Texas
    HemisFair '68, with pictures 386–89
San Francisco
    mass transportation 349
Sato, Eisaku 109
Saturn booster, with picture 305
Saturn V launch vehicle, with pictures 312–17
Saturn space flights 68
Saudi Arabia 245, 246, 248
Scenic trails and rivers 138
Schirra, Walter M., Jr. 67, picture 306
School desegregation 162, 220
Schools see Education
Schranz, Karl 341
Science, with pictures 282–93
    Antarctic discoveries, with pictures, 294–301
    hobbies 206–07
Scientific satellites 309
Scorpion, nuclear submarine 61, 69
Scott, Robert 295
Sculpture, with pictures 256–60
    Arco lamp, with picture 255
Seagren, Bob, picture 330
Seals and sealers 294–95
Sejna, Jan 26
Selective Service
    Supreme Court decision 219
Self government see Developing nations

Self-incrimination
    Supreme Court decision 219
Senate, United States see Congress, United States
Separatism, in Quebec 124
Service module, Apollo spacecraft 317
Sexual behavior of youth 46–47, picture 47
Shanker, Albert 67, picture 165
Sheepshearing, new method, picture 94
Ships and shipping
    Antarctica, pictures 294–95
    containerships and tankers, with picture 349

Shultz, George Pratt, labor economist, was named U.S. secretary of labor by President-elect Nixon on December 11, 1968. Shultz was born in New York City on December 13, 1920. He received his doctorate from the Massachusetts Institute of Technology. From 1962 until his appointment he was dean of the Graduate School of Business at the University of Chicago.

See also with picture 381

Shumway, Norman E. 50
Sibley, Antoinette, picture 177
Sierra Leone 79, picture 80
Sihanouk, Norodom 105
Silver certificates and coins 205
Simpson, O. J. picture 326
Sinclair, Upton 71
Sinyavsky, Andrei 22, picture 23
Sirhan, Sirhan Bishara 61, 366, picture 370
Skating
    Olympic Games 339, 341, picture 340
    statistics 328
Skiing 328
    Olympic Games 339, picture 338
Slama, Karel 287, 288
Slavery
    Mauritius 86
Sleep and dream studies
    Antarctica 299
Smallpox 235–36
Smith, Ian 80
Smith, Tommie 334–35, picture 335
Smrkovsky, Josef 21, 25, picture 26
Soccer 323, 329
Social conditions
    Canada's far north, with picture 126
    Protestant involvement 279
    youth revolution, with pictures 34–48
Somalia 80
South Africa 82
    Swaziland 89
    United Nations developments in 351
Southeast Asia 102–05
Southern Baptist Convention 280
Southern Yemen 245
South Korea see Korea
South Pole, Geographic 295, 298–99
South Vietnam see Vietnam
South-West Africa
    UN developments in 351
Soyuz spacecraft, with picture 307–08
Space
    signals from 290–91
Space Conference on Exploration and Peaceful Uses
    of Outer Space 310
Spacecraft, for lunar landing 312, 317
Space exploration, with pictures 302–17

T

U

V

Volpe, John Anthony, governor of Massachusetts, was named U.S. secretary of transportation by President-elect Nixon on December 11, 1968. He was born in Massachusetts on December 8, 1908. With little political experience, Volpe, a Republican, was first elected governor in 1960. He narrowly lost reelection in 1962, but in 1964 regained the governorship for a four-year term. Volpe had served for a year as a Federal highway administrator in the Eisenhower administration.

See also with picture 381

W

Wallace, George Corley, former governor of Alabama, was the presidential candidate of the American Independent Party in 1968. Wallace carried five deep South states and received 46 electoral votes (including one electoral vote from North Carolina, a state won by Richard Nixon). Wallace was born in

Clio, Alabama, on August 25, 1919. He received his law degree from the University of Alabama in 1942. Before serving as governor of Alabama (1963–66), Wallace was a member of the Alabama legislature (1947–53) and a judicial district judge (1953–58). Wallace's wife Lurleen, who was elected governor of Alabama in 1966, died in office on May 7, 1968.

See also 70, 359, 378, 380, picture 379

Y

Yost, Charles Woodruff, 61, diplomat, was named U.S. ambassador to the United Nations by President-elect Nixon on December 20, 1968. Yost served as deputy chief to the U.S. Mission to the UN (1961–66) and in the U.S. Foreign Service from 1930 to 1966, when he retired to become a senior fellow with the Council on Foreign Relations. A Democrat, Yost headed a study group on international organizations and peacekeeping for Vice-President Hubert Humphrey during the 1968 presidential campaign.

See also 353

Z

ILLUSTRATION CREDITS

The following list credits, by page, the sources of illustrations used in THE BOOK OF KNOWLEDGE ANNUAL. Credits are listed illustration by illustration—left to right, top to bottom. Wherever appropriate, the name of the photographer or artist has been listed with the source, the two being separated by a dash. When two or more illustrations appear on one page, their credits are separated by semicolons.

310	Hughes Aircraft	358	Dick Harvey
318	Ron McKee	360	William E. Shapiro
320	Claus Meyer—Black Star	361	Wide World
322	UPI	362	UPI
326	UPI	363	Gamma—PIX
327	UPI	364	UPI
329	UPI	365	Feiffer, Hall Syndicate
330	UPI	367	Morris McNamara—Nancy Palmer
332	UPI	368	UPI
333	Wide World; UPI; UPI	369	Wide World
334	Wide World	370	UPI
335	UPI	371	Robert Houston—Black Star; PIX
337	Marvin Newman	374	Don Getsug—Rapho-Guillumette; Claus Meyer—Black Star
338	Marvin Newman		
339	Marvin Newman	375	UPI
340	John G. Zimmerman, *Sports Illustrated*	376	Don Getsug—Rapho-Guillumette
342	Lee Balterman, *Life* magazine © Time Inc.	377	UPI
		378	Wide World
345	Boeing	379	Claus Getsug—Rapho-Guillumette; *The New York Times*
346	Sud Aviation Corporation		
347	Lee Balterman, *Life* magazine © Time Inc.	381	UPI
348	Charts courtesy of Transportation Association of America; Sikorsky Aircraft	385	Larry Krantz—Black Star
		386	HemisFair'68
349	Ishikawajima-Harima Heavy Industries Co.	387	HemisFair'68
350	UPI	388	HemisFair'68
353	Wide World	390	Jamaica Tourist Board
355	UPI	392	Kurt Scholz—PIX
357	United Nations